Demonizing the Qu

Chicago Studies in the History of Judaism
Edited by William Scott Green and Calvin Goldscheider

Demonizing the Queen of Sheba

Boundaries of Gender and Culture in Postbiblical Judaism and Medieval Islam

Jacob Lassner

The University of Chicago Press
Chicago and London

Jacob Lassner is the Phillip and Ethel Klutznick Professor of Jewish Civilization, director of the Jewish studies program, and professor of history and religion at Northwestern University.

The University of Chicago Press, Chicago 60637
The University of Chicago Press, Ltd., London

Printed in the United States of America

02 01 00 99 98 97 96 95 94 93 1 2 3 4 5

ISBN: 0-226-46913-1 (cloth)
0-226-46915-8 (paper)

Library of Congress Cataloging-in-Publication Data

Lassner, Jacob.
Demonizing the Queen of Sheba : boundaries of gender and culture in postbiblical Judaism and medieval Islam / Jacob Lassner.
p. cm. — (Chicago studies in the history of Judaism)
Includes bibliographical references and index.
1. Sheba, Queen of—Legends. 2. Solomon, King of Israel—Legends. 3. Rabbinical literature—History and criticism. 4. Islamic literature, Arabic—History and criticism. 5. Women in Judaism. 6. Women in Islam. 7. Judaism—Relations—Islam. 8. Islam—Relations—Judaism. 9. Tha'labī, Aḥmad ibn Muḥammad, d. 1035. Qiṣaṣ al-anbiyā. I. Title. II. Series.
BS580.S48L37 1993
296.1′42—dc20 93-7499
CIP

∞ The paper used in this publication meets the minimum requirements of the American National Standard for Information Sciences—Permanence of Paper for Printed Library Materials, ANSI Z39.48-1984.

For the best wishes

In memory of my father Kalman Lassner
and for Phyllis, Liz, and Jason
and my mother Ruth Lassner

Contents

Preface

The origins of this study are rooted in an age when students received their first instruction in Classical Arabic through a "kurzgefasst" or shorter grammar. In my case, it was the manual of A. Socin, which included in its chrestomathy a graded account of the Queen of Sheba and her celebrated visit to Solomon's court. The story adapted by Socin was based on the version of Abū Isḥāq Aḥmad b. Muḥammad al-Nīsābūrī, an author of the fifth Islamic century, better known by his nom de plume, al-Tha'labī. As did all students, I read the excerpt to acquire the rudiments of Arabic grammar. But attention to verbal forms and syntactical structures soon yielded to the overwhelming charm of the narrative because, even abridged and simplified, the tale of Solomon and the Queen of Sheba compelled the interest of readers. Years later, in search of material for instruction in Arabic literature, I turned again to Tha'labī, this time to the original, ungraded source, a longer, more richly textured version that invited comparison with parallel accounts and the matching of linguistic problems with literary and historical imagination.

My initial focus was on the nature of cultural diffusion. Embedded in the different versions of the queen's visit are discernible traces of Jewish lore. Literary artifacts of a more remote history, these residual materials were reshaped by Muslims to forge a sacred historiography of their own. And so what I had encountered years earlier as a grammatical exercise gave rise to an interest in Muslim uses of the Jewish past. Eventually, the story of the queen's visit became the skeletal structure of a project of intercommunal relations. For in appropriating Jewish experience to suit their own concerns, Muslims occasioned reaction from the older monotheists living among them. As a result, events and persons linking Muslim and Jewish sources became part of a wide-ranging discourse that determined polemical agendas; established boundaries separating the hegemonic majority from a tolerated Jewish minority; and, more generally, set the tone for relations between two closely connected faiths with competing claims to the past.

There is, nevertheless, a common theme that pervades the Muslim and

Jewish versions of the Solomonic legend, particularly in the exegetical literature. Readers will note that in all the commentaries on sacred scripture, Muslim or Jewish, the story of Solomon and the Queen of Sheba represents a contest of will and intellect between a crafty woman wishing to retain her independence and a privileged monarch anxious to subject her to his own authority. The authors are clear as to their sympathies in this contest: Jews and Muslims alike held that, regardless of rank, women must submit to men in accordance with the natural order of the universe. This view, which relegates all females to divinely assigned tasks, raises a second potential issue, namely, the role of gender in forming social identity.

Historians and literary scholars focusing on Near Eastern cultures would do well to consider female experience and consciousness as critical subjects of analysis—that is, whenever and wherever the data make such studies appropriate if not necessary. The tale of a female's audacious challenge to Solomon's authority is a case in point. Any analysis of the queen's behavior that fails to consider her alternative views of politics and natural order will not do justice to the larger tradition in either its Jewish or Muslim versions. The question of gender boundaries thus became a necessary concern of my own work, and with that substantive changes were required in the original design of the project. That is, what first took shape as a study of cultural diffusion has become a project with a broader conceptual framework and, I would imagine, a wider circle of potential critics.

In dealing with arcane and relatively inaccessible subject matter, one has to be conscious always of different audiences and their needs. The material in the pages that follow is likely to interest diverse readers engaged in cultural studies, but few of them will have knowledge of Hebrew, Aramaic, or Arabic, let alone the combination of all three languages. At the risk of appearing repetitive, I have translated for the benefit of those readers the most relevant texts analyzed in the general discussion. These translations are found in the appendixes. Generally speaking, I have tried to anticipate the concerns of scholars from fields other than Near Eastern studies, particularly social and literary theorists interested in the formation of tradition and, related to that, the shaping of attitudes towards the distaff side in premodern Muslim and Jewish societies.

As regards women and Judaism, there has been of late a plethora of articles and monographs dealing with classical texts. The sheer volume of publications and the chronological range of scholarly debate have proved daunting. No period of Jewish history has been ignored and no literary genre has escaped review. Where appropriate, I have noted feminist interpretations, particularly of the biblical narratives which have attracted much attention. Some general works dealing with feminist issues and Jewish life are listed in the bibliography.

Although there is no dearth of articles and collected essays on women in contemporary Muslim societies, much less has been written about the medieval period. Earlier studies of Muslim women in the Middle Ages were confined, by and large, to the politics of court and leading family circles. Moreover, this prototypical "feminist" writing failed to account fully for the didactic nature of contemporaneous sources. Upon close scrutiny, the tales of family intrigues are accounts of a world that should have been rather than a world that was. Today's investigators tend to wider interests and a more reflective approach to literary evidence. As distinct from earlier studies with their emphasis on the politics of ruling society, recent scholarship on Near Eastern women, medieval and modern alike, resonates to the current interest in broadly based social history. Moreover, cautious scholars, influenced by general trends in current literary theory, are more alert to problems of historicity in medieval writings. Still, for all intents and purposes, the place of medieval Islamic women in society remains terra incognita. We are still forced to speak more of values and attitudes than of actual states of the past, a point made clear by F. Rosenthal in his learned and reflective article "Sources for the Role of Sex in Medieval Muslim Society." Written in 1979, Rosenthal's study anticipates many current concerns and remains, in my opinion, the most useful discussion of what can be gleaned from classical Muslim writings as regards gender and sexuality. His article also has the advantage of discussing sensitive issues without resort to polemic or an opaque vocabulary.

A recent work edited by B. Baron and N. Keddie attempts to rectify a perceived neglect of the historical role of Muslim women, particularly in premodern societies. Of the seventeen studies in their collection, three fall under the rubric "The First Islamic Centuries" and an equal number under the "The Mamlūk Period." One of the essays, perhaps the most noteworthy, deals with hermaphrodites. Viewed as a group, the six pieces, however interesting, display a rather diffuse focus which is more descriptive than analytical. It goes without saying that much remains to be written about the role of Muslim women in history, particularly in the medieval environment.

It often happens that important studies appear too late to be integrated into a book that has gone or is about to go to press. Such is the case of T. Frymer-Kensky's *In the Wake of the Goddesses: Women, Culture and the Biblical Transformation of Pagan Myth* (The Free Press, 1992), which reassesses conventional notions of patriarchy and the ideology of gender as located in the biblical text. A study that also appeared too late to be integrated with my explication of the Solomonic legends, is F. Malti-Douglas's *Woman's Body, Woman's Word: Gender and Discourse in Arabo-Islamic Writing* (Princeton, 1991). This book represents the first major monograph to utilize an analytical framework derived from feminist studies while discussing women's issues in a wide range of medieval Islamic sources (Malti-Douglas links these sources to modern texts and concerns as well). The scope of her enquiry also cuts across boundaries of genre that tend to be artificial markers in medieval Arabic literature. Attention is thus drawn to belles lettres, philosophy, religious tradition, and even erotic manuals. *Woman's Body, Woman's Word* is a cornucopia of interesting material and includes as well an extensive bibliography of Arabic writings on gender and sexuality. The medieval period is also discussed in L. Ahmad, *Women and Gender in Islam: Historical Roots of a Modern Debate* (Yale, 1992). The relevant chapters are a reworked version of her contribution to the Baron-Keddie volume. As regards cultural borrowing, H. Lazarus Yafeh's *Intertwined Worlds: Medieval Islam and Bible Criticism* (Princeton, 1992) takes up the question of Muslim knowledge of the Bible, and related to that, Muslim attitudes toward Jewish scripture as seen from the larger context of Muslim-Jewish polemics. The author also includes a useful appendix on Jewish knowledge of the Qur'ān.

Some technical matters: The system of transliteration from Arabic is one commonly used in English publications and is, therefore, easily recognized. Hebrew, on the other hand, is transliterated in any number of ways. To avoid confusion, I have tried to render Hebrew terms as they would sound to the average ear. Nevertheless, certain conventional Western spellings, such as the names of Talmudic tractates, have been retained throughout. I trust that readers familiar with Hebrew (and Aramaic) are not likely to be offended by small inconsistencies of that sort. As a rule, I have employed Arabic terminology where it is not likely to confuse readers of English, for example, "wazīr" for "vezier" and "satans" rather than "devils" for Arabic "shayāṭīn." By citing the earliest link in the Islamic chain of receptors, I have tried to convey some sense of earlier authorities, suggesting thereby possible avenues of cultural diffusion. The various formulae that indicate the reception of an account, such as *ḥaddathanā, akhbaranā,* and so forth, although they differ in importance for Muslim scholars are all rendered by the symbol >. For example, > Abū Muḥammad stands for: "The tradition was received on the authority of Abū Muḥammad." In citing parallel sources to Arabic traditions, I have confined myself to well-known accounts from different chronological periods and reflecting at times somewhat different points of view. There is a voluminous literature of exegetical and belletristic texts, in manuscripts and printed editions alike, that illuminate the Queen of Sheba's visit to Solomon's court. The treatment of the Solomonic tale in this book is hardly exhaustive. Significant revision is inevitable, but I believe that my overall analysis has sufficient textual support to stand as it is.

Acknowledgments

Various segments of this book were originally presented as papers to learned societies, and some of its ideas were included in journal articles that appeared before publication of this volume. Needless to say, the final shape of the book reflects directly critical discussions generated by these earlier efforts. A number of colleagues expressed an interest in this project at various stages. Expressing gratitude to all of them would require a publication in its own right, but I would like to single out a few individuals whose encouragement and advice were significant: Peter Machinist; T. H. Breen; Rudi Lindner; Marvin Becker; W. M. Brinner; Bernard Lewis; Joseph Sadan; Joel Kraemer; M. A. Friedman; Etan Kohlberg; Ezra Spicehandler; and above all my wife, Phyllis, who was most instrumental in my linking issues of gender to the larger scheme of cultural diffusion. Our extended and often intense discussions were a constant source of challenge and reappraisal and no doubt of considerable amusement to many eavesdroppers at cafes in Ann Arbor, Oxford, and Tel Aviv.

Various stages of this book were written in different places and with the assistance of various grants. I should like to take this opportunity to thank the directors and staffs of the Dayan Center for Middle Eastern and African History at Tel Aviv University; the Centers for Jewish and Middle East Studies at Harvard; the Rockefeller Center at the Villa Serbelloni, Bellagio, Italy; the Israel Folklore Archives; the Oxford Postgraduate Center for Hebrew Studies; and my colleagues in the departments of history and religion at Northwestern University. I would also like to acknowledge support from the National Endowment for the Humanities and, last but not least, the support of Wayne State University for funding travel for research and for supplying me with released time.

Introduction

The Queen of Sheba heard of Solomon's fame . . . and she came to test him . . . (I Kings 10:1/II Chron. 9:1)

This study treats the Queen of Sheba's visit to King Solomon's court. To be more precise, it asks how and why the "historic event," a diplomatic mission recorded by the biblical chronicler, was reshaped by later Jewish and Muslim writers to accommodate contemporary values and newly defined concerns. By the Middle Ages, the main focus of the queen's visit had shifted from international to sexual politics and from diplomatic relations to the more complicated relations between men and women. That is, in its postbiblical and Islamic versions, the queen's joust with Solomon was portrayed as a dangerous attempt to subvert time-honored rules of gender.

For writers agitated by thoughts of an empowered distaff side, the queen's boldness in confronting the great Solomon had wide ramifications. At the least, her presumption in testing the hegemony of men was viewed as a challenge to orderly society. Were, however, that challenge not enough to cause anxiety, Jewish and Muslim writers provoked their audiences with more ominous thoughts. Combining arcane scholarship and a playful literary imagination, they transmuted the "historic" Queen of Sheba, a clever and politically astute sovereign, into a demonic force seeking to dissolve *all* boundaries of gender. In doing that, they linked the queen's striving for political power with the wholesale dissolution of sexually differentiated tasks. Seen in that light, her contest with the great Solomon was not a matter of redefining roles so as to allow women an honored place in the political arena. There was the danger that given political parity, if not advantage, she would tamper with the very essence of God's design. Any such attempt to alter nature's equilibrium was perceived as an obvious threat to all of humankind because, once liberated from their natural function, women may well decide against child rearing and even reproduction. Hence, the queen's brazen disregard for the roles that God assigned women resonated to concerns openly shared by all who had a stake in the continuity of the human species.

Anxious readers were, no doubt, reassured that the Queen of Sheba had chosen Solomon, of all men, to be her opponent. His heralded successes with women, concubines and royal ladies alike; his unique knowledge and intelligence; and more important yet, his mastery over natural and supernatural forces made him a worthy defender of the current order. No boundaries of gender were crossed where he ruled at God's behest. For a world dramatically changed by sexual politics is a world that neither the Almighty nor His authors were prepared to accept. No good can come of tampering with a universe as perfectly and elegantly conceived as ours. Thus, the wily queen will be humbled and the world will remain as it is and as it should be. In any event, that is the view of ancient and medieval authors who inscribed their own sensibility on memories of the historic past.

The current concern with empowerment and sexual hierarchy obliges us to move beyond the traditional outlook of these evocative legends. Readers interested in gender issues will want to know how the reshaping of the ancient tale reflects culturally constructed notions of men, women, and natural order in postbiblical Judaism and medieval Islam. It is likely that these readers will be drawn from diverse disciplines embracing a wide variety of perspectives. Investigations of sexual hierarchy now range from highly theoretical essays postulating the origins of gender in the paleolithic age to ethnographic studies that record and analyze living cultures. The central thrust of this multidisciplinary effort is to move beyond reductive explanations of sexual roles based on human biology and to focus more directly on the inner logic of cultural codes that reflect societal norms and influence behavior.

Richly textured and gracefully written, the accounts of Solomon and his female antagonist deserve their place in current discussions of gender and sexual hierarchy. But detailed as they are, the traditions of Solomon and the Queen do not yield easily to modern interrogators. While much can be done to sort out the underlying values of ancient and medieval societies, using literary sources to reconstruct social environments is problematic to say the least. There is no adequate way to interview or observe the dead and the silent. Authors, identifiable and anonymous, remain in the form of extant texts, but the response of contemporaneous readers to these sources and the historical contexts that inform written works are much less accessible. Recovering social transactions from a highly didactic literature conjures up images of traversing an epistimological minefield, mapless and barefoot. Scholars who would embrace remote chronicles, folkloric tales, religious commentary, or even law codes to discover and shed light on actual states of the past should exercise considerable caution. One must be prepared for likely divergences between the representation of ancient and medieval women in literature and how they were constituted in "real life."

In complex societies with a vast range of written forms and elaborate legal systems, there is generally a gap between public declarations and privately held views and between legally proscribed and privately sanctioned behavior. However much one can learn about contemporaneous values from the tradition of Solomon and the Queen of Sheba, the distance between declared values and social realities can be measured only with documents that record the minutiae of daily life combined, where possible, with the evidence of material culture—in other words, sources less subject to tendentious shaping. Although I have not intended to evaluate literary texts as historical witnesses in light of documentary evidence, a postscript on archeology and archives is appended to my discussion of gender issues and templates of behavior. In any case, one ought not forget that archival sources and evidence obtained from material culture are subject as well to vexing problems of interpretation and analysis.

There is also the question of voice. Whose values are reflected in the codes that give coherence to the Solomonic texts? If asymmetry favoring men is found in most if not all cultures, must we assume that the reports of Solomon's victory over the Queen and the manner in which it was achieved reflect a male-biased ideology? And if they do indeed reflect male bias, how would women have interpreted the tale? That is, is there a female subtext to these accounts that is not articulated in our written sources? Put differently, had ancient and medieval women been granted full license to elaborate on the biblical story, would the result have been a rather different tradition, perhaps one that is informed by a cultural code reflecting a female perspective or even different female perspectives?

Modern women have given additional if not entirely new meaning to the old traditions of the Solomonic saga. The Israel Folklore Archives contains two Moroccan versions of a particular episode in that story, one obtained from a man of Tangiers; the other from a female informant of the same city. Readers encountering these stories will observe that in the male version a haughty queen is put in her place by Solomon who is far too savvy to be bested by any female, even one so clever as the ruler of Sheba. Contrasted with that is the female account in which a wise queen encourages a vain Solomon to be all too clever by half, and having allowed the king to think that he has won the battle of wits, she tricks him into marriage—a romantic ending with many parallels in the popular literature of the Near East and elsewhere.

Reflecting a different sensibility, current feminists have made political icons of both the Queen of Sheba and the demonic Lilith, with whom the queen is explicitly linked in Jewish sources. As regards the queen, it is her intelligence; her desire for political independence; her sagacity in dealing with men at their own game; and above all her ability to make and enforce decisions about her own life that make her a kindred soul to the modern woman. The demonic Lilith provides in turn a model of sexual independence; a rejection of biological imperatives that relegate women to roles of procreation and nurturing; and, more generally, a defiance of male authority.

There is, however, a truly dark side to Lilith, an aspect of her behavior that inspired dread in women as well as men. She caused mothers to abort and strangled babies in their cribs. No subtext expressing admiration for Lilith was likely from women who wore amulets and recited incantations in order to protect themselves and their children from her. On the other hand, I can readily imagine an ancient or medieval version of the romantic story told by the woman of Tangiers. No doubt, Jewish and Muslim women admired the queen's intelligence, perhaps even her pluck, but would they have been enthusiastic about her competing openly with men or in seeking an active role in the public sphere? Or, to the contrary, would a change in rules governing the hierarchy of gender have been viewed by women and men alike as filled with risk? Would most women of stature have preferred to forsake the dangers of public space, even if somehow it was more available to them, in favor of power freely given them in the domestic sphere, that is, the area where they were responsible for producing and nurturing children to preserve prestigious family lines and managing large and complex households? Seen from that perspective, some Jewish and Muslim women would have had a stake comparable to that of men in Solomon's triumph and in the preservation of what was deemed natural order. All this, however, is speculation. If there was a distinct female perspective, it has been subsumed within a larger (male-oriented) world view. Feminists have argued that women's perspectives and ambitions have been constrained and conditioned by male hegemony, a point forcefully stated, generally well taken, and regarded by many as conventional wisdom. Scholars are constrained in turn by the available evidence, a point often made but not always appreciated in academic discourse. The silence of Jewish and Muslim women binds us, in this case, to texts produced by men; but can one say with confidence that the Solomon saga represents the views of men alone?

A wide variety of sources indicate that both Jews and Muslims shared concern about women's activity outside the domestic sphere. As a rule, women were confined to their household and its tasks. It was axiomatic to Jews and Muslims that men alone attended to matters of public life in accordance with that finely tuned universe that God had designed. Indeed, the preservation of an orderly world in which men and women knew their station and function was a universal concern in hierarchical societies of the ancient and medieval Near East. Where Muslims depart from Jews and others is in the need to rework issues of gender so that they blend in with specifically Muslim religious concerns and settings. Hence, the second major focus of this study: the Islamization of universal and, more specifically, Jewish themes. In the pages that follow, the dramatic account of Solomon and his female antagonist becomes a test case of how Jewish memorabilia penetrated the literary imagination of medieval Muslims. Seen in that context, the Solomonic saga reflects crossing boundaries of religious culture as well as gender. For however familiar to readers steeped in Jewish sources, the events and dramatis personae of the Muslim versions conformed to a newer and different religious sensibility. Absorbing biblical and postbiblical themes, Muslims refashioned the Jewish past and made it part of their own historic experiences and world view. As a result, a heritage common to two prophetic and closely linked faiths could and did become a bone of contention as well as a basis for shared values and mutual understanding. In such fashion, the story of Solomon son of David, the Jewish King, became that of Sulaymān ibn Dāwūd, the Muslim Prophet.

The appropriation of the Jewish past by Muslims forging a monotheist historiography of their own touches upon many concerns. It was crucial in shaping literary taste and polemical discourse; in forming attitudes about "self" and "other"; in establishing a convenient bridge for Jews converting to Islam; and, more generally, in setting the tone for Muslim-Jewish relations. No doubt, the material dealt with here will interest any number of specialists in Judaica and Islamic studies, particularly scholars of the ancient and medieval world. But it should also attract scholars more generally concerned with the transfer and absorption of cultural artifacts among societies that embrace a common past while competing with each other for sacred or ideological space.

What follows, then, is a study linked to two particular communities, Jews and Muslims, and to two loose settings in time, antiquity and the Middle Ages. The problems occasioned by this broad and complex linkage suggest the need for inventive and wide-ranging literary and historical analyses. Indeed, the specific focus of this study addresses concerns presently shared by a number of philologists, historians, and literary critics. I refer to a revival of interest in how traditions are formed and then embedded in sacred history and religious writing. Doubtless, scholars well versed in social science and those familiar with recent feminist investigations will want to add still other perspectives that are in keeping with their expressed interests. The prophet Amos declared: "I am neither a prophet nor the son of a prophet." I lay no special claims to anthropology, folklore, or comparative religion. Rather, as a philologist and historian, I have attempted to make available arcane traditions that some scholars otherwise might not be able to interrogate. In any case, researchers with wide-ranging analytical tools will have much to consider regarding the wondrous Solomonic saga, be it overarching theory or the minutiae of scholarly detective work.

I have no doubt that in the long run broadly based interdisciplinary studies will be widely acclaimed as a way of better understanding the diverse peoples and cultures of the Near East, Jews and Muslims among them. For the moment, there is for some researchers that tension-filled period which comes with voyages of discovery. Crisscrossing genre and discipline can be a humbling experience, one that may, or rather should, inspire circumspection. There is the danger that, overstimulated and in a rush to pass judgment, we may impose our own sensibilities on literary artifacts far removed in time and place. Rather than do justice to the past, we then will have imposed a contemporary interpretation on the story of Solomon and the Queen of Sheba, as did the rabbis and Muslim exegetes. My primary concern with ancient and medieval opinion is to recover the cultural attitudes that inform the legends of Solomon and the wily queen. I have tried, therefore, to be extremely sensitive to contemporaneous terminology, rhetorical strategies, and categories of definition. To be sure, there is much concerning the story of Solomon and the Queen of Sheba that shall never be recovered. Too much context has been lost with the passing of time; too many allusions that might have given meaning to difficult passages have become opaque to modern readers; too many sources pregnant with valuable material are known only through oblique references in the preserved literature. This important caveat aside, there is much that we do and can know about religious, belletristic, and historical texts that shed light, however dim at times, on the distant past.

One thing is abundantly clear. Our texts reflect a very different milieu from the ascetic Christian world of late antiquity described by Peter Brown or from that of pietistic circles in the medieval West. This is not to say that pietism and even ascetic forms of behavior did not find a proper place in Judaism and Islam or that various laws of purity did not restrict sexual activity at proscribed periods for observant Jews and Muslims. Philosophers also pondered questions of sexuality and love. Some, stressing the unimportance of materiality, preferred the exercise of the intellect to that of the body, creating thereby an ideal world marked by asexuality. But, as did George Bernard Shaw, most tried sex at least once and, unlike the Irish writer, who saw little in it, we may assume many continued to experience it. In any case, they understood all too well the importance of adjusting abstract ideals to societal norms and religious concerns. And so, in the interest of preserving divine order, which meant promulgating the human species, Jews and Muslims alike were enjoined to accept the responsibilities if not pleasures of carnal knowledge, however dangerous the consequences at times.

1 *Biblical and Postbiblical Accounts*

The Jewish stories, which tell of Solomon hosting a proud and powerful queen, are based on an ancient Hebrew tale that was destined to undergo many changes. More specifically, they are linked to chapter 10 of I Kings and its parallel, chapter 9 of II Chronicles, texts that record Solomon's extensive diplomacy; his conquests, territorial and matrimonial; the opulence of his court and the size of his retinue; and his great combination of wisdom and wealth. These are all themes directly treated in rabbinic and later Jewish lore as well as in the Qur'ān and other Muslim sources.[1] Our interest is also drawn to other biblical passages that treat Solomon's vast knowledge of the natural order, suggesting thereby an ability to communicate with all of God's creatures, a theme that also elicits considerable attention in Jewish and Muslim lore, including later versions of the story that preoccupies us here.[2] First of all, however, our concern is with I Kings 10:1–13, the intriguing and all too brief account of how the Queen of Sheba visited Solomon at his court in Jerusalem during a period of extensive diplomatic activity.

A. *The Biblical Account*

As described in the Hebrew Bible, the visit, occasioned by the growing influence of the Solomonic state, had an unusual twist. Having heard of Solomon and his efforts on God's behalf, the queen (a potential client) decided to test him with riddles.[3] And so she came to Jerusalem armed with a sharply honed intellect as well as an enormous army and, were that not enough, camels laden with tribute: great amounts of spices, gold, and precious stones. She tested Solomon, withholding none of her ploys, and he, in turn, replied without missing a trick. The queen was thus able to comprehend the extent of Solomon's wisdom and the magnificent edifice that he had created. Indeed, the opulence of his court and the splendor of his retainers, together with the sacrifices at God's Temple, all served to break her spirit. She confessed to the king that all that she had heard in her own land regarding his wisdom and deeds was indeed true. She had been skeptical at first, but she now saw with her own eyes that

that which she had been led to believe was not even the half of it. The queen blessed his people and servants, "those who stand always before you and listen to your wisdom."[4] Then she blessed the Lord, his God, who out of His eternal love of Israel, placed Solomon on the throne and made him king of his people to rule with justice and righteousness. Having done that, she presented the king with gifts that included 120 talents of gold and an enormous quantity of spices and precious stones. Indeed, the amount of spices reportedly exceeded anything seen since then. The text goes on to say that Solomon (reciprocating her tribute) satisfied all of her wants[5]—this aside from what he gave her in his official capacity as king. After receiving this largesse, she departed, all the wiser and more accommodating.

When I Kings 10:1–13 is read together with the rest of the chapter and the other biblical material on Solomon's reign, it becomes clear that the Queen of Sheba's visit was one of a series of diplomatic undertakings, each negotiated to strengthen the king's position. For it was in the reign of Solomon that the small and not always stable Kingdom of Israel became a powerful polity.[6] Nevertheless, the extent to which the king could exact vast tribute in manipulating even his relatively weak neighbors was no simple matter of coercion. The Israelites at the apex of their authority could not project power as did the great and venerable kingdoms of ancient Egypt and Mesopotamia. Solomon's real strength was his capacity to manipulate events and rulers largely through clever diplomacy, including the skillful use of matrimonial alliances.[7] Hence the king's reputation for probity, wisdom, and success with women. In any case, the Solomonic kingdom had found its glorious place in the sun. All this is lucidly described by the ancient chroniclers.

And yet, the biblical text gives rise to many unanswered questions. There is not the slightest hint as to the content of the queen's riddles nor of Solomon's replies. Nor is there any indication of what were "her wants" and how they might have been satisfied, but given Solomon's enormous learning, his proverbial wisdom, and not the least his capacity for making love (the king had seven hundred wives and three hundred concubines),[8] these questions occasioned discussion among the exegetes.

More generally, later commentators were struck by the extraordinary influence of the Israelite state and its king. Such influence, never so great before, nor duplicated since, stimulated the literary imagination of postbiblical Jewish authorities, thus giving rise to flights of exegetical fancy. The Solomon of later Jewish tradition is a ruler of truly fabulous wealth and power; a king who speaks to birds and animals; and the possessor of a magical signet ring which enables him to command a host of demons, satans, and jinn.[9] And so, the historic Solomon of the Bible—taking considerable license to call him that—was transformed into a legendary figure surrounded by a legendary court and partaking of legendary events, the visit of the Queen of Sheba among them. But it is not only Solomon, the King of Israel, that is transformed by the literary accretions of subsequent generations. The Queen of Sheba is similarly changed into a larger than human figure capable of offering him challenge. For without this appropriate challenge, the story would lose much of its appeal to later audiences.

The postbiblical accounts of the queen's visit are found in three texts: the *Midrash to Proverbs* (*Mishle*), the *Midrash ha-Hefez,* and the *Targum Sheni to the Book of Esther.* The two midrashim, written in Hebrew, contain short accounts dealing only with the riddles that are mentioned, but not described in the Bible; the material in the Aramaic *Targum Sheni* reflects a larger tale suggested by the ancient biblical chronicles. To these three accounts, one can add the brief reference to a particular moment of the queen's visit found in the *Stories* of Pseudo Ben Sira, a medieval work of wisdom and fables and, more recently, in various folkloric traditions.

B. *The "Midrash Mishle"*

It is not surprising that the midrashic text inspired by Proverbs, that quintessential statement of biblical wisdom, reportedly authored by Solomon himself, should draw attention to the game of wits between the all-wise Israelite king and the crafty Queen of Sheba.[10] Thus, the verse: *But wisdom where shall it be found* [*and where is the place of understanding*]?[11] was said to refer to the visit of the queen, more particularly to her riddles and Solomon's ingenious solutions.

According to Rabbi Jeremiah Bar Shalom, an unknown authority quoted by the midrash, the queen started with the intention of asking but a single riddle: "What is it? Seven depart and nine enter, two give drink but [only] one partakes." He responded, "No doubt, seven are the days of the menstrual period, nine are the months of pregnancy, two [refers] to the breasts that succor and one to the child born who drinks from them."[12] As the king provided her with an immediate and correct answer, she asked him permission to proceed once more. He acknowledged her request and so she asked, "What does it signify? A woman says to her son, 'Your father is my father. Your grandfather is my husband. You are my son and I am your sister.'" Solomon answered, "No doubt, the two daughters of Lot [in reference to the biblical tale of two women who slept with their father and became pregnant when they feared, following the destruction of Sodom and Gomorah, that there would be no men with whom to propagate the species]."[13]

Having been bested a second time, the queen prepared a more intricate challenge to the king's intelligence.[14] Various boys and girls, all of a tender age, of the same height and dressed identically were placed before him, whereupon she said, "Distinguish the males from the females." At Solomon's command, nuts and roasted corns were distributed before them. The boys, without any sense of embarrassment, gathered them and placed them in their garments; the girls, who were more modest, placed them in their headdresses. Thus, Solomon was able to distinguish between them. A less confident woman might have given up by now, but once again, the queen challenged the king.[15] This time she brought a group (of males) some of whom were circumcised and the others unclean. When Solomon was asked to separate one from the other (that is, without exposing their genitalia), he signaled the High Priest to open the Ark of the Covenant. Those who had been circumcised bowed down to half their height and the radiance of God's presence (*shekhinah*) lit their faces. The uncircumcised fell prostrate because, as Solomon explained, the manifestation of God's presence causes gentiles to lose control of their limbs as in the story of the pagan prophet Balaam.[16] Were the queen reluctant to accept this explanation, Solomon will convince her by citing the story of Job and his comforters, a tale of gentiles from a remote past.

Pressed by his colleagues, Job remarks: [*But I too have a mind such as you*]. *I do not fall below you* [*nofel . . . mikem*].[17] The intention of the biblical verse is to show that Job is as wise if not wiser than his interlocutors (as, indeed, Solomon is wiser than the queen). But, in this instance, the author of the midrash is prepared to squeeze additional meaning from the text. An exegetical gloss seems to indicate that *I do not fall below you* (meaning "I am not inferior to you"), should be understood as *Do I do not fall as you do* [*nofel . . . k^{e}motkhem*]? The interpolation suggests that Job, the righteous gentile, like Balaam, the pagan prophet with whom he is linked in Jewish legend, will fall fully prostrate in God's presence, reinforcing thereby the distinction between those who are circumcised and those who are not. However problematic this exegesis may seem to modern readers, it appears to have satisfied the queen. Finally realizing that she was unable to best Solomon, she recited the words attributed to her in I Kings 10:9; she recognized Solomon's wisdom and justice and praised God for having placed him on the throne of Israel.

As regards the larger message of the midrash: All four tests are linked to the natural order of things and the question of identity. The die is cast for all humans with the cycle that gives rise to birth (riddle 1). There are natural confusions as in the case of Lot's daughters (riddle 2); there may be attempts to disguise what nature has defined as the Queen of Sheba sought to do in dressing boys and girls to look alike, an act that reflects a questioning if not defiance of established gender lines (riddle 3); but nature—in this case really culture—runs a predictable course. Solomon, the wisest and most learned of men, understood this best of all. Thus, males can always be identified for what they are; the ritually pure, that is the Israelites, remain separate and superior (riddle 4); and the queen is forced to praise God and recognize the primacy of Solomon His King. In our text, it is the logic of the universe that women know their place and not try to best men; that the Israelites and their descendants are preferred to all others; and that the Queen of Sheba, because she is so wise herself, should give recognition to these facts.

C. *The "Midrash ha-Hefez"*

This source, basing itself on the authority of Rabbi Ishmael, the famous scholar (*tanna*) of the second century C.E., reproduces these same four tests with some very minor variations and then adds fifteen more.[18] The result is a more diffuse message that is almost lost amid the added content. Fourteen of the queen's additional probes are in the form of riddles. Of these, three have no particular Jewish referent; the others play with familiar events and personae of the Hebrew Bible. As with the *Midrash Mishle,* most of the additional tests are linked directly or indirectly to the natural order of things. Given the nature of riddles, there is also play with problems of confused identity. The fifteen additional queries begin with questions about God and the creation of the universe, and then speak of men, women, and objects. A theme common to several riddles is the preservation of family lines and, more generally, that of humankind, God's most sublime artifice.

Various questions put to Solomon concern the nurturing of the human embryo; the story of Jonah, with its emphasis on God's compassion for the people of Nineveh, originally slated for destruction; a second reference to the daughters of Lot and how they became pregnant by their father in order to preserve their bloodline; and perhaps the most interesting of the riddles, one that draws on the biblical story of Judah and Tamar, a tale of levirate marriage, an alleged "killer wife," and an incident of confused identity, all skillfully interwoven to form a plea for family continuity and the maintenance of divine order.[19]

Needless to say, Solomon answers each of the queen's queries with brevity and accuracy. Finally, she presents the all-knowing Israelite with a last test that requires his powers of observation as well as his capacity to reason. A sawn section of cedar is brought, and the king is asked at which end the root had been and at which end the branches. Once again, the test involves disguised appearances. A log altered so one cannot tell the difference between top and bottom is analogous to a woman pretending to be a man. By all appearances, both ends appear to be the same, but nature always seems to betray these deceptions. Solomon orders that the cedar be thrown into the water, whereupon one end sank and the other floated to the surface. At that, he declares, "That which sank was the root, that which floated was the end containing the branches."

I am not sure that I understand fully the scientific principles that guided Solomon, but he was, according to tradition, the quintessential naturalist.[20] He was thus capable of offering the correct response, reaffirming thereby the immutable laws that govern nature. Presumably, the area closest to the roots was considered more sensitive to moisture, causing it to absorb water and sink beneath the surface. In any case, what matters for the author and his readers is that the queen was impressed by his answer. And indeed she was. Thus, the Queen of Sheba was forced to recognize that Solomon's wisdom exceeded that which she had heard and she then blessed his God as in the Book of Kings.

My suspicion is that the *Midrash ha-Hefez* is the residue of a Yemenite oral tradition that, in this case, was committed to writing in the first half of the fifteenth century C.E. The individual riddles of that tradition, however, are no doubt very old and probably derived from a wide variety of written and oral sources. In addition to those passages that are linked to the aforementioned *Midrash Mishle,* there are possible references to Talmudic literature and two of the queries are written in Aramaic, all of which points to a diverse literary background.[21] It was as though this visit of the queen were almost completely lifted from history and biblical commentary and reconstituted as a folktale. The result is a story that dulls somewhat the gender issues raised by the Book of Kings and its racier exegetes.

D. *The "Targum Sheni to the Book of Esther"*

The third of our sources, the Aramaic *Targum Sheni* (or second Aramaic translation of the Book of Esther) embellishes the biblical account with considerable detail.[22] Interpolated into the story of Ahasueras and Esther is a wondrous tale of how the Queen of Sheba came to visit Solomon, a king who ruled over contingents of animals, birds, and demonic spirits; how she presented him with splendid gifts; and how she then probed his intelligence with three difficult tests, each of which he passed by answering her questions succinctly and correctly.[23]

It would appear that King Solomon was in rather jovial mood, having imbibed much wine. Feeling a need to impress his guests, the rulers of the neighboring countries (a barely disguised analogue to the extravagant celebration that Ahasuerus hosted at Susa),[24] Solomon ordered a muster of his bizarre army, a force that contained animals, birds, reptiles, and various demonic spirits. When reviewing the birds, Solomon was disturbed to find that the hoopoe was missing and he threatened the delinquent bird with punishment.[25] But the hoopoe appeared and explained his absence. Pleading on his own behalf, he explained that he had not neglected his duty out of self-interest. Indeed, he had gone without food and drink for three months, during which time he had taken to the sky in order to search for a realm which had not yet fallen under the great king's influence. To the east he had found a land of extraordinary wealth. The dust of its capital, Kitor, was more precious than gold, and its silver as prevalent as dung in the markets.[26] The bird continued, relating other wondrous things. Kitor was inhabited by men, each of whom wore a crown, and yet they were a docile lot, not knowing of war or even the use of bow and arrow. And (most amazing of all) they were ruled by a woman known as the Queen of Sheba. The hoopoe then offered to fly to Kitor, subdue its inhabitants, and bring them in chains to Solomon, his king. No doubt, the thought of birds subduing a kingdom seems rather strange; but then again what defense can be expected of people who are ruled by a woman, know not war, and are incapable of using the bow and arrow?

Solomon may have been deep into his cups, but he was sober enough to appreciate this plan. For it would add to his many clients the last kingdom not yet under his control. And so he had the royal scribes draft a letter (of demands), which he tied to the hoopoe's wing. At that, the hoopoe and the other birds took to the sky. When they reached Kitor in the morning, the queen was about to bow down in prayer to the (rising) sun, but its light had been blocked out by Solomon's force filling the sky. The queen became greatly disturbed and disoriented and (recognizing calamity) tore her garment. Then the hoopoe touched down, and she noticed the letter that was attached to his wing. She removed the missive which read:[27]

> From me, Solomon the King, who sends greetings. Peace unto you and your nobles, Queen of Sheba! No doubt you are aware that the Lord of the Universe has made me king of the beasts of the field, the

> birds of the sky, and the demons, spirits, and Liliths. All the kings of the East and West, and the North and South, come to me and pay homage. If you would come and greet me [that is, pay homage], I will honor you more than any kingly guest of mine,[28] but if you refuse and do not appear before me to pay homage, I will send out against you [my] generals, contingents, and riders. You ask, "What generals, contingents, and riders has King Solomon?" Then know that the beasts of the field are my generals, the birds in the sky are my riders, and the demons, spirits, and Liliths are my contingents who will strangle you in your beds. The beasts will slay you in the fields and the birds of the sky will consume your flesh.

When the Queen of Sheba read the contents of the document, a letter that seemingly left her few choices, she tore her garment once again and sent for the elders and great men of her realm. They knew not of Solomon and cared less for being his subjects; that is, they were prepared to ignore him. But the queen knew better, and so ignoring them, she assembled all the ships of her domain and loaded them with presents for Solomon—pearls and precious stones. She also presented him with six thousand young boys and girls, each born in the same year and month, and, were that not enough, on the same day and at the same hour. In addition, they were all of equal stature and dressed in purple raiment, that is, the royal colors. The targum gives no reason for the last rather curious gift, but it is clear from other stories, especially those found in Arabic accounts, that Solomon was asked to distinguish one from the other.[29] Had he failed to do that, she would have proved by the very nature of the test that women are indeed equal to men even when it comes to rule. Then she wrote to the king that she would hasten to see him, compressing a journey of seven years into three.

When she arrived at the appointed time, she was met by one of the king's servants, a man of unusual beauty that caused her to think he was in fact the Israelite monarch.[30] Clearly, it was not power alone that women found attractive in the king. Having learned of her error, she was brought into the presence of Solomon himself. The king was seated in a chamber of glass. She, thinking that the throne was situated in (a pool of) water, raised her skirt and bared her hairy legs, whereupon Solomon remarked, "You're a beautiful woman but hairiness is for men. You look absolutely disgraceful." However undiplomatic, the Israelite's remark sharply defines the point of the story: the queen has disturbed the natural order of the universe. She rules over men and disregards their advice when it is not to her liking. The hair on her legs thus symbolizes this reversal of gender roles and forewarns Solomon of the potential danger in her remaining independent.[31] It is clear that this Queen of Sheba will not be easily put aside; she has already emasculated her subjects. For, as the hoopoe reported, they are incapable of waging war or of even using the bow and arrow (objects with which boys prove their right to manhood). Now, she has prepared some tests for the king in order to see if he is in fact "like all other men." Her ploy is self-evident; if he is but another man she will handle him as easily as she handles her subjects. In her domain each man may be a king, that is, they all wear crowns—but it is the queen who wears the pants, so to speak.

The game of wits begins.[32] "What is it?" she asks, "A basin of wood and a pail of iron; it draws stones but pours out water." "A cosmetic box," he replies. She then proceeds to the next question: "It comes as dust from the earth and it feeds on dust. It is poured like water but lights the house. What is it?" "Naptha," he answers. Then she poses a last question: "It precedes all things; it wails and cries; it bends like a reed;[33] it is the glory of the nobles and the disgrace of the poor; the glory of the dead and the disgrace of the quick; it is the delight of the birds but the distress of fishes. What is it?" "Flax," he says (in reference to the sinewy plant from which all sorts of linen garments and shrouds are made; a plant whose substance is eaten by birds and whose fibers were used to make fish lures or nets).

As with the tantalizing riddles of the *Midrash Mishle,* a common thread runs through all her queries, namely our capacity to be misled by disguised appearances. Cosmetics change the face, naphtha changes substance, and flax may be used for conflicting purposes. But Solomon recognizes the world for what it really is. As defined by our authors, the universe is a construct of carefully delineated hierarchies. He, as no other man, understands this construct and speaks for its legitimacy. He will not be deceived or manipulated by a female acting as if she were a man, regardless of her wiles. Each of her riddles is answered correctly and with apparent confidence. The queen confesses, as in the biblical version, that she had been skeptical of the rumors of Solomon's wisdom, but now that she has seen it with her own eyes, she knows that she had been told but half the truth. When, as in the biblical account, the king then takes her on a tour of his magnificent palace, the queen has no recourse but to praise the eternal God of Israel for having set Solomon on the throne that he might rule with justice and righteousness. Her praise, a direct quote from the Hebrew Bible, is reinforced with a tribute of gold and fine silver and Solomon reciprocates by "satisfying all her desires." The transaction is therefore complete; she has become the king's client through an exchange of gifts.

E. *The "Stories of Ben Sira"*

The last of the Jewish sources to be discussed here, the so-called *Stories of Ben Sira,*[34] refers tangentially to the queen's visit, but this account even more than the others gives one a feeling for the dangers that such women represent. The segment of the book that interests us most focuses on a single, albeit illustrative detail of the larger story: the queen's excessive hairiness. Mentioned briefly in the *Targum Sheni,* Solomon's concern with the queen's hair is further amplified by the author of this medieval wisdom book while he is describing a game of wits between a certain Ben Sira and Nebuchadnezzar, the King of Babylon.

Like his analogue Solomon, Ben Sira was a child prodigy blessed with keen intelligence and extraordinary erudition. According to one version, by the time he was five, he had mastered the Hebrew Bible, the Mishnah, and the legal and legendary literature of the Talmud. Another version indicates that he learned the entire Torah in his first year; the Prophets, Mishnah, and Talmud in his second; and that by the time he was seven, his vast knowledge included such diverse subjects as gematriah, the discourse of the heavenly host and the jinn, and all manner of esoterica and natural phenomena.[35]

Upon hearing of Ben Sira, Nebuchadnezzar insists that the youth be brought to his court, and so he commands a thousand horsemen to deliver the seven year old into his presence.[36] Brave soldiers, capable of uprooting trees, they are nevertheless reluctant to engage in this task for fear of suffering the same fate that befell the Aramean hosts when they confronted the prophet Elishah.[37] They will go anywhere and contend with any people but a single wise Israelite is considered too dangerous. A confident Nebuchadnezzar seeks to relieve their apprehension. He proclaims, "The God of the Hebrews did not speak of the King of Aram as he spoke of me." Turning to the Book of Jeremiah, he quotes a passage referring to himself: [*Even*] *the beasts of the field I gave to him that they may serve him.*[38] Armed with Jeremiah's prediction, the king's troops set off to bring back the famous youth.

Ben Sira's reputation as a wise Israelite is fully justified. When informed of the king's request for his presence, which is based on a prophetic statement, he too will cite chapter and verse. Interpreting Jeremiah's *beasts of the field,* he says, "He [Nebuchadnezzar] did not send you for me but for a female rabbit of mine."[39] Ben Sira then produces a rabbit with a smooth bald head as white as an eggshell upon which is written: "Delivered as promised, one of the beasts of the field to serve you," followed by the verse itself. Ben Sira's response makes a mockery of the Babylonian's interpretation of scripture. It also mocks the king's vaunted power. What is one to make of a great conqueror sending a thousand cavalry to bring back a single female rabbit? Be that as it may, the king's interest is aroused by the bald creature. An astounded Nebuchadnezzar wishes to know how one makes the head of a rabbit so smooth. And so, he dispatches another troop to bring Ben Sira, this one greater and more distinguished.[40] They carry a new message requesting Ben Sira's presence, "if not for my sake then for that of your rabbit," an implied threat to the helpless animal that is calculated to raise the boy's anxiety. What child would not feel for his pet rabbit? Ben Sira will see the king.

At the Babylonian court, a series of tests and questions are put before the boy.[41] He turns his examiners aside with incredible ease and confidence and then reverses positions with them and becomes their interrogator. In the end, he emerges clearly triumphant and the king is duly impressed. He is prepared to make Ben Sira a ruler, but the latter does not wish to leave his native land [of Israel]. Nebuchadnezzar then proposes to kill Zedekiah, the King of Israel, and replace him with his newly discovered prodigy. Echoing Solomon at Gibeon, Ben Sira protests that he is too young.[42] In any case, Ben Sira claims that he is not a scion of the ruling house. In a last effort to retain the boy's company, the Babylonian asks him to remain seven more years at which time "I shall send you home in peace." Again, the king is rebuffed, but as if to compensate Nebuchadnezzar, Ben Sira answers twenty-two additional questions.

When asked about the source of his knowledge, the boy reverses the pronouncement of the biblical Amos, and proclaims himself "prophet and son of a prophet,"[43] a description that applies also to Solomon son of David in the Muslim tradition.[44] To probe Ben Sira's lofty claim to prophethood, the king will again test our protagonist regarding his knowledge and wisdom. These latest queries deal with biological and physical phenomena, subjects about which Solomon was, according to tradition, the most informed of men. Needless to say, the results once again favor Ben Sira. As in the stories of Solomon and the Queen of Sheba, each question and answer demonstrates the superiority of the Israelite and his God.

There is no doubt that the pseudonymous author of this medieval tract intended that Ben Sira and Nebuchadnezzar be seen as analogues to their famous predecessors. The implied relationship between Ben Sira and Solomon has already been noted. There is as well a direct relationship between the Babylonian and Solomon's female antagonist. For the text explicitly states that Nebuchadnezzar is the offspring resulting from a tryst between the Israelite ruler and the foreign queen, a union occasioned, to be sure, by her widely reported visit to his court. Not surprisingly, the Babylonian's ancestry is brought up during an exchange between him and the redoubtable hero of the book.

Asked how the head of the female rabbit was made smooth, Ben Sira answers, "miracle in lime."[45] Asked what that is, he replies that it is a depilatory made of lime solution laced with arsenic. "But if you really want to know," says Ben Sira, "ask your mother." "My mother!" says Nebuchadnezzar. The king's puzzled reaction certainly suggests the need for further comment, and so, by way of explanation, Ben Sira recalls the Queen of Sheba's visit to Solomon's court.[46]

It seems that Solomon was taken with the queen's beauty and desired her, but he found her exceedingly hairy.[47] The author asks us to remember that this historic encounter took place at a time when "no Israelite woman had hair on those parts of the body ordinarily covered by garments."[48] This last statement appears to echo a rabbinic discussion concerning women in biblical times. In any event, Solomon would not deny himself the pleasure of having the queen. No doubt, he had his reputation as a *surhomme du monde* to uphold. And so, he ordered his servants to prepare a depilatory, and in short order, the solution was applied and her skin was made "pure and completely free of hair." Solomon "then did with her as he wished."[49]

Note the use of language here: "Her skin was made pure" and "he did with her as he wished." The use of the verb *t-h-r* to indicate purity suggests not only that her hair was ugly, but that hairy women have to be cleansed or purified because there is something ritually unclean or unholy about them. Indeed, Pseudo Ben Sira suggests that, unlike contemporary females, biblical women shaved their pubic hairs because such hair was considered exceedingly dangerous to men. In any case, hirsute women are seen by our authors as anomalous to the God-given nature of the universe. That is, as the *Targum Sheni* indicates more explicitly, the abundance of certain hair on women is emblematic of reversed gender roles. Indeed, only after the Queen of Sheba lost her hair was Ben Sira's Solomon prepared or able to do with her "as he wished." As regards the relationship between men and women, there is still another point to be made in the subtle use of quotes. It would appear that by the Middle Ages (at least in this story), "satisfying all of her desires," the concern of the biblical Solomon, was confused with a rather different sensibility, namely, "taking her as he wished," that is, satisfying all of his desires. Moreover, Pseudo Ben Sira cannot imagine that the queen might have been put off by Solomon. As soon as the king is finished bedding her, she is made to exclaim, "I did not believe the things [that I heard about you] until I came and saw with my own eyes [in this context also experienced you physically] that what I had been told is not even the half of it."[50] As in the Hebrew Bible, these words illustrate the extent to which the queen has been moved by her visit. In the ancient chronicles, it is the king's wisdom and the splendor of his court and temple that causes her to sing the praises of Solomon and his God. In the spicy medieval version, she also waxes poetic over his sexual advances and prowess.

In any case, the queen's praise and her recognition of Solomon's dominance, the one theme that runs through all the accounts, are consistent with a world that is as it should be. For the ancient Israelites and their successors, God has created a universe that is intricately and perfectly designed. Its pattern reveals a quintessential harmony based on hierarchical structures; everything has its place and function. Who was this woman to think that she could alter the cosmic scheme by seeking rule over men, and, referring to the *Targum Sheni,* how significant is the sun, the subject of her worship, that its radiance can be blackened by a mere flock of birds? Just as God rules the universe including the sun, His chosen king, Solomon, will come to rule the upstart queen. With God's guidance, he commands her allegiance just as he demands allegiance from the demons, spirits, and Liliths—creatures who, unreined, could also distort the appearance of the natural order. In fact, various Jewish sources declare that the Queen of Sheba was not really a woman but a supranatural being with seductive sexual powers and an intention to kill infants in their cradles.

Solomon's Queen of Sheba was thus equated in midrashic and later Jewish mystical literature with the prototypical Lilith, Adam's original wife, who, according to legend, preceded the creation of Eve. But this first wife (who could have been the mother of the human race) refused to recognize her husband's status and held out for sexual equality if not dominance. She insisted on reversing positions and mounting him. Being disrespectful to Adam was serious enough, but this haughty challenge did not satisfy her. Boldly pronouncing the ineffable name of God (Yahweh), she abandoned the earth and threatened to harm newborn infants. When confronted about this threat, which is seen as running counter to the instinct and purpose of women, she defiantly proclaimed her destiny: She will alter the basic design of the universe. It is no wonder that, even to this day, amulets are worn to keep her from harming childbearing women and infants in their cradles and cribs. Seen in this context, the Queen of Sheba's desire to manipulate men and appropriate their rule is part and parcel of a larger and more ominous design: the abandonment of motherhood and, more generally, the rejection of any desire to nurture.[51]

The linking of Solomon's adversary with the demonic Lilith was not a matter to be treated lightly. Crowning the act of creation, God blessed Adam and Eve and ordered them "to be fruitful and multiply" and to "fill the earth and take dominion over it."[52] Following the flood and the near extinction of humankind and all living creatures, God repeated His blessing and reestablished, albeit with some modifications, the hierarchical nature of the universe. More than that, God established a covenant with Noah and gave notice that He would serve as the guarantor of the world as we know it. There would be no future destruction comparable to that of the flood.[53] The very same blessing of fertility reverberates in the later covenant between Abraham and God, an act that directly links the Almighty with those who will become his chosen people and their rulers, the Israelites and their kings. Should Abraham behave in a meritorious fashion, his Lord will maintain for all times "My covenant between Me and your progeny to follow."[54] And so, God's blessing was similarly granted to Isaac; to Jacob, the eponymous ancestor of the Israelite tribes; and by extension to the larger polity, the Jewish people.[55]

The hierarchy of God's creation and the survival of the species, matters of universal concern, thus became a special concern of Israel's society and its cultural guardians. By rabbinic times, procreation and dominion were considered by learned scholars as part of Mosaic legislation.[56] Hence, producing offspring was not only pleasurable and/or desirable, it had become incumbent on Jewish men (and women). What had been God's blessing to the seed of Abraham now had the force of substantive law, a statute that was part of a larger mandate to preserve a privileged community and its distinct ways. Legend had it that the refusal of a single Jew to conform to that mandate might occasion the Divine Presence to actually abandon the people called Israel.[57] In sum, there is among Jews a grand conception linking god, procreation, the hierarchy of nature, and the very special relationship between the people and their Lord.

Were the daughters of Israel to emulate a Queen of Sheba represented as Lilith, they would reject the basic design of God's creation and His commitment to preserve the world with its manifest hierarchies; they would prevent mankind from fulfilling God's commandment to be fruitful and multiply; and, were that not enough, that would compromise God's sacred and eternal covenant with His people.

To be sure, Pseudo Ben Sira allows the Queen of Sheba to become a mother, but only to give birth to a perverse child and for perverse ends. For it is through Nebuchadnezzar, her offspring, that she will ultimately best Solomon and usurp his authority. It is the hated Nebuchadnezzar who will destroy the temple that his father built and exile his father's people denying them sovereignty in their own land. They are thus left with neither house nor home. The other scions of the Israelites were expected to rule with "justice and righteousness" as did Solomon. But Nebuchadnezzar was his mother's child, the symbol of her perverse desire for power. Given the nature of mother and son, the survival of Solomon's Israelite progeny was in danger. The great king might have had his brief moment in the royal bedchamber, but the queen, at least in the story of Ben Sira, would seem to have had the last word. The irony of it all was surely not lost on medieval readers despite the skewed chronology linking Solomon with a son born some four hundred years later. The great exegete Rashi commenting on *and he* [Solomon] *satisfied all her desires* indicates that this refers exclusively to the acquisition of wisdom. Rashi's determination to cleanse the verse and story of any unpleasant sexual nuances is seeming proof that all too many others read the text as did Pseudo Ben Sira. An interpolation printed in Rashi's commentary reads: "*all her desires:* He (Solomon) had intercourse with her and she gave birth to Nebuchadnezzar who destroyed the temple."[58]

Stories of this dangerous queen featuring reversed gender roles and confused sexual identities continue to find expression in the folklore of diverse Jewish communities. The Jewish tales from Islamic lands will be presented below in a larger discussion of Jewish sources, Arabic texts, and the transfer of cultural artifacts.[59] Suffice it to say that the legend of this woman challenging the prerogatives of men, if not endangering mankind, has been adapted by Jews to fit a wide variety of cultural settings. The following account, recorded in Israel from a Polish informant, is an indication of just how widely the queen's strategies and tactics could travel without losing any of their frightening appeal.[60]

Our informant relates that some boys played along the banks of a river. "Suddenly, they heard a voice call out to them: 'Boys! Boys! Come to me and I shall give you lovely things.' The boys looked about and saw a gentile (*goy*) sitting in the water, a long pipe in his mouth. The lads didn't know that this was the Queen of Sheba in disguise. And so they approached [her] whereupon the Queen of Sheba immediately snatched them [and pulled them] into the water['s depths]." Perhaps for Polish Jews hairy legs were not unusual for women or, in any event, such hairiness was not unusual of Polish women in villages and small towns. But there was no confusing the long pipe. There was no doubt about it; this was certainly the Queen of Sheba. Dressed as a man and displaying an obvious symbol of her feigned gender, she lures the (foolhardy Jewish) youths (who should have stayed clear of the gentile stranger) and plunges them into a (dangerous) abyss. Some modern readers may wish to see a paradox in this rendering of the ancient tale: Here is the Queen of Sheba usurping phallic power while at the same time she uses water, a symbol of creative female fluid, as a destructive force.

Regardless of their provenance, these bizarre and wondrous tales, written texts and oral lore alike, suggest the same question. How did it come to pass that the biblical queen was transformed over time into the likes of Nebuchadnezzar's mother, the demonic Lilith, and even a pipe smoking woman, who disguised as a Polish man, lures Jewish children and drowns them in unfamiliar waters?

F. *The Origins of the Dangerous/Demonic Queen*

The later Jewish portrayal of Sheba's ancient sovereign hardly conforms to the "woman of valor" idealized in the sacred wisdom literature.[61] Nor does the later queen reflect any historic prototype from the Bible's depiction of specific Israelite women. Neither the ancient chronicler nor Proverbs, a book often critical of women, picture them as seeking to replace men or compete with them for political hegemony, let alone as abandoning procreation, child rearing, and other traditional female roles.[62] This does not imply, however, that, when called upon to act, women are incapable of dealing with men as men deal with one another in games of power.

One need only recall how Jael kills the Canaanite Sisera in a crafty and brutal fashion, a problematic and contradictory tale told in the Book of Judges in both prose and verse.[63] Having lulled the exhausted general to sleep with soothing milk and a surfeit of maternal concern, Jael drives a stake into his head, smashing his temple with such force as to cause the sharp end to exit at the other side of his head. In the poetic version, spiced with sexual imagery, he crumples before her, literally "between her legs," and dies. That the great Sisera was done in by a woman, as the prophetess Deborah had predicted, is a fitting touch of irony that mocks the proud Canaanite. Had he been victorious, he would have savored his victory by taking the women of Israel, as his proud mother expected: "They must be dividing the spoil . . . A damsel for the taking, one or two for every man."[64] Instead, he is ravaged with cunning and cold brutality by one symbolizing his intended conquests.

Citing the Canaanite tale of Aqhat, feminists suggest that Jael and Deborah should be linked to the warrior goddesses of ancient mythology. But, unlike Aqhat where patriarchal order is established against the threat of a wrathful female, the story of Judges is seen by S. Hanselman as subverting patriarchy at the behest and hand of a woman. However challenging, such a view is best examined with caution lest we place too much emphasis on Jael's savage act and the sexual allusions that spice the poetry of Judges 5. Whatever interpretation modern readers may wish to attach to the juxtaposing of captive women with a woman assassin and to the implement and grim method of execution, the biblical Jael, a married woman, is merely the instrument of God's will in a larger contest between the Israelites and Jabin King of Canaan. As portrayed in scripture, the slaying of Sisera does not challenge the social foundations or even mores of ancient Israelite society. The action is directed specifically against Canaanite hegemony and not the global hegemony of men. In any case, Jael's actions clearly do not disturb those responsible for traditional notions of patriarchy. The planning and execution of Sisera are justified completely by the biblical author and, more to the point, they were fully commended by later Jewish interpreters who had a vested interest in preserving gender boundaries. Whatever the prebiblical origins of the tale or its alleged links to goddesses of the ancient Near East, the later interpretation, which produced our demonic queen, preserves no certain echo of a remote mythic past.[65]

The rabbis do give the tale a sexual gloss of their own:[66] A remarkable beauty with a seductive voice to match, Jael prepares to attract the fleeing Sisera's attention. There are no verbal suggestions from Jael that she would actually encourage any advances. The signs are all visual but hardly subtle: seductive clothing, jewels, and a bed of roses for the exhausted Sisera to sleep away his fatigue. The Canaanite is immediately smitten by the comely Jael and is ready to bring her home to mother once he can safely get away, a commentary suggested by the biblical text in which Sisera's mother imagines her son taking Israelite women as the spoils of war. Despite the external trappings designed to stimulate Sisera's lust, there is no hint of sexual play in the rabbinic account. Jael, a proper Jewish woman, offers him only food and rest in return for an unnamed recompense. When he awakens, he asks for water. She gives him instead a drink with wine that has a soporific effect. Invoking God's name that she might have the (physical) strength to carry out his murder, she jostles him to see if he is capable of stirring. Assured that he is beyond response, she pulls him off the bed, and when he slumps to the floor, she drives the stake into his head.

In such fashion, the rabbis addressed the contradictory versions of Sisera's death in prose and verse. They suggest that he crumpled at her feet, as in chapter 5, because she dragged him off the bed while he was unconscious. Only when he was lying prone and immobile, as described in chapter 4, was she able to carry out the bizarre method of execution. They surely surmised that no female (indeed what male) could hammer a tent stake into a man's head while he was able to offer even the slightest resistance. In their version, the force of the blow shocks Sisera into consciousness. He recovers just long enough to bewail his ignominious fate at the hands of a woman. She acknowledges his last words with a final assault, this time administered verbally. What were her motives? The rabbis certainly do not conceive of her as striking a blow for the independence of women. She becomes a temptress and acts as she does only for the sake of her God and her people.

Nor is her contemporary, Deborah, the prophetess who issued the challenge to twenty years of Canaanite hegemony, a woman who challenges reigning notions of sexual hierarchy. There is a division of labor in the revolt of the Israelites. As prophetess and judge, she provides religious inspiration and leadership; the all-important military campaign is conducted by her male counterpart, Barak ben Abinoam. True enough, Barak is denied the glory of killing Jabin's general. Even before the fighting has begun, the prophetess foretells of Sisera's demise at the hands of a woman[67]—such is the power granted Deborah and Jael in this stirring account. Nevertheless, Deborah's opposition to the Canaanites is framed as a conflict between God's people and a rival polity, not a struggle between male supremacy and female ambition. Although she is both judge and prophetess, Deborah never renounces the traditional role of woman. Described as the wife of Lapidoth and referred to as "a mother in Israel,"[68] she is hardly the analogue of the female who gave birth to Nebuchadnezzar, let alone the rapacious Lilith who preys on pregnant women and murders infants in their cribs. Indeed, this story from the Book of Judges reflects the sensibilities of biblical mothers as well as battle-hardened warriors. In the final segment of her victory hymn, Deborah sings of Sisera's mother peering through the latticework of her window anxiously waiting for her son to return.[69] But she waits in vain to greet him and rejoice in his triumph. Instead, it is Deborah the "mother in Israel," who exults at the feats of her sons, Yahweh's warriors.

The postbiblical authorities were somewhat disturbed by the prominence of the Israelite women. The victory on the field of battle was that of Barak and the men, all praise to them, but Jael is clearly the most compelling figure of a tale that is, after all, Deborah's story. Moreover, Deborah was granted the status of a judge, a function otherwise reserved for men in the biblical narratives. The learned rabbis understood that women could be prophets, as were Miriam and Huldah, but political leadership was another matter. The postbiblical view of women and politics is best summed up by the dictum: "Woe unto the generation whose leader is a woman."[70]

Later sensibilities therefore called for a commentary that reduced Deborah's role. The rabbis stress that she was not only Barak's partner in the revolt, she was as well his partner in life.[71] But how can the wife of Lapidoth, of whom nothing is said in the biblical text, be transformed into the wife of Barak ben Abinoam? The authorities remind us that Barak had more than one name. It appears that he carried candles to the sanctuary at Shilo and so he was also called Lapidoth, that is "Flames." As if calling attention once again to the division of labor that characterized the revolt, the rabbis point out that while Barak provided the manly work of carrying the candles, Deborah supplied the wicks which she made so thick that they burned for long periods of time illuminating the house of God. In return, God appointed her prophetess and judge so that her light and fame should shine throughout the land.

The biblical prophetess and judge is portrayed, nevertheless, as a woman subject to the frailties and temperament occasioned by women's nature—that is, as the rabbis understood that nature. Resonating to the biblical text which informs us that Deborah rendered her judgments under a palm tree, the rabbinical authorities indicate that it would have been improper for her to see men in her house.[72] In any case, she allowed success to intoxicate her. She was insubordinate to her husband and a braggart. The rabbis thus explained why it is Barak who answers her summons in Judges 4:6 and not the reverse, and why the Song of Deborah, the stirring poem, which is chapter 5, speaks so much of herself: "Eminence is not for a woman." Indeed, God was so displeased with Deborah, He suspended her prophetical gift while she sang her own praises.[73] The rabbinic accounts suggest that, were the story of the revolt told in full and not colored by Deborah's self-serving version of events, Barak and the men of Israel would have emerged the major players. For Barak himself was a prophet but he was also a modest man. The postbiblical accounts, which picture Deborah competing with her husband and taking liberty with God's grace by rejecting the role designed for her by nature, are consistent with the more benign versions of Solomon's joust with the Queen of Sheba. Lest the authorities appear too critical of Deborah for modern readers, she is, despite her vanity, a heroine to the rabbis and a far cry from the demonic queens of our story.

Among the women described in the Hebrew Bible, various non-Israelites are clearly more representative of demonic females. Understanding these women requires juxtaposing their "otherness" as females with an "otherness" that is generally representative of foreign cultures and values. For it is that linkage to the non-Israelite world, rather than any overt desire to rule, which makes these foreign women dangerous if not lethal.

Delilah, presumed to be a non-Israelite, but not explicitly stated as such, seduces Samson, a Nazirite, into revealing the source of his extraordinary strength.[74] After teasing one another, he with false revelations, and she with sexual overtures but no lovemaking, they reach an agreement. In return for her love, he reveals his secret. Upon learning that, she emasculates Samson by having his head shaved. Having yielded his locks for the first time to a razor against his mother's pledge to the God of Israel, the Nazirite is rendered powerless. The man once capable of slaying a thousand Philistines with the jawbone of an ass has become the victim of his own unbridled passion.[75] And so, the vengeful Philistines are able to capture the weakened Samson and, finishing what Delilah had begun, render him completely impotent, or so they thought, by putting out his eyes.[76] The rest of this story rich in symbolism requires no telling here. Suffice it to say, as with the account of the worthy Jael, one should not be misled by the actions of a crafty woman. Delilah does not betray Samson because she seeks to displace men from rule but because she has been promised eleven hundred pieces of silver for uncovering the source of his strength.[77] An inherently dangerous female, she is surely the agent of Samson's demise but there is no question of her assuming his power.

Similarly, Jezebel, a sexually seductive creature and most certainly a foreign woman—in fact a Tyrian princess—is capable of the most insidious and evil influence.[78] She is portrayed as the gray eminence behind her husband Ahab, the Israelite King who scripture and rabbinic tradition alike see as the embodiment of corruption.[79] As Ahab's strong-willed and beloved consort, Jezebel occasions state policy without being granted the privilege of rule. Like Delilah and the Queen of Sheba before her, she knows only too well how to manipulate men with her feminine wiles. When the reformer Jehu puts an end to her husband's house, the line of Omri, she carefully applies her makeup, perhaps a last defiant gesture or, as traditional Jews are taught, in anticipation of seducing still another powerful Israelite.[80] Will she save her life and influence? This time she has met a man principled enough to withstand her. Having rebuffed her son-in-law Joram's offer of peace—"What peace can there be while your mother continues her endless whoring and witchcraft"[81]—Jehu acts against her. She dies in the presence of eunuchs, presumably immune to her charm, and her body parts are left to the dogs.[82] No woman is so vilified by the biblical historians and rabbinic commentators, but when all is said and done, the powerful Jezebel can exercise real authority only in concert with a male ruler. In this respect, she seems at first glance a far cry from the Queen of Sheba, whether the biblical or postbiblical sovereign.[83]

The closest biblical parallel to the demonic ruler of Sheba is Athaliah,

Jezebel's daughter, or in another tradition sister-in-law, who like Jezebel is a corrupt woman given to the foreign ways of the Tyrians.[84] Were that not enough to warrant condemnation, Athaliah is a unique affront to God's basic design for the sexes. Among the Israelites, men are called upon to be sovereigns, but she is a queen who rules by royal prerogative. In other words, she fulfills what may have been Jezebel's intent for herself, or at least represents the logical extension of Jezebel's own career. The only female to rule the biblical polity of Israel, she maintains power for six full years. What is more noteworthy, given the subject of our discussion, is the manner in which Athaliah seized control of her realm. When her son, King Ahaziah of Judah, was killed by the reformer Jehu, she instigated the murder of all the heirs-apparent save one grandson, Joash, who was spirited away unbeknownst to her. In such fashion she meant to clear the field of royal pretenders and pave the way for herself. The perceived absence of a scion from the ruling house may have allowed her to seize power but one should not underestimate what it meant for a woman to maintain that power. That her rule lasted a full six years is no doubt a tribute to extraordinary political skill and ruthlessness. Be that as it may, a palace revolt at which Joash reappears results in Athaliah's murder thus ending the only female stewardship in the history of the Davidic monarchy.[85]

Regrettably, the reign of Athaliah is treated by the biblical historians as an ephemeral if very unpleasant episode in the generally unpleasant story of Omri's line. The all too brief description of her tenure leaves us asking for more details of this remarkable woman and the circumstances that surround her life. Can she be compared with the remarkable woman of our enquiry, or might Athaliah even have been a prototype of the menacing postbiblical Queens of Sheba? She certainly has the instincts of Lilith. Witness the manner in which she destroys her own offspring. The biblical story being so terse, we can only speculate about Athaliah's political skills and whether or not she displayed Jezebel's lethal charm, a negative quality also associated with the illustrious Queen of Sheba. In any event, Athaliah is sui generis among women of the Hebrew Bible. Contrasted with her, biblical women are fearless in defense of their extended family, anxious to produce offspring, and supportive of their progeny once born. Even Jezebel, the quintessential dangerous female, never went so far as to indulge in infanticide.

Given that she is unique among Israelite women, it is perhaps surprising that Athaliah elicits little comment in later Jewish tradition. Might it be that the "historic" queen was considered too menacing and indeed too successful a female to draw detailed comment from men? There is no grudging respect for her nor is there any perceived need to endow her with legendary credentials as did later writers of the Queen of Sheba. The rabbis merely point out that she was one of but a handful of female rulers known to humankind and leave it at that.[86] It appears that there are no direct links between Athaliah and Solomon's antagonist or at least none that is stated by Jewish authorities. What, then, is the origin of the dangerous woman of postbiblical accounts, the Sheban Queen who acts as a man and presumes to rule over them?

The convergence of so many cultures in the Near East and over so long a time suggests a complex development to the portrayal of the postbiblical queen. The notion of a female wishing to defy time-honored gender roles is broadly based from Hellenistic times through the Middle Ages and beyond. Indeed, there are noteworthy examples of famous women who actually ruled: Zenobia, Cleopatra, the Byzantine Empress Irene, and the like.[87] Nor ought we rule out connections to the indigenous cultures of a more ancient Near East. Is it not plausible to go still a step further and assume that the ancient Israelites resonated more directly to dangerous female creatures, demons and goddesses alike, than official Israelite historiography was prepared to discuss?

It is true that, as a rule, biblical historians do not link women to demonic forces. It is, nevertheless, also true that beneath the surface of the historical texts there is real concern with the mysterious, hence dangerous elements of ancient Near Eastern culture. This concern is shaped, to be sure, by the highly judgmental attitudes of biblical authors. They saw a preoccupation with the mysterious and supernatural as a direct threat to the beliefs and well-being of their own society. Needless to say, they were equally critical of those who laid special claim to understanding and manipulating the world of spirits and the unknown: necromancers, wizards, false prophets, and the like.[88] The biblical agenda is not to give credence to supernatural forces, which are part and parcel of the world of neighboring polytheist cultures. They may not be used to explain human experience nor more generally the workings of the universe. The mandate of those who shaped the Hebrew Bible and who understood themselves to be the guardians of ancient Israelite religion was to demythologize ritual and history. The purpose of their enterprise was to promote monotheism, the ideological fulcrum of the Israelite polity. And so, the biblical chroniclers produced the first extensive and sustained historiographical enquiry that linked events of past, present, and future without a direct appeal to mythopoeic thinking or intentional reliance on supernatural personae. Even the cosmological segments, the ante- and postdiluvian accounts, and the patriarchal narratives of Genesis, texts that imitate mythic forms and retain references to mythic figures, have an unmistakable monotheist thrust. Again and again, the Hebrew Bible liberates the God of Israel from the limiting influence of cyclic occurrence and from the juxtaposition of natural forces with the divine. Unlike pagan divinities, the God of Israel is not compromised by chaos beyond his control, nor are his subjects absolved of their behavior by forces they cannot comprehend or master by their own moral strength. The authors of the biblical chronicles, or more correctly, the redactors of these biblical texts, created a sacred history that assumes a linear development according to a grand design of God's own choosing. Having done so, they gave the interpretation of historical events a religious perspective that could be consistently applied to past, present, and future episodes. To follow God's clearly established design, more particularly the law given to Moses, was to ensure the harmony of both individual and collective existence. To do otherwise was to risk divine retribution. No demonic forces were allowed to intervene freely in human affairs let alone compromise divine will or schema.[89]

Judging by their own testimony, the monotheist authors saw their ideological agenda as taking a long time to fulfill. For the residual influences of pagan culture remained bothersome long after the establishment of the Israelite monarchy. Ironically, Solomon himself is said to have impeded the eradication of pagan influence by erecting high places to please his foreign wives.[90] However tempting and easy it might have been in those circumstances to make a demonic creature of the Sheban Queen, Solomon's antagonist, the biblical authors, given their agenda to demythologize, presented her as an historic person and her visit as a real event. Be that as it may, Solomon's indiscretions reportedly led to the division of his great realm.[91] Subsequent rulers, even more accepting of foreign influence, were said to have suffered still greater calamities. To be sure, there are sufficient hints that following foreign ways was a rather complex phenomenon. A changing Israelite society that featured the increasing centralization of power and tangled political alliances could hardly be insulated from the encroachment of neighboring polytheist cultures.[92]

In shaping the history of ancient Israel, the monotheist writers were quick to condemn; there is the suspicion, nevertheless, that they did not wash all their dirty linen in public and that the specific details of past Israelite practices might have been more syncretistic than the Hebrew chronicles lead us to believe. One notes in this respect the particularly savage denunciation of King Manasseh, who, in addition to the usual litany of polytheist backsliding, is accused of making his son pass through the fire; of practicing soothsaying and divination; and of employing necromancers and conjurers (to consult spirits)—all this in an attempt to provoke God.[93] Were Manasseh's actions a general reflection of assimilationist tendencies in ancient Israel, we would be forced to conclude that, at least in certain courtly circles, the Israelites had not immunized themselves against the mysterious and demonic world of their pagan contemporaries.

The references to Manasseh notwithstanding, there is still no direct link between these assimilationist tendencies and the independent if not destructive nature attributed to the postbiblical Queen of Sheba. Perhaps it is too much to expect a direct connection. The very linkage of seductive powers and demonology and, more generally, of seductive women subverting God's design by their influence over men may be enough to suggest that the later portrayal of the Sheban monarch was inspired, however indirectly, by references to women in the Hebrew Bible. Jezebel may have required Ahab to carry out her agenda, but as far as the rabbis are concerned she had achieved power comparable to that of men as did three other remarkable women: Athaliah, Vashti, and Semiramis.[94] Interestingly enough, not included in their company is Queen Esther who manipulates Ahasuerus with her beauty and charms Haman into sowing the seeds of his own destruction. It would appear that righteous women, that is those who serve God, are identified with their own and that sexuality when it is employed to carry out God's design is commendable. Our concern here is, however, sexuality and evil as in the biblical accusation of Jezebel's pagan ways and more particularly Jehu's comment which links her "endless whoring and witchcraft."

One also recalls the "forbidden" or "strange" female, that rebellious and mysterious creature of the Book of Proverbs.[95] She is described as "the alien woman whose talk is smooth. [She] who forsakes the companion (*aluf*) of her youth and disregards the covenant of her lord [and master]. Her house sinks down to death (*mwt*) and her course leads to the rephaim [i.e., ghosts of the dead]. All who come to her cannot return and find the paths of life." It has been suggested that the enigmatic female of these passages is a distant echo of the avenging goddess Anath. In Canaanite mythology, the enraged goddess rips Mot (*mwt*) to shreds and then ravages humanity, wading hip deep in blood and gore.[96] However enticing, the proposed connection between the "foreign" woman of Proverbs and the goddess of the West Semites is problematic. In any case, it is not important that we have a mythic analogue to the later Queen of Sheba. The woman described in the biblical text has all the frightening qualities that we are looking for without necessarily being Anath's look-alike or, for that matter, the analogue of any other goddess from the ancient Near East. For those postbiblical readers who shaped the later traditions of Solomon and the Queen of Sheba, the "foreign" woman of Proverbs would have been enough to give cause for concern. For them, she would have been the quintessential seductress: her loyalty cannot be taken for granted; she is foreign and presumably foreign in her ways; and above all she is absolutely lethal. In sum, she has all the negative qualities ascribed by writers to the worst of the later Queens of Sheba. If there is no direct prototype for the woman who contests Solomon in postbiblical Jewish lore, it is because she is, like the seductive creature of Proverbs, a composite of all the dangerous women feared by men.

This fear of women has deep roots in many cultures. Among Israel's ancient neighbors, there is no lack of female beings defying natural order or endangering humankind, the aforementioned Anath among them. More specifically, scholars have attempted to trace the origins of the Jewish Lilith to the Lamaštu of Mesopotamian mythology and to the Canaanite/Mesopotamian demon Lil/Lilitu, a winged strangler of children.[97] The Hebrew scriptures are, to be sure, lacking in references to comparable demonic female creatures—the single reference to Lilith, that of Isaiah 34:14, mentions her only in passing. Isaiah's Lilith, together with various beasts of prey, will inhabit the wasteland created on the Lord's day of vengeance. There is, nevertheless, reason to believe that demonic creatures disturbed the imaginations of biblical men and women, as indeed they frightened others. The very need of Hebrew writers to suppress influences from neighboring cultures suggests the seriousness with which ancient Near Eastern traditions were viewed by Israel's monotheists. Still, there is a nagging question: Given the mandate of biblical historiography to cleanse its tradition of foreign influence and paint events and personae in human and Yahwistic terms, how is it that the postbiblical authorities were so explicit in portraying a demonic Lilith and so free generally in their use of mythic elements as later tales of Solomon and the queen reveal?

The rabbis, although they would hardly admit to it, had a different agenda from that of their biblical predecessors. It would appear that the battle for monotheism had been settled in their favor despite newer forms of paganism.[98] There was no doubt religious leakage, as indeed there always is, and there was no doubt concern over that, as there always will be, but in all likelihood the identity of the Jewish community was well formed. The inroads of foreign cultural influences still bore watching, but normative Judaism would not be blown away or even seriously altered by some polytheist heresy—certainly not in the great centers of Jewish life: the Land of Israel and Babylonia. Nor do there seem to have been major political or religious concerns with dissident Jewish sects after the calamity of the Roman wars—the rise of Christianity may be seen as a separate development. It was rather the links to the biblical past and the sense of legitimacy that was derived from that past that elicited the concern of the rabbis. How were they to establish their authority as if it did indeed represent what they claimed: an unbroken chain going back to Moses at Sinai? Similarly, how could they continue to make an historical case for the legitimacy of Israel following the dissolution of the polity and ritual center that bound their people? The biblical past had in many ways become an anachronism in the absence of a temple and a state and under otherwise changed historical conditions.

Betrayed by historical events that actually unfolded, the rabbis reversed the course of Israelite historiography and took to mythologizing the present and the distant as well as more recent past. The vivid and "realistic" portraits of biblical historiography give way to the legendary figures and events of rabbinic midrash. Connections that strain credulity for modern readers become the common fare of biblical exegesis. The extended realistic chronicle so ably developed by biblical historians is replaced by short anecdotal accounts long on fantasy, the stuff of enchanting folklore and legend. True enough, both biblical history and rabbinic midrash are thoroughly didactic, but there is a world of difference between them regarding substance as well as form. In a manner of speaking, one might claim that midrash is a literary process that freed Jewish authors to explore explicitly a mysterious world that the Hebrew Bible sought to suppress. This process was already in evidence among Jews before 70 C.E. and the destruction of the temple, as can be witnessed in various works of the Pseudepigrapha and the apocalyptical writings from Qumran. The Bible itself exhibits some features of midrash, particularly in the Book of Daniel. But no one ought confuse the previously mentioned forays into midrash with the exquisite, full-blown enterprise of rabbinic exegesis. One can hardly compare biblical historiography with the rabbinic ordering of historical events and persons. And so, the terse "historical" account of the Queen's visit to Solomon's court acquired legendary trappings.

In their broadest sense, the postbiblical stories of Solomon and the Queen, with their emphasis on confused roles and identities, have both ancient antecedents and contemporary analogues in many cultures.[99] Peeling away the Jewish material from the legend of the Israelite king and the wily queen, one uncovers a terrifying fear that has gripped men and women alike in traditional societies of the Near East: that is, left to their own devices, dangerous female creatures would change the nature of the universe as we know it. For in aping men and seeking political and even sexual parity with them, they may well rescind the obligations of mothering if not motherhood. The implications of this course are self-evident. If the danger to the newly born and those who would be born is realized, humankind will not be able to sustain the species and in time will become extinct. Therefore, it is imperative that men, and the women of their households as well, do everything to maintain the separate roles that nature has designed for them at God's behest. In any event, that is what texts ancient and medieval say they ought do.

From the perspective of our authors, there always will be, as there have always been, clever females who seek to undermine the "natural authority" of men. There are also, however, champions like Solomon who have the capacity to put them in their place, restoring thereby the divine order of the universe. It is Solomon, with his extraordinary understanding of nature's schema and his God-given power over the world of the supranatural, who commands attention from other peoples and cultures directly or indirectly familiar with the story of the queen's visit.[100] It is also this legendary Solomon who is the likeliest link between the Israelite king of the Hebrew Bible and the prophet of Muslim sources. For there is much in the Solomonic saga that speaks to the influence of Jewish themes on Islamic tradition.

2 *The Qur'ānic Story of Solomon and the Queen of Sheba*

As in Jewish tradition, the Islamic story of Solomon and the Queen of Sheba begins with sacred text. That is to say, it is first found in the Qur'ān, the public utterances of the Prophet Muḥammad. The relevant verses are situated in Sūrah xxvii, that section of Muslim scripture titled "The Ant" after a chance meeting between the great prophet Solomon and the humblest of God's creatures. Later Muslim anthologies generally begin the tale with the exegesis to verse 20 and end with 44;[1] however, the previous five verses, which also refer to Solomon, may be considered part of the story.

A. *The Account of the Queen's Visit*

The terse and disjointed Qur'ānic narrative, which has given rise to much fascinating, if not tortured, commentary, begins with Solomon's credentials. Like his father, David, also a prophet, he was preferred by God "to many believers" (15). Indeed, Solomon had been "taught the speech of birds" and "something of everything" had been bestowed upon him (16). This unique ability of his to communicate with (all) of God's creatures, to say nothing of his vast material possessions, is considered a sign of divine "graciousness made clear" (16). Who else could possess so bizarre and imposing an entourage, including "jinn and men and birds kept in order of rank" (17)? To command such resources is an enormous responsibility, for power and wealth so awesome can corrupt those who rule. One need not fear for this ruler, however. An encounter with the ants in their kingdom (18–19) illustrates Solomon's sense of gratitude for the beneficence that Allāh has bestowed upon him. As prophet, he wishes only to "be righteous in a manner [God] will approve."

Having defined the nature of the man and the vast resources that he commands at God's behest, the Qur'ān turns to the prophet's encounter with the Queen of Sheba. It all began with a muster of the air corps. In reviewing his army of birds, Solomon cannot locate the hoopoe (20), and so the normally tempered Israelite proclaims (in anger), "I will surely punish him severely or slaughter him unless he brings me a clear excuse" (21). Without commentary, that excuse is provided in the very next verse. The bird informs Solomon that he has come upon something that even the prophet has not seen. He has been to Sheba and has now come back "with tidings true" (22). An amazing tale begins to unfold, for the hoopoe has seen in this journey a land ruled by a woman. Moreover, like Solomon, she too "has had something of everything bestowed upon her" including "a great throne" (23). The reward of this material splendor would seem anomalous with her religious beliefs and practices; the hoopoe found the queen and her subjects "bowing down before the sun rather than God." The proferred explanation is that "Satan has made their [ungodly] deeds attractive to them thus blocking them from the true path." Hence, "they are not truely guided" (24), for "there is no God but He [Allāh] Lord of the mighty throne" (26).[2]

Solomon's interest is clearly aroused at news of this hitherto unknown ruler and her kingdom. He will find out whether the bird has "spoken the truth" or is "among the liars" (28). A missive will be sent with the hoopoe who will linger in order to bring back news of the queen's response.

The scene then shifts immediately to the queen's court. "O ye leading men," she addresses her entourage, "a noble letter has been delivered to me [29]. It is from Solomon and reads:

> In the name of God, the Merciful and Compassionate:
> Do not be haughty! Come to me submitting as Muslims [32]!

The sharp tone of the prophet's letter provokes her greatest concern and so she wishes the assistance of her nobles in responding. "Advise me in my affair," she says, "I decide matters only when you bear witness" (33). As great warriors, they indicate a readiness for fierce combat, but, in recognition of her authority, they leave the matter for her to decide (34). Having solicited their advice, the wise queen is cautious of blindly endorsing their martial sentiments, for she is well aware of the consequences of defeat. Conquerors transform "the greatest . . . people into the most debased" (34). Instead of arms, she will try diplomacy; a gift will be sent. The response to this overture will be a sign of her future dealings with the powerful Israelite (35). But Solomon is not easily dissuaded from his course of action. He upbraids the queen's emissaries for trying to reach him with (mere) wealth and bids them return to their masters (with a second message). Because the Queen of Sheba does not see fit to come to him and submit, she and her subjects can expect his arrival with irresistible forces; he "shall indeed expel them [from their city] debased and they shall be humbled" (37).

It would appear that the prophet is confident of changing her mind through this course of action. Surely, he expects that she will come to him in submission, for he inquires of his entourage, "Which of you will bring me her throne before they come to me submitting as Muslims" (38). A trustworthy and powerful ʻifrīt, one of the jinn, offers to bring it to Solomon before the latter concludes his assembly (39). Apparently that is not quick enough. One who has knowledge of "the book" then speaks out. "I shall bring it to you in the twinkling of an eye," he says. Upon seeing her throne actually standing before him, Solomon gives thanks to God in a rather puzzling statement, "This is the grace of my Lord in order to test me. Shall I give thanks or be ungrateful? Indeed my Lord is rich and generous" (40).

Possession of the throne, the symbol of the queen's authority, sets the stage for her eventual submission to the prophet and his God. At Solomon's command, the throne is disguised and a test is devised to see "if she is truly guided" (41). She will be asked, "Is this the likes of your throne?" When in fact the question is put to the queen, she answers, "It is as if it were." Why Solomon should have chosen this particular question and why the queen chose her seemingly evasive response is not indicated by the Qur'ānic text; there is, as a result, much tortured explanation from the exegetes.[3] Nevertheless, the basic thrust of the verse is clear. The loss of the emblem of her authority signals an end to her independence and that of her subjects. There is no place in the House of Islam for a ruler who worships other than God, a queen "from a people of unbelievers" (43). Her moment of truth is at hand. She is told to enter a court[4] "which she reckoned to be a pool [of water], and [so] she uncovered her ankles" (44). It is in reality, though, "a court made smooth of slabs of glass." Finally (in Solomon's presence) she proclaims, "My Lord, I have wronged myself. I submit through Solomon to Allāh, Lord of the Universe" (44). There is now no doubt as to the finality of her submission and the triumph of the prophet and his God.

B. *Muslim Scripture and Jewish Sources*

What view of the world is reflected in these verses and to what history, if any, does it resonate? At first glance, there are obvious similarities between the Qur'ānic version and the above-mentioned Jewish sources. Both Jewish and Muslim scriptures describe the visit of a proud and powerful queen to an even more powerful Israelite ruler; both indicate her plan to buy peace through payment of tribute; both require a test of intelligence between adversaries; and finally both sacred texts relate the ultimate triumph of Solomon. These shared themes aside, it is difficult if not impossible to establish any linkage between the biblical and Qur'ānic versions. In any event, one would hardly want to make a case for direct linkage based on these texts alone. The differences in content and mode are simply too broad ranging.

Even the shared themes reflect different outlooks. Unlike the Muslim prophet, the biblical King Solomon is anything but scornful of the queen's tribute; to the contrary, her wealth is part and parcel of his larger political designs. The biblical queen is skeptical of Solomon's legendary intelligence, and so she tests him with a series of riddles; in the Qur'ān it is the Israelite king who does the testing "to see if she is truly guided." Above all, the theological thrust of each account is different. True, both the Bible and the Qur'ān end with a triumph for Solomon and his God, but the nature of the victory reflects conflicting views. For the biblical king, success is that of his political agenda, signified in this case by her payment of tribute. For the Qur'ānic prophet, who is contemptuous of her tribute, it is her submission to Allāh, Lord of the Universe.

Regarding content, the *Targum Sheni* is a much closer parallel to the Muslim account.[5] As does the Qur'ān, the postbiblical source reveals Solomon's capacity to speak to all of God's creatures and vividly describes his army, a terrifying host of humans, animals, birds, and supranatural beings. Both accounts introduce the hoopoe, who is reported missing at Solomon's muster of the troops, an absence that causes the king or prophet to be enraged. In both versions Solomon threatens the bird but is mollified at hearing a wondrous tale of a hitherto unknown kingdom ruled by a woman. Moreover, the *Targum Sheni* and the Qur'ān both report Solomon's desire to reduce the Queen of Sheba and her people to subservience. Both accounts indicate that the hoopoe was commissioned to carry the letter containing his demands and that, upon reading the letter, she sought but did not follow the advice of her notables. Instead of defying the Israelite, she decides on tribute and a diplomatic course that will bring her to Solomon's abode. According to both accounts, it is there, in an amazing structure built of glass, that she finally confronts him and in the end is forced to recognize his primacy. All these common elements would seem to suggest a link of sorts between the Jewish legend and Muslim scripture.

Nevertheless, there are also pointed differences between the Muslim and Jewish texts, as indeed there are bound to be in any sort of cultural borrowing. One can hardly expect to see the Muslim Solomon threatening the absent hoopoe because he was somewhat into his cups while entertaining foreign heads of state. As pictured in the *Targum Sheni,* the king's joviality and rage, both occasioned by an excess of wine, are a reflection of Ahasueras's feast, the event which frames the interpolated material on Solomon and the Queen of Sheba. Quite obviously, the Muslim prohibition against drink does not allow God's prophet to be portrayed in so compromising a fashion. Nor would the Arab tribesman of Central Arabia, for whom nobility is intimately linked with military prowess, conceive of a leader soliciting advice from notables incapable of waging war, as does the *Targum Sheni*'s Queen of Sheba. The Qur'ān's advisors are brave warriors ready to do battle, if indeed for an ungodly cause. No doubt, the reader found it strange enough that a woman should rule over men.

Still, not all the differences between the Jewish and Muslim versions can be attributed to differences of cultural sensibility. It is clear that Solomon's acquisition of the queen's throne and his testing of her are central to the message of the Qur'ānic text, and yet there is no reference at all to this in any of the Jewish sources currently known. The Jewish sources speak only of the riddles she directed to Solomon and the answers with which he disarmed her. More significant yet is the different message conveyed by each source. The Book of Kings speaks, albeit implicitly, about the dangers of a wealthy and independent monarch to Solomon's political hegemony; the postbiblical texts, particularly the *Targum Sheni,* view the Queen of Sheba as nothing less than a threat to the natural order of the universe. Even if the queen were no Lilith, she is by her very nature and being a threat to the world as it is and should be.

No such dangers are manifest in the Qur'ānic account. Explaining his absence at the muster of Solomon's host, the hoopoe does not titillate the prophet with the discovery of a realm that has not yet fallen under the Israelite's influence. Nor is the Muslim prophet moved to subdue the Queen of Sheba because her capital is described to him as a city whose dust "was like gold and whose silver was as prevalent as dung in the markets."[6] The queen may possess great wealth, but what is that to Solomon who proclaims, "something of everything has been bestowed upon us"?[7] To be sure, there is something most unusual about a land ruled by a woman, but who is this woman to contest Solomon with riddles? It is rather the prophet who tests and probes in Muslim scripture. The Qur'ān's queen is clever indeed; she would have to be to rule over a society of men. But one hardly has the impression that her continued independence is so appalling a threat to the natural order. Why then does Solomon wish to subdue her in the Muslim version? It is not for wealth; he is contemptuous of her tribute. She does not threaten him politically; if she defies him, he can and will "certainly come [to her] with contingents too powerful [to overcome]."[8] It is not because he is threatened by her feminine wiles; there is never any question that he, unlike her subjects, is in complete control. The Muslim prophet wishes to subdue her for one reason and one reason alone: she is an unbeliever.

Having to excuse his absence, the hoopoe tells Solomon something that the prophet, despite his legendary knowledge, had not previously known. The bird begins speaking of a realm ruled by a woman of fabulous wealth, a queen possessing a great throne, but then switches to the heart of the matter. She and her people bow down before the sun rather than God. "Satan [a male figure] has made their deeds attractive to them thus blocking them from the true path," hence "they are not rightly guided."[9] The situation cannot be allowed to continue. Solomon sends the queen a message by way of his winged emissary. It is both short and to the point. Unlike in the *Targum Sheni,* he does not order her to appear and pay homage so that he can include her among his other collectibles, the subdued monarchs of the earth. "In the name of God, the Merciful and Compassionate," he proclaims, "Do not be haughty; come to me submitting as Muslims."[10] In the end, she has no recourse but to comply and, acknowledging the error of her ways, she calls out, "My Lord, I have wronged myself. I [now] submit through Solomon to Allāh, the Lord of the Universe."[11]

In I Kings 11:1–13, Solomon's romantic liaisons with foreign women occasion a rather tolerant attitude towards polytheism. "For it came to pass, when Solomon had grown old, that his wives turned his heart to other gods and he was thus not completely devoted to his Lord as was David, his father."[12] The harsh result of this flirtation with women and things foreign is the posthumous division of Solomon's kingdom and the pointed criticism of the ancient chronicler.[13] This compromise with non-Israelite practices, however, was the mistake of a monarch grown old and not the vigorous ruler of the previous chapter. In his version of Solomon's encounter with the Queen of Sheba, the biblical historian expresses no doubt of the king's strict adherence to the ways of his Lord. Nor is there any discussion of, let alone concern for, the queen's religious preferences, whatever they might have been. Stripped bare of theological interpretation, I Kings 10 is an account of realpolitik and patronage. The aforementioned postbiblical texts go much further. Demonstrating considerable play in interpretating the past, the midrashic stories completely transform a particularist sacred history into legends of universal interest.

The Qur'ān could not be so casual about the dangers of polytheism. The battle against unbelief waged by the earliest Muslims was marked by a great sense of immediacy. The struggle to gain recognition for the one true God was intricately tied to diplomacy and warfare as well as to social and religious developments. It is no small wonder then that this battle is the central focus of Muḥammad's public utterances, including the story of Solomon and the sun-worshiping queen. But is this surface meaning of the text all that there is, or are there other themes embedded somewhere in the Qur'ānic version? And if this were so, might the relevant passages of Sūrah xxvii reflect also broad-ranging themes of confused gender and a disturbed cosmic order, the very themes that inform the Jewish midrashic sources? Or, to phrase this question somewhat differently: Is the Qur'ānic story compressed from a larger and more detailed tradition that links Muslim scripture and the legendary postbiblical accounts?

C. *The Nature of the Qur'ānic Version*

The case for a story that is compressed from a larger and more detailed version begins with the inaccessibility of the Qur'ānic text. Unlike the extant Jewish versions, which are fairly straightforward, the rather loose narrative of Muslim scripture creates a host of interpretive problems for current readers of Sūrah xxvii. Shorn of all exegesis, verses 15–44 represent a seemingly disjointed account more reminiscent of an opaque folktale than historical narrative or a didactic midrash based on an ancient and oft-read chronicle. Moreover, the Qur'ānic version remains elusive and ahistorical even after considering the scattered references to Solomon that are found elsewhere in Muslim scripture.[14] Relying on the Qur'ān alone, the modern reader will have difficulty reconstructing even the detailed outline of a story that has a beginning, middle, and end, all of which hang together. The thread that would tie together all these disparate parts is somehow missing. It is as though the Qur'ānic account were torn out of a larger tale known to contemporary audiences but beyond our grasp. Without the background material (that is, the missing larger story) available to these early readers and listeners, we are unable to tease meaning out of particularly vexing passages. Simply put, too many questions are left unanswered in the Qur'ānic version for it to have been a cohesive account of Solomon's joust with the queen. There must have been a more detailed and broadly focused account that informs the scriptural version.

A case in point: What is one to make of the events leading up to her conversion? We are told that at Solomon's command the queen's throne is disguised "to see if she is truly guided."[15] In other words, he will soon find out whether she has had a change of heart (and will submit to him as a Muslim). She is asked if the throne is hers (or the likes thereof) and, responding to the test, she answers, "It is as if it were."[16] How are we to understand this response? Is the queen genuinely confused by the altering of her throne, or does she answer evasively in order to avoid acknowledging that the prophet has acquired the very symbol of her authority? For that matter, how does the next passage relate to what we have learned? That is, now that the queen has or has not recognized her throne, we are informed: "Knowledge was brought to us prior than her. For we were Muslims."[17] The reader can only ask, knowledge of what? The assumption might be knowledge of the true path, for the following verse reminds us that she was (and still is) an unbeliever, though this interpretation is at best implicit. Finally, in verse 44 the queen "submits through Solomon to Allāh, Lord of the Universe" after having been led to a court of glass resembling a pool of water. Thinking that the surface is actually water, she uncovers her ankles. One can understand why she does; she surely would not wish to get her garment wet. But what is the point of this and what does it all have to do with the major theme of the story, her renunciation of unbelief? And what is it that ultimately forces her to realize that further resistance is futile? She seemingly remains proud until the very last moment. Can the architectural oddity of the glass court be a reason for the great queen to bend to the will of a foreign ruler and his God? The text begs for an explanation.

The need for commentary is not untypical of "biblical" narratives in the Qur'ān. Muslim scripture often appears disjointed, with little if any evidence of sustained and unified composition.[18] This pervasive feature of Qur'ānic style may be explained in several ways, including the manner in which the final versions were formed. The search for the authoritative text was a complex process of collecting, collating, and establishing correct readings. According to Muslim tradition, the editors were contemporaries of the Prophet who produced a version thoroughly consistent with his public utterances. At the conclusion of their effort, they presented the faithful with a Qur'ān that they and future generations regarded as a coherent document written in the most lucid language.[19]

As a rule, Western scholars have a more critical view of this editorial process;[20] some even express skepticism that current versions represent Muḥammad's public utterances, let alone a very early text that preserves much semblance of its original order.[21] Indeed, one scholar has recently proposed that there were in fact three Qur'āns, each the product of a different geographical region and cultural environment: A Ḥijāzī text reflecting the views of Muḥammad's Arabs; a Syro-Palestinian text preserving Christian material; and an Iraqi text which presents Jewish themes. All three versions were then combined into a single document during the reign of the Caliph 'Abd al-Malik (d. 705 C.E.).[22]

Taken as a whole these last propositions may raise more than a few eyebrows before and after the evidence, such as it is, is fully digested. Needless to say, one can prefer more cautious ground and still hold the redactors accountable for disjointed narratives and problematic verses. Indeed, this critical approach can be useful in explaining textual difficulties, much as the documentary hypothesis has been used to explain various confusions in the Hebrew Bible.

Surely, though, more can be said here of Muslim scripture and the editorial process, particularly as regards the problematic verses of Sūrah xxvii. An inherent feature of Qur'ānic style, the disjointedness may also be intended.[23] Is it then possible that the story of Solomon and the Queen of Sheba may be a carefully crafted text, collated from diverse manuscripts by a board of editors sometime after the Prophet's death? Some scholars maintain that Muḥammad spoke in a clipped and highly allusive rhetorical style, the kind of style that is allegedly consistent with the delivery of prophetic utterances.[24] Were this in fact the Prophet's intention, then the seemingly disjointed references to the hoopoe, the throne, the court of glass, and the like, may have all reflected a story that was known to both him and his contemporaries. Mixing great rhetorical talent with a similar economy of words, the Prophet, speaking for God, could have triggered the extensive memory of his audience. A few well-chosen lines pregnant with meaning might have been sufficient to command their attention; at the least, they would have enjoyed matching his allusions with their extensive literary associations. Given his forceful delivery, Muḥammad's message was likely to have been riveting if not mesmerizing to knowledgeable listeners in Mecca and Medina. They may even have become part of the performance, lending him vocal assistance as he delivered a recognizable message.[25]

In any case, let us assume that the earliest Muslims read the Qur'ān as if it were a coherent text, much as ancient Jews read disparate traditions of the Hebrew Bible even before the advent of rabbinic Judaism. For the sake of argument, let us assume also, as did Muslims, that the story found in the Qur'ān replicates the Prophet's (i.e., God's) speech and represents all that he had to say about the subject of Solomon and the Queen of Sheba. Let us assume further, again following the believers, that the sequence of verses, however disjointed for modern readers, corresponds more or less to the original order of Muḥammad's utterances in God's name—that is to say, the disjointedness is not the result of loose editing but is characteristic of the original design. Assuming all that, we are obliged to ask, how does this stylistic peculiarity factor into Muslim interpretations of the Qur'ānic account? How did Muḥammad's contemporaries and subsequent audiences understand passages that seemingly beg for clarification (at least to modern readers) in the Book, which proclaims itself "abundantly clear"?[26] Did they see only the polemic against unbelief that lies close to the surface, or did they perceive other themes within the text?

What subsequent Muslim readers understood is a lesser problem because there is an extensive literature that reflects their views; this commentary, which is often highly tendentious, will be treated with interest in the pages that follow. But what of Muḥammad's community? Does the later exegesis also reflect their understanding of the Qur'ānic story, and if so, what is there in that later commentary that informed the story for them? Or, more pointedly, what is the relationship between the sparse Qur'ānic narrative and a more extensive tale of Solomon and the Queen of Sheba that would have been familiar to the Prophet's audiences? Needless to say, scholars interested in the Islamization of Jewish themes will also want to know if Jewish sources are directly or indirectly linked to any larger tale that might have illuminated the Qur'ān.

To be sure, there is no hard evidence that a larger story of Solomon and the queen directly informed Muslim scripture during the Prophet's lifetime; nor is there any sure way of determining the response of contemporary audiences. The case for such a text and its influence remains rather hypothetical to say the least. But this need not prevent us from imagining the broad implications of what has been proposed. The allusive and highly disjointed discourse of the Prophet suggests not only the existence of a larger tale; it suggests as well that the links between the Qur'ān and later exegetical developments are more subtle than some Western scholars are prepared to imagine. The classical commentaries and other writings that are textually intertwined with them may also preserve echoes of how the earliest Muslims really understood the Qur'ān. In such fashion, Muslim exegesis may be a significant repository of early memories as well as literary artifacts of subsequent generations. The possibility then exists that the argument against unbelief, although the dominant theme of the Qur'ānic story of Solomon and the Queen of Sheba, is not the only theme that readers perceived. There may be subtle traces of other themes for those with sufficient learning to read the text. The exegesis to Sūrah xxvii: 15–44 and the historical and belletristic accounts that serve as further commentary are rich in all sorts of allusions to the universal themes that dominate the postbiblical Jewish sources. Indeed, this may be an instance where Muslim scripture is influenced by the aforementioned Jewish midrashim, or what is more likely, by an as yet undiscovered tradition or cluster of traditions that link these Jewish sources, the Qur'ān, and Muslim exegetical literature. That being the case, this study, which explores gender related issues, must focus as well on problems of cultural transmission and borrowing. We are obliged to ask how the postbiblical story of the queen's visit became an Islamic tale and, as part of that query, how Shelomo ben David, the king of the Hebrew Bible and Jewish lore, was transformed by Muslims into Sulaymān ibn Dāwūd, the prophet of Islam.[27]

For modern scholars, the critical problem is that of distinguishing between early memory and later imagination. That is to say, sorting out and recovering elements of the original tale that supposedly informed the Qur'ānic text (i.e., the memory of Muḥammad's contemporaries) from later accretions reflecting new literary creativity (i.e., later imagination). Influenced by changing times and carrying its own cultural baggage, each generation of exegetes, chroniclers, and litterateurs found new problems and produced new commentary in reading and editing old sources. Unfortunately, this ongoing and highly tendentious process tends to obscure as well as clarify how texts were understood at any given time, particularly in genres that Muslims did not consider fully part of religious scholarship. In history, biography, and belles lettres, the continuous fusion of the new and the old resulted in clustered and multilayered traditions of great complexity. Recovering discrete Muslim versions of Solomon and the Queen of Sheba is therefore a challenging salvage operation.

3 *Later Muslim Versions*

At the least, one could say that Muslim exegesis to the Qur'ānic story is considerably enriched by literary elements traceable to Jewish tradition. One might even think that, with common points of reference, the postbiblical and postqur'ānic stories of Solomon and the Queen of Sheba are well suited to comparative analysis. The literary history of these accounts, however, is at best elusive because the chronological relationship of texts and segments of texts to one another is anything but certain.[1] To cite but one example, what influence can be claimed for the *Targum Sheni,* a work that has been dated by various scholars to the fourth, sixth, seventh, eighth, and eleventh centuries C.E. (this without any authoritative edition to guide them)?[2] How then does one chart the development of Muslim and Jewish versions and their relationship to one another when there is no sure or even convenient point of entry into the larger story of Solomon's encounter with the visiting queen?

Without an informed consensus on the dating of important individual traditions, I have chosen to begin with a richly textured Muslim source of later times in order to work backwards through layers of interpretation and meaning until reaching the Qur'ān and the relevant Jewish sources. The version chosen is that of Aḥmad b. Muḥammad b. Ibrāhīm al-Nīsābūrī, the eleventh century author better known by his nom de plume, al-Tha'labī. His charming anthology of biblical tales, the *'Arā'is al-majālis,* serves as a useful point of departure because it represents, perhaps, the most detailed story of Solomon told in continuous narratives.[3] Moreover, as Tha'labī also preserves chains of transmission, if not substantive material going back to early generations of Qur'ān commentators, there seem to be better chances of uncovering the stratigraphy of this text, that is, the chronological layers that comprise the larger story and give it meaning. Tha'labī's rendering of Solomon and the Queen of Sheba also contains allusions of Jewish materials so that among the different Muslim versions that have been published it offers the most promising clues for tracing possible paths of Jewish influence.

For the benefit of readers not familiar with Arabic, the relevant passages of the *'Arā'is* are presented here in a mixture of loose translation and summary that is interspersed with my own personal observations. A fully annotated translation is found among the appendixes. The Qur'ānic passages, which serve as a skeletal frame for the author's account, are italicized; the verse numbers are set off by parentheses. Readers of the Arabic text will note that I have tried to preserve as much ambiguity as possible in order to illustrate the playfulness of exegetical imagination while highlighting the need for the extensive modern commentary.

A. *Tha'labī's Account*

Our author begins his story in Jerusalem, the capital of the Israelite Kingdom. Quoting unnamed scholars versed in the history of the ancients, Tha'labī relates that when Solomon finished building the Temple, he decided to leave for the sacred land (*arḍ al-ḥaram*). Lest one be confused because Solomon was already in Jerusalem, the reference here is to the Ḥijāz and more particularly the sanctuary of Mecca. Preparing for the journey, the prophet gathered his usual retinue of humans, jinn, satans, birds, and wild animals, an army that extended one hundred parasangs (*farsakh*).[4] (As was his custom, he and his retinue mounted the magnificent carpet that served as their vehicle for rapid transit); then, at Solomon's command, the gentle wind carried them to their destination.[5] Arriving at the sacred area, he set about offering sacrifices and fulfilling the (prescribed) rites of pilgrimage. The occasion also served a didactic purpose. Solomon brought his people glad tidings of the coming of the Prophet, Muḥammad. He informed them that Muḥammad is (to be) the Lord and Seal of the Prophets, that is the best and last of them, and that that truth of Muḥammad's future prophethood is fixed in their own biblical scripture.[6]

After that, Solomon set out for the land of Yemen. Leaving Mecca on the morn, he guided himself by the star Canopus, and subsequently arrived at Ṣan'ā'[7] when the sun was high. That was (for ordinary people) a month's journey, but given Solomon's unique mode of transportation, travel time was compressed into mere hours. Having reached his destination, he saw a beautiful land lush with green foliage[8] and decided to camp in order to worship and partake of the midday meal. The traveling entourage sought water (to quench their thirst and perform the ablutions required for prayer) but didn't find any. And so they sent for the hoopoe, Solomon's remarkable guide. This fantastic bird could see water beneath the ground, thus enabling the satans to draw it to the surface.[9]

B. *The Missing Hoopoe*

Given his immediate need of water, Solomon sought the hoopoe, but his guide was missing at the muster of the birds.[10] With his master preoccupied, the hoopoe had said to himself, "Solomon is surely busy setting up camp." With that, he lifted himself up to the sky and looked right and left over the length and breadth of the earth. Then he saw the garden of Bilqīs (the Queen of Sheba) and made for greens. Suddenly he came upon the hoopoe of the Yemen and touched down next to him. Solomon's hoopoe was named Ya'fūr, the hoopoe of the Yemen 'Afīr. The latter questioned Ya'fūr about his visit, and he replied, "I have come from Syria with my master Solomon son of David." The local hoopoe continued his questioning, asking, "Who is [this so-called] Solomon son of David?" Ya'fūr shot back, "The ruler of the jinn and of men and of satans and of wild animals and the winds." Now it was his turn to question the Yemenite. The latter indicated that he was native to the region, and, responding to Ya'fūr's question about its ruler, he explained that the Yemen was governed by "a woman." The visitor probed further and discovered that her name was Bilqīs.[11] Then, as if to establish proper credentials for his queen, 'Afīr proclaimed, "If your master [Solomon] possesses a mighty domain, Bilqīs has no less than he. For she is ruler of all the Yemen. Twelve million provincial rulers [*qayl*] serve at her behest and each is served by 100,000 fighting men." An invitation is proffered to allay all skepticism, "Why not join me so you can observe her rule?" But the visitor is aware of his unique talents and hence responsibility, "I fear Solomon will miss me at the time of worship when he has need of water." Not to be turned aside, the Yemenite hoopoe offers a compelling rejoinder, "He will surely be gladdened if you bring him news of this queen." So the hoopoe went off with 'Afīr to see Bilqīs and her realm and did not return to Solomon until the time of the evening prayer.

To be sure, all this was unknown to Solomon who anxiously awaited the bird so that he and his retinue could quench their thirst and carry out their ritual obligations. Solomon then grew angry and said: *I shall surely punish him severely or slaughter him unless he brings me a clear excuse* (Qur'ān xxvii:21). Following that, Solomon summoned the eagle, Lord of the Birds, and ordered the hoopoe brought at once. The eagle lifted himself beyond the sky until he clung to the outer reaches of space. Scanning right and left, he looked at the world as if it were a bowl placed before a human. Suddenly, he came upon the hoopoe approaching from the direction of the Yemen and he took off in pursuit of the errant bird. When the hoopoe noticed that the eagle was after him with a mind to do him harm, he invoked God's protection saying, "By the law of Him who has empowered you and made you stronger than I am, would you not pity me and approach me without harmful intent." The eagle then turned aside and said, "Woe unto you! Your mother is about to become childless because the prophet of God, Solomon, has sworn that he will punish you or slaughter you." Then the two set off, flying towards Solomon.

Upon reaching the encampment, they were met by the vulture and the other birds. They asked the hoopoe about his whereabouts and informed him of Solomon's threat. The hoopoe asked, "Didn't the prophet of God allow for an exception?" "Indeed," they replied, "He said: *unless he brings me a clear excuse.*" The hoopoe and the eagle then flew on until they came to Solomon who was seated on his throne. When the hoopoe approached the prophet, he lifted his head and lowered his tail and wings, dragging them on the ground in humility before his master. Solomon stretched out his hand towards the hoopoe's head and pulled it forward. Then he said, "Where have you been? I will surely punish you severely!" The hoopoe replied, "O prophet of God! Remember, you are standing before Allāh." Solomon trembled on hearing that and forgave him.

When the prophet's anger subsided, he asked the bird, "What kept you from me?" The hoopoe replied: *I have encompassed what you have previously not encompassed*—that is, I have learned something that you do not know.[12] *And come to you from Sheba with tidings true. I have found a woman ruling over them. She has had something of everything bestowed upon her* (Qur'ān xxvii: 22–23).

C. *Bilqīs*

Tha'labī continues, citing her name (Bilqīs)[13] and her lengthy and disputed pedigree.[14] It would appear that Bilqīs's father, named al-Bashrakh and nicknamed al-Hadhhādh, was a king possessing great influence. As ruler of all the Yemen, he considered himself superior to the provincial dynasts (*mulūk al-aṭrāf*) and refused to marry among their people. Thus, they paired him off to a woman of the jinn—unlike present times, men of that era could see the jinn and cohabit with them. She subsequently bore him Bilqīs and as fate may have it, he had no other offspring.

When Bilqīs's father died, she, forging claim as his heir, coveted rule and sought to have her people render the oath of allegiance to her. One group obeyed but others turned against her. Unwilling to be ruled by a woman (let alone a woman of such dangerous lineage; she was after all the daughter of a jinni), they chose a man in preference to her and made him their king.[15] And so, the people (of the Yemen) split into two factions, each holding dominion over part of the land. But the man they had chosen to rule them behaved abominably, having gone so far as to violate the womenfolk of his subjects. As a result, his followers wished to depose him, but found themselves powerless to do so.

When Bilqīs saw this, she was overcome by horror and concocted a complicated scheme for his downfall. First, she sent word to the king offering herself to him. The stunned king responded favorably, if somewhat timidly, "I would have initiated a proposal had I not despaired of your [likely] refusal." Seeking to reassure him, she answered, "I cannot turn away from you [now] for you are surely equal to me in nobility." She then requested that he gather her representatives and propose marriage through them. With that, he gathered them and, addressing them (directly), he proposed marriage. Her notables were incredulous at the turn of events. "We do not envision her doing this," was their response. "But," he countered, "it was she who first contacted me!" Not to be denied, the king insisted on hearing her own response and bid them to relay his intentions. When they asked her about the alleged offer, she exclaimed, "I loved the boy.[16] I did not respond to him previously because I preferred not to marry, but now I give my consent to him." Having been so informed by the queen herself, they took the first step towards consummating the union. The two monarchs of the divided Yemen were married, albeit in absentia (according to custom).

She then left her palace and made her way to him with a vast retinue of servants and attendants that she brought as part of the bridal procession. So vast was her entourage that his residences and palaces were crammed full of those serving her. When finally she came to his private chamber, she offered him wine, and he partook of it until falling into a drunken stupor. Then she cut off the head of her helpless rival and slipped away under cover of night. Upon awakening, the notables saw that the king was slain and that his head had been hung from the gate of the palace. Then they knew that these nuptials were a deception concocted by her. Gathering to her they said, "You are worthier than anyone of this realm." She responded, "Were he not branded by his disgrace, I would not have killed him. But, when I saw how corrupt he had become, I was seized with rage and did with him as I did." With that explanation, they chose her to govern and her rule became firmly established throughout the (entire) realm.

Clearly this was a most unusual set of circumstances, one that could hardly escape the notice of later Muslims. Indeed, the author points out that when someone mentioned Bilqīs in the presence of God's Messenger, Muḥammad remarked, "No society (*qawm*) prospers that allows a woman to rule over them."[17] But here was Bilqīs now firmly entrenched as ruler over all the Yemen. As if to reinforce her recently acquired position, she surrounded herself with the trappings of power: an impressive palace and a magnificent throne. Both structures are described by Tha'labī.[18] Of particular interest is the author's detailed description of her elaborate throne room. The throne itself, the emblem of her rule, could only be reached after passing through seven chambers, each of which was protected by a locked gate. The detailed description provides us with an intended analogue to Solomon's incredible throne, a legendary structure also described in detail by Tha'labī in a previous account.[19] As did Solomon, *she had something of everything bestowed upon her* (Qur'ān xxvii:23). As the author explained this verse, she had all the implements required for rule.[20]

All was not well, however, in the Kingdom of Sheba. To be ruled by a woman is one thing; the hoopoe also *found her people bowing down before the sun rather than God* (Qur'ān xxvii:24). She had asked her wazīrs, "What did my ancestors worship?" When they answered, "The Lord of Heaven," she then asked for signs of his presence. "How shall I worship him when I cannot see him? I know of nothing more powerful than the light of the sun. We should give precedence to the sun as the object of our worship." So she worshipped the sun rather than Almighty God and obligated her people to do likewise at sunrise and sunset. When the hoopoe related that to Solomon, he became aroused and said: *We shall see if you have spoken the truth or are among the liars* (Qur'ān xxvii:27).

D. *A Noble Letter*

A letter was then sent to Bilqīs;[21] a letter that was, per Solomon's custom, both eloquent and to the point. Indeed, that is how all the prophets dictated their correspondence. They preferred short, expressive statements to long, detailed accounts. And so, the letter read:

> From God's servant, Solomon son of David, to Bilqīs the Queen of Sheba: *In the name of God the Merciful and Compassionate* (Qur'ān xxvii:30). Peace is for those who follow the rightly guided path. *Do not be haughty! Come to me submitting as Muslims* (Qur'ān xxvii:31).

When the prophet completed his letter, he dabbed it with musk and sealed it with the impression of his (famous) signet ring—that is, the ring from which he derived so much of his power. Having done all that, he said to the hoopoe: *Go with this letter of mine and deliver it to them. Then turn away,* but stay close to them *and see what they come back with* (Qur'ān xxvii:28), that is, the answer that they give in response. The hoopoe took the letter and took it to Bilqīs who was at a place called Ma'rib[22] some three days journey from Ṣan'ā'.

According to one authority, when the hoopoe reached her palace she had already locked the gates and gone to bed. When she went to sleep, it was her custom to lock the gates and place the keys beneath her head. The bird came to her as she slept on her back and dropped the letter on her neck. Another scholar relates that the hoopoe carried the letter in his bill and flew about until he was directly above her (as she sat in audience). He flapped his wings for a while, attracting the attention of the notables, until she lifted her head, at which point he dropped the letter on her bosom. Still another scholar reports that she had a window in her bedchamber, that is an arched aperture facing the direction of the sun. At sunrise, light would strike the window, filling the room. Then, seeing the sun, she would bow down before it. On this occasion, the hoopoe came to the window and blocked it with his wings so that the sun rose without her being aware of it. Sensing the delay in the sun's coming, she got up in order to look, at which point the hoopoe dropped the letter in her lap.

In any case, Bilqīs, who (unlike other women) was literate, took the letter in order to read it. When she saw the seal, she trembled and bowed down because Solomon's great power was in his signet ring and she thus knew that he who sent this letter was a greater sovereign than she.[23] "Any ruler who uses birds as his emissaries is indeed a great ruler," she said. Then she read the letter as the hoopoe lingered not far away. Following that, she went off to sit on her throne and gathered the leading men among her people. They were twelve thousand provincial rulers (*qayl*), each of whom was served by a hundred (thousand) fighting men. She would (ordinarily) speak to them veiled, but when some matter distressed her she would strip the veil from her face.

When they came and took their places in the assembly, Bilqīs addressed them: [*O ye leading men*], *a noble letter has been delivered to me* (Qur'ān xxvii:29). *It is from Solomon and reads: In the name of God the Merciful and Compassionate. Do not be haughty. Come to me submitting as Muslims* (Qur'ān xxvii:31–32). Then *she said: O ye leading men, advise me in my affair* and offer me counsel concerning that which has been proposed to me. *I only decide matters when you bear witness* (Qur'ān xxvii:32), that is when you are present. *They said* in response to her: *We are possessed of power and fierce fighting spirit* when called to combat. *But the matter is yours* [*to decide*]. *Consider that which you will command* (Qur'ān xxvii:33). You will find us obeying your order. When they offered themselves for combat, Bilqīs declared: *Indeed, when rulers conquer a city, they corrupt it, transforming the greatest of its people into the most debased* (Qur'ān xxvii:34). Thus the queen pointed out that foreign conquerors humble nobles and great men so that they can establish their own authority. The Qur'ān verifies this statement, for God says: *That is what they do* (Qur'ān xxvii:34).

Capturing this sense of xxvii:34, Tha'labī quotes the following verse attributed to the father of Abū al-Qāsim al-Junayd:[24]

Wheresoever kings come to settle they vanish
There will be no shelter for you under their wings.
What hopes do you entertain from a group enraged
They oppress you, impatient, even if you satisfy them.
Praise them, and they suppose you deceive them
They find you burdensome as they do everything.
Ask God that for your sake you do without their portals
For he who stands at their door is surely debased.

Unsure of her capacity to best Solomon in combat, the queen will devise a subtle stratagem. She surely had the intelligence and resources to pursue an innovative plan as her late but not lamented husband found out much to his regret. Moreover, she had already trained the leading men of her people to conform to her wishes and was fully capable of asserting herself as well as manipulating her subjects indirectly. And so she said: *Indeed I shall be sending them a gift* (Qur'ān xxvii:35); that is, to Solomon and his people. By this she meant a gift with which she would attempt to dissuade him from seizing her authority and through which she would determine whether he is king or prophet. Were Solomon a mere king, he would take the gift and depart. But were he a prophet, he would not be satisfied "until we follow his religion." And so it came to pass that she sent him a gift of slaves consisting of young lads and maidservants (*wuṣafā'* and *waṣā'if*) as well as gold and spices and a special bauble designed to test Solomon's intelligence.

When word of that reached Solomon, he ordered the jinn to fashion bricks of gold (*ājurr*) and then have them strewn everywhere along the road so that they could be seen by the queen's emissaries as they approached his camp. The prophet's contempt for wealth was not lost on the visitors. The discovery of Solomon's gold bricks strewn about indiscriminately made them realize the trivial nature of the wealth they carried. The real test awaiting Solomon, however, would be the game of wits that Bilqīs had prepared.

Citing authorities who read (sacred Hebrew) texts,[25] Tha'labī relates that the queen called for a number of maidservants and an equal number of young lads.[26] According to one tradition, she dressed the former as young lads in tunics and sashes. The latter she dressed as maidservants, placing bracelets and necklaces of gold around their forearms and necks. In their ears she inserted earrings for the upper and lower lobes, each inset with various kinds of gems.[27] Then she placed the maidservants on five hundred steeds and the young lads on an equal number of nags. She also called for a box and placed in it a costly pearl (*durrah*) that was perfectly smooth, as well as a shell (*kharazah*) that had been perforated, but whose perforation had been crooked. Having done all that, she wrote a letter containing an inventory of the presents[28] and sent it along with her handpicked emissaries, men noted for their reason and intellect.

In the letter she stated, "If you are a prophet, distinguish between the maidservants and young lads, tell us what is in the box before opening it, perforate the [smooth] pearl evenly, and string the crooked shell." Leaving nothing to chance, Bilqīs ordered the young lads, "If Solomon addresses you, speak to him in an effeminate way, as if imitating the speech of women." Similarly, she ordered the slavegirls to speak to him roughly in a tone that resembles the speech of men.[29] Then she said to her chief emissary, a certain al-Mundhir b. 'Amr, "Look at the man when you enter into his presence. If he gives you an angry look, then know that he is a [mere] king and do not let his gaze frighten you, for I am greater than he. But, if you find him to be pleasant and kind, then know that he is a prophet that has been sent [by God]." She then instructed her ambassador to "understand his words and return with [news] of his response." The emissaries then departed with the gifts. The hoopoe, following Solomon's orders, lingered nearby, observing everything. Then he hurried (back) to his master and told him the entire story.

E. *The Mission to Solomon*

Continuing his account on the authority of the (Hebrew) scholars, Tha'labī points out that Solomon ordered the jinn to make him bricks (*ājurr*) of gold and silver.[30] Then he ordered them to use the bricks in paving a single review ground that extended nine parasangs[31] from the spot he (presently) occupied. Around the review ground, they were to place a prominent wall of gold and silver. Then he asked them about the most beautiful pack animals that they had ever encountered. They told Solomon of multicolored animals from a certain sea, exotic creatures possessing wings, combs, and forelocks. Solomon had them brought to him immediately. When the animals arrived he commanded, "Hitch them to the right and left of the review ground on the bricks of gold and silver and scatter fodder on it for them." With that done, he ordered the jinn to bring forward their children. A large throng gathered and he positioned them to the right and left of the review ground. While Solomon sat on his throne in his place of assembly, four thousand chairs were placed to his right and an equal number to the left. At his command, the satans formed rows several parasangs long, as did the humans, the wild animals, the beasts of prey, the reptiles, and the birds. When the emissaries approached, drawing near to the review ground, that is, when they beheld Solomon's domain (*mulk*) and saw the pack animals, the likes of which they had never seen, defecating on the gold and silver bricks—an obvious sign of contempt for the wealth of this world—they panicked and threw aside the gifts that they were carrying.[32]

Some reports indicate that when Solomon ordered the review ground paved with bricks of gold and silver, he commanded the jinn to leave along the way an empty space equal to the number of bricks carried by Bilqīs's agents. Seeing that the place for these bricks was empty while the rest of the ground was paved, the queen's emissaries feared that they would be accused (of having taken them).[33] So they placed what bricks they were carrying in that empty place.

When they came to the review ground and saw the satans, Bilqīs's representatives were greeted by an awesome look that frightened them. And yet, they were told to enter without fear. Passing squadron after squadron of jinn and of men, of birds and of beasts of prey and wild animals, they finally stood before Solomon. With kind looks and cheerful countenance, he asked them their purpose. The leader of the delegation indicated to Solomon what they had brought and gave him the queen's letter. After looking at it and reading it aloud, Solomon asked, "Where is the box?" When it was brought to him, he shook it, whereupon the angel Gabriel came and informed him of its contents.[34] Thus Solomon said, "It contains a costly pearl without perforation and a shell that is perforated but whose perforation is crooked." "Correct," said the emissary. "Now perforate the [smooth] pearl evenly and run a string through the shell."

To a large extent, the prophet's great power rested with his ability to match the right creature to the right task. So Solomon called out, "Who can perforate this for me?" He asked the men but they lacked the knowledge to do it. Then he asked the jinn, but they too lacked the knowledge thereof. After that, he consulted the satans who told him to send for the earthworm. When the earthworm came, it seized a hair and, placing it in its mouth, it passed through the pearl until exiting at the other side. A grateful Solomon asked the earthworm to name its heart's desire. The earthworm responded, "Let my daily sustenance (*rizq*) be provided by the brush [I inhabit]." He graciously consented. Then the prophet asked, "Who can thread this shell?" A white fruitworm spoke up, "I can do it O Prophet of God." The worm then took the thread in its mouth and, after entering the perforation, exited at the other side. That accomplished, Solomon asked the fruitworm to name its heart's desire. The fruitworm responded, "Let my daily sustenance be provided by the fruits." Once again, Solomon responded to a modest request. Like the prophet himself, his subjects were more interested in serving their master than acquiring material wealth.

Having solved the test of the box, Solomon distinguished the maidservants from the young lads by ordering them to wash their hands and faces. For, as a rule, a maidservant takes water from a vessel with one hand and, after transferring it to the other, splashes it on her face. Moreover, a maidservant pours water on the inside of her forearms while a young lad does it on top of them. Also, a maidservant (actually) pours water, whereas a young lad lets it run down his forearms. Thus, did Solomon distinguish among them.[35]

Then Solomon returned all the gifts saying: *You reach out to me with wealth. Has not God given me better than what he has given you? And yet, it is you who rejoice with your gift* (Qur'ān xxvii:36) because you are a people given to boasting and the acquisition of material wealth. You know nothing else. The earthly world is not among my needs, for God, may His name be exalted, has already allowed me to possess that. He has bestowed upon me riches that he has given to no one else in the universe. Were that not enough, God, may He be praised and exalted, honored me with the gifts of prophecy and wisdom. Solomon then said to al-Mundhir b. 'Amr, the leader of the delegation: *Return to them* [*with the gifts*], *for we will most certainly come to them with contingents too powerful for them. We shall indeed expel them from it* [*the city*] *debased. And they shall be humbled* (Qur'ān xxvii:37) if they do not come to me submitting as Muslims.[36]

F. *The Queen's Visit*

When Bilqīs's emissaries returned and informed her of what had happened, she exclaimed, "By God! This is no king! We are powerless to deal with him."[37] So she sent word to Solomon that she and her provincial rulers would be visiting him shortly to consider his command and the call to his religion. Then she ordered that her throne be placed in the most remote of her palaces in the last of seven chambers, each enclosing one another. Following that, she locked the gates and appointed a security force to stand guard with explicit orders that no one be allowed to look at the seat of her rule, let alone have access to it. Clearly, she was concerned lest someone usurp her authority. Then Bilqīs set off for Solomon with twelve thousand provincial rulers from among the kings of the Yemen, each of whom was served by one hundred thousand fighting men.[38]

When the queen and her entourage drew near, Solomon went to his contingents and asked: *Which of you can bring me her throne before they come to me submitting as Muslims* (Qur'ān xxvii:38), that is obedient and subservient. Why did the prophet order the throne brought to him on such short notice? Tha'labī turns to this puzzling question and indicates that the authorities are at odds with one another on this point. Most said it was because Solomon knew that when she submitted to Islam, her property would be forbidden to him (by law). Therefore, he wished to seize her throne before her conversion.[39] One scholar maintained that it was because he was amazed at the hoopoe's description of the throne and thus wished to see it before he saw her.[40] It has also been said that he did it to demonstrate to her, through the miraculous delivery of the throne, God's power and the greatness of His dominion.[41]

But how was the throne to be brought and by whom? An 'ifrīt,[42] one of the jinn, the most powerful of the spirits, spoke: *I will bring it to you before you arise from your place* (Qur'ān xxvii:39), that is, from the assembly at which you issue judgments—every morning Solomon held an assembly, issuing judgments until midday. *For indeed I have the power to do it and am trustworthy* (Qur'ān xxvii:39), that is, he had to be trustworthy in addition to being capable because the jewels which embellished the throne might prove tempting. That, however, was not quick enough. "I want it faster than that," Solomon called out. *One who had knowledge of the book then spoke* and indicated that he would bring it in *the twinkling of an eye* (Qur'ān xxvii:40).[43] Here, too, there is disagreement among scholars.[44] Some said it was Gabriel; others, it was an unspecified angel that God had sent to assist his prophet; still others held it was rather a human being. Those scholars who maintained that the speaker was human disagreed as to his identity. Most exegetes opined that it was Asaph son of Berechiah son of Shimea son of Malchijah. A truthful man, he knew the mightiest of God's names. When he summoned the Lord with that name, God answered. Moreover, if asked anything when summoned by that name, God granted it. When Asaph prayed and summoned God (invoking his mightiest name), he said to Solomon, "Look afar and make out what you can at a glance." Solomon then looked far to the right and God sent the angels on their mission. They carried the throne, tunneling underground, until they burst from the earth, the throne appearing before the prophet.

Other authorities attest that the *one who had knowledge of the book* was a righteous man (*rajul ṣāliḥ*) from an island in the sea. On the day in question, he went forth to serve the inhabitants of the mainland to see whether or not they worshipped God. As a result, he found Solomon and when he invoked one of God's names, there was the throne already transported. It had been brought to Solomon *in the twinkling of an eye* (Qur'ān xxvii:40).

Some say that the mysterious person having knowledge of the Book was Usṭūm; others that it was Malīḥā,[45] but, according to Muḥammad b. al-Munkadir, it was rather Solomon himself, for God had given his prophet knowledge (*'ilm*) and understanding (*fiqh*). Apparently, one of the authorities among the Israelites told Solomon: *I shall bring it to you in the twinkling of an eye*. When Solomon asked him to do that, the Israelite then said, "You are a prophet and the son of a prophet. No one is more highly regarded by God than you. Were you to call God, you would have it." Solomon, realizing the obvious truth of these words, invoked God's name and the throne was brought to him immediately.[46]

The invocation also occasioned disagreement among the Muslim authorities. It is reported that the mightiest name (of God) invoked by Asaph was "Yā! Ḥayy! Yā! Qayyūm!" On the other hand, it is also maintained that the *one who had knowledge of the book* invoked, "Our Lord and Lord of everything. The Lord is One. There is no Lord but You. Bring me her throne." Still another scholar said he called out, "O Possessor of greatness and generosity."[47]

When Solomon saw the throne standing before him— it had been brought in the twinkling of an eye—he said: *This is the grace of my Lord in order to test me. Shall I give thanks or be ungrateful? Indeed my Lord is rich and generous.* (Qur'ān xxvii:40). Then he said: *Disguise her throne for her.* That is, the prophet ordered substituting the upper and lower parts for one another. *We shall see if she is truly guided* to her throne and recognizes it or is among the ignorant, (meaning) *those not truly guided* to it (Qur'ān xxvii:41).[48]

According to Tha'labī, Solomon disguised her throne in order to test her intelligence.[49] Citing various authorities, our author reports that the satans feared a union between the two rulers. Because if Solomon were indeed to marry the queen, he (of all men) could make her desirous of bearing children. She would then disclose to him the secrets of the jinn (which she had acquired from her mother). As a result, the jinn (who were subservient to Solomon alone among men) would never rid themselves of him and his offspring to follow. Wishing to incite him against her, they painted a distorted picture of this truly exceptional woman. They maligned her intelligence and claimed that (because her mother was a jinni) her ankles are hairy and her feet "are like the hooves of a mule."[50] But the prophet, who preferred to draw his own conclusions, was not so easily put aside; he decided to test the claims of the satans.

When Bilqīs arrived, [*she*] *was asked: Is this the likes of your throne? She said: It is as if it were* (Qur'ān xxvii:42). Then she compared the altered throne to the one she had left behind in a chamber of seven locked gates while she herself retained the keys.[51] Sensing that there was something behind the question, she was, to say the least, extremely evasive. She did not confess that it was hers and yet she did not deny it. And so, Solomon knew the extent of her intelligence. There still remained, however, the question of her ankles and feet. And so, Solomon devised a second and equally elaborate test to verify whether the satans had indeed told him the truth.[52] At his command, the satans built him a court (*ṣarḥ*)[53] of glass resembling white waters. Beneath the floor, they placed real water stocked with fish. Following that, Solomon had his magnificent throne placed along the central axis (*fī ṣadrihī*). He then took his seat with the birds, jinn, and humans arrayed about him.

When Bilqīs finally arrived in Solomon's presence, *she was told: Enter the court! When she saw it, she reckoned it to be a pool* most of which was filled with water. *And* so, *she uncovered her ankles* (Qur'ān xxvii:44) to wade through the water on her way to Solomon. Solomon gazed at her. Clearly, the satans had been partially mistaken. She resembled no mule. Indeed she had the most beautiful ankles and feet that any human could have, but her ankles were hairy. When Solomon saw that, he turned his eyes from Bilqīs and informed her that there was no water on the surface. *It is a court made smooth with slabs of glass* (Qur'ān xxvii:44). Presumably, she then lowered her skirt and Solomon was spared the sight of her unbecoming hair.

The queen may have been put on the defensive by Solomon's elaborate tests, but she was prepared to continue the game. When seated, she turned to the prophet, "O Solomon, I wish to ask you something." As he responded affirmatively, she continued and queried him "about [drinking] water which is neither in the ground nor in the skies." Now, when something came up that Solomon did not know, he asked the humans. If they had knowledge of that, good and well, if not, he would ask the jinn. If they knew, fine, and if not, he would ask the satans. In this case he was forced to turn to the satans who said,

"Simple! Order horses to race and then fill the vessels with their sweat." Solomon replied, "The sweat of horses." Needless to say, the prophet answered correctly once again.[54] And so, Bilqīs (resigned to the inevitable) enquired about the God she could not comprehend and therefore could not worship. "Tell me about your Lord's [very] being," she asked.

Of all her queries, this one, probably asked in all innocence, reversed completely the course of the game. Unable to answer what was in essence unanswerable, Solomon leapt from his throne, prostrated himself, and lost consciousness. She stood aside as his contingents broke ranks in panic. Intentionally or not, Bilqīs had trapped Solomon in a position from which he could not extricate himself; it would appear that she had finally bested him, with all that this implied for the faith and faithful. But Allāh does not abandon his messengers. The angel Gabriel came immediately to the Israelite and said, "O Solomon, your Lord is speaking to you. Whatever you want is yours." The prophet answered, "O Gabriel, my Lord Knows better of what she said." The angel then proclaimed, "God orders you to return to your throne." Gabriel then instructed the prophet to replay the event as if nothing had taken place.

When Solomon returned to his place and all the others that had been present to theirs, he inquired of Bilqīs, "What was it that you asked me about?" "About water that is neither in the earth nor in the sky," she responded. He continued, "What else did you ask?" "I asked nothing else," she said. Following that he asked the same of his contingents and they responded as she did because God, may He be exalted, caused them to forget her question. Erasing the past, God protected Solomon from having to answer.[55]

Now, Solomon called upon her to become a Muslim. Having witnessed what had happened concerning the hoopoe, the gifts, the messengers, the throne, and the court of glass, she responded affirmatively, saying: *My Lord, I have wronged myself* through unbelief. *I submit through Solomon to Allāh, the Lord of the Universe* (Qur'ān xxvii:44).

G. *The Fate of Bilqīs*

What happened to Bilqīs after her conversion to Islam?[56] Most authorities report the following. When Bilqīs became a Muslim, Solomon wished to marry her. When he mulled over the idea, however, he became disenchanted because of her thick ankle hair. "How disgusting this is," he said. Then he asked the humans how (ankle) hair is removed, and they told him that it was done with a razor. The woman protested, "No blade has ever touched me." So Solomon was against using a razor for fear that "she'll cut her ankle." He turned to the jinn, but they knew of no other method to remove ankle hair. Finally, he asked the satans who feigned ignorance and said the same (as they wanted to prevent the marriage at all costs). When pressed by Solomon, however, they claimed, "We'll employ a technique for you that will make her ankles appear like highly polished silver." And so, they prepared her depilatory and bath. It is reported that was the first time a depilatory was used.[57]

There is disagreement about what followed. Some authorities believed that the prophet and queen were married.[58] They report that Solomon was very much in love with Bilqīs and so he allowed her to remain as ruler over her dominion. As if to reinforce his connection with the Land of Sheba, he ordered the jinn to build three fortresses in the land of Yemen, the likes of which were never seen as regards height and grandeur. They were Salḥīn, Ghumdān, and Baynūn.[59] Following that, he would travel back and forth from his residence to the Yemen, visiting her once a month for three days.

There are, however, other scholars who reject the reports of this marriage. They indicate that, once Bilqīs had converted, Solomon decided to marry her off. And so, he instructed her to "Choose a man from your own people."[60] She protested, "O Prophet of God, should the likes of me marry among [mere] men when I have already possessed such authority as I have in my domain and among my people." Her protest went unheeded as Solomon insisted that "submission to Islam requires that you not prohibit what God has declared as lawful." Now reconciled to her fate, she married Tubba' the Elder, King of Hamdān. The prophet then returned her to the Yemen and established Dhū Tubba' as ruler over what had been her kingdom. When he did that, he summoned Zawba'ah, the commander of the Yemenite jinn, and said, "Do whatever I require of you for Dhū Tubba' in the Yemen." And so, the latter remained there, ruling with a free hand until Solomon died. With the death of the mighty Solomon, the jinn were set free, and the reign of Dhū Tubba' and his (consort) Bilqīs came to an end, as does our story.

Did sophisticated Muslim thinkers give credence to the fantastic tale of Solomon and the Queen of Sheba? Sprinkled here and there in various sources there are expressions of doubt. Elements of the tradition are regarded as *gharīb,* "strange" or "fantastic," and *abāṭīl al-Yahūd* "fairy tales of the Jews." Still, there were authorities, perhaps the majority of religious scholars, who were prepared to privilege these texts. When the great Qur'ān exegete Ibn 'Abbās related the story of the hoopoe and his ability to locate water underground,

Nāfi‘ b. al-Azraq said to him, "How can it see water underground when it cannot see a trap laid under a few inches of dirt?" Ibn ‘Abbās replied, "Woe! When fate intervenes, sight turns to blindness." Put somewhat differently, Ibn ‘Abbās held that when faith intervenes sensory perception is not required for engaging the truth.[61]

4 *A Reading of Tha'labī's Solomon and the Queen of Sheba*

It is no small task to recognize, let alone do justice to medieval sensibilities. Arabic texts of the period can be extremely allusive. In order to understand what they read, contemporaneous Muslims were obliged to combine vivid memories of events and personae with vague literary referents. But such memories have dimmed with time, and so important texts and subtexts once pieced together by knowledgeable audiences have become opaque documents even to the most learned modern readers.[1] Before we become too self-critical, we may note that later generations of Muslim authorities also had trouble with the fine detail. Moreover, Muslim religious scholars had a cultural agenda of their own; explication was linked to religious doctrine and practice. As a result, many universal themes were filtered out of religious scholarship or given much less importance in the formal analysis of texts.

One should not assume, however, that these universal themes did not retain a strong hold on the literary imagination of Muslims. There are sufficient hints strewn about the sources that medieval Muslims could and did draw upon literary associations that traversed the boundaries of their religion and culture. That residual interest in widespread and time-honored themes concerns us here. Utilizing a voice that is, I trust, broadly consistent with the manner in which medieval Muslims produced and read narrative, I shall examine Tha'labī's tale from two related perspectives: as an expression of broad concern for an orderly universe—a concern that embraces anxiety-provoking issues of gender—and the need to Islamize that concern when it is encountered in non-Muslim settings, such as the Jewish sources previously cited.

A. *Concern for an Orderly Universe*

As do the authors of those postbiblical accounts, Tha'labī reaffirms the efficacy of a world created in accordance with God's grand design. There is a certain presumption in this, for although praising divine handiwork, humankind, as a rule, lacks the requisite understanding to appreciate its intricacy. That is, the remarkable edifice that God has fashioned truly defies explanation. If comment is necessary, suffice it to say that the universe, of which we and our world are an integral part, is an expression of quintessential harmony derived from God's total control over the natural order. There is a seeming paradox in this last assertion, as we can easily detect all sorts of chaos in the world about us. How then does one explain this seeming flaw in such a carefully sewn tapistry?

For monotheists, there can be no competitors that challenge the Lord of the Universe. If nature is perceived to be unkind at times, it cannot be that the Almighty has relinquished any measure of control. Unlike the divinities of the ancient Near East, the God of Israel and of Islam does not suffer the ravages of winter only to be born anew every year with the emergence of vegetation in the spring. There is no equivalent of the Babylonian New Year's festival that celebrated the resuscitation of the gods above and their counterparts, the earthly kings below.[2] Among Jews, the agricultural significance of the major festivals shares importance with historical events firmly rooted in their collective memory:[3] the Exodus from Egypt, the tabernacles in the wilderness, and the events at Mount Sinai. The Jewish New Year, celebrated in the fall, occasions somber reflection and penitence concerning relationships between man and man as well as man and God. The importance of changing seasons has even less impact on the ritual calender of Islam. To be sure, there are residual traces of a more distant Near Eastern past, and given the importance of agriculture one can hardly dismiss Mother Nature out of hand. The seasons and other natural phenomena are commemorated in a variety of ways, but always with the understanding that the natural order of things, even when there is apparent disorder, has been and will continue to be bent by a superior will. Should seeming disorder appear incongruous with our perception of harmony, it is because we lack the capacity for understanding the divine will. For reasons best known to Himself, the Almighty has allowed a certain latitude for extraordinary intervention in the workings of the universe, be it by natural agents, the supernatural, or by the most sublime of His creations, humankind. Thus, everything, including unexplained disorder if not chaos, is part of God's ineffable scheme.

Seen from the perspective of ancient and medieval audiences, the harmony of the universe is characterized by carefully balanced realities that often form reverse images. Some comport to observable reality, others reflect mysterious, unseen forces known only because of their impact on the world around us. Contemporaries who read the literature in question perceived the eternal difference between night and day, the various flora and fauna, male and female, and the like. That part of God's grand design they could by and large comprehend and appreciate. They knew that this design also accounts for rain and drought, scarcity and plentitude, and various kinds of natural calamities and blessings. More puzzling were abstract forces such as good and evil, but they too could be understood as God's way of allowing humankind a more active role in their world.

Perceiving the familiar in a timeworn way, ancient and medieval people adjusted to circumstances as best they could, and following long established precedents, sought to live harmoniously with their sometimes discordant surroundings. The mysterious and the unseen present humankind with a less sure path to adapt to God's order. Like a genetic code gone awry, the familiar and predictable in nature is at times disrupted by forces of the supernatural. Although these forces are also subject to God's will, humankind is often powerless against them. Who among Tha'labī's contemporaries actually witnessed satans, devils, and their various subspecies? There was a time when humans actually consorted with the jinn but, as the author reminds us, that was long ago.[4] Even then, could humans be expected to hold their own against the likes of such creatures? Confronted by the dark side of reality, humankind must be considered vulnerable; on such occasions the balanced and time-honored place of human beings in nature's larger scheme cannot be taken for granted.

The exception is Solomon. Of all men in all times, only he was granted the knowledge to comprehend god's universe in all its dimensions, the dark side included. For he was "given something of everything," including unparalleled knowledge of flora and fauna, the natural sciences, and, uniquely, the complex and mysterious world of the supernatural. If anything can be assumed of Tha'labī's audience, it would be their familiarity with the tales of Solomon's unique understanding and the extraordinary power with which that understanding was linked. Among humans, only Solomon had the capacity to communicate with all of God's creatures. He knew all the tongues of mankind, could converse with the lowly ant, negotiate with the earthworm and fruitworm, and discourse with every kind of bird. This was no small trick, for each subspecies of bird spoke its own dialect or language.[5] But the most remarkable of Solomon's gifts was his control over the darker forces: the various species that spawned the culture of the devils, satans, and jinn. Reluctant subjects, they were forced by God to serve Solomon, the possessor of the mighty signet ring. Whether king or prophet, Solomon's mastery over these creatures draws considerable attention in both Jewish and Muslim writings and is among the most ubiquitous themes of the extensive and much-coveted Solomonic folklore. This aspect of Solomon's power was no accident, no fortuitous polishing of a magic lamp or innocent opening of a mysterious and potent vessel. For Muslims, the prophet's extraordinary control over the world of the spirits was destined from birth. Thus, it came to pass that on the day Solomon was conceived, a voice cried out to Iblīs, *the* Devil, informing him that his children were soon to be enslaved. An enraged Iblīs gathered his cohorts from distant regions and then went off to intervene on their behalf. Fortunately for humankind, he found himself presented with a fait accompli; Bathsheba had already conceived. That being the case, the attending angels informed Iblīs of his impending slavery and that of his seed. Returning to his legions, he was melted by grief into the likes of molten lead.[6]

B. *The Prophet's Mandate*

Those who read Tha'labī's tale or heard it from popular preachers were likely to have known that extraordinary and wide-ranging dominion is a rare gift that carries special obligations. Solomon's immense power had to be balanced by wisdom and the learning the determine that is both legal and proper in God's world. A precocious child, the future prophet absorbed immediately everything that this father recited from the Torah and the Psalms. He studied sacred writings at the age of three and memorized all of the Torah within a year. At four, he performed a hundred genuflections (*rak'ah*s) a day while reciting a verse from Hebrew scripture.[7] Accounts picture him as a young boy shaping his father's thinking, thus enabling the great Israelite ruler to render more effective judgments. The polite and loving manner in which the boy influenced his father during the latter's audiences, may be seen as a sign of his maturity and the nature of his temperament.[8] A mere boy influencing a great ruler could not go unnoticed. When the notables of Israel saw young Solomon holding court with his father, they grew jealous, whereupon David had the boy clothed in the white garment of the prophets and invited the religious personae to pass judgment on his abilities. They were astonished at the boy's erudition and his eloquence and wisdom. And so, despite his tender years, all came to recognize his standing.[9] There are other versions of this event, but however the story is told, the results are always the same: there is wide recognition of young Solomon's talent.[10]

By the age of twelve or thirteen (as in Jewish accounts), he had been chosen to rule. This is the view of Tha'labī and others.[11] According to Kisā'ī,[12] like Tha'labī a major source for the tales of the prophets, Solomon had to pass two tests before succeeding his father. When Solomon was seventeen, Gabriel came to David with a gold quire on which were inscribed a series of questions. The questions were to be submitted to David's offspring; he who answered correctly was to be designated the prophet's successor. Of course, it was Solomon who bested his older brothers. Then, when the aged David died, the angel appeared once more, this time to indicate that Solomon could have his dominion but only at the expense of wisdom. Faced with this choice, the would-be ruler of the Israelites preferred "the most precious possession" to authority. Having declined his father's earthly inheritance on God's terms, he apparently passed the test before him. Solomon was indeed worthy of all the gifts that the Almighty had intended for him and was thus given rule along with knowledge, reason, and a perfect disposition.[13] The prophet's choice and God's subsequent largess also has its parallel in Jewish sources.[14]

One should be aware that, in coming to power, Solomon did not inherit the domain of an earthly king. In replacing his father, Solomon acquired extraordinary power over the forces of nature and the unnatural alike. Kisā'ī[15] indicates that the winds came to pay obeisance in accordance with God's wishes. Following them were representatives of the animal kingdom. But what of the darker side of the universe, the world of the satans, devils, demons, jinn, and other spirits? To ensure Solomon's domain over forces natural and supernatural, Gabriel dusted off the signet ring of God's Vice Regent, which had been lying about Paradise almost since time immemorial. That is, when Adam had been expelled, it flew from his finger and returned to its place of origin.[16] As did the magic seal of Jewish sources, this ring contained extraordinary power. Its unique signet contained four points that shone as brightly as the stars in the heavens. Indeed, it shone so brightly that none save Solomon could look directly at it. Each point contained an inscription. The first read: "There is no God but God"; the second: "Everything will perish except His countenance"; the third contained the words: "His is the kingdom, the power, and the glory"; and finally, the last proclaimed: "Blessed be God, the Best Creator." The points also indicated dominion over God's different creations. Thus, the first, "There is no God but God," was addressed, quite appropriately, to the world of rebellious demonic spirits; the second to the birds and beasts; the third to the rulers of humankind; and the fourth to creatures inhabiting the sea and mountains. Such was the power literally placed in Solomon's hand; he had indeed been "given something of everything."[17]

Armed with the ring and the mandate for rule that went with it, Solomon began his reign. At his command, the Israelites took up arms.[18] Then, with Gabriel's assistance, the various subspecies of demonic spirits, numbering four hundred and twenty in all, swarmed about the prophet. They were a testament to their unnatural being. Produced by a fornicating Iblīs and bent by a multitude of sins against the Almighty, they were grotesque distortions of God's orderly creations. Some were half human, half animal, some formed bodiless heads, others headless bodies. I might add parenthetically that medieval Muslims were much fascinated by this distortion of the natural order and gave visual expression to the darker side of the universe in graphically illustrated manuscripts. It is no wonder that Bilqīs's emissaries were frightened out of their wits upon encountering these creatures for the first time. At the least, they are a seeming affront to the exquisite symmetry of God's fauna. Still, if they cannot be reshaped, they can certainly be yoked. Why not have them serve humankind and find a useful place in a more orderly world?

The sources indicate that Solomon placed his seal on their necks and that they all became compliant; that is except Ṣakhr the Rebellious, the Muslim analogue of Judaism's legendary Ashmedai.[19] But Ṣakhr, who escaped to a distant island, found freedom short-lived. Only Iblīs himself was beyond the prophet's control. For some reason God allowed the Devil his independence until the day of resurrection and the first blast of the heavenly trumpet. So the quintessential manifestation of the supranatural remains at large to prey on humans not receiving divine protection. But this is not the same free-spirited Iblīs. With Solomon's emergence, he has been shorn of his minions.[20] The darker forces have been made good, or at least compliant, citizens of the orderly world. They will become unusually efficient *gastarbeiter* whose men engage in many crafts and trades. They are particularly good at digging wells and construction, and Solomon will use them extensively in building his temple and palaces. Their women, too, are excellent workers who produce different varieties of cloth and weave carpets. However unnatural they may be, both male and female of the species conform to traditional gender roles.[21]

Together with the humans, the wild animals, the birds, the reptiles, and various support contingents, they constitute the most powerful military array ever formed. Their tactical mobility is unmatchable. At Solomon's command, they mount in precise order and formation an enormous carpet that carries his magnificent throne. Then, once again at his command, the winds that have been subjected to his will deftly lift the carpet skyward, as the birds fly overhead shielding him from the sun. Having been borne aloft in such fashion three thousand years before vertical takeoff craft, the prophet now shifts his means of transport into high gear. Still another command is given, whereupon powerful winds gently but speedily propel prophet and entourage alike, compressing month-long journeys into a matter of hours. The strike time and tactical radius of this army would be the envy of modern strategists. Needless to say, in battle the combined force is invincible, hence Solomon's reputation as the great conqueror on God's behalf.[22]

One might wonder how such a disparate fighting force is kept in line and battle-ready given the wariness of humans towards demonic creatures, reptiles, and wild animals. Indeed, since Adam's fall from Paradise, all of God's creatures have been engaged in struggle with one another. In this respect, man's propensity to engage in conflict with his own kind is the microcosm of an even wider struggle. How then did Solomon avoid the feuds that dominated politics and dismembered armies in the Caliphal era?

Medieval readers were surely aware of the debilitating effect of *'aṣabīyah,* or excessive group loyalty, on the body politic of Islam. The chronicles of the times are replete with accounts of tribal and other forms of internecine strife. And yet, Solomon's contingents seem to be organized along tribal lines. For example, the eagle is the *sayyid* of the birds and the vulture their *'arīf,* both titles used to signify tribal functionaries.[23] When the hoopoe's punishment is discussed in order of increasing severity, the worst that is envisaged, other than being unable to serve Solomon, is banishment from his species. That is to say, he will be exiled as were the incorrigible troublemakers of tribal society.[24] Moreover, in organizing his entourage, Solomon always placed his subjects in discrete places, each according to rank and group.[25] For imaginative readers, this division of forces might have jostled memories of an Islamic state beset by internal strife.

In its broadest sense, the arrangement of Solomon's legions follows the pattern of early Arab settlement in the *amṣār,* or garrison towns, where each tribal association staked out and patrolled its own territory within the larger urban setting. This separation of fighting forces was required to minimize conflict among groups of warriors who jealously guarded their own prerogatives. Whatever stability resulted from this policy of settlement in the first century A.H. was compromised by the cumulative effects of *'aṣabīyah* and the anarchic conditions that tribalism fostered. At best, the central authorities could contain and cajole the tribesmen; they had no mandate to demand, let alone insure, loyalties. As a result, the caliphs of the second and third centuries A.H. sought to replace tribal units with larger regional forces. The creation of this new army was designed to counter the pernicious effects of extreme tribal loyalties by creating associations of fighting men more inclined to follow centralized authority. But in time, new contingents, displaying their own measured sense of independence, subverted the authority of the caliph and created new disorder.

Thus, military reforms that were designed to mitigate the effects of *'aṣabīyah* also tore at the fabric of Muslin society.[26]

Tha'labī's readers who were familiar with the role of the military in Islamic times might have wondered how Solomon managed to keep his own bizarre contingents subservient to him and at peace with one another. Comparisons are often misleading. For all their talents, the rulers of the Islamic world were not Solomon when it came to statecraft. More important yet, they lacked the magical signet ring and the mandate to rule that came with it. However much Solomon's instruments of conquest resembled traditional military forces—what other models would medieval Muslim writers turn to?—they could hardly chart for themselves an independent course. His possession of the Vice Regent's authority guaranteed that. There is no outward expression of *'aṣabīyah* in the prophet's camp, only a sense of that harmony that pervades the larger universe. Each species and subspecies knows its place and function and finds satisfaction in that. That is, except for the creatures of the supernatural who yearn for their independence. but even they are forced to submit to Solomon and accept his authority as long as he lives. The hoopoe scouts for water; the satans draw it from the ground;[27] the jinn fashion bricks and build palaces;[28] an 'ifrīt moves objects from one place to another at great speed;[29] even the tiny creatures, the earthworm and fruitworm, have their specific functions to fulfill. When Solomon, who has the material wealth of the world at his disposal, offers the worms "their hearts' desire," they accept only what nature has ordained for them. Even these lowly creatures are capable of recognizing that there is a divine scheme and it is best to live in harmony with that which god has ordained.[30]

All this was made possible by the acquisition of the signet ring, an "historic" event that took place, according to Kisā'ī, on the last Friday of Ramaḍān. And rightly so, for we learn elsewhere that it was on the very same day of the very same month that Adam, God's first and only prior Vice Regent, had been expelled from Paradise so long ago. The ring had been entrusted to Adam, but as he was no longer worthy of it, it flew from his finger and returned to paradise. The result of Adam's fall had catastrophic effects. The harmony of God's universe had been tampered with, and worst of all, humankind would soon succumb to idolatry. But the world now had a new champion and so when Solomon was born, it laughed once again.[31]

As does Jewish tradition, Muslim sources emphasize Solomon's statecraft. This is quite understandable in view of the biblical and Qur'ānic narratives. And yet, there is another side to the Solomonic legend, one that is also linked to the power of the signet ring. Having been entrusted with preserving the natural order of things, the prophet is the quintessential conservationist. Even as a boy, he was extremely concerned with the maintenance of God's handiwork; he was in effect the defender of creatures large and small. When his mother instructed him to kill an ant that had attached itself to his garment, he picked it off instead and spared its life. The incident, which foreshadows the more celebrated Qur'ānic encounter with the ants in their valley, is an indication of a certain sensitivity to nature's delicate balance and an appreciation for how all living creatures serve their Creator. He put it very well to his mother, "Every animal will have its say on the Day of Resurrection. I would not like this ant to say, 'Solomon the son of David killed me.' "[32]

Ka'b al-Aḥbār, allegedly a learned rabbi who was an early convert to Islam, tells a poignant story of Solomon's deep concern with the preservation of all species.[33] As with the previous incident, the episode took place during the future prophet's childhood. One day, when Solomon was with his father, a dove appeared and perched itself before the boy. It complained of having no offspring to hatch. This was not simply another barren mother, but apparently the last of the species. There was then the danger that one of God's noblest and most beloved creations would disappear from His landscape. At once, Solomon extended his hand to the bird's womb and said, "Off with you, and may God cause you to bring forth seventy chicks from your womb! May your offspring increase [in turn] until the Day of Resurrection!" Ka'b goes on to note that all the turtledoves in existence are the issue of this formerly barren bird. One need only add that the dove was instrumental in reestablishing order following the great flood. It is therefore only proper and just that Solomon enabled it to witness the coming Day of Resurrection, when the world will be reestablished once again. His gracious act is consistent with the exquisite symmetry of God's design.

Power did not alter Solomon's appreciation for the rational design of the world nor did it diminish his efforts to sustain that rationality. Similar stories are thus told of Solomon the great ruler and other creatures to be preserved. A composite of parallel accounts tells of a lark who was denied mating by a female of the species. When he implored her that he only wished to sire a living being that would mention the Lord, she finally relented. At the proper time, she laid her egg along the roadside so as to protect it from passersby. Suddenly, Solomon appeared with his entourage and the birds feared that they would crush the unhatched egg (preventing the species from replicating itself and paying homage to the Creator). According to Tha'labī, the would-be father's concern was allayed by the female of the species; she knew only too well of Solomon's reputation.[34] Indeed, the prophet assigned one of the jinn to guard the egg by gently shielding it with his foot. And so, Solomon's army could pass without causing injury. In appreciation, the larks went to Solomon bearing gifts. Jazā'irī[35] informs us that the prophet received them graciously and patted their heads, whereupon the larks grew the combs that distinguish them today. There is a last, but most significant point to this story. Having finally consented to mate, the female of the species came to recognize her position vis-à-vis her partner. It is no coincidence that when the two larks were admitted to Solomon's presence, he placed the male in the privileged position to his right while the female sat to his left. This too is God's design for all societies, human or animal, medieval Islam among them.

C. *The Danger of Crossing Gender Boundaries*

It is against this background that we turn to the Queen of Sheba, a proud and presumptuous woman whose very presence threatens to jar Solomon's balanced and harmonious world. She too chooses to deny men their due; she too will have to be put in place. From her father, the King of all the Yemen, she inherited her sense of independence if not haughtiness. Feeling himself superior to the regional princes, he declined marriage to any of their daughters. Instead, he chose Rayḥānah bt. al-Shukr, a woman of the jinn.[36] There is danger in consorting with creatures from a mysterious world that one cannot know, let alone master. So the King of all the Yemen, the possessor of enormous wealth and power, produces no heir who will command total allegiance from the regional princes. He sires but one child: a girl named Bilqīs.[37] Clearly this marriage has denied him God's blessing.

The daughter of a jinni, Bilqīs is not prepared to accept the place of a woman among humans. Nor will she be confined, as are the jinnis held in servitude by Solomon, to a life of spinning cloth and weaving carpets. Belonging neither to the society of humans nor of spirits, hence an anomaly in a world otherwise delicately balanced, she seeks the unnatural in coveting rule. But who would have a woman rule over them? The question of succession became a source of dispute between rival parties. For whatever reason—perhaps because she alone represented the line of the previous ruler—some constituencies of the kingdom obeyed Bilqīs and rendered her the oath of allegiance. The others preferred a male to lead them. And so, the unity of the Yemen was shattered by female ambition, and a polity that had previously known peace and harmony was split into two factions, each holding dominion over part of the land.[38]

One may wish to argue that choosing a male in preference to Bilqīs was in principle the correct decision. Why should one wish to serve a woman, let alone a woman who was descended from the jinn? No doubt, Muḥammad put it best when he reportedly said, "No group prospers that appoints a woman to rule over them."[39] But in this case, conventional wisdom was clouded by an unwelcome reality. The new king turned out to be corrupt and went so far as to violate the womenfolk of his subjects. In rejecting a woman as capable of leading them, the second faction had chosen a man that compromised their own women. That is, they had selected for themselves a person whose behavior clearly violated the accepted norms of human relations. Ironically, it was the human king and not the queen descended from the jinn that had tampered with God's design. Faced with this king's abomination, his subjects now wished to depose him, but the men were discovered impotent. Not so Bilqīs. Overcome with rage she concocted a brilliant plan to kill him.

Interestingly enough, there is no indication of what it was that particularly disturbed her. One may assume that the jinn also regarded their women as inviolable, in which case the king's actions merited her most severe reaction. But is there more to consider? Could her anger have been occasioned also by empathy for the other women? There is, alas, no evidence at all that she harbored any such sentiments. Might we be more correct in assuming that her rage was colored by disgust with the very crudeness of his unbridled use of authority? The extent of her rage would seem to suggest more than anger over a political aesthetic that had become debased—it was rather his outrageous disregard for the norms of society. Her adversary had completely overstepped the boundaries of what was acceptable from a ruler, even in medieval Islamic society where despotism was preferred to anarchy in troubled times such as those depicted in our story. Hence, the king's disaffected followers will swing their allegiance to Bilqīs. But first there is the matter of his murder.

Her stratagem calls for catching the king alone and unawares; her tactic is to take the initiative and propose marriage. It is no doubt a bold act for a woman to approach a man in so direct a fashion—this was not the manner in which marriages were ordinarily arranged by Thaʿlabī's readers. The king is flabbergasted at her offer and responds that he would have initiated a proposal (of his own) had he not despaired of her (likely) refusal. What is it that caused him to assess his chances so negatively? The author leads us to believe that she, as was her father before her, is haughty and not about to marry among the mere likes of the regional princes, if at all. What manner of man can be allowed to domesticate the offspring of the jinn? Clearly, her adversary will need some convincing and so she writes, "I cannot turn away from you for you are surely a noble equal [now]. So gather my notables and propose a marriage through them."[40] Her retainers, kept in the dark about her plans, are incredulous at the king's proposal. He insists in turn that it was her idea to begin with. When they come to her, his proposal in hand, she gives her assent.

What explanation does she proffer to her aides for this startling turn of events? Given the political background of these machinations, we would expect that the two contestants decided to unite the kingdom through marriage and rule as king and consort. In any event, that was a likely way to sell the proposed marriage to all concerned. An alliance of convenience based on matrimony had the advantage of restoring harmony to the strife-town Yemen. Indeed, her opening diplomatic ploy was to declare her adversary "a noble equal." But that is not her explanation for proposing the match. Asked why she did it, she says to her skeptical advisors, "I loved the boy (*aḥbabtu al-walad*)!"[41] These four words (only three in Arabic) speak volumes, though they are not tomes of love. *Aḥbabtu al-walad* drips with contempt for a usurper too young and immature to exercise power. His sexual excesses suggest reckless attempts to compensate for inadequacy borne of failure to develop a true sense of manhood. Who is this pup to contest the likes of (the mature) Bilqīs, daughter of the late King of all the Yemen and a (noble) woman of the jinn? No wonder that he could not imagine she would be interested in him. It was not acrimonious politics that caused him to despair of her interest; she was simply out of his league and no doubt that held for all the other men of the Yemen. Even Bilqīs, the consummate politician, is hard pressed at justifying the match. At best, her reason seems lame: "I did not respond to him previously because I preferred not to marry [at all], but now I give my consent."[42]

When the nuptials are completed, the queen is escorted to her husband by a vast retinue of servants and attendants. It is in his royal bedchamber that he will finally take possession of her, thus restoring the Yemen and, by implication, a larger world to its previous balance: one kingdom; one polity; and, above all, no independent queen of dangerous ancestry. Such may be his thoughts, but his own highhanded actions have tampered with the orderly nature of things. And so, he will not live to conquer the wily queen, either in the bedroom or stateroom. As if to foreshadow future events, his palace literally chokes on the multitude of retainers that she has brought with her. Meanwhile, in the privacy of his chamber, she offers him wine until he falls into a drunken stupor. She has completely disarmed the overreaching boy by taking advantage of his immature and, from her view, unwanted passion. In a move symbolic of removing his improperly overactive genitalia, she severs his head and hangs it from the palace before slipping away under cover of night. When the notables saw the head, they realized that the nuptials were a deception. They gathered unto her and said, "You are worthier than anyone of this kingship."[43]

Even with such an acknowledgment, it was no simple matter for her to claim rule. To an audience familiar with the realities of blood feud and more generally the delicate side of political behavior, her action, no matter how justifiable, would not have ended the political crisis. Regicide was not something medieval Muslims could easily defend. A presumptive case had to be made justifying her bold and deceptive action in legal as well as moral terms. She also had to calm any fears that might arise from her being a woman and more particularly the daughter of a mixed marriage with a jinni. Given a choice, the good people of the Yemen who wished for a return to order would no doubt be reluctant to accept anyone with so controversial a history. And so, she claims, "Were he not branded by his disgrace, I would not have killed him. But when I saw that this corruption had become widespread, I was seized with rage and did with him as I did."[44] She was only acting as she had a right to do, for he had forfeited rule with behavior that defied all accepted norms. As to her being a woman, and half jinn at that, apparently that was a risk the notables were willing to take to restore order. For Muslims whose polity was frequently racked by disorder, anarchy was a condition that called for stringent measures. A highminded and ferociously independent woman with ties to the darker side was no doubt preferable to continuing chaos. Tha'labī's readers would surely have understood the notables' decision. In any case, there was still Solomon to bring her to heel and fully restore the natural order of things.

They chose Bilqīs to govern them and she surrounded herself with the trappings of authority: a magnificent palace and an equally magnificent throne. The palace, briefly described, is an enormous structure set aside on a hillock overlooking Ṣan'ā', the capital.[45] Like the Abbasid palace complex overlooking greater Baghdad, it is built of burnt brick and gypsum, a combination that makes for sturdy building materials that are resistant to seepage when applied with quicklime.[46] The golden domes that surmount the palace at each corner are reminiscent of the Round City,[47] the center of Abbasid government which became in time the most famous monument of their rule. Similarly, the (interior) rooms along the side of the structure, which housed her chamberlains, security forces, and a wide variety of attendants, recall vaguely the arrangement of the inner ring of the Round City. If the great Abbasid government center was not indeed the model of Tha'labī's palace, it probably would have suggested some link between the two structures for his knowledgeable readers.[48] In any case, hers was a dominion that was extraordinary, something that could not help but catch the attention of the hoopoe and stir Solomon to action.

As the story unfolds, her throne will be seen as the more important symbol of rule. It is in fact described in resplendent detail, much as the author treats Solomon's even more magnificent throne in an earlier account.[49] Protected by a series of locked chambers, whose keys never left the queen even when she slept, the throne platform was a full 120 feet in length and rose to an equal height—coincidentally, the same height as the Abbasid audience chambers in the Round City. It was constructed of precious metals and stones and had four legs: one of rubies, one of green corundum, one of emeralds, and one of black pearls. The seat itself was covered with gold. There could be no question that anyone possessing so magnificent a throne wished to be regarded a legitimate ruler.[50] Of all the implements that became symbols of Solomon's authority, none, including perhaps the signet ring, received such prominence in so wide a variety of cultures as did his legendary throne.[51] That she too possesses a magnificent throne foreshadows the impending conflict between them and his need to obtain her most prized possession. As did Solomon, *she had something of everything bestowed upon her and has a great throne* (Qur'ān xxvii:23). The patterned doubling, a salient feature of the text, should not be misunderstood. Bilqīs may be coupled with Solomon but that does not make them equals.

As did other Muslim authorities, Tha'labī understood the Qur'ānic quote to mean that she had the requisite implements for rule, not the extraordinary gifts that God had bestowed on Solomon alone. The exegetes also make it clear that her throne was considered great because of its dimensions (and not because it gave her license to rule).[52] In that case, should she be allowed to continue ruling? Solomon is a man, chosen by God no less, and she, a woman and half jinn, is chosen by mere mortals in difficult if not desperate straits. His mandate is to preserve God's orderly world for all of humankind; hers is simply to rule by whatever means. The reader is obliged to give her her due. She is exceedingly clever, there is no doubt of that. She may be highhanded and overly proud, but she is certainly an improvement over her rapacious predecessor. A great beauty, she can have any suitor of her choice. She has, however, two unacceptable failings: she spurns the natural state of marriage and obeisance to man. Hence, this creature descended from the jinn is incongruous with the way the world ought to be. Were that not enough, her unbelief, that is, her failure to pay obeisance to God, will require her to bend to a new reality. After much resistance, she will submit both to man and God, consistent with the way of the world. And so, the great prophet and the Queen of Sheba are fashioned by our author into doubles representing reverse images of reality. There they are, bigger than life itself, with matching hoopoes, somewhat similar thrones,, and great domains. As 'Afīr, the hoopoe of the Yemen, said, responding to the boasts of Solomon's Ya'fūr (both names are derived from the same Arabic root), "If your master possesses a mighty domain, Bilqīs has no less than he."[53] It is inevitable that Solomon and the Queen of Sheba will spar with each other as did their servants, the hoopoes.

'Afīr's loyalty to his queen is understandable: but neither bird nor master have yet to comprehend the prophet's mandate to uphold God's grand design. Upon hearing of this kingdom ruled by a woman, Solomon is galvanized to action. As in the Jewish *Targum Sheni,* the prophet cannot tolerate her independence.[54] He will test the hoopoe's report and the queen as well by sending her a letter sealed with the signet ring (of God's Vice Regent). No diplomatic niceties are intended. There is no need to obfuscate the issues in highly elusive language. The missive is exceedingly short and to the point.[55] He warns her not to be haughty towards him but to submit instead. It also arrives in the most direct manner. As in the Jewish text previously cited, the letter is delivered by the bird, a mail service that duly impresses Bilqīs as does the letter's widely recognized seal.[56]

According to Qatādah, whom Tha'labī quotes, the queen had been sleeping on her back when the hoopoe dropped the letter on her neck. As was her custom, she placed the keys to the palace beneath her head upon retiring. Indeed the keys, which gave access to her throne—that is, her rule—never left her.[57] Modern readers familiar with Western culture might be inclined to see these zealously guarded objects as a symbolic barrier against the unwanted attention of men. Be that as it may, in this instance it also calls to attention the mysterious delivery of the letter, a missive calling on her to give up her independence and submit to Solomon and his God. She had personally locked the gates behind her, thus denying any direct access to her bedroom. Bilqīs was not exactly the trusting sort; one need only recall the circumstances in which she brought about the demise of her late but not lamented husband. Those who are prepared to play Judith and Holofernes have to be cautious lest others reverse the rules of the game. Readers empathetic with the queen must have shuddered as she discovered the letter on her neck in a locked bedroom. Indeed most readers would have connected this danger on her neck with the unspecified implement with which she beheaded the sleeping king in his bedchamber. Did the letter so purposefully and deftly placed foreshadow retribution for having seized rule from a male, albeit a male given to heinous corruption? Solomon certainly knew how to make a dramatic statement.

D. *The Queen's Challenge to Man and Divine Order*

Now it is Bilqīs's turn to react to events; she assembles her so-called advisors. Unlike the passive lot in the Jewish *Targum* who are simply willing to ignore Solomon's provocation,[58] they are prepared to do battle and advise her accordingly. They may be possessed of *fierce power and fighting spirit* (Qur'ān xxvii:33), but she did not gain the throne upon which she sits by direct confrontation with a powerful enemy. She dismisses summarily the advice of brave but foolish men in favor of a more subtle course. The wily queen will attempt to buy him off with gifts while at the same time testing his intelligence. In her own clever way she will determine if he is, as he says, a prophet or is a mere king, that is, simply another man to be manipulated. Were he a prophet, he will return the gifts and press for her submission. A mere king might be satisfied with her lavish tribute.[59] In any case, she will determine his intelligence through a series of intricate tests. Matching wits with men plays to her strength and has already proven to her advantage. As our author put it, "She had already trained (*sāsat*) the leading men to conform [to her wishes] and was experienced at . . . manipulating authority."[60] The use of the Arabic *sāsa* to signify her manipulation of men is instructive. While the verbal noun (*siyāsah*) comes to mean 'politics' in the conventional sense of administering government, it denotes more generally the training of horses and the domestication of animals. This is a woman who literally has great fighting men eating out of her hand. Now it is Solomon's turn to be handled as were the previously unbroken stallions.

Once again, Tha'labī's account mirrors the Jewish sources. Citing a well-known expert on Judaica and other scholars familiar with sacred (Hebrew) writings,[61] he discusses in detail the snare with which the queen will test Solomon's mettle. As in the *Midrash Mishle* and the *Targum Sheni,* the game of wits between God's Vice Regent and the ruler of all the Yemen will be emblematic of the joust between man and woman. At a more cosmic level, the major test that Bilqīs has prepared signifies an attempt to disrupt if not reverse God's design by deliberately confusing gender, the most identifiable marker of natural order.

She has called for a number of maidservants and an equal number of young lads and has dressed them as if reversing their gender.[62] To complete the deception, the disguised maidservants will ride steeds with gold saddles and brocade blankets. The heavily bejeweled lads were in turn mounted on nags. When the bizarre group arrives, Solomon is asked to distinguish male from female (without examining their genitalia). To make Solomon's task even more difficult, she has instructed the girls to speak harshly as do men; the boys are told to affect an effeminate manner of speech. The expectation is that Solomon will blunder and will be unable to distinguish among them. His failure will signify not only her triumph but the inherent foolishness of defending a natural order that is so easily confused. Why then should she, a woman, not be the uncontested ruler of her domain? But nature does have a way of keeping the sexes discrete against disguised appearances. At so young an age, beardless youths with high-pitched voices might not be taller than girls, and so dressed in the raiment of one another they may appear indistinguishable. but the body language of the sexes is well established early on. The prophet orders the group to wash their hands and faces. At that, the maidservants took water in one hand and, after transferring it to the other, splashed their faces. The lads, being males, took it with both hands and then did the same. In addition, the girls poured water on the inside of their forearms; the boys performed the reverse. Recognizing the body language only too well, Solomon was able to answer the question that should have thwarted him. In doing so, he demonstrated convincingly that men and women have distinctive roles to play in God's ordered world. No amount of posturing; no gameplaying; and above all, no usurping of gender roles can change what the Almighty has decreed.

The other tasks are child's play: The prophet, with Gabriel's help, will determine what is inside a closed container, and with the assistance of a fruitworm and earthworm, he will thread a shell with crooked perforation and a costly pearl with none at all. What foolishness has this Queen of Sheba devised? Two of God's most humble creatures can perform these last tasks, a reflection of the inexplicable genius of His creation. Given the option of any reward, both the fruitworm and earthworm prefer to live as God has ordained for their humble kind, for everyone and everything has its respected place and role. In due time, Bilqīs will come to understand the logic of that choice and the wisdom of God's design.[63]

Having dispensed posthaste with her trivial tests, the prophet will return the gifts with which she hoped to bribe him. What is mere wealth to Solomon? The material world is not among his needs; God has already bestowed riches upon him that he has given to no one else. Moreover (as Solomon had been prepared to foreswear all power and wealth), the Almighty also gave him prophecy and consummate wisdom. What then have her ambassadors with which to tempt him? Bringing all sorts of precious objects to impress a king, the visiting delegation finds instead a prophet who mocks their queen's offering. Gold bricks are strewn about indiscriminately like loose paving stones, and then, were that not enough, there are the exotic beasts of burden. Brought from a faraway sea, these wondrous creatures have been deliberately stuffed with fodder in order to make them defecate on a lavish review ground that had been made especially for the visit. And so, the queen's emissaries witnessed beasts, the likes of which they had never seen before, fouling an area paved with gold and silver that extended some thirty miles.[64] That carefully arranged theater was the expression of Solomon's contempt for her paltry gifts and her addiction to earthly rule. The prophet's contempt is matched only by his warning: She and her people will indeed submit (to God's order), *or we shall certainly come to them with contingents* and *shall indeed expel them from* [*their city*] *debased* (Qur'ān xxvii:37). Having learned of this threat, she has no recourse but to seek a personal meeting with Solomon. Hence, she journeys with her entourage to meet him, but only after safeguarding her throne. That is, the symbol of her rule is kept in a well-guarded place entered through several locked chambers; the keys are safely secured by her. Clearly, she has as yet no intention of giving up her domain.[65]

Now it will be Solomon's turn to test her. Miraculously, the locked chambers housing her throne are penetrated, and the object itself is brought to him in the twinkling of an eye. At his command, it will then be disguised by substituting elements of the structure for one another. More specifically, the lower sections will be exchanged with the upper parts of the throne, as if to indicate that the proud Bilqīs will soon have her world turned upside down.[66] But will she be astute enough to recognize changed realities? When she arrives, she will be asked: *Is this the likes of your throne* (Qur'ān xxvii:42)?

As we have noted and shall note again, the episode of the throne elicited considerable discussion among medieval authorities.[67] They were puzzled by the sequence of events, the mysterious dramatis personae, and why Solomon required the symbol of her rule so quickly. At face value, there does not seem to be much need of interpretation, at least as regards altering the throne and testing whether Bilqīs will then recognize it. The exquisite symmetry of the world that the prophet is pledged to defend requires that he mirror the test previously put before him. In a game of disguised appearances, Bilqīs sought to demonstrate that women are the equivalent of men and that she, therefore, was entitled to the great domain that she had obtained and now rules with female cunning. It turns out that Solomon was more than equal to her, and so she failed. She has still not drawn the necessary conclusion though, and instead of submitting, has taken every precaution to hang on to her realm. But now the great Solomon has reversed the game of disguised appearances; he has altered her throne and asked her whether it was the likes of hers. The question is carefully constructed. She will fail the test and lose the game whether she answers affirmatively or negatively. Should she respond that it is not, she would proclaim herself a proper ruler with an authentic symbol of authority safely locked in her palace. However, Solomon could then expose her folly were she challenged to produce her throne. Were Bilqīs to accept that the disguised throne is indeed hers, she will have acknowledged that the prophet possesses the very object that gives her license to rule.[68] If nothing else, this queen is extremely perceptive. She seems to grasp the essence of his ploy, and so, according to various scholars, she responds evasively: maybe it is and maybe it is not. The game is still on.

Some authorities, including the Yemenite, Wahb b. Munabbih, link the episode of the throne to the dark side of the woman's ancestry.[69] It appears that the satans were fearful that Solomon might be enticed into marrying the formidable queen. Lest one misunderstand, they had no concern for the prophet that had imprisoned them; quite obviously, he can take care of himself. It was the power that she possessed that caused them to worry. At Solomon's death they will be set free; such is their destiny. But should he wed Bilqīs, even for diplomatic reasons, she might further entice him into having offspring. As the issue of the dark side, she had knowledge of their secrets. What was to prevent her from passing this knowledge on to her progeny? Indeed, if this were to be the case, they would be enslaved to Solomon's family for all eternity. It was therefore best to dissuade Solomon from any matrimonial adventure.

Their strategy was to degrade Bilqīs by distorting what was praiseworthy about her. In a manner of speaking, they too are involved in disguising appearances. They claim that there is something wrong with her intelligence and that her feet are like the hooves of a donkey. As a result, Solomon put their testimony and her intelligence to the test by having her questioned about the disguised throne. Through her clever answer she has managed to allay some doubts about her wits, but there is a final test for her to pass in the presence of Solomon himself. Once again she will be confronted with disguised appearances. At the prophet's command, the satans build for him a court of glass resembling white waters. The impression that this is in fact a pond is reinforced when the area under glass is filled with water and stocked with live fish.[70] She, who presumes to rule over men in defiance of nature, should at least be able to distinguish nature's handiwork from an artificial creation. But this she cannot do. Thinking the court to be a real pond, she lifts her shirt in order to wade through without wetting her garment. She has failed this test and her chances against God's prophet have all but slipped away. The reader is led to believe that it is only a question of time before she submits to Solomon and his Lord, thus restoring the Yemen and beyond that the larger world to its accustomed and rightful state.

There is an additional nuance to the game as it is unfolding. In raising her skirt, the queen has revealed her feet and legs. It is now clear to Solomon that the satans have told him but half the truth. Although her ankles are indeed hairy, they, like her feet, are as beautiful as any human possesses. To be sure, Bilqīs was half jinn but she does not have hooves instead of feet; she is not one of those grotesque creatures that could be found among the spirits. No doubt, medieval readers were clever enough to understand that the satans did not depict Bilqīs as they did simply to elicit Solomon's disgust. There would seem to be a larger message embedded in their deception, one that goes well beyond sexual attraction. Taken symbolically or as fact, the queen's link to a female donkey denotes potential disaster, that is, if Solomon hoped to propagate through her the future rulers of the Israelite dynasty. Were a stallion such as Solomon to mate with a donkey-like Bilqīs, the result of that union would be a hinny, a hybrid creature incapable of reproducing itself. For Solomon to marry Bilqīs means the certain end of his biological line, much as her failure to seek marriage and children dooms the line of her father, a great king in his own time. At a more cosmic level, marriage to Bilqīs means the abrogation of Solomon's mandate to preserve natural order. If, as a modern reader, I am not abusing this intricate text, that would seem to be the compelling argument with which the satans hoped to convince the mighty Israelite.

There still remains the issue of her hairy ankles. True the prophet looked aside at the sight of them, but this, too, is not simply a matter of aesthetics as some medieval scholars suggest. Although not explicitly stated, as in the Aramaic *Targum Sheni,* the hair is symbolic of her bold and successful attempt to usurp the natural authority of men.[71] She has already seized rule from a husband that she callously murdered and has continued to hold it in a society of great warriors. Until her adventure with Solomon, the Queen of Sheba had not the slightest inclination of bending to the expectations of a male-directed society.

Only because her ploys are exhausted does she contemplate the inevitable. Her last probe, a question put to Solomon about drinking water which is neither in the ground nor in the skies, seems at best a feeble attempt to prolong her independence.[72] She will submit, but the unshaved hair, symbolic of reversed gender roles, will have to come off in order too give legitimacy to her submission. The only question was how to remove it.

When the prophet inquired about this, he was told to have her use a razor. But the woman protested, "no blade has ever touched me."[73] So Solomon was against the razor for fear that she would cut her ankles. Men who ordinarily do not use a blade or have allowed their hair to grow coarse before shaving will fully understand Solomon's empathy. Nicking her delicate skin would have been, however, only the most obvious and indeed innocuous result of having to use a razor. Again, if it is not forcing a medieval text to yield more than it can, there is a more dramatic explanation for her not taking to the blade. Might Tha'labī's male audience have attributed her reluctance to their fear of castration? After all, she was in their view, the very model of a phallic woman. Thus, the shaving of her hair was clearly indicative of an impotence linked too her forced submission. Or, from their perspective, might the blade itself be taken as a symbolic instrument of male dominance? That no blade had touched, let alone penetrated the queen, would then signify that she had until then successfully deflected all male advances. Her late husband made it to the bedchamber, but drunk and then decapitated, he never quite made it in bed. No wonder the virgin queen fears that the razor will cause her to bleed. In this reading of the text, blood is a sign of violation.[74]

Whatever interpretation is preferred, Solomon has decreed that the hair must be removed without using a blade. The technique for doing that, however, is unknown to the prophet and most of his retinue. The satans, who are familiar with depilatories, feign ignorance, hoping that aesthetic considerations will prevent the marriage. Their tactics, nevertheless, prove fruitless. In the end, they are forced to reveal that, using an alternative to a razor, they can "make her ankles appear like highly polished silver." And so, Bilqīs, soon to be shorn of all power, was now shorn of all ankle hair as she became the first human—actually half human—to employ a depilatory. Freshly bathed and beautiful in all respects, she will give up the last manifestation of her dogged resistance to God's design.[75] She will become a woman in a man's world by submitting to a real marriage. This time, the union will not end so dramatically to her advantage.

E. *Submission to Male Authority*

All the authorities concur that she did in fact take a second husband and that the marriage lasted quite a number of years. There is, however, much disagreement about the bridegroom. A tradition attributed to the redoubtable Wahb b. Munabbih is consistent with the larger story as it is explicated here.[76] Wahb thus reports that Solomon finished with Bilqīs when she recognized her past errors and then offered her submission to God through his prophet. That done, he instructed her to choose a husband from among her own people. This choice could hardly have been much consolation to the humbled queen who, but a short time earlier, haughtily rejected the institution of marriage out of hand. She certainly had not intended to compromise her fiercely won independence by sharing herself or her domain with a man. To be sure, there had been an unexpected development; she did not anticipate the results of her encounter with Solomon. Still, her image and some of her power might be preserved by marriage to the prophet himself. There was no disgrace in such a union. He was, after all, more than her equal, as she reluctantly came to acknowledge. The choice available to her was something else, however. As seen by the readers, she must have felt terribly degraded in having to marry among former subjects previously rejected as unsuitable. No wonder she protests, "O Prophet of God! Should the likes of me marry among [mere] men when I have already possessed such authority in my domain and among my people?"[77] Given the prophet's mandate to preserve the natural order of things, his response is both firm and predictable; she will not prohibit, by her presumption, what God has declared lawful (and indeed natural). She will be bent to God's design.

Left with little choice, she consents to marry Tubba' the Elder, King of Hamdān. But that is not the end of her indignity. Dhū Tubba' established residence in the Yemen where he ruled in her stead, no doubt a constant reminder of the glory that was hers but not hers to keep. In order to guarantee respect for the new ruler's authority, Solomon assigned to him Zawba'ah, commander of the Yemen's jinn, with explicit instructions to carry out the king's wishes. Zawba'ah's assignment is the final act of retribution for her having usurped the prerogatives of men. The jinn, from whom she is descended, will be the ones to ensure that she never again aspires beyond her station.[78]

If the extensive Muslim lore about Solomon rang true, readers might have detected still another ironic touch to the queen's downfall. This haughty woman who had never been touched by a "blade" and who had trained great men as if they were wild stallions to be broken, will be rejected outright by the greatest stallion of them all. By all accounts, Solomon was the greatest of all lovers. He had the sexual potency of forty men and clearly needed all of it, because as in the Jewish tradition, he had no less than one thousand concubines and wives.[79] Indeed, on one occasion, he proclaimed that he would make the night rounds with a thousand women and would impregnate each and every one of them. True enough, the tradition was suspect because Isḥāq b. Bishr, one of the links in the *isnād,* or chain of authorities, was not entirely trustworthy. But there were other impeccably sound traditions that spoke of impregnating seventy, ninety, and even one hundred women, all in a single evening. Alas for Solomon, he forgot to finish his declaration with, "God willing!" And so, for all this prodigious lovemaking, he could produce only a single pregnancy, the result of which was a half-formed fetus.[80]

One has to put this event in historical perspective, as did the Muslim authorities. The prophet was not given to idle boasting or self-gratification, be it about his lovemaking or anything else. It is true that Solomon had an almost insatiable appetite for sex, but his needs did not include ravaging women against their wishes, as did Bilqīs's first husband, "the boy." His actions were dictated by the constant desires of his multitude of wives and concubines as well as his service to God. For in impregnating the women, he assumed that each would carry "a horseman [or sword-wielding hero] who, following God's path, would wage holy war." In this case, the references to "sword" and "horse" can probably be taken at face value. The striving on behalf of God was no doubt directed against the polytheists and not women, recalcitrant or otherwise. In losing to Solomon, Bilqīs was forced to give up more than her power over men.

F. *Postscript: Universal versus Particular*

Seen from the perspective of man's concern for his rightful authority—a concern shared also by women preferring their own specific place in nature's scheme—this tale of Solomon and the Queen of Sheba has a certain universal ring to it. Aside from the interpolation of Qur'ānic references and the transformation of Solomon into a prophet, there is, at first glance, little to distinguish Tha'labī's account from the likes of the Jewish stories previously cited. The version of Kisā'ī, which relies exclusively on the Jewish convert, Ka'b, and the Hebrew scholar, Wahb, offers even less Islamic material to consider. Indeed, his rather tame treatment of the queen's early history gives little indication that Bilqīs is any threat at all to the divine order. Kisā'ī's is a rather sweet story, the likes of which draws an acceptable rating for bedtime fairy tales.[81]

Briefly put, the king, in this case no boy but a manly tyrant, rules all the Yemen with total despotism. When angered, he likes nothing better than to ravage the virgins of the realm. Bilqīs, a ravishing beauty, is the daughter of a jinni as before, but her father is only a political appointee of the king. Having lost her mother at an early age, she is raised by the ladies of the jinn. But upon reaching her majority, she wishes to break with the spirits of her past and live in the world of the humans. There is, however, a problem. The king, having learned of the innocent girl, wishes to marry her. Her father quite rightly is in a quandary. Were he to give his daughter to this tyrant, the latter will do with her as he pleases. Should he refuse, the despot will do with him as he pleases. There is, however, no cause for alarm. She tells her father, "Marry me to him, for I shall kill him before he [so much as] touches me."

The plot is set in motion. She connives to have the king come to her palace and spend time with her alone, whereupon she gets him drunk by deftly mixing his wines and then proceeds to cut off his head. Following that, she invites the wazīrs and informs them that the tyrant is about to ravage their wives and daughters. When they grow rebellious, she reassures them that she can handle the situation by herself were they to concede rule to her. When they agree, she returns shortly thereafter with the severed head. Needless to say, they rejoice at the tyrant's fall and, being men of honor unlike the king, they hold true to their bargain. A beautiful child of mysterious background who wishes to join the society of humankind has proved her mettle by eliminating a king unsuited to that society. Taken as a whole, the introduction reads like one of those tales to which university professors assign a number and place in the cosmic taxonomy of folklore.

Given the specific thrust of the Qur'ānic version, that is, its condemnation of polytheism, it is rather remarkable that the tales of the prophets and even more formal exegetical works preserve so much in the way of universal themes. Presumably, the gender-related issues that link Muslim and Jewish sources were so powerful and so spoke so directly to Muslim concerns that they became central to the larger Islamic saga of Solomon and the queen of Sheba. Be that as it may, the theological agenda of the Qur'ānic text and the need to Islamize the ancient history of the Jews creates a parallel story requiring a second explication of the text.

5 *Islamizing Universal and Specifically Jewish Themes*

Returning to Tha'labī, we are obliged to ask what it is that makes his account a Muslim story. To begin with, there is the Qur'ānic infrastructure that supports the larger tale. The interpolated passages from "The Ant," which include all but one verse, clearly indicate the exegetical nature of Tha'labī's writing. His version of the Solomon story thus links the universal theme of the Jewish sources with the Qur'ān's salient message against polytheism. As noted, the Jewish texts show little interest in the queen's religious preferences; they emphasize instead her defiance of men in an attempt to overturn the natural order. Tha'labī adds to that an even greater concern, the condemnation of her unbelief, a practice that represents the quintessential defiance of God's grand design. Moreover, she was not satisfied that she alone should worship the sun instead of the Almighty. In her arrogance, she forced her subjects to deny their very own ancestors who paid homage to the God of Heaven.[1]

It should be clear that for Muslims the unicity of God and the uniqueness of his creation is not a truth that came to be slowly realized. Humankind did not turn to monotheism because it recognized a need for a more sophisticated understanding of the universe. The God of Heaven is not a human artifice, carefully shaped over time, in order to give the world moral and intellectual coherence. As worshipped by Muslims, the Lord of the Universe represents an indescribable reality that transcends human experience and understanding and is thus more true than anything observable in His creation. At the very outset of humankind when Adam and Eve were linked in harmony to their surroundings, all of nature's creatures recognized the one true God and the efficacy of His design. Only those jinn who descended to earth chose to disobey Him and even these rebellious creatures originally knew their place. It is only later that men and women turned to polytheism.[2] Giving "partners to God" is in fact *the* human artifice and an abomination against the natural order of things. Seen from this perspective, Bilqīs has erred on two counts: She has, in taking rule of the Yemen, usurped the natural place of man. But more seriously, in forcing her people to worship the sun, she has made them withdraw recognition from God, their one true ruler.

It cannot be said that the Queen of Sheba had not heard of the Almighty. When she asked her wazīrs what her ancestors worshipped, they answered, "the Lord of Heaven."[3] When she then asked where he was, they pointed out that He was in heaven above but that the manifest signs of His presence are here on earth. Such as it was, the explanation of God's whereabouts did not prove satisfactory. The queen, not about to be impressed with something that she could not personally envisage, chose instead to worship the sun, whose rays were more powerful than anything she had experienced. Were that not enough to brand her, she obligated her people (who had previously been monotheists) to do the same. It thus came to pass that they bowed to the sun in devotion at sunrise and sunset. Such disbelief, compounded by her disrespect for God's design, was a most serious provocation.

Oddly enough, among the storytellers and exegetes, only Tha'labī is willing to condemn the queen for denying a truth already received and forcing her subjects to do the same. The other authorities make her a victim of her own ignorance and that of her people.[4] Following holy scripture, she is made to be an unbeliever *from a people of unbelievers* (Qur'ān xxvii:43). She knew no better; she simply worshipped the sun (and moon) "according to the religion of her people and ancestors." It is perhaps no accident that the Qur'ānic verse (43), which is the proof-text for this argument, is the only verse of the scriptural account not interpolated into Tha'labī's version of events. One might wish to argue with the author about his thoroughness, but there is no question that, in making Bilqīs culpable for denying God and forcing her people to do the same, Tha'labī offers a more compelling story of her unbelief and the prophet's response.

Upon hearing that news directly from the hoopoe, the prophet is forced to change her ways and policies. And so, he will send her a letter in which he warns her not to display haughtiness towards him but to come in submission. The Arabic word that demands she submit is the active participle of the verb *aslama,* which can mean, and does mean in this case, submission to both man and God. That is to say, this woman, who presumes to rule over men, has been instructed to surrender to Solomon, the greatest ruler among men and the upholder of the natural order. But, as she has also presumed to deny the rule of God, not only to herself but to her subjects, she will also submit to Allāh. There can be no doubt that the double entendre was both intended and understood. When Bilqīs finally submits, her various ploys to remain independent exhausted, she proclaims: *I submit through Solomon to Allāh, Lord of the Universe* (Qur'ān xxvii:44).[5]

That Solomon's missive is a religious pronouncement as well as a political directive is also suggested by its very terseness, for as Tha'labī indicates, prophets, as a rule, write in summary fashion rather than long detailed accounts.[6] Moreover, the salutation is the familiar *basmalah* that all Muslims utilized in writing.[7] And so, the document begins, "In the name of God, the Merciful and Compassionate." Sending the letter in such an extraordinary fashion was bound to catch the queen's attention: "Any ruler who uses birds as his emissaries is indeed a great ruler." It is, however, the power of the signet ring, the seal of God's Vice Regent, that forces her to acknowledge Solomon's true greatness. He will not be as easy as was her late husband, "the boy," but she has a plan to retain her position even as she doubts her unbelief. Although at each step Bilqīs will face proof of her folly, she will persist in denying what should have been obvious to her with the delivery of the letter: that Solomon, a man, is her superior, and that all her devious schemes will have absolutely no effect on the ultimate outcome of her life. Her fate, which is in God's hands, will be determined according to His wishes because compared with the Lord of the Universe, the mighty sun, the original object of her veneration, is nothing.

The delivery of the letter should have been instructive, for as in the Jewish *Targum Sheni,* the presence of a bird (in the *Targum* an army of birds) makes a mockery of her belief.[8] She worships the sun in preference to God because she can directly perceive the sun's power through the presence of its rays. The mysterious God who is in heaven is beyond direct comprehension and is thus known only through his signs on earth. How is it that a woman as clever as Bilqīs cannot recognize these signs? How is it that a woman as skeptical as she is about the Almighty can worship an object that is driven to cover under the darkness of night? As if to foreshadow the queen's presumptuous joust with Solomon, the hoopoe, a lowly bird, will demonstrate her faulty thinking. According to Wahb b. Munabbih, the queen had a window in her bedroom that caught the morning sunrise.[9] In such fashion, it served as nature's alarm clock. That is to say, when the first rays entered her room, she awakened and bowed down before the object of her veneration. On this day, however, the hoopoe spread its wings blocking the sun, so the darkness continued. Sensing that the time for daylight had already passed, Bilqīs got up to investigate. At that, the bird dropped the prophet's message in her lap. To a discerning person like the queen, all this should have been an object lesson. How can she continue to worship the sun if the source of its strength can be negated by a single defenseless bird—an obvious question also suggested by the Jewish *Targum,* albeit referring to an army of birds?[10]

Still, the queen is not moved to submission. Although she has witnessed the amazing delivery of the letter and the seal of the Vice Regent's signet ring, presumably signs on earth of the God in Heaven, she is yet to be convinced that Solomon is actually His prophet. She will test the Israelite with gifts to see if he is but a king, in which case, she can and will deal with him. But if he is a prophet (doing God's bidding), there is no doubt trouble ahead because prophets are only satisfied when they oblige others follow their cause. Indeed, other sources informed the medieval reader that Solomon searched the earth for domains yet unconquered so that he could force them to submit to his religion.[11]

The return of her disgraced embassy gives indication of future pressure. Moreover, as Bilqīs has learned that Solomon is no king, she is powerless to confront him. To forestall the impending attack of the world's most formidable army, she will come to him as commanded. Nevertheless, Tha'labī's audience might have perceived a certain lack of conviction in her compliance. The ambiguous wording of her message seems to suggest that she still harbors some reservations. She comes, not to surrender to the Israelite's wishes, but "to consider your command and the call to your religion."[12] The queen does not strike us as willing to give up everything in obedience to Solomon even though she may submit to his God. Presumably, additional signs of the Almighty's intervention will be required to effect a final change in her attitude. However Bilqīs may feel as regards her future spiritual development, she is not about to let it interfere with her current political status. She still cannot bring herself to surrender unconditionally. To forestall any loss of power, she has taken elaborate measures to safeguard her precious throne. But here too she will be thwarted, as Solomon will have the symbol of her authority brought to him before the queen's arrival.[13]

A. *The Significance of the Queen's Throne*

Various scholars maintain that Solomon called for her throne so that he could demonstrate to her "the power of God . . . and the greatness of His dominion."[14] If, as they seem to suggest, she needed still another impressive sign of God's presence, Solomon surely provided it. By invoking Allāh's mightiest name,[15] he transferred her most precious object from its secure resting place. What greater sign would she require now that she has seen before her very eyes the throne that she left safely guarded in her palace? Were that not enough, these scholars could have added an additional proof of God's presence: the miraculous fashion in which her throne was disguised and turned upside down, a clear signal to the reader that, in due time, the same would happen to the status she has privileged for herself. A final test in Solomon's presence and the game will be ended to the satisfaction of the prophet and his Lord.

For some exegetes, the ambiguity surrounding Bilqīs's changing relationship to Allāh and his prophet informs the most difficult verse of the Qur'ānic tale: *Knowledge was brought to us min qablihā. For we were Muslims* (Qur'ān xxvii: 42). Medieval scholars were especially perplexed by the phrase *min qablihā,* which has been left untranslated here. Various luminaries understood the verse to mean: *Knowledge was brought to us* of her obedient arrival *min qablihā,* that is, *prior to her coming. For* [unlike Bilqīs, who had not yet submitted] *we were Muslims,* obedient and subservient to God, may He be exalted.[16] Although the reading seems at best problematic, it is consistent with the basic thrust of Tha'labī's account regarding the queen's arrival and the ensuing events. She had come to Solomon prepared to declare her submission if need be; but only after a formal declaration to him would she truly become a Muslim.

A second explanation is proffered by commentators who link the verse with a positive inclination by Bilqīs to recognize the God of Heaven.[17] They claim, contrary to opinions previously expressed, that she was not so evasive when confronted by the altered throne. They claim instead that, in her own way, she acknowledged the object to be hers. There was no reason for her to deny that Solomon held the symbol of her authority, with all that that implied concerning her status and power, because, according to them, she had already decided to recognize his prophethood and submit to him and his Lord. Presumably, this second group of authorities opined that she had had enough of God's signs, beginning with the arrival of the hoopoe and continuing with the ambassadorial visit.[18] Seen from this perspective, the speaker in the verse is Bilqīs rather than Solomon; the knowledge possessed is her knowledge of Solomon's prophethood rather than his of her arrival; and the most problematic phrase *min qablihā* is rendered "prior to this last wonder," in reference to the transfer and altering of her throne, and not "prior to her coming."[19] The enigmatic text thus reads: *Knowledge was brought to us* of your prophethood even *prior to this last wonder* of the throne. *For we were Muslims* simply verifies that she had already submitted (in her heart though not in deed) before she arrived at Solomon's court. In one respect at least, this second interpretation is also consistent with the basic thrust of Tha'labī's account. The queen's visit will enable her to give

Solomon formal notice of her submission. Through her personal declaration, she will become subject to the rights and responsibilities of the Muslims.[20] There is no indication of how scholars holding this view explained the queen's further questions and her determination to hold on to her throne, the very symbol of her authority.[21]

Viewed as a whole, the passages concerning the throne (verses 38–42 of the Qur'ān) are without doubt the most perplexing of the tale. As such, they are the subject of considerable discussion and conflicting views among medieval authorities. Nevertheless, the commentary is consistent in one respect. The episode of the throne, which has no parallel in the extant Jewish sources, is always presented in a distinctively Muslim context. We have already shown that establishing Solomon's hegemony as a man and upholding nature's order is not enough of a story for the exegetes. As in sacred scripture, Bilqīs's presumption invokes a larger concern: her denial of Solomon's prophethood and beyond that her earlier denial of Allāh.[22] Unlike the political upstart of the Jewish versions, the Queen of Sheba must bend to the God of Heaven, whom she personally rejected and caused her subjects to abandon. In doing so, she must recognize the legitimacy of Solomon's prophetic vocation, not simply the power of his worldly rule. No self-respecting Muslim could have accepted less of her if the tale were to ring true.

B. *Muslim Markings*

Even this religious message did not go far enough in Islamizing the account. The universal themes that link the Qur'ān and its exegesis to Jewish sources had to be embellished with specific religious markers easily recognized in contemporary Muslim society. As a result, the issues of gender gave way to a different concern, that of creating a discrete Muslim tale. Appropriating the Jewish past, Muslims reshaped ancient "events" to accord with their own familiar customs and practices. Seen in this context, the Arabic story of Solomon and the Queen of Sheba shifts interest from the queen's challenge to natural order to Solomon's status as a practicing Muslim.

Referring to the transfer of the queen's throne, some religious scholars wondered why Solomon needed to have it, as she was prepared to declare her submission. What prompted him to ask: *Which of you can bring me her throne before they come to me submitting as Muslims* (Qur'ān xxvii:38)? For Muslim scholars, the immediate need of the queen's throne suggested more than a contrivance to impress Bilqīs. There is more to this miraculous demonstration than a skirmish between the sexes. Nor was the related issue of her submission merely a question of recognizing Solomon's vocation through God's signs on earth. The Muslim view of the world, combined with the pyrotechnics of Muslim scholarship, called for a more arcane analysis of this and other verses of the Solomon story.

It seemed eminently reasonable to medieval Muslim scholars that Solomon, an analogue to the Prophet Muḥammad, would have been guided by the principles of Islamic law as they studied and practiced it. Thus, according to most exegetes, the extraordinary timing needed to acquire the throne was dictated by the prophet's respect for the law as they understood it. That is to say, there were two ways by which one submitted (to Islam): by force (*'anwatan*) or by peaceful means (*sulḥan*). The former, in which the enemies of Islam were forced to capitulate, often resulted in forfeiting rights to livestock, produce, landed property, and all means of household chattel. The defeated forces, if polytheists, might themselves be regarded as slaves awaiting formal conversion. If they were monotheists, for example Christians taken during the summer forays across the Byzantine border, they might be held towards a future exchange of captives, or redeemed as part of a financial transaction. On the other hand, monotheists who surrendered their territory peacefully to Islamic armies, or, for that matter, any peoples who freely embraced the conqueror's religion, remained free and were entitled to retain their property. Indeed, no Muslim, whether born free or manumitted, could be reduced to servility. From the vantage point of a medieval Muslim jurist, the issues raised by Tha'labī and the Qur'ānic tale on which his account is based suggest the need for a legal analysis of the verse in question.

Why then did the Solomon need her throne *before they come to me submitting as Muslims?* Because once Bilqīs submitted to God through his prophet, that is converted to Islam, she was entitled by legal precedent to retain her property. As a result, Solomon would have been denied the spoils of their conflict.[23] The queen herself seems to have understood the implication of resisting Solomon with military force. She rejects the counsel of her brave but foolish warriors that she seek combat and rely on their prowess. The various commentaries make it clear that defeat will entail destruction, humiliating status, and loss of property.[24] According to Ibn Kathīr, she informed her notables that the burden of an aggressive response would be borne directly by her. As the author put it, "She was more levelheaded in sorting things out than were they."[25]

We can surely understand the queen's decision, but does Solomon, who has "something of everything" and who had dismissed her material possessions earlier, need this luxurious bauble to add to his regalia?[26] Qatādah's view that the prophet had been amazed by the hoopoe's description and therefore wanted to see the throne seems quite naive and not at all convincing. Can we seriously believe, given Solomon's incomparable throne, that he would have been anxious to look at hers?[27] Moreover, what was to prevent Solomon from seeing it after she had become a Muslim? In this case, the need to have the story comport to the world of Muslim scholars produces a tendentious commentary that obscures the more likely point of the original tale. There can be no doubt that the prophet was beyond material needs; nevertheless, he was bound to recognize the symbolic importance of the occasion. Allowing the queen to retain the symbol of her authority implies that she will continue to rule all of the Yemen even if she submits to Solomon and his God. As noted before, various Muslim scholars could not conceive of Solomon giving his consent to that. In their view, her past indiscretions, if that is strong enough a word, demanded the forfeiture of power. Another monarch will be chosen to wed Bilqīs and rule in her stead.[28]

To be sure, there were also scholars who maintained that Solomon allowed Bilqīs to continue as ruler of the Yemen. They also say, contrary to the aforementioned opinion, that the prophet fell in love with the queen and married her himself, and that having wed her, he commanded the jinn to build her three magnificent fortresses.[29] But even here, Muslim law and custom will inform opinion. It appears that the prophet was too busy with the affairs of state (to say nothing of all his other wives) to set up an exclusive household with Bilqīs in her land. As one might have expected, the Israelite preferred to live in Syria (at his recently built capital, Jerusalem). It would have come as no surprise to Tha'labī's readers that he placed Solomon in Syria, or to be more precise, the province called in Arabic al-Shām, rather than in the Land of Israel, as ancient Palestine was known among Jews. Medieval Muslims were only too aware that Palestine was part of Syria and governed from the provincial capital in Damascus.[30]

As regards the alleged marriage between the prophet and Bilqīs, there is still one more point to be made. Having married the queen and having established a separate domicile for her, the prophet was obligated by Muslim law to arrange for visitation rights. And so, as did all good Muslim husbands, Solomon traveled to this wife (among others) and, in his case, spent three days a month with her in the Yemen. This was no small undertaking.[31] Jazā'irī reminds us that every one of his thousand royal women had a domicile of her own and, as the proper head of his house, Solomon was obliged to keep them all sexually content.[32] One has to believe that, in spite of that, the prophet managed just fine. Given his unique mode of transportation, a fully equipped administrative center borne by the winds like a modern airliner, this was one commuter marriage that was likely to have survived the enervating effects of jet lag. Could one say that the marriage was a success? There is perhaps the hint that it was ultimately a mistake, for Kisā'ī reports that the issue of this union was Rehoboam (Solomon's only son and successor). Scholars knew only too well that this son's foolish policies strengthened idolatry and brought permanent division to the illustrious kingdom of his father.[33]

Not surprisingly, other aspects of the Solomonic story are also informed by Muslim customs and legal practices. Commenting on the verse *And Solomon inherited from David* (Qur'ān xxvii:16), the exegetes, Tha'labī among them, indicate that this inheritance was not shared by David's other eighteen sons.[34] Readers familiar with Islamic practice would have been surprised that the Israelite ruler had not given all his male offspring their proper share of his wealth. This seeming incongruity between the laws of inheritance practiced by Muslims and David's bequest to Solomon as understood by Qur'ān scholars clearly demanded an explanation. Ibn Kathīr thus points out, "The intention (in verse 16) is not that Solomon inherited wealth [to the exclusion of his brothers] for David already had sons other than him and would not have apportioned his wealth without specifying them."[35] Indeed, prophets do not appoint heirs to their worldly possessions (*māl*). And so, after death, their wealth is not distributed among relations as with others, but is converted instead to alms (*ṣadaqah*) for the poor and needy. Nevertheless, the Qur'ān explicitly states: *Solomon inherited from David.*[36] Because the latter could hardly have disregarded the time-honored practice of his religious vocation, scholars held that Solomon's inheritance was limited to prophethood (*nubuwwah*), knowledge (*'ilm*), and rule (*mulk*). To reinforce this contention, Ibn Kathīr cites two proof-texts, both traditions ascribed to the Prophet Muḥammad. The latter allegedly said, "What we leave behind [after death] we do not leave as inheritance. Rather it is [reserved for use as] legal alms (*ṣadaqah*)." Were that statement not sufficiently clear in specifying who is meant by "we," the author adds a second comment. Muḥammad also said: "We, the company of prophets, leave no inheritance." Once again, a self-evident Qur'ānic passage—in this case, a verse calling attention to a unique occurrence, namely that both father and son were prophets—is embellished by religious authorities to reflect the concerns of medieval scholarship.[37]

C. *Islamizing the Story of the Hoopoe*

Even the hoopoe's relationship to Solomon takes on a distinct Muslim coloring. Ibn Kathīr states explicitly that every species (*ṣinf*) of birds assisted Solomon just as military contingents serve (temporal) rulers.[38] Collectively, their duty was to fly above Solomon and his entourage, thus shielding them from the discomfort of the sun. As regards the hoopoe, it was his specific function to guide Solomon to water, a task for which this bird was uniquely suited because, flying high above the earth, he could locate subterranean cisterns with remarkable precision. Once the place of water was determined, it was a simple matter for the satans to draw it from the earth.[39] However charming, this tradition concerning the hoopoe was not without its critics. There was skepticism that a creature ordinarily caught in a shallow trap could locate water situated at great depths beneath the ground. One notes that the response occasioned by this flawless logic seems more informed by humor than acrimony. The critics were told, "When fate intervenes sight turns to blindness." Clearly, medieval scholars had a graceful way of distancing themselves from legendary accounts when challenged.[40] Be that as it may, Muḥammad himself allegedly said that it was forbidden to kill the hoopoe, as the bird had been Solomon's guide to water. And so, the hoopoe reportedly joined the ant, the bee, and the sparrow hawk on the Prophet's list of protected species.[41] Whether or not pious Muslims actually followed this dictum and refrained from hunting the bird cannot be ascertained. Suffice it to say, the hoopoe's special talent was generally acknowledged by religious scholars. There is serious dispute, however, as regards the circumstances of his absence. Because that dispute is relevant to the Islamization of the larger tale, it is, along with the bird's water-seeking abilities, a topic for discussion here.

Some scholars maintain that, as in the Jewish account of the *Targum Sheni*, Solomon first noted the bird missing during a review of the air corps.[42] On that occasion, the prophet was not shielded from the sun as he should have been. A ray of sunlight shone through the spot vacated by the hoopoe. As a result, the prophet became enraged and threatened the bird with extreme violence. There is something disquieting about this explanation. The prophet's response to the bird's dereliction of duty seems rather excessive. What if the prophet was struck by a ray of sunlight? Did that require severe punishment, perhaps even death? True enough, the Qur'ān does say: *I will surely punish him severely or slaughter him unless he brings me a clear excuse* (Sūrah xxvii:21). Nevertheless, there is nothing in the story which follows to explain the ferocity of Solomon's anger.[43] Indeed, the majority of the exegetes must have been puzzled by the severity of his response, particularly the prophet's threat to kill the hoopoe. Of all the commentators that I consulted, only Zamakhsharī discusses slaughtering the bird;[44] the others respond with what seems embarrassed silence. Most authorities hold that, in threatening to *punish* the hoopoe *severely,* Solomon intended to pluck the bird clean and lay him bare on an ant hill. Some envision a more gruesome punishment, others a punishment less painful, but none seem concerned for the hoopoe's life lest he not produce a clear excuse for his shocking absence. Killing the guide to water was not an option that elicited much commentary.[45]

Still, the threat to the hoopoe's life was uttered for all to hear and, according to Tha'labī, the birds did indeed take that threat at face value. In escorting the hoopoe to Solomon, the eagle tells his compatriot, "Woe unto you! Your mother is about to become childless." There is no reason to believe that in this instance the commander of the birds was speaking metaphorically.[46] The Jewish king of the *Targum Sheni* could act menacingly when he missed the hoopoe at the flypast of the birds; he was, after all, drunk and anxious to impress his guests, the assembled monarchs of the earth. But on no account could any Muslim prophet be given to drink or ostentatious display. For those who read the verse literally, a more suitable reason would have to be found to explain Solomon's great rage and, beyond that, his threat to slaughter the hoopoe. The seed of this explanation may perhaps be found in a second version of these events.

Another group of scholars maintains that the bird was needed to find water at the time of prayer.[47] That is, without the hoopoe's special gift, the prophet and his entourage would have been unable to perform the ablutions required for worship. For on this occasion, there was no water at ground level and none save the hoopoe had the ability to locate it. It was then that Solomon sought his guide but could not find him. There is, to my knowledge, no explicit reason for this second version of events. It is in no way suggested by a literal reading of the Qur'ānic text which mentions neither water nor prayer. Why then did these exegetes explain the verse as they did? One could claim that, whatever its source (perhaps some lost text), the second accounting of the hoopoe's absence provides ample reason to slaughter the bird. To be sure, that reason is never stated explicitly, but the new reading of events alters completely the nature of the charge against the hoopoe. Through his negligence, Solomon's guide to water was not merely guilty of offending his ruler on earth; his behavior made it impossible for the Israelites to perform their obligations to the Heavenly Ruler. Medieval readers might then understand why Solomon reacted as he did. It was not that the hoopoe had offended the prophet; it was rather his offense against God that so rankled Solomon and the medieval Muslims. One can respond that this explanation of the prophet's anger is based entirely on inference but, after all, inference was and is a mode of reading well suited to highly allusive medieval texts. In any case, no better explanation has been offered.

Having speculated rather freely as regards Solomon and the hoopoe's absence, I would be judged no more guilty for doing the same about their face-to-face meeting, an event that also speaks to Muslim religious sensitivities. Standing humbly before the prophet and certain to be punished unless he had *a clear excuse,* the hoopoe enjoins Solomon to remember that he himself stands before Allāh. At that, the prophet "trembled and forgave the bird" even before hearing the reason for his absence. This response is also puzzling. Given the gravity of the hoopoe's negligence and the corresponding nature of the prophet's threats, why should Solomon have forgiven the bird without further inquiry? We can understand that justice is best served in an atmosphere not heated by rage, but how can Solomon issue a proper judgment without first hearing the bird's testimony? The reason offered by Tha'labī, namely, that Solomon decided not to slaughter the hoopoe out of mercy for the latter's parents, is at best forced. Clearly, the prophet's judgment is affected by the hoopoe's plea, but what has the bird said that causes the mightiest ruler on earth to change his mind so dramatically? What did it mean for Solomon to be cognizant that he himself was "standing before Allāh"?[48]

When interpreting a particular Qur'ānic verse, it is often profitable to invoke other scriptural passages, for the Qur'ān has a way of commenting on itself. In the sūrah named "Ṣād" we are told of an earlier incident in which creatures of the animal kingdom caused Solomon to miss the time of prayer. To be more precise, three opaque verses (xxxviii:31–33) are held by the exegetes to describe such an incident:

> *Behold there were brought before him at eventide swift horses that stand on three legs while brushing the ground with the fourth* [*31*]. *He said: Instead of mentioning my Lord, I have loved the love of good* [*things*] *until it* [*the sun*] *was concealed by the veil* [*of night*] [32]. *Bring them* [*the horses*] *back to me! Then he began to pass* [*his hand*] *over shanks and necks* [33].

Leaving much tortured commentary aside, we are obliged to ask if these veiled allusions to animals and missed prayer can be made to inform the hoopoe's later plea to Solomon? In other words, is the earlier incident described in sūrah "Ṣād" reflected in the hoopoe's remark that the prophet (ought not act rashly but should instead) remember that he is standing before his Lord? And if so, what is there in the hoopoe's statement that would have caused the mightiest of all earthly rulers to tremble and then forgive the bird against his own solemn pledge?

As regards the relevant passages of "Ṣād" the following story can be gleaned from the comments of Tha'labī and others: It would appear that Solomon had acquired a number of magnificent horses. Some scholars say they were taken as booty in a raid against Naṣībīn; others that he obtained them from his father who had taken them from the Amalekites; still others[49] maintain that they were winged creatures that came originally from the sea.[50] In any case, having completed the midday prayers, the prophet ascended his throne and the animals were paraded before him. The beasts, described as *ṣafināt,* that is horses that stand three legs planted with a fourth brushing the ground, were marvelous to behold. But, more than that, they are also described as swift of foot. The prophet became completely enraptured by the parade of *ṣafināt* before him. Indeed, he was so absorbed with the display, that he did not notice it was time for the late afternoon prayer.

Upon realizing what had happened, Solomon grieved that his love of beautiful things, namely the horses, had prevented him from noting that the sun had become veiled.[51] As a result, he had neglected to mention his Lord, for he had inadvertently missed the time to worship. He called for the horses and they were brought back at which point *he began to pass* [*his hand*] *over shanks and necks*. This vague passing of the hand over the body parts of these magnificent animals was understood by various exegetes as a sacrificial act performed with a knife.[52] That is to say, having missed the prescribed time of worship, the prophet sought to make amends with offerings to God. But, according to Tha'labī, quoting Ka'b, the learned Jewish convert, killing the animals was a wrongful act and God punished Solomon by removing him from his throne. He was thus without rule for fourteen days, one for each animal slaughtered.[53] Although neither Tha'labī nor his source indicate it, the reference to Solomon's temporary exile is seemingly suggested by the following verses of the sūrah: *We tried Solomon and placed a body on his throne. Then he* [*Solomon*] *repented. He said: O my Lord! Forgive me and bestow upon me rule* [*the likes of which*] *will be unsuitable to any* [*ruler*] *after me. Indeed, You are The Bestower* (Qur'ān xxxviii:34–35). The proposed link certainly makes for a coherent story: Having erred in slaughtering the horses, Solomon was exiled. But having done penance, he was allowed to return to his throne and was subsequently rewarded.[54]

This facile reading, which links the commentary of one sūrah with verses of another, is not without difficulty. Scholars disagree whether the passing of hand over shanks and necks actually refers to sacrifice.[55] Others accept that Solomon sacrificed the horses but disagree that God was displeased. To the contrary, many authorities hold that the offerings were accepted and that God compensated Solomon for the loss of his fleet *ṣafināt* with dominion over the swiftest creation of all, the winds.[56] But, most important, the verses of "Ṣād" that speak of Solomon's punishment, that is his temporary loss of rule, are linked by most exegetes to events other than killing the horses.

The majority hold that verses 34–35 reflect an episode in which a compassionate Solomon allowed one of his wives to erect a statue to her deceased father. Intended as a bereaved child's remembrance of a beloved parent, the statue soon became an object of idolatrous worship. When the prophet then went off to do penance for his foolish if kindhearted deed, a satan emulating Solomon's image obtained his magic ring and ruled in his stead.[57] This is how these exegetes understand the cryptic allusion to a *body on his throne*. Other authorities refer to a very different incident with the world of the spirits. We are informed that Solomon was blessed with a child, thus causing the satans to fear that they would be forced to serve Solomon's progeny as they serve him. So they planned to kill the child or cause him to be demented. In either case, they would have been set free upon Solomon's death. Having learned of this, Solomon had the child raised in a cloud but did not personally ensure safety for his heir. The child was subsequently killed and the *body* placed *on his throne*. In such fashion Solomon realized that he had been judged and punished for his failure to enlist God's aid in this matter.[58]

Quite obviously, these interpretations run counter to the elaborate argument that we have constructed. Let us assume, however, that Tha'labī was inclined to follow Ka'b's interpretation whether or not it was actually suggested by verses 34–35.[59] Such being the case, our author would have believed that the prophet slaughtered the horses and paid for what was considered a blameworthy act with the temporary loss of his domain. How might this interpretation inform the hoopoe's plea to Solomon? In asking the prophet to remember that he is standing before his Lord, the bird would have jostled his master's memory. Solomon's thoughts would then have turned to that previous episode when creatures of the animal kingdom caused him to miss the proscribed time of prayer. On that occasion, his attempt to make amends by sacrificing some of the animals led to unanticipated calamity. In his current rage over missing prayer, he was in danger of repeating a foolhardy act. Were he to execute the hoopoe or, what is more likely, offer him in sacrifice, he will run the risk of losing his kingdom once again. It is no small wonder that Solomon trembled and forgave the bird even before hearing his story.

There is, nevertheless, a disquieting footnote to this line of argument. However neatly these two episodes of missed prayer and animals may fit together, the Muslim exegetes did not bother to make the connection, nor, to my knowledge, did they even hint that the circumstances of "Ṣād" might have had any bearing on the story of Solomon and the Queen of Sheba. For the time being, the modern reader is asked to accept that connection on faith alone. Nevertheless, it does seem plausible that medieval readers would have linked Solomon's threat to slaughter the derelict hoopoe with the lack of water to perform the ablutions before prayer. Hence, an interpretation rooted in a Muslim practice was given equal footing with an explanation linked to a Jewish midrash.

Which of these interpretations rings most true? Did Solomon first notice the hoopoe's absence when he needed the bird to perform the rites of prayer or was the bird missed when he failed to show up for his patrol in the sky? The great historian and exegete Ṭabarī managed to validate both views, when, exercising the most graceful logic, he maintained that both interpretations might be correct because there was no way of establishing the validity of one over the other.[60] In such fashion, an episode linked to a universal Jewish tale could take on a distinct Islamic flavor without any sense of contradiction.

D. *Jewish Themes and Settings*

The gender issue that connects specific midrashim with Muslim versions of this celebrated tale has been duly noted. There are, however, other Jewish themes and settings that are reflected in the Muslim story and in the larger saga of Solomon the prophet. Readers will recall that Solomon assumed rule at the age of twelve or thirteen (depending on which Muslim authority is followed).[61] However circuitously, this Islamic tradition, linked to still another rabbinic midrash, is seemingly based on a more distant echo of the Jewish past. Our attention is thus drawn to an event described in the Book of Kings.[62] As portrayed by the biblical chronicler, Solomon was at Gibeon when God came to him in a dream and informed him that he would rule (in preference to his older brothers). Solomon then exclaimed, "O God my Lord! You have chosen [me] your servant to rule replacing my father David, but I am only a young lad who will not know his way."[63] He then pleads with God to give him an open mind with which to distinguish between good and evil, "for who can judge this populous people of yours."[64] God was taken with this seemingly modest request for wisdom. As ruler of the Israelites, Solomon could have asked for long life; for the lives of his enemies (a veiled allusion to his stepbrother Adonijah and the cabal that sought to undermine an aged David's rule); or more particularly, for great wealth. Because Solomon asked only for the wherewithal to make sound judgments, God granted him wisdom that none before him had attained and to which none after him could aspire. Were that not enough, God chose to honor Solomon with the very gift that he had not sought, namely, unparalled earthly wealth and honor. Readers will recall that the lad's preference for wisdom over wealth and the unanticipated largesse that this choice occasioned from God is a theme that is also reflected in the Muslim account of young Solomon. According to Kisā'ī, when asked explicitly if he would prefer dominion (*mulk*) to knowledge (*'ilm*), Bathsheba's son replied, "O my Lord! Knowledge is more precious to me than dominion." At that, God revealed himself to Solomon and granted him dominion as well as knowledge, reason, and a perfect temperament (to rule).[65]

God's double gift to Solomon made him sui generis among monarchs. Not only was the wise Solomon the quintessential ruler of an earthly domain; having acquired a magical ring, he was also given control over the supernatural. Prominently featured in Jewish lore, the signet ring and Solomon's legendary jousts with various spirits have direct parallels in Muslim literature. Be it a story about the Jewish Ashmedai or his Muslim analogue, Ṣakhr, the tale often remains outwardly the same. Both the Muslim prophet and Jewish king are portrayed as using the jinn for highly specialized tasks, most notable among them, the building of God's temple in Jerusalem. These are, nevertheless, creatures not entirely happy with their work. In both Jewish and Muslim sources, the spirits held captive by Solomon are restless and yearn for their freedom. Indeed, they will have their brief moment. In both religious traditions, Solomon will suffer a loss of power as he finds himself without his signet ring. Similarly, both Jewish and Muslim tales will celebrate Solomon's return to the throne once the ring is restored to him. The stories of Solomon and the spirits may be somewhat different and the dramatis personae may appear under different names, but the Jewish and Muslim accounts are clearly connected, however difficult it may be to trace the path of that connection.[66]

E. *The One Who Had Knowledge of the Book*

The tale of Solomon and the Queen of Sheba also reflects some less obvious links between Jewish and Muslim sources. These connections, if they are indeed more than the playful imagination of a modern scholar, would seem to represent an extremely subtle process of Islamization. Consider the opaque reference to *the one who had knowledge of the book* (Qur'ān xxvii:40). The exegetes and storytellers were clearly puzzled by the mysterious personage and book mentioned in scripture and were left to wonder about the manner in which he came to assist a beleaguered Solomon. Who was he and how could he have managed to produce the queen's throne *in the twinkling of an eye* when one of the most powerful of the spirits would have required no less than an entire morning to bring it from the Yemen to Jerusalem? Not surprisingly, the Qur'ānic verses gave rise to considerable discussion. Muslim scholars agree that knowledge of God's mightiest name, the so-called *ism al-a'ẓam,* was required in order to produce the needed throne in so miraculous a fashion. According to tradition, Allāh never denied a request in which that particular name of His was invoked—the delivery of the queen's throne in the twinkling of an eye being a case in point.[67] There is no consensus, however, as regards Solomon's unnamed interlocutor; the untitled book whose contents that person (alone) was familiar with; and the mightiest name of God that the exegetes linked to special pleadings.

The reference to Solomon's interlocutor presented readers of the Qur'ān with an apparent paradox. Here was the great ruler of the Israelites, a prophet in Muslim tradition and without question the most learned man of his time if not all times, in desperate need of someone who had knowledge of a book that was linked in some way to God's mightiest name. Can it be that Solomon, who knew all manner of things natural and supernatural, and who was invested with Adam's signet ring, the sign of God's vicar on Earth, did not know the mysterious book and by implication the mightiest name of his Lord? And if the learned Solomon, of all people, lacked that knowledge, how could anyone else have been privy to it? But the Qur'ān is seemingly clear: a second person was required to assist Solomon in his moment of need.

Although verse 40 cannot be interpreted otherwise, at least not without straining what seems obvious, Muḥammad b. al-Munkadir was not prepared to admit that, for lack of any special knowledge, the great Solomon, seeking a special pleading, had to rely on someone else to summon Allāh. And so, Ibn al-Munkadir builds his case, however specious: Had not God given the Israelite knowledge (*'ilm*) and understanding (*fiqh*)? It was surely Solomon himself who summoned God by invoking His mightiest name. What then are we to make of *the one who had knowledge of the book?* The mysterious figure of the Qur'ān was an anonymous Israelite (undoubtedly acquainted with Hebrew scripture) who offered to bring Solomon the queen's throne in the twinkling of an eye. He did this, however, without any specific knowledge of God's mightiest name. He merely suggested to Solomon that as a prophet and the son of a prophet no one was more highly regarded by God than was Solomon himself. The prophet had only to call upon Allāh to have the queen's throne as desired. In such fashion, the unnamed figure having knowledge of the book—here seemingly identified with the Hebrew Bible—served only to galvanize the all-wise Solomon into making his own plea. However ingenious, this reading of scripture, which salvages the prophet's reputation as being all wise and all knowing, is not without obvious difficulty for it twists the verse well beyond its apparent meaning.[68]

Most exegetes were more faithful to the literal meaning of Qur'ān xxvii:40. They provided Solomon with an intermediary capable of intervening with God on the prophet's behalf. Some authorities claimed that Solomon's interlocutor was Gabriel;[69] others, an unspecified angel chosen by God for this occasion.[70] No doubt, it seemed reasonable to these scholars that the heavenly host would have been required to accomplish that which a most powerful spirit could not. There is ample testimony in a wide range of Muslim sources that Gabriel was specifically assigned to protect the interests of God's chosen messengers.[71] Those familiar with the Arabic tale of Solomon and the Queen of Sheba would have recalled several incidents in which the archangel came to Solomon's aid, most particularly during the visit of the queen's ambassadors and again during the visit of the queen herself. It was Gabriel who informed the prophet as to the contents of a gift box, thus enabling Solomon to convince the queen's emissaries of his proverbial wisdom and prophetic calling. Similarly, when Solomon fell prostrate and his legions were scattered, it was Gabriel who advised him to carry on as if nothing had happened. As a result, Bilqīs eventually submitted to the prophet and his God, the Lord of the Universe.[71]

On the other hand, some authorities suggested that the one with knowledge of the book was a mere mortal, a righteous man from an unspecified island in an unnamed sea. Among Muslims, as indeed among other peoples, islands in a distant sea are generally the source of mysterious beings and events. In this case, our enigmatic personage had come to visit the habitations of the mainlanders in order to see whether or not they worshipped Allāh. Fortuitously, he came upon Solomon who was in need of instant help. The obliging stranger then summoned Allāh by one of His names (presumably the *ism al-aʿẓam*), and, behold, the throne was transported to the prophet in the twinkling of an eye. Who was this islander?

According to various exegetes, he was a certain Usṭūm, which suggests rabbinic Hebrew *s^{e}tam,* meaning "an anonymous author or redactor" and by extension any unnamed person. Were that indeed the case, the mysterious proper name "Usṭūm," which is not derived from any known Arabic root, would have been fashioned from a Hebrew technical term. Other scholars refer to a Malīḥā or Balīkhā, also strange names to suit a mysterious islander.[74] Still another possibility is al-Khiḍr, who is mentioned as one who may have had knowledge of the book. From other sources we learn that al-Khiḍr did indeed live on an island in the sea and that he allegedly possessed learning unknown even to his companion Moses, the great prophet of Israel.[75] What better candidate to summon God by His mightiest name than a shadowy figure who knew what even Moses did not know. In any case, the theory of a mysterious visitor to the mainland remains problematic and not the preferred interpretation of most commentary.

F. *Asaph Son of Berechiah*

The majority of Isrā'īlīyāt scholars favor Asaph son of Berechiah as *the one who had knowledge of the book.*[76] However, they reveal little of him or his background. He is reported to be the son of Solomon's maternal aunt but, to my knowledge, no more is known of his origins.[77] In truth, the Muslim reports of Asaph seem to be limited to his brief role in the Solomon saga. Be that as it may, what is said of him is very impressive. A truthful man (*ṣiddīq*), he was, according to reports, Solomon's wazīr and/or scribe (*kātib*).[78] Indeed, it was Asaph who took a sheet of gold and wrote upon it Solomon's invitation to the Queen of Sheba.[79] But Asaph was more than a court functionary. He was sufficiently talented to carry on in Solomon's place for the better part of a year. That was after the Prophet had died but before the news of his death had become known. There are even hints that he might have been groomed to succeed the prophet, an extraordinary claim considering that Solomon had a son to carry on after him.[80] On at least one occasion, Asaph is portrayed as the prophet's conscience. When Solomon foolishly allowed one of his wives to erect a statue of her father, it was Asaph who dared tell him the consequences of his action. Standing before the Israelites, the scribe of the mightiest ruler on earth, chastised his master by praising the Lord's prophets and omitting Solomon's name. When the seeming insult was explained to the prophet, he realized the error of his ways and took measures to redress his ill-conceived behavior. Later, when a satan usurped Solomon's authority, it was Asaph who discovered the pretender and refused to write out his decrees, thus saving the Israelites from transgressing God's ordinances.[81]

It is also said that the son of Berechiah was extremely learned (*'ālim*) and that his learning included esoteric knowledge (*ghuyūb*).[82] He knew all the law of the ancient Israelites by heart and on at least one occasion he used that knowledge to thwart dangerous supernatural spirits.[83] No doubt, this specific tradition of Asaph's legal and esoteric learning was meant to be linked with his alleged knowledge of God's mightiest name. As a result, Asaph was able to obtain the queen's throne for Solomon. For, as soon as he invoked that name, a band of angels sent by God tunneled their way underground from the Yemen and transported the symbol of her authority to the prophet's court in Jerusalem.[84]

Readers familiar with the Hebrew Bible could easily identify the Arabic Āṣaf b. Barkhiyā as the important Levite who lived in the time of David and Solomon.[85] And yet, there is nothing in the biblical record to account for Asaph's statesmanship. The Hebrew Asaph was a temple singer and not a political functionary as in the Muslim sources. The Book of Kings does mention a certain Asaph as being the father of Joah, the secretary (*mazkir*) of King Hezekiah, but it is asking a great deal to believe that this second Asaph and his son, the secretary, were somehow confused with the Levite who lived four hundred years or so earlier.[86] There is a biblical figure somewhat analogous to the Muslim Asaph; namely, Benaiah son of Jehoiada.[87] A great warrior who served both David and his son, Benaiah shepherded young Solomon through his troubled succession and guarded the king's interests once he was firmly established in power. He even plays a role in the *Targum Sheni*'s account of Solomon and the Queen of Sheba. The midrash portrays Solomon as sending Benaiah to greet the queen when she arrives at his court in Jerusalem. Following that, it is also Benaiah who escorts her into the king's presence.[88] The son of Jehoiada was, in short, a valued confidant of the world's mightiest ruler. That Benaiah is missing from the Arabic accounts requires no explanation; any number of biblical persons, major as well as minor figures, find no place in Muslim tradition. But why choose a temple singer to replace him? Was there anything about the Jewish Asaph, be it in the biblical or postbiblical traditions, that suggests a place of prominence for him in the Muslim account of Solomon? And, related to that, why did Muslim scholars favor this Levite as one who had knowledge of the book and along with that the *ism al-a'ẓam?* There is no evidence to suggest why a temple attendant should become a political secretary. A more compelling though highly speculative case can be made, however, for linking Asaph's cultic activity, as described in the Bible and postbiblical texts, with his knowledge of God's mightiest name in Muslim sources.

A descendent of Gershom son of Levi, Asaph was one of the Levitical singers responsible for bringing the ark to Jerusalem in the time of David.[89] Following that, he and his brother were given permanent charge of servicing the ark, which eventually came to rest in the Holy of Holies, the most sacred compartment of Solomon's temple.[90] Asaph's descendant's continued to serve as custodians of the temple well into the monarchy; one notes that only singers of his family appear on the list of returnees from the Babylonian Exile.[91] Among the temple servants, Asaph appears to be the one most closely connected with the ruling family. He alone is mentioned as composing hymns to the Lord with David. Indeed, Psalms 50 and 73–83 are preceded by a superscription that identifies them as Asaph's compositions. In any case, that is how the rabbis understood "To Asaph," for they maintained that the Levite assisted David in writing that holy book.[92]

For those who accepted Islam as followers of Muḥammad and his faith, the Psalms were not simply a collection of hymns in praise of God. The Zabūr,[93] as that book was known to them, was elevated to a status roughly equal to the Torah and was believed to contain predictions of the future course of Islamic history. When Solomon came to Mecca after having completed the temple in Jerusalem, he prophesied the advent of Muḥammad based on scriptural evidence from the Zabūr.[94] The use of Psalms as a prophetic text reminds us, albeit indirectly, that Asaph and his descendants are identified in the Hebrew Bible as seer and prophet, or whatever the designations of *hozeh* and *nabi* might have meant to ancient readers.[95] We can assume that learned Jewish converts with access to Muslim scholarly circles knew of Asaph's contributions to sacred discourse as well as his cultic activities and "prophetic" vocation. May we also suppose that this learning was accessible in some form to Muslim scholars interacting with Jewish converts and, as regards the biblical passages, through Arabic translations of scripture, be it from the original Hebrew or some intermediary source? Were all this indeed the case, the "Jewish" Asaph was likely to have stimulated the imagination of Muslims. They were seeking a person who was both linked to Solomon and had the credentials to invoke a miracle on short notice. One could understand how the most revered custodian of God's temple might know God's mightiest name. If only the Muslim sources had linked Asaph more directly to the figure described in the Hebrew Bible, one could be more assertive in these claims.[96] A brief reference to his temple service or better yet his reputation as a prophet or seer would explain how Asaph came to know the mightiest name of God. For the time being, our explanation of Asaph's role in the Muslim accounts will have to be taken on faith like so much else.

G. *The Mightiest Name of God*

According to Jazā'irī, this most mysterious of names contains seventy-three letters of which only seventy-two are known to humans.[97] Asaph knew but one of these letters (presumably the one that is missing) but apparently that was enough to summon the Almighty. Jazā'irī seems to indicate that we are not likely to witness such a miracle again as only God knows the final letter and He has made it inaccessible to current Muslims (and undoubtedly generations to follow). The basic thrust of these comments can be found as well in Jewish sources, which indicate that God's (mysterious) name consisted of numerous letters. At first, all the Israelites were familiar with these letters, then only the righteous, and finally none at all.[98] It was, no doubt, unseemly that humankind should continue to possess such intimate knowledge of the Creator. Be that as it may, Muslim scholars were not dissuaded from indulging in learned speculation about the mightiest name.

Authorities were clearly intrigued by the Qur'ānic passage and freely commented about the invocation that summoned God and occasioned His miraculous intervention on Solomon's behalf. One view maintained that it was: "Our Lord and Lord of Everything, the Lord is One. There is no Lord but You!" and that this was then affixed by the statement "Bring me her throne!"[99] Another indicated that the unnamed figure of the Qur'ān called out: "O Possessor of greatness and generosity!"[100] No doubt, he then added to this formula Solomon's specific request. There is little point in trying to trace these invocations to any specific formula known from Jewish or indeed any other religious sources. The sentiments expressed in these statements are commonly shared by all monotheists and are found in any number of texts and traditions.

What is of particular interest, given our concern with the Islamization of Jewish themes, is a third formula, the one linked specifically to Asaph. It is reported that the mightiest name of God invoked by Solomon's companion was: "O Living! O Eternal! [*Yā Ḥayy Yā Qayyūm*],"[101] an expression that reflects two divine attributes mentioned in the Qur'ān.

"The Cow" and "The Family of Amram," sūrahs richly decorated with

Jewish cultural icons, contain the passage: *Allāh, there is no God but He, the Living, the Eternal* (ii:255; iii:1). A variant in Sūrah "Tā' Ḥā'" reads: *On that day, no intercession will be of any avail except from him to whom the Merciful grants compassion and whose word He approves. He* [that is, God] *knows what is before them and what is behind them but they have not the knowledge to comprehend Him. Faces shall be humbled before the Living, the Eternal* . . . (xx:108–111).

The larger context that frames these verses of "Tā' Ḥā'" is the Day of Judgment, a dramatic event when all mankind will appear before the Merciful. Lacking both knowledge and words to plead for themselves, God's subjects will require an approved intermediary to appeal on their behalf. Moving from the Day of Judgment to Solomon's day of reckoning with the Queen of Sheba, we note that, able as he was to discourse with all of God's creatures, the learned Solomon could not properly implore the Almighty when in need of a miracle. Apparently, that special gift was reserved for the mysterious interlocutor with the Living and Eternal. Considering Solomon's sudden and urgent need to obtain the Queen's distant throne, the exegetes rescued him by referring indirectly to the circumstances of that special day described in "Tā' Ḥā'." Fortuitously, an interlocutor analogous to the one mentioned in Sūrah xx was a fixture at the Solomon's court. And so, Asaph, who had the requisite knowledge that Solomon lacked, put it to good use by invoking God's mightiest name. That the learned Asaph should address the Lord of Heaven as *the Living, the Eternal* is clearly suggested by the epithets denoting God in verse 111 and, as we shall soon see, by the text and commentary of Sūrahs iii:1 and more particularly ii:255, the so-called "Throne Verse," which is closely linked to the passage cited from "Tā' Ḥā'."

It is indeed the "Throne Verse" that commands our most serious attention. The relevant text reads: *Allāh, there is no God but He, the Living, the Eternal . . . Who is there to intercede before Him except he who receives His permission? He* [that is, God] *knows what is before them and what is behind them. They comprehend of His knowledge only that which He wishes. His throne extends over the heavens and earth* . . . As in the variant "Tā' Ḥā'," the larger context of the "Throne Verse" is the Day of Judgment. Again, as in Sūrah xx, there is reference, albeit more obliquely, to the knowledgeable interlocutor who will intercede with God for humankind. With such passages to draw on, it is no wonder that the exegetes had Asaph, the analogue of this intermediary, invoke God with the divine epithets *Yā Ḥayy! Yā Qayyūm!*—if you will allow the pun: The "Throne Verse" of Sūrah ii is invoked to explain a difficult verse about a throne in the Solomonic story of Sūrah xxvii. Indeed, the queen's throne and the Throne of Heaven are actually juxtaposed in the scriptural account of her visit to Solomon's court. She is described as the possessor of a mighty throne (*'arsh 'aẓīm*); and God as the Lord of the Throne Supreme (*al-'arsh al-'aẓīm*).[102]

There is more with which to link Bilqīs and the "Throne Verse." The so-called *āyat al-kursī* gave rise to considerable commentary. For example, when Muḥammad's companions were discussing *the* most excellent passage of holy scripture, 'Alī (b. Abī Ṭālib) recalled that the Prophet had said to him, "O 'Alī, the lord of humankind is Adam; the lord of the Arabs is Muḥammad—no boast intended; the lord of speech is the Qur'ān; the lord of the Qur'ān is 'The Cow' [Sūrah ii] and the lord of 'The Cow' is the 'Throne Verse' [255]." No wonder, then, that whoever recites this verse after every prescribed prayer is guaranteed Paradise after death and, were that not enough, God Himself will receive the soul of the reciter.[103]

Given our interest in the Queen of Sheba and the supernatural—Bilqīs was, according to Muslim tradition, descended from the jinn[104]—we are obliged to point out that the "Throne Verse" was thought to have magical properties that protected human beings against evil spirits. When it was revealed, idols collapsed and crowns flew from the heads of prostrating kings. Satans ran about aimlessly in confusion until they rallied about Iblīs, who sent them forth to determine what had happened. When they came to the Prophet's city, they were informed that the "Throne Verse" had been revealed. Thus, whenever the Prophet recited this verse, the satans fled the building for thirty days and wizards, male and female, were denied entry for forty nights. Similarly, when the Caliph 'Umar b. al-Khaṭṭāb defeated one of the jinn in a wrestling match, he agreed to let go of his adversary. In return, the jinni told him how humans might protect themselves from creatures such as himself. That is, he instructed 'Umar and those like him to recite the "Throne Verse." Indeed, many are the legends that surround this privileged text and those who cherish it; too many indeed to cite here.[105]

To be sure, medieval Muslim authorities were familiar with these accounts and in all likelihood would have recognized the relevance of the *āyat al-kursī* and verse 111 of "Tā' Ḥā'" to the Solomonic saga. Given the need for a special pleading with God in order to secure the queen's throne, imaginative scholars would have linked *the one who had knowledge of the book* with the knowledgeable interlocutor of Allāh, the Living and Eternal.[106] With their great command of religious literature and their uncanny instinct for literary associations, medieval Muslim scholars would have been able to piece together the shreds of evidence that seemingly linked the Queen of Sheba's throne with that of God; Asaph with the critical interlocutor of the Day of Judgment; a mysterious book with special pleadings; and the mightiest name of God with *Ḥayy* and *Qayyūm*, epithets attributed to the Almighty when the ultimate destiny of humankind hangs in the balance, as did Solomon's on the day of Bilqīs's visit.

Assuming that all these connections are not the product of a hyperactive modern imagination, one may wish to ask in what way these conjectural comments, which focus on Qur'ānic texts and commentary, reflect traces of Jewish material in the Solomonic tale. Or, put somewhat differently: How does the wondrous account of the Queen's throne reflect the process of Islamization that is our primary concern here? As regards these questions, our inquiry is best served by turning first to Asaph's enunciating the mightiest name of God: O Living [*Ḥayy*]! O Eternal [*Qayyūm*]!

H. *Traces of Jewish Themes*

Being superb philologists and grammarians, Muslim scholars were intrigued by *Qayyūm* and realized the difficulty in considering it a *fa'ūl* form of Arabic. Some authorities considered a changed reading based on the precedent of the Caliph 'Umar (b. al-Khaṭṭāb), who recited *al-Qayyām* albeit with the same meaning as *Qayyūm*, that is, "Eternal God." Others understood *Qayyūm* to signify *al-Qayyim*,[107] meaning "God supervises" or "tends to the affairs of humankind." Still others followed the general sense of this last reading by explaining *Qayyūm* as meaning "The Overseer [*al-Qā'im*] of everything." Rāzī,[108] who is highly antagonistic to Christians and Jews, bristled at a far more sensible suggestion namely that [*Yā Ḥayy!*] *Yā Qayyūm!* as read by 'Umar, is ultimately a borrowing from the well-known Hebrew epithet *'el hay ve-qayyam* "Living and Eternal God." He also rejects a second possible connection, one that links *Qayyūm* with Aramaic, here designated as *Siryānīyah* or Syriac. Rāzī's reaction notwithstanding, the very mention of borrowing from other Semitic languages raises an obvious question. Could it be that the unnamed authorities holding the views cited by Rāzī really had, in this instance, some knowledge of non-Muslim sources, and in the original no less? If so, what are the larger implications of cultural borrowing?

The designation "Living God" appears with some frequency in the Hebrew Bible, but the juxtaposition of both divine epithets is limited in scripture to a single Aramaic passage in the Book of Daniel: "I hereby command that throughout my royal domain, men must tremble before the God of Daniel, He [Who is] the Living and Eternal God [*'elaha hayya ve-qayyam le-'almin*]."[109] One notes also that the equivalent forms *qayyom* and *qayyoma* are found in Palestinian Aramaic[110] and Qayyom appears as a proper name in the medieval documents of the Cairo Geniza.[111] The Hebrew expression *hay ve-qayyam* "living and eternal" finds currency in tannaitic (third century C.E.) and later postbiblical Hebrew texts. If the Hebraisers among the Muslim exegetes are correct, it is from that body of literature that the combined Jewish epithets "living" and "eternal" most likely made their way to Muslim sources, however circuitous the journey might have been. Assuming that *Yā Ḥayy! Yā Qayyūm!* is an artifact borrowed by Muslims from Jews, can one also explain invoking the mightiest name of God, in this case a special pleading by a special intermediary, as a reflection of Jewish literary tradition and/or ritual practice?

Jews also referred to a special name of God, one that connoted greatness and awe. Indeed, it was not to be pronounced except under specifically designated circumstances. Perhaps, not coincidentally, these circumstances were also associated with special pleadings. The reference is to the Tetragrammaton, the personal name of God, written in the Hebrew Bible with four consonants (*YHWH*).[112] Ancient ostraca make it clear that the name was pronounced at one time in Israelite history, but already in the third century B.C.E. the pronunciation of *YHWH* was to be avoided. The current vocalization found in pointed biblical texts, that which is rendered in English as Jehovah, is a contrivance to avoid uttering the original name, presumably Yahweh. As it were, this contrivance gave birth to others, and so *YHWH* was read *'Adonai,* "my Lord" or "the Lord." When the combined form *'Adonai YHWH* is found in Jewish scripture it is pronounced *'Adonai 'Elohim. 'Adonai* was in turn superseded by *ha-Shem,* literally "The Name" and then much later by *'Adoshem;* similarly, *'Elohim* gave way to *'Elokim.* The latter contrivances continue to find expression among traditional Jews when they are not engaged in liturgical or other formal religious practices. Such was the power associated with the mighty ineffable name of God.[113] The need for all this circumspection was apparently based on a stringent reading of the third commandment: "You shall not take the name of Yahweh your God in vain."[114]

There were, however, occasions when the name of God was in fact uttered; this took place during special pleadings by the priests of Israel on behalf of the larger community and on the most solemn of all occasions by the high priest.[115] The latter occurred once a year—and only then—during the ritual of Yom Kippur, the Jewish Day of Atonement, when the God of Israel sits on His celestial throne in judgment of His people. The temple ritual of that solemn day is described in detail by the rabbis of the Talmud and is recalled in the liturgy that replaced temple worship following the destruction of Judaism's most sacred shrine.[116] For nine days (following the New Year's festival), the high priest prepared himself for that sacred moment when he would enter the Holy of Holies to plead on behalf of his people. In full view of his constituents, he read the sacred law aloud and consecrated himself for that solemn occasion. Quite naturally, he himself was overcome with fear and awe given the enormity of the mission with which he was charged; the mystery and danger that was attached to the most sacred of the temple's chambers; and presumably the ineffable name of God that he was obliged to pronounce. It was in the Holy of Holies that the ark and by implication God's presence was situated. On the ninth day of the cycle of repentance, the High Priest partook of various ritual functions and after a modest meal, spent the night with his priestly associates expounding every aspect of the law.

With the arrival of the tenth day, Israel's intercessor, now clothed in special garments for the occasion, began his sacred pleading and the sacrifices that accompanied it. On three occasions he beseeched the Almighty: first on his own behalf and that of his household, then on behalf also of the (priestly) sons of Aaron, and finally on behalf of all of God's house, the people of Israel. On each of these three occasions, he would summon God by His ineffable name (*ha-Shem*) as "the priests and the people stood in the courtyard. And when they heard the glorious and awesome name [*YHWH*] pronounced [as it is written] from the mouth of the High Priest, in holiness and purity, they would bow down until fully prostrating themselves while saying: Blessed be the name reflecting his glorious sovereignty forever and ever." As those assembled in the temple court recited this blessing, the High Priest slowly enunciated the ineffable name of God[117] in order that he might finish when they completed their longer statement. And so, the "glorious and awesome" name of the Lord was invoked to secure compassion for His people on the Day of Judgment (*yom ha-din*).

Can it be that traces of this ancient ritual are somehow reflected in those Muslim sources that command our attention: the two Qur'ānic passages about the Muslim Day of Judgment (*yawm al-dīn*) in "Tā'Ḥā'" and the "The Cow" and the account of a mysterious stranger who intercedes with God by uttering his mightiest name in the wondrous tale of Solomon and the Queen of Sheba? In all likelihood, Arabic (*Yā*) *Ḥayy* (*Yā*) *Qayyūm* is indeed based on the older Hebrew (*'el*) *hay* (*ve-*)*qayyam*, as some Muslim exegetes surmised. But how can *Yā Ḥayy! Yā Qayyūm!* be linked to *YHWH*, the ineffable name of God pronounced by Israel's intercessor?

In discussing the *ism al-a'ẓam,* the Qur'ān commentator, Ṭabarsī, proffers the usual explanations.[118] But, in mentioning *Yā Ḥayy! Yā Qayyūm!* he gives what he considers the Hebrew translation of God's mightiest name in Arabic script. The transliteration reads *'a-h-y-a sh-r 'a-h-y-a,*[119] "I Am what I Am" (or "I Shall Cause to Be What Shall Be"). In this instance, Ṭabarsī reproduces an actual text of the Hebrew Bible, a statement found in the enigmatic passages of Exodus 3:13–15 where Moses says to God, "Suppose I go to the Israelites and say to them, 'The God of your ancestors has sent me to you' and they ask me, 'What is His name?' Then what shall I say to them?" God answers by giving the etymology of *YHWH* based on the Hebrew verb "to be," (*h-y-h* derived from *h-w-h*). Speaking of Himself, God says *'Ehye,* "I Am" or "Shall Be," or as some scholars read *'Ahye* "I Shall Cause to Be." Speaking of God, the Israelites say *YHWH,* "He Is What He Will Cause to Be [*YHWH*]." God then instructs Moses, "Say to the Israelites. '*YHWH,* the God of your ancestors, the God of Abraham and of Isaac and Jacob has sent me to you. This is My name for all time, the name by which I am to be remembered from generation to generation.'"[120] And so, the mysterious names of the Almighty, the Qur'ānic (*Yā*) *Ḥayy,* (*Yā*) *Qayyūm* and *YHWH* of the ancient Israelites are linked directly in Muslim exegesis to holy scripture. The linkage of Asaph to the High Priest of the temple service is, however, less secure.

The Asaph of biblical and post-Jewish tradition had all the credentials to understand temple ritual. He and his family serviced the ark before and after it came to rest in the Holy of Holies, that most sacred precinct of God's sanctuary. Moreover, he was, as previously indicated, a composer of Psalms and some sort of seer and prophet. Nevertheless, he was not the High Priest of rabbinic tradition.[121] Nor does there seem to be any explicit statement which might suggest that the full range of Asaph's temple activities were known to Muslim scholars. Still, I cannot help feeling that, however faint, there are echoes of a Jewish past in this Muslim tradition. The circumstantial evidence linking the Days of Judgment, Jewish and Muslim; the mightiest name of God and the Tetragrammaton; the intercessor required to plead before the Almighty; the Jewish Asaph son of Berechiah with Solomon's Muslim companion; and, more generally, the story of Solomon and the Queen of Sheba with all the above is simply too strong to be dismissed out of hand.

I. *Muslim Uses of the Jewish Past*

The specific problem of Jewish readings and Muslim sources is reserved for a subsequent discussion. At this point, the analysis of the Solomonic tale calls for a general comment concerning Islamization and more particularly the Muslim interest in Jewish themes. Muslims were no doubt fascinated by the accounts of the ancient Israelites and they read them with much interest and profit. But these accounts of the Jewish past were not considered arcane legends of the sort that interest modern scholars of comparative religion. Whatever Muslims thought of things Jewish was directly linked with the need to legitimize their own beliefs and practices.[122] Because there was intense competition to occupy the center of a stage held sacred by both monotheist faiths, the Jewish past could and did become part of a polemic against contemporary Jewry.[123] Thus, the story of the ancient Israelites, the episode of Solomon and the Queen of Sheba included, was a history that Muslims appropriated and refashioned to suit their own historic consciousness and world view.

For the followers of Muḥammad, Islam was not a new departure, an entirely new religion to be offered to humankind. From the outset of prophecy there was only one true faith, albeit a faith revealed through different authentic revelations and languages. The faith of David and Solomon, as with all the Israelite prophets and their followers, was the faith of Islam. Put somewhat differently, Solomon and his Israelites submitted themselves totally to God in accordance with the wider meaning of the Arabic verb *aslama,* the verbal noun *islām,* and the active participle *muslim.*[124] Given the perspective of Muslim tradition, beginning with the Qur'ān, the ancient monotheist prophets were themselves Muslims or, invoking the broader application of that term, perhaps it would be more correct to describe them as proto-Muslims. But the distinction between Islam, capital *I,* meaning the system of beliefs and practices expounded by Muḥammad and a more broadly defined islam, lower case *i,* practiced by earlier monotheists in accordance with the authentic revelation of Israel's prophets, was not always maintained by medieval authorities. As we have seen, Muslims tended to view an ancient Israelite past as the mirror image of the last and most perfect development of monotheism: the Islam that began with Muḥammad's revelation. Indeed, according to Muslim authorities, the truth of this contention is to be found not only in the literature of current Muslims but in the sacred writings of the Banū Isrā'īl or ancient Israelites.[125]

How is it, then, that the Jews do not recognize the Prophet Muḥammad and the authenticity of his revelation? It is because they reject their own scripture. Following a tampered version of the Hebrew Bible, the Jews suppress disclosure of their own true past and in doing so deny the validity of Muslim claims. Medieval Muslims had no difficulty with the physical space occupied by Jewish communities nor was there great concern about their political temper after

Muḥammad defeated the recalcitrant Jewish tribesmen of Khaybar.[126] It was rather the Jewish failure to accept the authentic Muslim versions of an ancient Israelite past and with that their denial of Muḥammad's mission and his place among monotheist prophets, venerated by Jews and Muslims alike, that required the concern, indeed the condemnation, of true believers.

Regarding Tha'labī's version of the Solomon legend, the text clearly reveals a Muslim need to preempt the Jewish past and make it consistent with Muslim paradigms of history. One notes that his story of Solomon's encounter with Bilqīs begins when the mighty Israelite finishes building the temple in Jerusalem. We are informed that, having completed the great city and sanctuary of his father, an undertaking described by the author in considerable detail, the prophet left for the sacred land (*ard al-ḥaram*).[127] We have already pointed out how Muslims, conforming to their own geographical reality, placed Jerusalem in al-Shām, an area comprising a large territorial entity ruled from Damascus and not in the Land of Israel as Jews called ancient Palestine.[128] Similarly, the expression *ard al-ḥaram* did not refer to the Holy Land of the Jews (and Christians) but to the sacred precincts of West Arabia.[129] That is to say, no sooner had Solomon constructed the temple that was symbolic of his rule and to which Jews came in pilgrimage three times a year, than he himself left for Mecca, the holiest shrine of Islam.

The juxtaposition of these two events is not accidental nor is there any doubt as to what Solomon was doing in the Arabian Peninsula. Having completed the great monument of his people, he immediately set off on a pilgrimage to the more ancient and venerated sanctuary in the Ḥijāz. According to Muslims, the Ka'bah,[130] the holiest shrine of all, was built originally by Abraham, who in the Muslim tradition was not the first Jew but a *ḥanīf,* that is, a precursor to the later monotheists.[131] By going to Mecca immediately after completing the temple, the Israelite prophet acknowledged the primacy of Muḥammad's future birthplace and its shrine.

When asked about places of worship (*masjid*), Muḥammad indicated that the earliest was established at Mecca, the next was built in Jerusalem, and that forty years separated one from the other. The tradition, which resonates to the politics of early Islamic history, puzzled medieval scholars. Their sense of chronology, being closer to modern opinion, placed Abraham "more than a thousand years prior to Solomon." Nevertheless, the point of the alleged response was all too clear: Jerusalem was sacred, but Mecca was the most sacred of all.[132]

Among the multitude of traditions that attest to Mecca's primacy is a comment suggested by a verse in the aforementioned sūrah, "Ṣād." Referring to Solomon and the temple in Jerusalem, Muḥammad reportedly said: "When he built the Holy City [*Bayt al-Maqdis*], he asked his Lord to satisfy three needs but the Lord Almighty granted him [only] two. We hope that the third will be ours. [That is] Solomon asked God for wisdom to administer justice. And He granted him that. Then he asked God *for rule* [*the likes of which*] *will be unsuitable to any* [*ruler*] *after me* (Qur'ān xxxviii:35). And He granted him that. [Finally] he asked for that place of worship which everyone would choose as his own because after leaving it, that person would be free of sin as he was on the day he was born. [That was not granted. Having rejected Solomon in this matter,] we hope that God will have granted that [house of worship] to us." The reference to sinless birth may be rooted in complex theological disputations between medieval Muslims, but the larger meaning of the tradition seems all too clear. It was Muḥammad's hope, if not expectation, that Mecca would be preferred to Jerusalem and that the Arabian sanctuary would take precedence over the Israelite temple.[133]

Solomon's agenda in Mecca certainly reinforced the sacred importance of that place. Judging by Tha'labī's account, the Israelite's journey to the Ḥijāz was no mere pleasure trip. Upon arriving at the sacred precinct, the prophet "remained as God wished, offering sacrifices (*qurbān* pl. *qarābīn*) and fulfilling the rites of pilgrimage (*manāsik*).[134] Zamakhsharī is even more explicit. He states that when Solomon finished building the temple, "he prepared for the *ḥajj*." And having arrived at Mecca, he sacrificed daily five thousand she-camels, an equal number of cattle, and twenty thousand sheep.[135] The irony of it all would not have been lost on readers familiar with the Hebrew Bible. Just as the great high place at Gibeon had been superseded by the temple of Solomon in Jerusalem, that temple, however important a shrine, was of secondary importance to the sacred Ka'bah in Mecca. Still, it was not enough that Solomon should have favored Mecca over his own beloved Jerusalem. According to Tha'labī, the Israelite used the pilgrimage to inform his people of Muḥammad's future vocation. In bringing glad tidings of the Meccan's prophethood, he informed the accompanying Israelites that "Muḥammad is [to be] the Lord and Seal of the Prophets," as Muslims later claimed. This was no fanciful tale or idle speculation. Solomon made it clear that the proof of Muḥammad's future calling is actually found in the sacred scripture of the Israelites.[136] In still another journey, this one from Persepolis to the Yemen, Solomon is said to have traveled to the Prophet's city (*madīnah*). There, at the second of the *Ḥaramayn* or sacred precincts of the Ḥijāz, the ancient Israelite again informs his entourage of Muḥammad's future coming: "This will be the settlement [*dār hijrah*] of a prophet at the end of time [*fī ākhir al-zamān*]." By way of explanation, God Himself indicates that He will give special sanctity to that place: There, at the "end of time" He will reveal an Arabic Qur'ān and send forth "the most beloved of My prophets."[137] Medieval Muslim readers saw nothing surprising in these comments. They held that the authentic Jewish scripture foretold Muḥammad's future mission and addressed the qualities of his people. Correctly understood, as the learned Solomon surely understood it, the authentic biblical text contains proof of the legitimate link between Muḥammad and the ancient Israelite prophets. Solomon's call for recognizing Muḥammad was no act of largesse. The Qur'ān, in a problematic verse that I have treated elsewhere, speaks of a covenant with God that was binding on all the Israelite prophets. At the time of their missions, they were called upon to affirm their faith in Muḥammad's future coming and to assist him in that mission by calling attention to the substance of their agreement with God. When asked: *Do you accept* [*the conditions of this agreement*] *and take upon yourselves the burden I have charged you with? They said we accept . . .* (Qur'ān iii:75). And so, Solomon, as did all the prophets revered by the Jews, not only believed in the coming of Muḥammad and the legitimacy of his revelation, he, along with the others, transmitted these convictions to his coreligionists, as required of them by God. Not surprisingly, Solomon did this citing chapter and verse from Hebrew scripture, for that truth is *revealed in book and wisdom* (Qur'ān iii:75). Thus, if the Jews rejected Muḥammad and continue to reject him, it is against their own authentic scripture and beliefs.[138]

With these references, the story of Solomon and the Queen of Sheba comes full cycle from the biblical account of a little-known diplomatic mission, to postbiblical tales that articulate widespread concerns about gender boundaries and an orderly universe, to the Qur'ānic admonition against idolatry, and finally to a Muslim exegetical tradition that links all these themes while at the same time creating a discrete and self-serving Muslim vision of man, woman, prophecy, and God's universe.

6 *The Transfer and Absorption of Cultural Artifacts*

Beginning with A. Geiger's doctoral dissertation, published one hundred fifty years ago, various scholars have grappled with the Islamization of Jewish themes.[1] Given what we now know about the transmission of cultural artifacts, there is much in Geiger and his early successors that will strike us as naive and judgmental. The vaguest similarities in Jewish and Muslim traditions were often considered proof of direct cultural borrowing; differences were ascribed to textual distortion or even perversion. In effect, the learned orientalists charged medieval Muslim writers with failing to quote accurately or footnote adequately Jewish traditions that were said to inform Muslim texts.[2] This charge, whether stated or implied, rests upon two assumptions: that the transmission of literary artifacts was consciously initiated and carefully programmed and, related to that, that the artifacts themselves were always discernible to those borrowing them. Neither assumption reflects the complex process of closely linked cultures interacting with one another.

One should not be misled by this seemingly harsh assessment of Geiger and those who followed in his path. The search for Jewish origins in Islamic sources was hardly a frivolous enterprise, nor was it intended to offend Muslim sensibilities. The orientalists had too much integrity, too much scholarly acumen, and certainly too wide a learning for that. Rather, they were, as we are all wont to be, consumers of contemporary intellectual fashion. Fueled by a positivist outlook, armed with well-honed scholarly tools, and supremely confident of their research methods, an earlier generation of scholars went about the task of stripping sources bare in order to expose the textual and ideological strata. The purpose of this reductive enterprise was the recovery of earlier sources and kernels of ideas that had embedded themselves in a new literary environment—in this case, Jewish themes in Muslim texts. A kind of literary archeology, this method was favored in any number of disciplines and so it informed research on such diverse subjects as biblical prophecy, Aztec myths, and European fairy tales. In each case, the object was to discover a different culture rather than inscribe contemporary values on it. To claim, as some recently have, that "orientalist" scholars were engaged in a cultural conspiracy would be silly if it were not patently self-serving and deliberately mischievous.[3]

That Jewish and Muslim sources are directly and indirectly linked is an indisputable fact from which proper conclusions should be drawn. For one, the use of Jewish memorabilia did not at all compromise the magnificent creative imagination of medieval Islam. Muslims themselves understood this only too well, particularly during the formative stages of Islamic civilization when scholarly contact between Jews and Muslims was more likely to have been marked by curiosity and interest than by outward antagonism. Well aware that Jewish scripture and lore deeply penetrated their own tradition, Muslim religious authorities engaged in a sharp discussion as too the potential impact of this borrowing. There were those among them who maintained that the Hebrew Bible was not to be cited because it had been inaccurately transmitted and deliberately falsified. Hence, there was danger of leading the faithful astray, a possibility that was taken seriously by more stringent guardians of the faith. However, other Muslims, no less suspicious of Jews, regarded the Torah (*Tawrāt*), currently revered by the latter, as an authentic document of God's revelation, a Hebrew version of scripture comparable to the Arabic Qur'ān. From this second perspective, there was no compelling reason to exclude references to the Bible from Muslim writings. To the contrary, the benefits of citing the Hebrew Bible were significant. In addition to foretelling Muḥammad's mission, the Torah contains a description of him and indicates that Moses had instructed the Israelites to obey him. Similarly, the Psalms of David (*Zabūr*) were said to address the future mission of the Prophet.[4]

The transmission of nonscriptural Jewish materials, also a subject of considerable discussion among Muslims, was generally looked upon with even greater favor. Traced back to at least the second Islamic century, this discussion revolved around an alleged statement of the Prophet: "Transmit on my authority even if it is but one verse [of the Qur'ān]. Narrate [traditions] about the Israelites for there is nothing objectionable in that. But, he who lies on my authority, let him take his place in hell!"[5] It is clear from the extended commentary on this proof-text that it was considered permissible to transmit certain narratives about the ancient Israelites provided that the faithful would not be led astray. For properly understood, the nonscriptural traditions were said to predict the coming of the Prophet as does the Bible. They also foretell events of a later Islamic history. In fact, the learned Jew (or Christian) was often seen as a sage character who interprets mysterious apocalyptic texts of his own tradition and thus predicts with remarkable accuracy future happenings in the world of Islam.

Such accounts, when transmitted, are likely to lead to the edification of Muslims. To narrate traditions about the Israelites was, therefore, desirable in addition to being licit. In any case, whether or not they actually read Jewish texts, Muslim authors cited them. Similarly, Jewish themes appear in Muslim writings without indication of their origins.[6]

A. *Islamizing Jewish Memorabilia*

A century and a half of modern scholarship notwithstanding, the process by which ancient Jewish themes became linked to a later Islamic literature remains elusive. This is particularly true of the earliest stages of cultural borrowing before the advance of Islam brought the new faith out of Arabia and into sustained contact with the centers of normative Judaism. Because little is known about the Arabian Peninsula in late antiquity and less yet of its Jews, there are many tantalizing questions to tease the historian's imagination. We speak broadly of Jewish influence, but what Jewish culture is likely to have influenced Islam in its formative stages? Can we be sure that the literary and even religious traditions of Rabbinic Judaism remained essentially unchanged as they diffused from the center to the periphery of Jewish settlement? Or did the distance between Arabia and the Jewish heartland in Palestine and Babylonia stimulate the development of a regional and more exotic Jewish culture? Related to that, was there significant conversion to Judaism among the indigenous Arabs, and if so, how were Jewish cultural artifacts mediated by their traditions? What role might local Christians have played in the interpretation and transmission of a Jewish past that they, too, had appropriated? Given the current state of our knowledge, it is not likely that these questions will elicit informed answers.[7]

One might think that scholars interested in cultural borrowing would be on safer ground following the Arab conquest when rabbinic Judaism became more directly accessible to Muslims. A good deal is known about the leading rabbinical authorities and the prestigious schools of learning in Palestine and Babylonia. Indeed, the world of the rabbis has been the central focus of Jewish scholarship for some two thousand years. Still, much remains obscure about Jewish-Muslim contacts and the actual process of cultural borrowing. Again, there are tantalizing questions. What did medieval Muslims know of the various compendia of Jewish law and of rabbinic exegesis, that voluminous literature of legal and historical traditions forged over centuries? In particular, how were Muslims affected by rabbinic views of the biblical past, a past whose events and personae they also revered? Given what we actually know, these sorts of wide-ranging questions also remain largely unanswered, if not indeed unanswerable.

Moreover, there is always the possibility that Muslims borrowed Jewish themes indirectly from other monotheist communities. In certain instances, one is hard pressed to determine whether the so-called "biblical stories" of the Qur'ān and later Islamic writings (*Isrā'īlīyāt*) are in fact directly attributable to Jewish sources and not to Christian discussions of biblical events and personae. For, in addition to the Hebrew Bible, numerous texts of Jewish origins were accessible in varying degrees to learned Christians of the East. Indeed, all sorts of claims have been pressed by modern scholars searching for the prophetic roots of Islam. As a rule, those raised in rabbinic sources have opted for some sort of Jewish influence; others trained in Christian texts have made the case for traditions held in common by Judaism and Eastern Christianity.[8] More recently, there has been the suggestion of Christian influence from Abyssinia (mediated perhaps by a local Jewish tradition in the Yemen, if not in Abyssinia itself?).[9] With so little hard information, it is no small wonder that scholars can speak of an Islam influenced by ill-defined groups of Eastern Christians or by a hypothetical Jewish circle of pietists residing in seventh-century Medina.[10]

Surely, more than one monotheist tradition could have provided Muslims with themes, if not whole tales based on the Hebrew Bible and its exegesis. But, of all the exegetical traditions that could have influenced Muslim renderings of the biblical past, the Jewish tradition seems the most pervasive when there is presumptive evidence of cultural borrowing; that is, when there are actual rather than hypothetical texts to compare. It is my opinion that the *Isrā'īlīyāt* are sprinkled with material that has been channeled through post-biblical Jewish sources, and so various prophetic tales of Islam can be more richly understood as adaptations of familiar Jewish themes and stories. To be sure, each text will have to have to undergo careful examination and analysis before opinions can give way to more substantive claims. In any case, the *Isrā'īlīyāt* are most certainly informed by Jewish traditions, as we have seen from the evocative story of Solomon and the Queen of Sheba.

In similar fashion, the murky process of transmission needs to be clarified. One cannot assume, as did some learned men of the past, that the transmission of cultural artifacts is consciously initiated and carefully programmed, and that the artifacts themselves are always discernible to those who borrow them. Indeed, there are moments when it may not be all that clear that a text actually reflects cultural borrowing. There are, after all, themes that are widely, if not universally, shared by the most disparate cultures. On the other hand, there is the danger of exaggerating the ubiquity of universal themes and the extent to which stories that seem similar are really the same—a misuse of Proppian typology that caused one scholar to quip that, in effect, all of history and literature is the story of Cinderella, told and retold again and again. The pungent comment makes an obvious point. Because universal themes are so often fitted to narrowly defined concerns, there is sometimes greater profit in analyzing seemingly familiar accounts as the discourse of a specific place and time.

Assuming that in certain cases it is correct to speak of linkage between Jewish and Muslim sources, one is obliged to ask how the older material penetrated Islamic writings? Were ideas and themes simply in the air, so to speak, or were they absorbed via sustained contact between Jews and Muslims, or between Muslims and intermediaries who were both familiar with Jewish lore and capable of transmitting it without altering it beyond recognition? What role might Jewish converts have played in bringing elements of their heritage to the new faith? And, related to that, how did those learned in Judaica receive Muslim texts that could be informed by "Jewish" readings?[11] Above all, how did the material appropriated from Jewish sources serve Muslim needs? In our case, how did a Solomonic saga, so well known among Jews, become part of Islamic tradition?

B. *The Queen's Visit: Some Methodological Considerations*

The search for Jewish links to the Islamic story ought to begin with Arabic translations of older Hebrew or Aramaic texts. One may suppose that the most likely translators of any such texts would have been Jewish converts who were both familiar with Arabic and knowledgeable in their own scriptural and postbiblical traditions. What impetus might there have been for converts to translate Jewish sources? Would the intent have been polemical, that is, was the object of translation to provide Muslims with access to Jewish tradition so that they might use it against other Jews still clinging to their faith? Or, might there have been more subtle and decidedly less polemical reasons to connect the translation of Jewish texts with conversion to Islam?

There can be no doubt that Jewish cultural artifacts were refashioned to legitimize the Prophet Muḥammad and more generally to promote the Islamic faith. At first glance, this may strike us as a rather parochial enterprise with clearly defined aims. The use of the Jewish past to suit Muslim concerns, however, may have been shaped as well by complex relationships among Jewish converts and between them and Jews who retained their beliefs and practices. For Jewish converts, finding familiar themes in Muslim religious sources would have provided great comfort, especially for recently confessed Muslims having residual sympathies for their former faith and brethren. These former Jews need not have felt guilt over abandoning the religion of their forefathers. To the contrary, in converting to Islam, they would have seen themselves as establishing authentic ties with the ancient Israelites and their leaders. According to Muslim doctrine, Muḥammad was the "Lord and Seal" of the monotheist prophets, a figure with direct links to Noah, Moses, and a host of other biblical personae. Even as they abandoned rabbinic law for Islamic legislation, Jewish converts could still retain the very broad outlines of their history and continue to revere their cherished ancestors. Simply put, for the converts, Islam was not an entirely new faith; it was rather the continuation of a genuine monotheism that was deeply rooted in their past.

One wonders, then, whether Jewish themes could have percolated into early Muslim tradition as part of an internal discourse among Jewish converts seeking reassurance for having chosen Islam and/or as part of an informal dialogue between them and former coreligionists with whom they wished to remain in contact. Unlike some later converts to Islam and Christianity who sought to distance themselves from their Jewish past and who were extremely hostile in disputing their previous faith,[12] the early transmitters of Jewish tradition among the Muslims might well have tried to build bridges with the Jewish community in order to retain familial and other social ties. The integration of well-known Jewish themes in Muslim tradition would have made Islam more compatible to believing Jews; at least that is what the converts might have wished. Seen from this perspective, the identification of self and other becomes somewhat ambiguous.

These views are, of course, highly speculative. Before pursuing further the notion of "bridge building," a good deal more would have to be known about the social and intellectual dynamics of conversion, particularly during the ascendance of Islam. That, however, is a subject about which we know precious little. To be sure, Arabic sources mention various converts as having discussed *Isrā'īlīyāt* with the first generation of Muslims, but shadowy former Jews, such as Ka'b al-Aḥbār, frequently mentioned as a transmitter of Solomonic stories, and 'Abdallāh b. Salām, who reportedly served as an informant on Judaism to the Arabs of Medina, remain elusive along with their literary activities.[13]

Be that as it may, there is no compelling reason to believe that only converts from Judaism would have been active in translating and otherwise transmitting material from Jewish texts. The Arabic sources indicate that Muslims actually studied with practicing Jews; the extent of these lessons, if that is the correct word, and the knowledge acquired by Muslim pupils is, however, not known.[14]

It also has been suggested,[15] although without any shred of evidence and not without considerable circumspection, that Jewish traditions were recorded in the Arabic language by communities of Arabic-speaking Jews even before the advent of Islam. If true, this would simply that Muhammad and his contemporaries could have had direct access to written Jewish sources in a language they could read, assuming of course that there was widespread literacy among the early faithful. Were all that indeed the case, these Jewish materials could have been integrated into early Islamic writings in order to validate Muḥammad's mission and his claims of a prophethood directly linked too the Israelite past. Because not a single line of this hypothetical literature has been recovered—nor for that matter have any Arabic prose texts contemporary with the Prophet—the dramatic suggestion of an early Jewish-Arabic literature accessible to pre-Islamic Arabs has to be taken for what it is: rank conjecture. Still, it is a notion that titillates scholarly imagination.

There remains yet another group that could have translated Jewish sources into Arabic, namely Christian scholars who had acquaintance with Hebrew and Aramaic or of languages into which Jewish sources might have been translated earlier, that is Greek or Ethiopic. One might even suppose that there were learned Jews who first converted to Christianity and then turned to Islam as the true faith. Upon embracing Islam, such converts could have brought with them a knowledge of Jewish sources learned before their first change of religion, as well as anti-Jewish biases acquired thereafter. While learned double converts may be likelier agents of cultural transmission than authors of a proto-Jewish Arabic literature still to be discovered, there is as yet no presumptive evidence to indicate an ongoing and intensive translation effort by Jews who converted to Christianity before embracing Islam.[16]

In any case, there is little to suggest, as regards the tale of Sulaymān and Bilqīs, that Muslims had direct access to translations of Jewish material. Indeed, in all the Muslim literature about Solomon, I have found but one likely translation of a Jewish source. The reference is to Ya'qūbī's account of Solomon's reluctance to take power, a short text clearly based on young Solomon's dream at Gibeon in I Kings:5–14.[17] That Muslims did not quote the Hebrew Bible more extensively in their versions of the Solomonic tradition is not all that surprising. Although literate Muslims could and did read Arabic translations of Hebrew scripture—there is certainly evidence of that—the Jewish tales of Solomon are by and large postbiblical creations. It is much less likely that the Muslims, who were generally unlettered in Hebrew and Aramaic, would have known of Solomonic lore via direct access to later Jewish literature.

And so, we are obliged to ask how Muslims could have become acquainted with the postbiblical material that informs so much of the Solomonic legend, the queen's visit included. Again were are forced to conjecture; however, this time based on something more tangible than the proposed proto-Jewish-Arabic literature previously discussed. Among the early Muslims, there is ample evidence of widespread oral transmission. Let us then assume that much of the Solomonic material was made available to Muslims through folkloric tales and that, based originally on written sources in Hebrew and Aramaic, these tales, which were part of oral presentations in Arabic by local Jews, were later transcribed and thus became part of Muslim literary tradition.[18] That being the case, the process of transmitting and absorbing Jewish cultural artifacts is likely to have been circuitous and, as such, it will be extremely difficult, if not impossible for modern scholars to retrace in detail.

By its very nature, oral prose tradition is susceptible to the mediating influence of multiple transmitters, each inscribing on the tale cultural/political agendas and rhetorical strategies. The process of transmission is reminiscent of a game played by schoolchildren in a number of cultural settings. An anecdote is whispered in the ear of a student who is obliged to relate it in the same fashion to a second child. The chain of transmission continues until all who are assembled have finished relating the story. The last recipient is finally called on to reveal the anecdote, which is then compared to the original version. Despite various controls that might be built into the game, such as meaningful rewards for accuracy, two very dissimilar stories always seem to emerge. Where there is a likeness of detail between the first and last versions, it is invariably marked by some confusion.

Keep in mind that this game is played by a group of children, all of the same age and sharing common experiences and values. One can readily imagine the changes in the story once it travels to other groups and regions. The only control that will prevent even greater, if not total distortion of the original account is to reformulate the anecdote as a written text early in the history of its transmission. Even then, if the target audience were to reach a theoretical limit, or if the game were to continue for an indefinite period of time and over an extended landscape, there would be difficulty in recovering the earlier versions. Without formal commentary to preserve contemporaneous understanding, historical and philological memories will grow dim and then dimmer with each passing generation. Following that, the loss of topical information or the meaning of critical words may prevent the reader from discerning the internal logic of the tradition. When the meaning of an early text becomes obscure, later transmitters often begin extensive editing to make it more comprehensible; and so, traditions will come to reflect the experiences and values of contemporaneous communities as well as their language. Where distance and cultural settings vary widely, the original anecdote might even become an entirely new tradition, or, in any case, a tale that would have been thoroughly unfamiliar to the original audience.

There is no reason to assume that the *Midrash Mishle;* the *Midrash ha-Hefez;* the relevant segments of the *Stories of Ben Sira;* or even the *Targum Sheni* to Esther, which is perhaps the closest analogue of the Arabic sources, were known to the authors of the Islamic story as they appear in their current Hebrew and Aramaic editions.[19] However similar in theme and content, there are sufficient differences between the Jewish and Muslim accounts of the queen's visit to suggest that the link between them is not direct but based on older Jewish traditions that are no longer extant and from which both Jewish and Muslim versions are ultimately drawn. That we shall ever retrace the stemma of this larger manuscript tradition is doubtful because in literature as in coinage, there is a tendency for new currency to displace the old. Only canonical texts have a way of transcending time, but even those privileged sources are, more often than not, the residue of considerable editing when, at a formative stage, they are first shaped from a larger body of material into a cohesive literary and religious tradition. Recovering that early material is elusive because the very process of canonizing religious texts creates immutable literary artifices that are meant to transcend chronological boundaries. Most Muslims embraced the doctrine of an uncreated Qur'ān; for Jews, the entire Hebrew Bible and the oral law were revealed concurrently at Sinai—a single corpus given at a single moment in history. Medieval Jews and Muslims had license to comment about scripture, but they could not suggest that holy writ is the composite of numerous literary and linguistic traditions that had evolved over long periods of time. In theory, noncanonical texts could be subjected to more stringent analysis, but it would appear that the power of scripture extended to all religious writing and so believers hesitated to excavate written sources in order to expose their chronological strata. Analyzing the content of textual traditions to trace their history was not a concern of medieval Jews and Muslims.

All the Jewish versions of the Solomonic tale are embedded in texts with a clouded and problematic literary history. The *Midrash Mishle,* which contains a close parallel to one of Solomon's tests, an episode reported in Qur'ān commentary but not in the Qur'ān itself, is, as are all the medieval Jewish sources, a text of uncertain date and provenance. B. Visotzky, who has provided the most recent analysis of the midrash's manuscript traditions, argues that it was compiled "somewhere along the caravan routes linking the . . . communities of Babylonia with the Land of Israel." Surveying the works that quote the midrash and those that it quotes and with which it shares material, he fixes the date of the text "somewhere between the late eighth and late tenth centuries." His more precise suggestion, based on a close analysis of form and thematic content, is for a ninth-century date. That is to say, Visotzky argues that the midrash resonates to the disputes of that time between Rabbanite Jews and Karaite schismatics, a development clearly linked to intellectual trends in the Islamic world, principally the development of Qur'ān commentary.[20]

The date and provenance claimed by Visotzky should not lead us astray in searching for Jewish influences on the Muslim literary environment. Midrashic works are compilations of texts, shaped usually by anonymous redactors choosing material from a multitude of sources. Hence, Visotzky's ninth-century date, which seems plausible, does not serve, in all instances, as a precise chronological marker of style or content. It reflects only the sum of the parts. The *Midrash Mishle* cites material based on the authority of earlier talmudic scholars and contains numerous and extended passages from rabbinic texts that predate the rise of Islam by several centuries.[21] There is no reason to suppose that Solomon's tests, which are of interest to us, are not rooted in a version earlier than the Islamic parallels. Indeed, one of the riddles cited in the story—albeit not a test found in the Arabic accounts—can be traced to an Aramaic version in *Ekhah Rabbah,* an exegetical midrash of the fifth century.[22] Moreover, the story commonly shared by the *Midrash Mishle* and the Arabic exegetical tradition, namely how the Queen of Sheba tested Solomon by asking him to distinguish between boys and girls who were dressed in identical fashion, has parallels in the Aramaic *Targum Sheni,* a work of Palestinian origin that most likely dates to the sixth or seventh century.[23] Admittedly, there is no definitive evidence linking the various accounts of this test to still earlier Jewish sources. But, given the propensity of the midrash to quote material from those sources, it is certainly possible that the story of the queen's disguised servants derives from Jewish materials that are no longer extant and that serve ultimately as a common source for the Hebrew, Aramaic, and Arabic versions now available.

The Hebrew satirical work attributed to Ben Sira is a highly fragmented medieval text that appears in some one hundred fifty manuscript versions.[24] Modern scholars are generally agreed that the work originated somewhere in the lands of Islam; the suggested dates are the tenth and eleventh centuries.[25]

One scholar, M. Gaster suggests that the date be pushed back still another two hundred years.[26] In any case, there is little doubt that the *Stories,* in its current versions, is originally the product of an Islamic milieu. One need only note the substitution of Baghdad for Babel. That is, the capital of the Abbasid Caliphate built by al-Manṣūr in 762 C.E. replaced ancient Babylon, the city of Nebuchadnezzar, who, in the relaxed chronology of this work, is declared the son of Solomon and the Queen of Sheba despite some four hundred years that separate the two kings.[27]

One might with to characterize this medieval work as a somewhat irreverent belletristic undertaking. But in describing medieval Hebrew and Arabic prose texts, it is often difficult to assign descriptive labels. That is because religiously informed themes, if not direct quotations from religious sources, have a way of penetrating all of prose writing. The *Stories* of Pseudo Ben Sira has little of the exegetical thrust that one associates with midrash. And yet, it too is the repository of older rabbinic material, including material derived from legendary sources no longer known. The rabbinic literature at our disposal is often compared to a vast sea, but it was originally part of a much larger ocean.

The segment of Pseudo Ben Sira that interests us is the short description of Solomon's meeting with the queen, more especially his desire to remove all her unsightly body hair, a theme that is also found in Muslim exegesis but not in the Qur'ān.[28] What is especially noteworthy about this Hebrew description of the event is the author's analysis of the depilatory paste that was used to make her skin "pure as polished silver," a substance made of arsenic and lime and declared nothing short of miraculous. The same formula for the depilatory is found in two Muslim Qur'ān commentaries.[29] Moreover, in both Hebrew and Arabic sources, the word for arsenic is *zrnykh,* presumably a loan word from Persian also known from the Babylonian Talmud.[30] With shared detail of this sort, one would have to assume some connection between Hebrew and Arabic texts, but once again the path of influence is anything but clear.

Arguably, the most important of the Jewish parallels is the story told by the *Targum Sheni* or second targum to Esther. For unlike the other Jewish sources, it contains elements of both the Qur'ānic account and its commentary. In addition to the test in which Solomon distinguishes between boys and girls who have been disguised to look alike, there are references in the targum to the derelict hoopoe; to Solomon's threat against the bird; to the hoopoe's explanation of his absence; to his mission bearing the king's letter of warning; and most important of all, to the mysterious glass structure that forces the queen to reveal her hairy legs. As previously noted, there are substantive differences between the targum and Muslim scripture (and commentary) but there can be no doubt that the Aramaic and Arabic texts are somehow connected.[31]

Again, the presumption is that the Jewish and Muslim sources are not directly linked but derive in some fashion from a common Jewish text. The path leading back towards that conjectured text has no identifiable signposts nor even an established point of entry. There is as yet no reliable edition of the *Targum Sheni,* let alone a thorough analysis of its language and contents. The imminent and long-awaited appearance B. Grossfeld's edition, which is based on some sixteen manuscripts, will finally allow scholars to begin more meticulous studies of this important work. His preliminary treatment of the text, which includes an annotated English translation; a list of Greek loan words; and a tabular breakdown of the sources found in the extant manuscripts, is the first step in that larger interpretive effort. It also enables us to hazard a more informed judgment as to the possible date of the targum, a key to tracing potential paths of influence.[32]

The existing manuscripts are relatively late (post–twelfth century) and written either in either Ashkenazic or Italian script; that is, they are of European provenance. A Yemenite source, which combines elements of both the first and second targums as well as material that cannot be identified with either version, also exists. There is no consensus as to the date of this composite text, but it too fits within the general chronology of the aforementioned manuscripts. All that should not preclude a much earlier date and a Near Eastern setting for the *Targum Sheni* currently in our possession.[33] According to Grossfeld, the lexical character of the Aramaic is Galilean, the western dialect of ancient Palestine. He cites the basic vocabulary, the numerous Greek loan words, and various grammatical constructions. The particulars of Grossfeld's linguistic judgment are left for the Aramaists to decide; it is the date of the Palestinian text that is our primary concern here.[34]

As regards that date, Semitists have reached very different conclusions. It has been dated to the fourth century (S. Gelbhaus); the seventh (L. Zunz and P. Churgin); the ninth (S. Posner); and the eleventh (S. Munk).[35] In each instance, scholars drew conclusions based on the relationship between the *Targum Sheni* and parallel sources, an approach that is bound to mislead because dating the parallel accounts is also problematic. Later midrashic compositions often utilize earlier works, while more recent versions of early texts may include intrusive material that postdates the original composition. Not surprisingly, some scholars speak of an urtext, a *Targum Rabbati* (*Rabbah*) mentioned by a sixteenth-century authority when referring to the second targum to

Esther.[36] Leaving aside whether there is any validity to the notion of *an* urtext, the layered nature of midrashic accounts presupposes some earlier source that brings together various traditions of the Esther story. But given the chaotic nature of our extended manuscript traditions, it is highly unlikely that any such source will be recovered from an analysis of the texts currently at our disposal.

If there is a way to arrive at a more certain date for our *Targum Sheni,* it is not the further examination of parallels and linguistic peculiarities but of context. In a significant passage, the targum displays clear evidence of a Christian polemic while drawing reference to Christian acts of persecution against the Jews of Palestine.[37] Given the provenance of the targum, we can most likely assume that the reference here is to the religious intolerance and persecution that, at times, characterized Byzantine rule. Assuming that to be true, it is possible that the *Targum Sheni* in our possession reflects the last of these anti-Jewish activities, the persecutions inflicted by Heraclius against the Jews during the first part of the seventh century, events that were concurrent with the rise of Islam.[38] The variable intervention of the Persian monarch Ahaseuras; the demise of the wicked Haman and his followers; and the redemption of the Jews in trying circumstances of an earlier time and Persian milieu, all themes of the Book of Esther, would have been appropriate subjects for Jews responding to long established Byzantine practices against them. There is reason to suspect that the Jews regarded the Sasanians as their allies if not saviors when the latter took the offensive against the Byzantines in various campaigns. Indeed, the Jews are accused of assisting the Persians and of conducting other anti-Christian actions when the Sasanians conquered Palestine in the second decade of the century. Whatever the truth, the accusation explained for Christians Heraclius's anti-Jewish policies following the reconquest of the Holy Land in the 620s.[39] There is ample evidence in the Qur'ān that the Prophet followed closely events beyond the northern frontiers of Arabia.[40] A delicious if highly speculative thought thus comes to mind: Might some elements of the current version of the *Targum Sheni* have reached Muḥammad and the Muslims? Were that indeed the case, might the targum's tale of Solomon and the Queen of Sheba, presumably an oral and somewhat altered version of the current story, have informed Muslim scripture and its subsequent commentary?

C. *Cases in Point*

By its very nature, cultural borrowing requires the adaptation of received traditions to make them consistent with the perceived needs of those who borrow.

One may suppose that is all the more so for two cultures that contest the same sacred heritage as did Judaism and Islam. In absorbing biblical and postbiblical themes, Muslims refashioned the Jewish past and made it part of their own experiences and worldview. Similarly, Jews borrowing from Muslim scholarship and literature did so to suit their own religious needs and aesthetic sensibilities. Doubtless, the stakes were quite different for the believers in each faith. For the older monotheist community, there was, as ever, the question of its spiritual, if not physical survival. There was the danger that Muslim artifacts improperly used might detract from faith and observance and lead ultimately to schismatic meanderings or, worse yet, conversion. Nevertheless, learned Jews were greatly interested in Islamic scholarship and were attracted by the intellectual vitality of Muslim culture. A more confident hegemonic Muslim society sought to legitimize its prophet and faith as the final, indeed the quintessential link in the long history of monotheism, an agenda that occasioned much curiosity about the ancient Israelites and their times.

We are obliged to ask if there were any discernible rules that governed Muslim uses of the Jewish past, or, put somewhat differently, what guided the process of Islamizing Jewish cultural artifacts? Quite naturally, Islamization begins with the creation of a monotheist history in Arabic. Perhaps the most remarkable aspect of the Islamic conquest was not the rapid and thorough manner in which Arab tribal armies managed to dislodge the Byzantines and Sasanians from the vast domains they had governed for centuries. Rather, it was the way in which Arabic superseded Greek and the more ancient linguistic traditions of the central provinces, Egypt, and the Islamic West. In sum, Arabic became both the spoken and official written language of the Muslim lands that lay between the Iranian provinces and the Iberian Peninsula. To the east, in the far-flung territories that had comprised the empire of the Banū Sāsān, the inhabitants resisted Arabic in favor of local linguistic traditions, but the major spoken language of he Iranian peoples was altered greatly by the intrusion of Arabic vocabulary and grammatical forms. Even when this new Persian became the language of a remarkable literary culture, Arabic remained the centerpiece of religious instruction and an important, if not the most important, vehicle for scholarly expression.

Not surprisingly, stories from the biblical narrative are retold in the hegemonic language and presumably fused with snippets of information from a more ancient Arabian folklore about which we know very little indeed. And so, in our case, Sh^{e}lomo (Solomon) ben David ha-Melekh, the Israelite king, becomes Sulaymān ibn Dāwūd al-Nabī, the Muslim prophet. In turn, the unnamed Queen of Sheba of Jewish tradition becomes the mysterious Bilqīs, a name and person with possible links to memories of the ancient Yemen as well as Jewish sources. Also important, is the consideration given by Muslims to sacred geography. The Arabian Peninsula becomes the cradle of monotheism; its shrines become the oldest and most venerated for the recipients of God's revelation. Thus, Muḥammad was given to rule Mecca and the holy Ka'bah, a place and shrine denied even the great Solomon, that ruler who was said to have "something of everything."[41] Muslims encountering *Isrā'īlīyāt* traditions also found in them unfamiliar if not jarring cultural perspectives that could not be left unchallenged. The leader of the Israelites cannot threaten the absent hoopoe under the influence of excessive wine as he does in the *Targum Sheni;* Muslims are prohibited from drinking intoxicating beverages. Nor is his anger directed at the bird because the latter's absence has prevented the Israelite from showing off his might before the world's rulers, those sovereigns who gathered at Solomon's court in Jerusalem to pay him homage. Unlike the Solomon of the targum, Muslim prophets are not given to false pride and self-serving displays of wealth and power. Moreover, prophets like Solomon do not anger easily in Muslim tradition, and when angered for good reason, they are capable of great compassion and forbearance. The Muslim hoopoe's absence does not compromise Solomon's grandeur or diminish his reputation as the world's greatest ruler, a gentle man that commands the animal world as well as that of humans. If the Muslim Solomon was furious with his winged servant, it was not because of a personal slight that offended a false sense of dignity. The hoopoe's dereliction of duty might have caused the Muslims, Solomon included, to miss the prescribed time of prayer—the bird was the prophet's guide to water, which was needed for the ritual ablutions. Seen from that perspective, the bird's actions, or rather lack thereof, were an offense to God. These and other references to the Islamization of the Solomonic story have been treated in detail earlier.[42] In each instance, be it the Muslim accounts of Solomon or indeed those of any other biblical figure embraced by the Muslims, the fundamental rule of adaptation is clear: Where there is a conflict between Muslim custom and religious practice, the substance of the Jewish text must be altered to make it consistent with Islam. Where the venue of the event can be tied to the sacred geography of Islam, it is apt to be changed. Where the detail cannot be understood because it is linked to unfamiliar social practices or opaque literary allusions, it is likely to be omitted or altered beyond recognition.

More often than not, the literary allusions in Jewish sources draw heavily on the Hebrew Bible. While some Muslims were generally familiar with the biblical text by way of translations, it would have been difficult for them to sense the playful manner in which well known biblical passages become the basis of the queen's riddles, for example, the references to the daughters of Lot and to Balaam and Job in the *Midrash Mishle*.[43] References to postbiblical sources and to Jewish ritual practices were most likely beyond recognition to the overwhelming majority of Muslim scholars who were not themselves the recipients of a traditional Jewish education, that is to say, who were not learned converts to Islam. The various elements that are common to both the Muslim and Jewish accounts tend to be innocuous, such as the test by which Solomon is asked to distinguish between servants who have been disguised to conceal their sexual identity. Nevertheless, even in this case, a cultural artifact seemingly devoid of issues worth contesting became the subject of Islamization. The gender-related issues that are at the heart of the Jewish accounts and much of the Muslim exegetical literature are virtually excised from the Qur'ān. As was previously noted, Muslim scripture was little concerned with the queen's challenge to the hegemony of men and, related to that, her rejection of natural order. It is her idolatry that galvanizes Solomon to take action and teach her the error of her ways. In neither the Hebrew Bible nor its numerous commentaries was there any marked concern that the King of Israel established close relations with the queen because she was an unbeliever. Only later, when Solomon allows his foreign wives to introduce their idolatrous practices within Israel itself does the biblical and postbiblical tradition express concern and condemnation. Muḥammad could make no such concessions in his triumphal campaign on behalf of monotheism.[44]

D. *Islamized Artifacts Entering/Reentering Jewish Tradition*

The transfer of culture also involved the absorption of Muslim artifacts by Jews, a task made easier by the sharing of a common language. Following the great Muslim conquests of the seventh and eighth centuries, there was a comparatively rapid and almost complete diffusion of Arabic in the Fertile Crescent, North Africa, and Spain. One cannot underestimate the impact of this development on the Jews of Islamic lands. A dialect of Arabic written in Hebrew characters became, alongside Hebrew, their main vehicle for religious and scholarly discourse. The Judeo-Arabic dialect also served to record the minutae of daily transactions, the kind of letters and laundry lists that record the rhythms of contemporary life. One should be clear, however, about the Jewish use of Arabic; Jews did not simply adapt to the host language. A wide range of

Muslim writings informed Jewish concerns, be it the development of Jewish philosophy and mysticism, the creation of Hebrew poetry, comprehending the natural and physical sciences, and not the least the study of the Hebrew language itself. It is hard to exaggerate the continuity of Judeo-Islamic civilization with the Jewish past, particularly as regards religious law. That, however, should not lull scholars into undervaluing the widespread and persistent encroachment of Muslim influence on Jewish life and letters.

Among medieval philosophers, the most eminent guardians of so-called "high culture," there was a general consensus as regards the issues of the times. This was a consensus openly agreed upon and knowingly embraced by Muslim and Jewish scholars alike. In similar fashion, Hebrew poets in Islamic Spain were influenced by developments in Muslim literary circles. At first, they translated from the Arabic, but then, in a bold departure, they produced a vibrant if at times imitative Hebrew poetry, rich in allusions to biblical verses. Other aspects of Jewish culture were similarly informed by the realia and literary artifacts of the host environment. The Islamic influence on popular culture in the Middle Ages is more difficult to measure given the gulf that separates us from ordinary Jews and Muslims of the period. But the evidence, such as it is, may surprise more than a few scholars; certain distinctively Muslim traditions appear to have become common coin of the realm. How else can one explain a Jewish folklore about the Caliph Hārūn al-Rashīd?[45] It would appear that the stuff of *The Thousand and One Nights* was consumed by a highly receptive Jewish community. Can it then be that the Muslim versions of the Solomonic sage might have influenced the Jews of Islamic lands or, what is perhaps more interesting yet, that Islamized Jewish themes might have reentered Judaism by way of folklore commonly shared with Muslims?

That question brings us to three short Hebrew accounts that comprise a later (1702 C.E.) Yemenite tale of Solomon and the Queen of Sheba.[46] The accounts, published by Y. Avida, are taken from a unique manuscript at the Jewish Theological Seminary of America.[47] Nothing is known of the author, a certain Saadiah Ben Joseph. Unlike his famous namesake, the great Gaon of the tenth century, this Saadiah does not appear to have been particularly erudite. Nevertheless, he was well versed in the Bible as Yemenites generally are.[48] His account is embellished, often with great ingenuity, with expressions and phrases that seem deliberately borrowed from Hebrew scripture. The use of biblical imagery is particularly effective in those segments of the account that deal specifically with Solomon. Despite the literary flourishes, one has the distinct impression that, on the whole, the material is folkloric and that it represents a pastiche of different oral and written traditions of Jewish and Islamic origin.[49]

Avida divided the tale into three distinct episodes for which he provided the following rubrics: "The Story of the Queen of Sheba and How She Acquired the Realm"; "Solomon's War With One of the Island Kings"; and "King Solomon and the Queen of Sheba." The latter two episodes appear sequentially in the manuscript; the story of the queen's origins, although part of the larger tale, is recorded separately many pages removed from the segments pertaining to Solomon.[50]

E. *The Queens Origins: A Late Yemenite Version*

The queen's story[51] is introduced with a slightly altered opening verse from the account of the Book of Kings: "The Queen of Sheba heard of Solomon's fame and [on account of God] she came to test him with riddles."[52] The author then proceeds directly too the one major element of the larger story that is not found in any of the Jewish sources previously cited, namely the story of the queen's origins. Citing learned scholars, he notes that the queen, whose mother was a jinni (*shed*), married the King of Sheba and served as his consort until the time of his death. The Arabs then set her on her late husband's throne in recognition of her wisdom and sagacity. "As regards those qualities, she had no equal [among the Shebans]."[53]

The late king himself had been much impressed with intelligence, not the least his own. It was his custom to present the notables of his realm with riddles, insisting that they answer his queries in a prescribed period of time or forfeit their wealth (or even life). He asked these riddles until all the great men of his kingdom had become impoverished. Among those presented with a riddle was the future father of the queen. Needless to say, the latter was unable to provide a satisfactory answer in the time allotted. Recognizing that his victim was without wealth, and not wishing to kill him (on account of that), the king obliged his subject to undertake a state mission in lieu of payment. That journey ordinarily took three months but, utilizing one of the swift steeds, a stud bred of the royal mares, he could make the journey in thirty days. The successful completion of the journey within that period of time would then cancel the debt owed by subject to sovereign. And so, the man agreed and set off with a time schedule set by the punctilious ruler: ten days going; ten days staying; ten days returning—thirty days in all.

En route to his destination, the king's emissary came upon a wondrous sight.

Two snakes, one black one white, were locked in mortal combat. The black snake was about to be victorious because the other was exhausted from lack of drink, but the latter approached the man who slaked its thirst, causing it to revive. Immediately, the two snakes were poised to enter combat again. When the battle ensued, the white snake gained the upper hand and killed its adversary. The king's agent then continued with his mission. Arriving on schedule, he presented the local official with the diplomatic correspondence that he carried. The latter read the documents, took responsibility for their contents and promised to carry out the king's command. He answered all the emissary's questions, attended to all his requests, and sent him home filled with joy.

When the king's agent was four days distance from that city, he encountered a handsome man flanked with servants. The man's impressive bearing indicated honor and majesty. The stranger entreated him to visit his home so that he could reciprocate a previous act of loving kindness. The would-be host claimed that in the past the king's agent had rescued him from death. This invitation drew a puzzled response because the agent did not recognize the kindly dignitary but he accepted his hospitality nonetheless. The regal stranger then indicated that he would reveal his identity when his guest decided to return home.

And so, the king's agent spent the night meeting the entire household of his mysterious benefactor, and on the morn he bid them all goodbye, as time was running short and he had to hold too the prescribed schedule. He was, however, reassured that there was no need to worry for he could be delivered to his city in no more than a moment, that is, he was enjoying the hospitality of the jinn. With that disclosure, the agent's host revealed what had transpired between them. The mysterious stranger was (or to be more correct, had taken the form of) the white snake that had done combat with the black. The latter, a servant, had sought to kill his master in order that he might perform illicit sexual practices with his master's family. When confronted, the servant fled until he and his master met up at that very place where the king's agent saw them locked in a death struggle. Had it not been for the agent's kindness, the servant and not the master would have carried the day, with all that that implied. It is no wonder that the entire household, women and children alike, gratefully kissed the head and feet of their honored guest.

Now it was time for the jinn to come to the assistance of their friend. They had heard of the king and the manner in which he asked riddles in order to enrich himself at the expense of his subjects. The king's agent was told not to worry because the solution to his problem was at hand. He will marry the jinni's sister, a young virgin of unequaled beauty and brains to match. She will in turn enrich him with her wisdom and advice and provide him with solutions to all his sovereign's queries. In such fashion the kindly emissary will be able to save himself and his fellow men from impoverishment and death at the hands of their rapacious king.

Upon hearing that, the king's agent immediately married the beautiful virgin of the jinn and delayed his return, remaining with his new kin (an additional) seven happy days. His bride then mounted a slant serpent while he took to his swift steed and, loaded with various gifts, raiment, spices, and the like, the couple set off for his city accompanied by her kin. The new relations assured him once again that he had nothing to fear as they would never be far away. Indeed, they intended to visit frequently. In this instance, they escorted him to his residence and nary a person saw them or their sister (as they, being jinn made themselves invisible). The king's servant then appeared before his sovereign to pay obeisance and hand over the diplomatic pouch. Upon reading the correspondence, the king was gladdened and big his emissary to return home in peace.

As was his custom, the king sat on the throne and, from time to time, presented his subjects with riddles. But the people now came to this man who, after consulting his wife, provided them with solutions. In return, they provided him with suitable recompense. Needless to say, the king was startled at this turn of events. In the meantime, the sister of the jinni, who was with child, gave birth to a daughter, the likes of which had not graced the world. Upon seeing the child, people realized that the man was married, and it soon became known that his wife was descended from the jinn. In the meantime, the child grew up and when she reached the age of twelve (that is the age of marriage), she excited the interest of the Sheban king. She was sweeter and wiser than her mother and could even solve riddles more successfully. Moreover, the young girl was breathtakingly beautiful. Finally, he asked her father for her hand in marriage, and having then taken her as his wife, the king of Sheba gave her the royal crown and made her his consort. In addition, he placed all his possessions at her disposal. Humans and jinn alike gravitated to her, asked about her well-being and "satisfied all of her wants."[54] With the death of her mother, she was proclaimed Queen of the Jinn by her maternal kinsmen, replicating thereby the grand status that she already held among humans. Thus, it came to pass that news of her became known the world over.

Among the Queen's of Sheba previously mentioned, Saadiah's is clearly the most meritorious. She is no Lilith destroying her young and threatening humankind. Nor is she the Muslim Bilqīs. This queen does not murder her spouse, although he too is a tyrannical ruler, as was Bilqīs's first husband.[55] To be sure, Saadiah's king has to pay a price for his indiscretion of impoverishing his subjects by subjecting them to riddles they cannot solve and threatening death when they cannot satisfy his appetite for wealth. Guilty of misusing intelligence for his own ends, he is rendered proper punishment. He will indeed be smitten. But Saadiah's queen will not need a sharp dagger to make his lose his head. Just as her mother bested the king earlier, she will manipulate him through her beauty and precocious intelligence. Later, when the king died, she sat on the throne of the kingdom as various dignitaries, officials, and provincial rulers bowed before her. Aided by her relatives, the jinn, her armies set out and subjugated more towns and strongholds than had her late husband, the king. She is certainly a most worthy adversary for her double, Solomon, the master of the jinn and the greatest conqueror of all.[56]

Is there anything in this story that addresses issues of cultural borrowing, and, more particularly, the possible influence of Muslim tradition on Jewish folklore? Were this tale not written in Hebrew or attributed to a Jewish author, it would hardly be identified as a Jewish artifact. Nor, at first glance, is there much in this rendering of events that is directly attributable to the world of Islam. Saadiah's account of the queen's origins has all the markings of a generic folk tale. But, if it is such a tale, it is certainly informed by Muslim tradition.

Commenting on Tha'labī's version of the queen's origins, Diyārbakrī, a sixteenth-century C.E. Muslim author, produced two traditions as to why Bilqīs's father married a woman of the jinn.[57] The first of the Arabic accounts reports that the king (of all the Yemen) liked to hunt, and while hunting he trapped some jinn that had transformed themselves into fawns. Having released the fawns, he earned the eternal gratitude of the King of the Jinn, who became his friend and gave him his daughter in marriage. There is at best a vague similarity between this tradition and the aforementioned Hebrew tale. It is, however, the second Arabic tradition that commands our attention here. In that version, the hunter-king came upon two vipers locked in mortal combat. As in Saadiah's account, one was black, the other white. The black snake had gained the upperhand when the king intervened and killed it. Then he carried away the living viper and after reviving the snake by giving it water, he set it free. Upon returning to his palace, the king sat in solitude when a handsome fellow appeared before him. The sudden, indeed miraculous appearance of the fellow frightened the king. There was, however, no need for concern. The mysterious visitor, a jinni, explained that he was the white snake that the king had revived. His enemy (who had taken the form of the black viper) was a rebellious slave who had killed one of the royal family. The grateful jinni then offered the king wealth but the latter declined, opting instead for marriage to the jinni's daughter. And so, they were married and the woman of the jinn gave birth to Bilqīs, the future Queen of Sheba.

There can be no question of the similarity between Diyārbakrī's rendering of events and that of Saadiah ben Joseph more than a century later. Both accounts tell of mortal combat between jinn taking the form of snakes, one black, one white. Both indicate that the white snake, exhausted and about to perish, was saved by a kindly passerby who revived it with drink. Both relate that the victor was rendering justice to an insubordinate servant that had disgraced the honor of his master's family. And similarly, the Hebrew and Arabic stories relate that the grateful jinni later appeared to that kindly person in the form a splendid male and shortly thereafter offered the human his beautiful daughter in marriage. Nevertheless, there are also obvious differences, so one can hardly claim that Saadiah relied directly on this Arabic tradition. Moreover, there is much additional detail in the Jewish account of the queen's origins. It is more likely, therefore, that both accounts are linked to a common folkloric tradition, one that has wide currency in a number of cultures. Indeed, Diyārbakrī's account has an older Muslim parallel, a brief version of the story told by Mas'ūdī, a writer of the tenth century who cast his net far and wide in search of interesting material.[58] Given the cultures that are known to have been in contact in the Yemen, it would not be surprising if Saadiah had come upon his story by way of a Muslim source, be it written or, what is more imaginable, oral. In any case, similar links between Saadiah and Muslim sources can be found in his subsequent episodes of the Solomonic saga.

F. *Solomon's Campaign against the Island King*

Mention of the Queen of Sheba's military triumphs, which ends the segment on her origins, is a convenient lead-in to the second episode, the story of Solomon's campaign against the island king.[59] At the outset of this second account, we are informed of the unique way in which the great Israelite ruler waged war. When confronted by a distant military objective, be it a location separated from him by land or sea, Solomon immediately arranged for the wind to transport him (and his forces) while holding to a path between heaven and earth. In turn, the animals were instructed to follow on the ground while the various species of birds flew cover over head. (So gentle was the manner in which the wind transported them that) Solomon and his entourage had the sensation of never having left their dwellings.[60]

It appears that on one occasion Solomon heard of an island king possessing a daughter of unmatched beauty. And so, the Israelite sent that king a missive, the text of which is preserved in Saadiah Ben Joseph's account.[61] In this letter, which is sprinkled with references to Hebrew scripture, Solomon proposes a marriage between himself and the king's daughter. There is, however, a caveat; the king himself must convert to the Israelite faith and his subjects must unite in turn with the Israelites: one religion, one people, and presumably one all-embracing polity under Solomon's tutelage. Should the distant ruler entertain thoughts of resisting, Solomon made clear his credentials. He was the son of King David, anointed by God, the Lord of Israel, to be prince (*nagid*) of His people.[62] In addition the Lord of Heaven empowered him to rule over all the kingdoms of the earth,[63] and were that not enough, gave him dominion over the jinn, and over animals and birds.

This aforementioned ruler had an idol in which there dwelt a jinni. It was the king's habit to bow down before the idol and perform other ritual acts. When the king, visibly disturbed by Solomon's letter, approached that idol, the jinni enquired why he was so crestfallen. The king then told him the nature of Solomon's demands. He was hardly disturbed at handing over his daughter that she might serve the Israelite king; that meant nothing to him. So much for marriages forged out of love. It was the demand that he destroy the idol and embrace the faith of the Jews that was so upsetting. Upon hearing these words, the jinni became enraged. He urged the king to hold on for Solomon was a charlatan who lacked the capacity to contend with either one of them. Then the jinni offered to assemble all his brethren. In addition, he would instruct the wind to wreck any ship carrying Solomon. There was no need to fear; this jinni was as stalwart as the enemy, saying "We shall indeed prevail for our people and the cities of our God."[64]

When he heard these words, the island king found resolve, and raising his hand, he swore by his god that he would wage total war against Solomon. Now it was his turn to address the Israelite. He would send Solomon a diplomatic note that urged him to mind his own business. He warned the Israelite not to let his heart sway him. He, that is Solomon, cannot rely on his wisdom and realm nor on his silver and gold. This was one king that had the means to resist Solomon, or so he proclaimed. Speaking sovereign to sovereign, he advised Solomon to leave the island and its god alone lest the Israelite (and his forces) be annihilated. "I will not bow down or bend before your God nor will I give my daughter to be your woman. Do as you will!"[65]

Having received this reply, Solomon burned with anger.[66] It was now his turn to raise his hand and swear by God. This idol will be surely smashed. He, Solomon, would not rest until he brought this island to full account and fed the carcasses of the king and all his people to "the birds of the sky and the beasts of the earth."[67] But enough of vows; circumstances called for action. Solomon commanded the four winds to transport the Israelite army to its chosen destination. The various contingents of animals and birds were also called to muster and made ready for war. And so, the Israelite strike force assembled from all directions, and the wind transported them between heaven and earth until it dropped them off at that very island.

The island shook mightily at "the sound of the steeds neighing" and at the roar of the young lions and wild animals.[68] A shaken and confused king ran immediately to his idol and relayed (what was happening) for the king still held fast to his wickedness. The jinni egged him on, saying, "Assemble all your troops and take the field against him. Behold! I declare [myself] his adversary and go forth to gather my forces. I shall wage war against him."[69] And so, the king and jinni went off to do combat.

The (armies) gathered in the midst of that island (arriving) from the north and from the sea, whereupon Solomon ordered the wild animals (to attack). The latter penetrated the (enemy) camp, tearing it apart and "leveling the tall cedars and choice cypress trees."[70] The survivors "fled to the hills"[71] but could not save themselves, as Solomon's troops captured the king alive and annihilated his people.[72] The captured monarch was then brought before Solomon and the latter "rendered judgment upon him."[73] The Israelite asked him why he dared answer as he did, and the island king told him of the idol that had encouraged his defiance. A boastful jinni speaking from the form of that idol had declared, "He [Solomon] can do nothing for I have greater means at my disposal than they do."[74] At that, Solomon sent one of his own jinn to bring the presumptuous spirit back alive so that he, God's chosen ruler, might also render justice upon him.

When the local jinni caught wind of that, he fled seeking to save himself from Solomon. But the Israelite's jinn were in full pursuit. Finally, they caught the fugitive and brought him before their master. Solomon, passing judgment on the rebel, ordered his servants, the jinn, and the commanders of the troops to escort their captive to the place they had found him. Following Solomon's orders, they then hung him from an iron beam upon which was inscribed the ineffable name of God. The author goes onto say that the jinni, who had the temerity to challenge Solomon, remains suspended from that beam to this very day. With the jinni out of the way, Solomon laid the island waste, hung the rebellious king, and making off with the king's young daughter, he returned home.

As with the first segment of Saadiah's tale, the story of the island campaign and the king's beautiful daughter calls to mind a well-known Arabic tradition. This tradition, mentioned in passing earlier with regard to Asaph b. Berechiah,[75] is treated more fully here, where it is presented as a composite of several divergent accounts.[76]

According to Kisā'ī,[77] Solomon received word of a king who lived on one of the sea islands. This King Nūriyah (Tha'labī calls him Ṣaydūn)[78] had gathered about him a company of satans and jinn and thus angered the mighty ruler of the Israelites. Surrounded by a vast sea, the wealthy island king was secure from attack, or to be more precise, he was secure from all but Solomon who, alone among men, could rely on the wind to transport him. And so, Solomon mounted the flying carpet with his forces and set course for that distant isle and its presumptuous ruler. As one would have expected, the Israelite was victorious. He killed the island's ruler and made off with his daughter, a woman of unmatched beauty called Shajūbah (according to others she was known as Jarādah).[79]

Solomon wanted her and so he proposed that she become a Muslim, which she did—according to Tha'labī, out of fear rather than conviction.[80] Some scholars maintain that she refused to accept Islam and threatened suicide so the prophet relented. In any case, Solomon married the dead king's daughter. There was no question that he was madly in love with Shajūbah (or Jarādah) and that he preferred her to all his myriad other women. He gave her her own palace and elevated her to a unique status. This exalted position did not satisfy her. She was filled with grief over the loss of her father and was given to constant tears. When Solomon learned of this he tried to comfort her; he pointed out that God had given her more than she had left behind on her distant isle. But the girl could not be consoled. She pleaded with Solomon to allow her a representation of her father (Kisā'ī adds the mother)[81] so that she might be reminded of him and thus distracted from her grief. Filled with a surfeit of compassion (and no doubt a desire to give vent regularly to his sexual urging), the Israelite relented and had the satans make her an image of her father. The likeness was extraordinary, and when they dressed the statue with her father's clothing it was exactly as he was, except of course that it was inanimate.

When Solomon left her chambers, she would bow down before the image just as she had bowed to graven images with her father when he was king. Of this Solomon knew nothing, but his wazīr, Asaph, caught wind of the idolatrous behavior and called it to Solomon's attention in a clever way. The wazīr sought and received permission to mount the pulpit and in his sermon praised all of God's prophets, but in mentioning Solomon, he called attention only to his early reign, leaving aside mention of more recent events. The ruler of the Israelites understood that something was very wrong. He then discovered that his favored wife had paid homage to the statue of her father on no less than forty consecutive mornings. An outraged Solomon entered her chamber, destroyed the idol, and punished her and her servants. Recognizing the error of his original decision, Solomon placed ashes on his head and donned garments of purification. Those garments, made by virgins, were never touched by menstruating women. He then spent forty days away from court, one for each day of the girl's idolatrous worship. During this absence, his signet ring and throne were taken by a jinni that had assumed the prophet's form. The subsequent episode of how Solomon's signet ring was stolen and his throne occupied by a usurpacious jinni is discussed earlier.[82] Suffice it to say, the jinni who had disguised himself as Solomon was discovered and then permanently incarcerated in a watery prison for his audacious behavior.

There is much to be said of this richly textured account. Of particular interest is its insight into the psychology of a bereaved woman forced by fear to abandon her culture and marry the very man who destroyed her father and his kingdom. There is also the image of the world's greatest ruler and lover, himself love-struck and stymied by another's lingering memories of the lesser king whose blood he shed. In broader terms, there is the issue of a husband competing for his wife's affection and loyalty with her beloved father. However interesting, these themes are not our concern here. We are obliged to ask whether there is a link between Saadiah's account of the island campaign and the Arabic tradition of Solomon and his idolatrous bride.

When examined together, the Arabic and Hebrew texts seem to complement one another. Both Jewish folklore and Muslim tradition tell of a distant island; an idolatrous king who is surrounded by jinn; an airborne assault by Solomon's unique army; the conquest of the island and the execution of its ruler; and finally the exquisitely beautiful daughter that the Israelite seeks as his woman.

Indeed, Saadiah's rendering of Solomon's conquest may be seen as setting the stage for the later events that Muslim accounts record as having taken place in Jerusalem: Solomon's marriage to that woman; her loyalty to her dead father and his culture; Solomon's fall from grace; the triumph of the usurpacious jinni during the prophet's absence; and finally the resolution of the tale in which the jinni is incarcerated for all time, with Solomon returning to his throne.

There is an apparent symmetry to the Jewish and Muslim tales when they are read in sequence. It were as though the Arabic sources begin their story by recapitulating the essential events of Saadiah's account and finish by drawing upon familiar themes also represented in the Yemenite tale: The triumph over idolatry and the subjugation of a rebellious jinni who is incarcerated for all time. There is no doubt that in this instance the Hebrew and Arabic versions are linked. The question that remains is whether Saadiah has cited hitherto unknown elements of a larger Muslim tale or supplied a Jewish introduction to a well-known Muslim story.

G. *Solomon and the Queen of Sheba According to Saadiah Ben Joseph*

The last segment of the tale, that of Solomon's encounter with the Queen of Sheba, begins with the Israelite's return from his successful campaign against the island king.[83] Only then did he realize that the hoopoe had not set out with him nor had it come to battle his foes during the hour of God's victory. And so, he sent for the lords and officers of (all) the birds and admonished them over the hoopoe's dereliction of duty. Then he ordered them to bring the lord (*melekh*) and officers (*sar*) of the hoopoe so that he might punish their species. The reference to the lord and officers of the hoopoe recalls the words of the prophet Ezekiel 17:12: *Say to the rebellious breed: Don't you know what this means? The King of Babylon came to Jerusalem and carried away its king* [*melekh*] *and officers* . . . By referring to the biblical verse, Saadiah seems to convey the gravity of the hoopoe's absence (perceived initially as rebelliousness by Solomon) and the consequences of that behavior for the leading birds of the species, presumably exile. When the hoopoes arrives, they pleaded with Solomon: "Do not think of us in that way. God forbid! We are not about to rebel against your rule or defy your wisdom. Nor are we about to deny those gifts that God has granted you; gifts with which He has given you dominion over all his creatures great and small alike." As to their absence, they had not been aware of his proclamation (to mobilize) nor indeed has any (official) directive "reached us yet."[84]

They then told Solomon a fascinating story about a woman who had raised them from their youth. That was the Queen of Sheba, ruler of a kingdom acquired from her deceased husband. Hers was a land blessed with goodness and righteousness. Knowledgeable, wise, kind, and beautiful as well, she reportedly judged the birds with justice and fairness while raising them in their youth and until the present day. She was a mother unto them and they were sons unto her. Hence, they followed her command, not as subjects in awe of their ruler, but out of respect for her righteousness. The author would seem to indicate that the hoopoes were visiting in the Land of Sheba when the order to mobilize was announced (in Jerusalem). As a result, there could be no claim that that were derelict of duty. There was no way that they could have known that Solomon was marching, or to be more correct, flying off to war. In any case, Solomon was touched by the birds' eloquence and sincerity and bade them to go in peace.

The hoopoes returned to the Queen of Sheba and informed her of Solomon's exploits. They spoke of his bravery and his campaigns and how he vanquished the island king and its God. They also told her that he had annihilated the island's populace and laid it bare, putting the torch to everything. As to that king's jinni, the birds revealed that he was hung at the very place where he had been taken captive and that he remains alive and suspended there until this very day. They finished speaking of Solomon by noting how compassionate he had been when they begged forgiveness: "Through forebearance a ruler may be won over; a gentle tongue can break bones."[85]

When the Queen of Sheba (and her subjects) heard all that and "all the stories of his power and bravery as well as the full account of [Solomon's] greatness,"[86] they were overcome with awe "and their hearts were filled with utter dismay. It were as though those hearts melted and turned to water."[87] The queen then announced that she would go to Solomon to hear directly his wisdom and see firsthand the wonderful and awesome things that he alone among humans could accomplish. As in the biblical account, she took with her one hundred and twenty talents of pure gold, great quantities of spices, precious stones, and sandalwood and set off for Jerusalem.[88]

Having arrived at the Israelite's court, she tested Solomon's famed intelligence with a number of riddles, all of which are reported in earlier Jewish sources. There can be no doubt that in this third segment of Avida's text, Saadiah Ben Joseph has turned to his own tradition to complete the larger tale of Solomon and the Queen of Sheba. "What are they?" she asked. "Seven depart and nine enter; two give succor but only one partakes." The riddle, familiar too us from our previous discussion of the *Midrash Mishle,*[89] elicits a contemptuous response from "the wisest of all men." The king, whose wisdom surpasses that of Ethan the Ezrahite, of Heman, Chalkol, and Darda, the sons of Mahol, and indeed of all the legendary wise men of the East, will not be troubled by so trivial a question.[90] Does she expect to stump him with the (idle) prattle of females? For, as the author reminds us through Solomon, such riddles are the fare of women chatting in the moonlight.[91]

We are not informed why this particular riddle suggests a moonlight chat between two females. Readers might then permit me license to offer an extended, if highly speculative explanation. Can it be that, in this case, the reference to the moon (*l^e vana*) is meant to suggest a period of the month (*libun*) when women, not certain of their ritual purity, are denied their husband's company? Speaking of ritual impurity, scripture refers to seven days of menstruation to which the rabbis added additional days when women "wore white" (*libun*) while continuing to examine themselves for residual signs of blood.[92] One is tempted to entertain an intriguing notion that is derived from these admittedly loose connections. Does Solomon's rather caustic comment suggest a concern that the Queen of Sheba might have come to Jerusalem when her purity was in doubt? Our Yemenite author was surely aware that Jews are supposed to avoid contact and even idle conversation with women during their monthly cycle. And, as he was aware of that, would he not have assumed that Solomon also would have known of God's intention and would therefore have embraced the attitude and sentiment expressed by the rabbis? Commenting on the biblical verse: "Do not approach a woman when she is impure in order to reveal her nakedness,"[93] the authorities ask, "May her husband perhaps embrace her or kiss her or engage her in idle chatter?" The question, a rhetorical device to explicate a principle of rabbinic jurisprudence, namely that of constructing a hedge around the law (*s^e yag la-Torah*), evokes a swift and final response: "Scripture says, 'Do not approach.'" One could then understand why Solomon's first inclination was total avoidance.[94]

In this case, however, there is a danger in following the dictates of Jewish practice. Lest the queen think that failure to respond reflects an inability to do so, the king must give answer to her question. Had he not written in his own Book of Proverbs, "Answer a dullard in accord with his folly lest he consider himself wise"?[95] No! She will not have any excuse to be haughty. Turning to the business at hand, the king responds more or less as he does in the *Midrash Mishle:*[96] "Seven depart refers to days of 'wearing white' [when marital contact is prohibited]. Nine enter refers to the nine months of pregnancy. After the woman gives birth, the two breasts give succor to the child." The answer, correctly given, indicates how appropriate the riddle is to women amusing a friend or relative observing her menses. Solomon may think this the prattle of females, but for the impure woman it speaks of a happy time to come. Soon, she will have no need of lady friends with whom to chat in the moonlight; the period of waiting will be over; she will return to the bed of her husband. If all then goes well, she will become pregnant and give birth, and having done that, will nurture her child. In such fashion, she will fulfill what God has ordained for her. Childbearing and nurture are the proper roles for women as the riddle suggests.

The Queen of Sheba is no ordinary woman, however. The ease with which Solomon answered her did not dissuade her from pursuing her agenda. And so, she questioned the Israelite once again: "[To what does this refer.] A child asked his mother, 'Who is my father?' She answered, 'Your father is my father and your grandfather is my husband. You are my son and I am your sister.'" As in the Jewish sources, where this riddle is previously cited,[97] the king answers succinctly and with confidence: "No doubt, the reference is to Ammon and Moab who were descended from Lot. They were the offspring of Lot's [incestuous] daughters [who slept with their father to become pregnant when they feared for the survival of their family]." The queen was still not satisfied. Following the pattern in other Jewish (and Islamic) sources once again,[98] she presents Solomon with a visual problem. She dressed and bejeweled male and female children in identical fashion and then asked the king to distinguish between the sexes. This he did by distributing roasted grains and nuts among them. The boys grabbed them and, running off, went about their merry way. Boys will always be boys. On the other hand, the girls placed them in their laps and sat well behaved. Needless to say, girls will always be girls. As in all the accounts previously cited, especially the *Midrash Mishle,* disguised appearances cannot hide what nature has decreed even in childhood before the sexes are more prominently differentiated by hairiness, voice, physical stature, and the like. Once again, Solomon read cultural (or as our author understood them, natural) codes with consummate accuracy. In God's design, aggressiveness and power are reserved for the male species. No doubt, the Queen of Sheba is a most impressive woman but she cannot master the most impressive of men. In any case, that is the conventional wisdom of this tradition and all the others previously cited.

Were Solomon's responses not sufficient to demonstrate the foolishness of women seeking to best men, the last of the queen's riddles will prove no more difficult for him than the previous tests. This time Saadiah Ben Joseph draws upon the Aramaic *Targum Sheni* to Esther.[99] The queen asks in Hebrew: "Tell me! What is it? A copper basin, an iron pitcher; it raises dust and sucks water?" Solomon answers in Aramaic, quoting directly from the *Targum:* "A cosmetic box [*guvta d^ekohala*]." Once again, she has lost the game of wits and with that will concede the match. Our Yemenite author indicates that the queen was now persuaded of Solomon's learning and the quality of his mind. Paraphrasing the well-known verses of the biblical text, she confesses that she had been skeptical of what was said about Solomon in her land, but now that she had encountered him in person, she saw that all the marvelous things said about him were but half the truth.

As we noted earlier, Saadiah's queen is no Lilith. To the contrary, she has motherly instincts, witness her relationship to the hoopoes. Unlike Bilqīs, the Muslim Queen of Sheba, she does not lure her husband to his death on their wedding night in order to seize his throne.[100] She is a loving wife who seems to have had a positive effect on a rapacious tyrant. It is he who arranges for the most beloved queen to rule after him—that on account of her wisdom and character. And rule she does with compassion and righteousness. Of all the Queens of Sheba, clearly Saadiah's is the most admirable. Nevertheless, she is still a woman who rules men. Indeed, her reputation as a conqueror of peoples and domains exceeded that of her husband. There is something unnatural in a woman holding forth as if she were a man. And so, even this the most admirable Queen of Sheba will have to submit to Solomon. Moreover, she will have to submit to him in a fashion that clearly establishes his primacy over her, and with that, the primacy of man over woman. This conquest will take place in the royal bedchamber.

She is currently unmarried, hence available;[101] moreover, she is exceedingly beautiful. But there is a rumor that occasions Solomon's great concern. As in other accounts,[102] he has heard that she has hairy legs (a symbol of her arrogating the male's prerogative to rule and more generally a mark of ugliness in women). And so, Solomon is compelled to investigate by means of an elaborate scheme, also familiar from other accounts.[103] He made a marble clearing two hundred cubits square and placed an orchard on one side. Water was then splashed on the marble,[104] giving the impression that the entire floor was a pond. The queen, convinced that she faced a real body of water, was then asked to cross over to the orchard. As a result, she lifted her garments and revealed her hairy legs. At that, Solomon supplied her with cosmetics (to make herself alluring) and a depilatory with which to remove the (unsightly and unbecoming) hair. It would appear that in the Yemen, as elsewhere, women are expected to preen themselves in anticipation of male company. Then she came to him suitably feminine, hence disarmed and desirable, and he slept with her.

In the end, this moment of pleasure will come to haunt the Israelites. As in the account of Pseudo Ben Sira,[105] the queen becomes pregnant and gives birth to Nebuchadnezzar. The implications of Solomon's unbridled passion were perfectly clear to Saadiah Ben Joseph, as indeed they must have been to other Jews familiar with this tradition of Nebuchadnezzar's birth. The Babylonian ruler will destroy the temple and house of Solomon, his father, avenging thereby the indignity that had been brought upon his mother. The author ends his account of the love tryst with a clever and most appropriate postscript based on Isaiah 49:17: *Those who ravage you and leave you waste will depart from you.* Any learned Jew would have recognized the biblical passage and its larger context. Read in full, Isaiah 49:17 reads: *Swiftly your children are coming. Those who ravage you and leave you waste will depart from you.* The verse itself is part of an extended text in which the prophet foretells the redemption of Zion, previously laid waste by the Babylonian monarch. The children swiftly coming is thus a reference to the return of the Babylonian exiles to mother Zion; the departure of those who ravaged and laid waste refers to defeat and withdrawal of Jerusalem's Babylonian conquerors. Saadiah is not interested, however, in happy stories of redemption. His is the tale of the world's wisest monarch who was not wise enough to keep his distance when dealing with this clever female. Solomon should have been content with besting her in a game of wits. The contest in the royal bedchamber shifted the match to a playing field in which women are all too dangerous. In this instance Solomon won the game and bedded the queen on his terms, but she won the match when Nebuchadnezzar laid his father's kingdom waste. And so, the words of Isaiah are cited by Saadiah Ben Joseph as if they were stood on their head. *Those who ravage you and leave you waste* still refers to the Babylonians, or in this case, Nebuchadnezzar himself. But the phrase *shall depart from you* [*mimmekh yeze'u*] is understood by Saadiah to mean *shall issue forth from you.* Hence, the reference is not to the flight of the Babylonians but to the birth of their monarch, the tyrant sired by Israel's most illustrious king.

Having analyzed Saadiah's ingenious explication of the prophetic text, perhaps we should attempt our own postscript to the story. Returning to the theme of ritually impure women and the need of men to distance themselves from such females, we can underscore Solomon's most inappropriate, indeed most sinful behavior—behavior that is nevertheless understandable considering this legendary reputation as a surhomme du monde. When it came to making love, Solomon was known to take excessive risks. Commenting on the biblical text: . . . *among the many nations there was not a king like him . . . yet foreign wives caused even him to sin.*[106] Rabbi Eliezer son of Jabbi Jose the Gallilean explained: "The verse informs us that Solomon had intercourse with them when they were ritually impure and would not inform him [of their condition]."[107] It was one thing to forgo disdain and engage the queen in conversation as it was necessary to put her in her place. It was another matter to bed her, especially if there is a suggestion that she might have been in a state of impurity, or, in any event, that Solomon thought she might have been "wearing white," that is, examining herself for residual discharges. If indeed this were the case and the point of Saadiah's story, the king's behavior was exceedingly dangerous. By having intercourse with a woman during her monthly cycle, he was putting his own ritual purity at risk. The blood of the female was a pollutant to men who came into direct contact with it. To have risked that knowingly, was a grave offense according to Jewish law.

For observant Jews, the extraordinarily complex laws of purity were not frivolous.[108] These were not arcane regulations stemming from a distant biblical past that invoked curiosity but little more. The evidence clearly suggests that ritual purity was a serious matter at all times and in all Jewish societies before Jews began assimilating the values of a secularized modern Europe. To have risked going against the law, even to establish male dominance, was a most reckless act. Whether or not she was actually impure is besides the point. Solomon should not have taken the risk. Clearly, the king's passion ruled his senses—that is if, in this case, Saadiah's account does indeed suggest that the queen was suspected of still being impure. To be sure, this reading of Saadiah's intentions is highly speculative, perhaps even improbable considering the very slender evidence that supports it. Nevertheless, the temptation to stay with the suggested reading is very great, as there would then be a marvelous irony to the manner in which this folkloric tale is revealed. In putting the queen in her place, Solomon is carrying out God's charge to uphold the world as it is and as it should be. Men are meant to rule over women. That, being the natural order of things, is a biological as well as political imperative. But, by creating a complex biology for women, God has established a natural order that grants them extraordinary power that it denies men. That is, the biological cycle of women allows for both procreation and ritual pollution.

The elegant and subtle use of biblical passages; the obvious connection between this account and the various Jewish versions of the Solomonic tale; the

Aramaic quotation from the *Targum Sheni,* which rules out in that instance any borrowing from Muslim Arabic sources; and the reference to rabbinic customs of purity all indicate that, unlike the first two episodes, this third segment of Saadiah's tale is a Jewish story through and through.

H. *Recent Jewish Folklore*

The engaging tales of Solomon and the Queen of Sheba continue to find expression among Jews, be it in oral or written versions. The Israel Folklore Archives contains a significant number of traditions about the Israelite King, including several accounts of the queen's visit to Solomon's court. Most of the Solomonic lore is based on informants from Muslim lands including the yemen, Syria, Egypt, Tunisia, Morocco, Iraq, and Persia. Unlike the written versions, which are intricately designed and filled with literary allusions, the Jewish folktales recorded by Israeli researchers have, as one would expect of that genre, a directness that reflects the immediate experiences of the folk. Only the Jews of the Yemen, with their legendary and well-deserved reputation for memorizing scripture, integrate written sources with playful oral discourse.

For Alizah Anidjar, a woman from Tangiers, Morocco, the story is ultimately one of love and the recognition that a worthy man is worth pursuing.[109] Reflecting Muslim rather than Jewish parallels, she indicates that Solomon sent the queen a missive because she worshiped the stars (instead of the God of heaven). When the skies are then blackened by Solomon's birds, as in the *Targum Sheni,* she makes plans to visit the Israelite King. The queen is immediately struck by his handsome bearing and falls in love with him. How does a woman capture a man of Solomon's stature? She plays to his vanity. He is the wisest of men. Present him with a complicated task that challenges his powers of reasoning and observation, such as differentiating young boys and girls of identical age "who resemble one another as do drops of water." He will no doubt accept the challenge. Offer him marriage and your domain should he have the solution. Then, when he rises to the occasion, as indeed he most certainly will, he will be trapped by the bargain into which he has entered. And that is how Solomon was indeed maneuvered into marrying the Queen of Sheba—at least according to Alizah Anidjar of Tangiers.

The same basic tale told by Avraham Benisti, a man from Tangiers, tells a very different story.[110] He does not titillate with romantic notions. Rather, as in the aforementioned midrashim, his account of the queen's visit focuses on the competition between the sexes. Indeed, Benisti's queen has an arrogance that is not characteristic of the literary texts. Where the queen might have been skeptical, he portrays her as haughty; where she is clever, he makes her out as aggressive. There is no indication here of a love-struck woman plotting to get her man. For this man of Tangiers, the story of Solomon and Sheba is still another version of that veritable truth: Women must know their function and station in life. It is not clear what wider conclusions might be drawn from comparing these two Moroccan folktales, but the disparity between the accounts causes us to wonder whether some ancient and medieval women may have romanticized or otherwise changed the stories of the queen's visit, as did Alizah Anidjar.

Regarding the Israel Folklore Archives, the disproportionate number of accounts from Islamic lands should not mislead us. The Solomonic saga has residual charm for Western Jewry as well. I have no empirical data with which to illuminate this point, but it seems to me that the engaging tales of the wise king, the queen, the hoopoe, the demonic spirits, and all the other figures of the Solomonic saga are broadly familiar to Jews of European descent who have had a substantive and traditional Hebrew education. The biblical tale is read by all Jewish students deeply engaged in Hebrew studies, usually when they are eight years old or thereabouts. It is part and parcel of a religious curriculum that acquaints them with the dramatic history of their kings and prophets in most ancient times. More remarkable is the extent to which these children are generally acquainted with the content of various midrashic accounts. There is no claim that young students read the original sources, let alone understand them in the context in which they are discussed here. Nevertheless, there is every reason to assume that oral versions of Solomon and the Queen of Sheba have been circulating continuously since ancient times. Moreover, there has been a conscious effort in this century to make Jewish legendary literature more accessible to persons lacking direct familiarity with rabbinic texts.

No doubt, the most significant contributor to this effort was the Hebrew poet laureate H. N. Bialik (d. 1934). Myriad Jewish children raised on Modern Hebrew have become acquainted with various aspects of rabbinic lore through Bialik's anthologies, the *Sefer ha-Aggadah* (with Y. Ravnitzky) and *Vay^ehi ha-Yom,* a posthumous work that included many items hitherto published separately. Coincidentally, the latter also includes various Muslim tales, among them a rather deft translation of Tha'labī's version of the queen's visit to Solomon's court.[111] Bialik himself knew no Arabic; he relied instead on the efforts of others which he adapted in a way that befit a great poet of the Hebrew language. In this case, he had the work of J. Klausner published in the Hebrew periodical *Ha-Shiloah* (1904), where Bialik was literary editor. And so, as regard the story of Solomon and the Queen of Sheba, readers of Modern Hebrew have access to translations of Aramaic and Arabic versions as well as texts written in rabbinic Hebrew. Bialik's anthologies are not simply collections of diverse traditions assembled and reproduced under a single title. Many of the sources are extensively edited and adapted for modern reading audiences, producing thereby new folkloric texts. That these texts have taken root as if they represent a continuous tradition from ancient times is a tribute not only to Bialik's artistry but to the excitement generated by the encounter between the great Israelite King and his beautiful and talented rival. Theirs is a story which transcends the boundaries of time and culture.

Postscript

The extent to which ancient and medieval sources reflect, let alone influence, behavior is far from certain. Readers would do well to recall my cautious comment in the Introduction about gaps between public declarations and privately held views and between legally proscribed and privately sanctioned behavior. However much we can learn of contemporaneous values from literary sources, such as those that describe the Queen of Sheba's visit to Solomon's court, the gap between declared values and actual behavior must be bridged with documentation and/or the evidence of material culture—that is to say, materials reflecting the transactions of daily life.

A recent work based on archeological data and social science research has occasioned a new and vigorous view of Israelite women and their historic role in traditional family settings Modifying textually based feminist paradigms, which highlight biblical women as chattel in an abusive patriarchy, Carol Meyers stresses instead the vital activity of women in pre-monarchic Israel.[1] Viewed in their own place and time, the hill country of ancient Palestine, Meyer's women are portrayed as active and full-fledged partners with their men in the social and economic milieu.[2] In the individual households that were the building blocks of clan and tribal associations, women are said to have achieved parity with men as regards an extraordinarily wide range of economic tasks. True enough, the biblical record offers little if any evidence of the complex role of pre-monarchic women and indeed of women in general, but that is because that record is the literary production of the monarchic period and the attitudes and values of its urban elites. One supposes, based on Meyers's skilled reading of archeological data, that had the pre-monarchic Israelites articulated their attitudes, as did their successors, their description of women would have been that of true partners shouldering the burdens of life and earning the fullest respect of men.

The demographic shift from country to city that accompanied the development of kingship are said to have brought about significant changes in the function and status of women.[3] The economic rhythm of the newly established cities and towns reflected the emergence of political hierarchies and bureaucratic elites. Those families that moved to the centers of power witnessed social stratification and a material culture that reflected cleavage between the newly affluent and those less well to do. Meyers writes of urban women who became less essential to household economies as their husbands, cogs in the expanding machinery of government, gained access to external resources. Indeed, the rise of the state initiated a process that eroded the centrality of the household as the dominant social unit of Israelite society. To be sure, traditional households continued in the agrarian communities, but, as previously noted, rural society was also affected by the centralization of power. In due time, the position of women was irrevocably altered and with that, attitudes towards them became more negative. As Meyers puts it:

> The locus of power moved from the family household, with its gender parity, to a public world of male control. The establishment of the nation-state meant the growing prominence of the military and the state and religious bureaucracies controlling economic development. These institutions are typically public and male controlled; whenever they become an important part of society's organization, female prestige and power recede.[4]

What attitudes emerge as a result of these far-reaching changes? One would be hard pressed to identify a single view of women on the basis of the Hebrew Bible. Meyers refers generally to the negative portrayal of females in the book of Proverbs,[5] a text of a sophisticated urban milieu. But she also indicates that the attitudes towards women were extremely complex, as indeed Israelite society itself became increasingly diverse.

The convergence of so many disparate cultures in the Near East makes for an even more complex picture of Jewish women in postbiblical times. On the balance, postbiblical texts tend to portray women in a more negative light than Hebrew scripture; that is the impression based on a literal reading of incidental statements sprinkled throughout the sources.[6] Some feminists argue that the change for the worse was occasioned by the influence of the Hellenistic world.[7] To paraphrase Meyers ending her study: Greco-Roman culture brought a dualistic way of thinking to the Semitic world: pairs such as body and soul, evil and good, female and male became aligned. The female descendents of Eve, the mother of humankind, were thus linked to body and evil and were more generally associated with negative aspects of life.[8]

As with all thought-provoking research, Meyers's work raises questions. Are the economic tasks purportedly shouldered by the Israelite women of the rural hill country an indication of true parity with men, those who bore the responsibility of defending household and homeland? Were women stronger and more significant actors performing tasks in a rural economy than they were managing the day-to-day aspects of wealthy urban households? If nothing else, the negative portrayal of women in Proverbs is an indication of the power that some urban ladies wielded, at least in the imagination of men. Without disparaging the innate dignity of rural Israelite women, we might ask who was likely to have been the more independent and forceful actor: Jezebel or Naboth's wife.[9] In short, what is really meant by parity and how is that notion reflected in attitudes towards women? Whether the views of the misogynist Greeks, boldly expressed and popularized by many authors, reflect accurately the values of Hellenistic society is best left for classicists to debate. Similarly, Hebraists will have to issue a balanced verdict on the larger issues of postbiblical attitudes towards women, particularly if these judgments are based on didactic statements that are difficult to contextualize. To cite perhaps the most egregious case: What exactly did Jewish males mean when they first blessed God for not having made them female, a statement that persists in the liturgy until today?

To extent to which negative views of women influenced behavior between the sexes is debatable. Ancient papyri, scrolls, and epigraphic evidence speak of a different social reality from that indicated by legendary and juristic rabbinic texts. Or, more cautiously stated, they indicate the existence of a more complex social reality than a reading of traditional sources suggests at first glance. The further one travels geographically from the centers of normative Judaism in ancient times, the more diverse women's lives seem to be.[10]

As for Jewish women in the medieval Near East, the most compelling documentary evidence, the materials of the Cairo Geniza, also portrays a community far more diverse than literary and juridical sources seem to describe.[11] The Geniza, now being mined by an increasing number of scholars, represents a remarkable aperture through which to view private as well as public lives from the tenth through fourteenth centuries C.E. In hundreds of thousands of documents and fragments of documents there is hard evidence with which to recover the interstices of a medieval Mediterranean society composed of Jews, Muslims, and also Christians. Among the multitude of documents thus far uncovered are numerous texts that refer to women, including more than a hundred letters which resonate with their own voices. Be that as it may, the Geniza community is deeply rooted in talmudic Judaism and, as regards women, tends to reflect traditional values and norms despite occasionally diverse social and even legal practices. Our accounts of the queen's visit, some of which are contemporary with the world of the Geniza, are linked to both the values and social reality of that world—in short, a world where women knew only too well their place and function.

Oddly enough, we know a good deal less about the actual position of women in medieval Islam. There are as yet no major studies of medieval Muslim women that combine detailed historiographical investigation with a sensitivity to gender-related issues. Such studies that have appeared tend to be highly schematic and take at face value fragile and highly didactic sources.[12] The discovery of a large cache of Mamlūk documents (ca. fourteenth century), combined with more than a hundred thousand Arabic papyri that have been collected at major repositories, should open new horizons for Islamists as did the Geniza for scholars interested in the Jewish communities of Islamic lands. In interrogating these Muslim texts, researchers will have to determine if social realities described in the archival sources are broadly consistent with attitudes expressed in literary works. Or, put in the form of a question: Is there significant divergence between that which litterateurs wrote about women and how relations between the sexes were actually conducted, particularly in the privacy of shared domiciles? One might then compare in detail the position of Jewish women described in the Geniza with that of women from the dominant Muslim culture. That is, however, the subject of a future project.

Appendix: Texts in Translation

A. *The Queen's Visit: I Kings 10:1–13*

The Queen of Sheba heard of Solomon's fame through the name of Yahweh and she came to test him with riddles. (2) She arrived in Jerusalem with a very large retinue and with camels bearing spices, a great quantity of gold, and precious stones. When she came to Solomon, she asked him all that was on her mind. (3) Solomon had answers for all of her questions; there was nothing that he did not know nor anything to which he could not given an answer. (4) When the Queen of Sheba observed all of Solomon's wisdom and the palace that he had built (5) and the fare of his table, the seating of his retainers, the service and attire of his attendants, his wine service, and the burnt offerings that he offered at the House of Yahweh, it broke her spirit. (6) She said to the king, "The report that I heard in my own land about you and your wisdom was true. (7) But I did not believe the reports until I came and saw with my own eyes that what had been told me was not even the half of it. Your wisdom and wealth surpass the reports that I heard. (8) How fortunate are your people and servants, those who stand always before you and listen to your wisdom. (9) Blessed be Yahweh your God who delighted in you and set you on the throne of Israel. It is because of Yahweh's eternal love for Israel that he made you king to administer justice and rule with righteousness. (10) She then presented the king with 120 bars of gold and an enormous quantity of spices and precious stones. Never again did so vast a quantity of spices arrive as that which the Queen of Sheba gave Solomon. (13) King Solomon [reciprocated] satisfying all the Queen of Sheba's desires in addition to what he gave her in his official capacity as king. Then she and her retainers left and returned to her own land.

B. *The Queen of Sheba in the* Midrash Mishle *(Proverbs)*

Another interpretation: The verse: *But wisdom where shall it be found. . .* refers to the Queen of Sheba, who, upon hearing of his (i.e. Solomon's) wisdom, said: "I shall go and see whether or not he is wise." And how is it that she heard of his wisdom? Scripture says: *The Queen of Sheba heard of Solomon's fame through the name of the Lord and she came to test him with riddles*. And what is meant by *with riddles?*

Jeremiah Bar Shalom relates: She said to him, "You're the Solomon about whom I have heard? The Solomon whose kingdom and wisdom have come to my attention?"

"Yes," he replied. Then she said, "You are a wise man. Would you be able to answer a question of mine were I to put it to you?" He responded: *For the Lord gives wisdom; from His mouth comes knowledge and understanding*. And so, she asked: "What are they? Seven depart and nine enter, two give drink but only one partakes." He responded, "No doubt, seven are the days of the menstrual cycle, nine are the months of pregnancy, two [refers] to the breasts that succor and one to the child born [who drinks from them]." She then said to him, "You are a wise man! Would you be able to answer another question of mine were I to put it to you?" He responded [as before] *for the Lord gives wisdom*. And so, she asked: "What does it signify? A woman says to her son, 'Your father is my father. Your grandfather is my husband. You are my son and I am your sister.'" He answered her, "No doubt, the daughters of Lot."

She now offered another type [of challenge]. She presented him with very young children of equal height, all of whom were dressed alike. "Distinguish the males from the females," she said. Solomon signaled to his attendants and they brought him nuts and roasted grains which he began to spread before the youngsters. The males, who were not embarrased, gathered them and placed them in their garments. The females, who were modest, placed them in their headresses. Whereupon, he replied, "Those are the males and those, the females." At that, she said, "You *are* a wise man!"

She offered him [still] another type [of challenge]. That is, she brought a group [of males] some of whom were circumcised, the others unclean. "Distinguish the circumcised from the unclean," she said. Solomon immediately signaled to the High Priest who opened the Ark of the Covenant. The circumcised bowed down to half their height and at once their faces were lit with God's radiance. The uncircumcised among the group fell fully prostrate. At once, he responded, "Those are the unclean and those, the circumcised." The queen then asked him, "How is that you knew that?" "I knew that from [the story of] Balaam [the pagan prophet]," he said. For it is written: [*The word of Balaam son of Beor, the oracle of a man whose eye is opened. The oracle of him who hears the word of God,*] *who sees the vision of the Almighty, prostrate but with opened eyes*. Had Balaam not fallen he would have seen nothing. If [in this instance] the example of Balaam is not acceptable to you, you may take instruction from the story of Job. When his friends came to comfort him, he immediately said to them: *I too have a mind such as you. I do not fall below you* [*nofel . . . mikem*]. In this case, the text should be read: "Do I not fall as you do [*nofel . . . k^e^motkhem*]?"

[Returning to the story of Solomon and the Queen of Sheba: Upon hearing Solomon's reply,] the queen immediately said to him: *I did not believe the reports until I came and saw with my own eyes that what had been told me was half the truth. Your wisdom and wealth surpass the reports that I heard. How fortunate are your people and servants, those who stand always before you and listen to your wisdom. Blessed be The Lord, your God who delighted in you and set you on the throne of Israel* [etc.].

C. *The Riddles of the* Midrash ha-Hefez

The following story is told by Rabbi Ishmael: This is the wisdom of Solomon whose reputation extended from one end of the world to the other, as it is written: *He was wise*[*r than all men; than Ethan the Ezrahite, than Heman, and Chalkol and Darda, the sons of Mahol*]. *And his fame spread to all the surrounding peoples*]. The verse *But wisdom where shall it be found and where is the place of understanding?* This refers to the Queen of Sheba, who upon hearing of his wisdom, said, "I shall go and see whether or not he is wise."

Rabbi Jeremiah [Bar Shalom] relates: She said to him, "I have heard about you and your wisdom. Would you be able to answer a question of mine were I to put it to you?" *He responded: For the Lord delivers wisdom; from His mouth comes knowledge and understanding*. And so she asked: "Seven depart and nine enter, two give drink but only one partakes." He responded: "The seven days of the menstrual cycle depart, the nine months of pregnancy enter, the two breasts of the woman give succor and one refers to the child born [who drinks from them]." She then said to him, "You are a wise man!" She questioned him again: "A woman says to her son, 'Your father is my father. Your grandfather is my husband. You are my son and I am your sister.'" He answered her, "No doubt, that is the daughter of Lot who spoke thus to her son."

She went on. She brought him males and females and asked him to distinguish between them [without examining their genitalia]. At once, he signaled to his attendants, and they brought him roasted grains and nuts. The males, who were not embarrased, took them open-handed. The females took them by extending a gloved hand from inside their garments. He replied, "Those are the males and those, the females."

She now brought him a group [of males] some of whom were circumcised, the others unclean. "Distinguish between them," she said. Solomon immediately signaled to the High Priest who opened the Ark of the Covenant. The circumcised bowed down to half their height and at once their faces were lit with God's radiance. The uncircumcised fell fully prostrate. He then responded, "Those are the circumcised and those, the unclean." She then said, "You *are* a wise man."

She continued her questions [and he his answers]:

> "Who was neither born nor died?"
> "The Lord of the Universe, Blessed be He."
>
> "What land has seen the sun but once?"
> "The land upon which the waters were gathered
> on the day when the seas were formed."
>
> "What is the enclosure with ten gates—
> When one opens, nine are shut.
> When nine open, one is shut?"
> "That enclosure is the womb of a woman.

The ten gates are the ten orifices of human beings:
Eyes, ears, nostrils, mouth, the apertures for the
discharge of excreta and urine, and the navel.
When the child is an embryo, its navel is open and the
other orifices are closed.
When the child is born, the navel is closed and the
other orifices are open."

"Alive, it does not move; when its head is cut off it moves."
"A boat in the water [made of beams that were once trees]."

"To what does this refer?
Three neither ate nor drank nor did they have any
life breathed into them and yet they saved three lives."
"Those who did not eat were the seal, thread, and staff.
The lives they saved were those of Tamar, Perez, and Zerah."

"To what does this refer?"
Three entered a cave and five exited from it."
"Lot, his two daughters and their two sons."

"To what does this refer?
The dead lives, the grave moves, and the dead prays."
"The dead person is Jonah, the whale is the grave, and
the person who prays is [also] Jonah."

"To what does this refer?
Three ate and drank on earth but
they were born neither male nor female."
"The three angels that appeared before Abraham our father."

"To what does this refer?
Four entered a place of the dead and emerged alive.
[Two entered a place of life and came forth dead]."
"The four were Daniel, Hananiah, Mishael, and Azariah.
The two were Nadab and Abihu."

"To what does this refer?
He was born but he did not die."
"This refers to Elijah and the Messiah."

"What was unborn yet given life?"
"This refers to the Golden Calf."

"To what does this refer?
It is produced in the ground but humans produce it."
Its food is of the fruit of the ground."
"This refers to a wick."

"To what does this refer?
A woman is wedded to two men and has two sons.

But the four have but one father."
"This refers to the story of Tamar.
Tamar was married to two men: Er and Onan.
She bore two sons: Perez and Zerah.
The one father refers to Judah."

"To what does this refer?
A house filled with dead [that is, a cemetery].
No dead are brought there, no living emerge from there."
"This refers to Samson and the Philistines."

In addition to these riddles, she ordered that a sawn [section of a] cedar tree be brought and asked him, "Tell me! At which end was the rock and at which end were the branches." He ordered her to cast it in the water, whereupon one end sank and the other floated to the surface. He then answered, "That which sank is the root; that which floated is the end containing the branches." She immediately responded: *Your wisdom and wealth surpass the reports* [*that I heard*]. *Blessed be* [*the Lord*] *your God* [*who delighted in you and set you on the throne of Israel*]. Thus, it is said: *And the Lord gave wisdom unto Solomon.*

D. *The Targum Sheni to the Book of Esther*

One time, when King Solomon was under the influence of too much wine, he issued invitations to all the kings of the East and West who were near the Land of Israel and lodged them at the royal palace. Still under the influence of wine, he ordered that the stringed instruments, cymbals, tamborines, and harps, upon which his father David played be brought to him. A jovial Solomon also commanded the appearance of the wild beasts, the birds of the sky, the reptiles of the earth, and the demons, spirits, and Liliths. He did so that they might dance before him showing thereby his greatness to all the kings in his presence. The royal scribes called out their names and all the creatures gathered about him of their own free will, unfettered and not led by any human.

At the time, the hoopoe was sought but it could not be found among the birds. So the king who had been angered commanded that he appear lest he be killed. The hoopoe responded saying, "Listen, my lord King of the Earth so that my words may reach your ears. It was three months ago that I conceived of a scheme that I put into effect. During that time I took neither food nor drink but flew all over the world looking about. I said to myself, Is there a land or kingdom that does not pay obeisance to my lord the king? Then I looked about and saw a land to the East whose capital was called Kitor. Its dust is more precious than gold; its silver more prevalent that dung in the markets. Its trees, planted during creation, are slaked by the waters of paradise. There are great throngs of people there, all of whom wear crowns on their heads. They come from paradise and know not of war or [even] the use of bow and arrow. I have even seen a woman who rules over them all. She is called the Queen of Sheba. And so, if it pleases my lord the king, I shall gird my loins like a warrior and rise up and go to the city of Kitor, to the land of Sheba, where I shall bind its kings and fetter its governors in chains of iron. Then I shall bring them to my lord the king."

These words pleased the king and he summoned the royal scribes, whereupon a letter was written and tied to the hoopoe's wing. At that, he took to the skies, picking up along the way the other birds who accompanied him to the city of Kitor in the land of Sheba. With the coming of morning, the Queen of Sheba went out to worship the arrival of the day but the birds blocked the sun. Astonished and perplexed, she tore her clothes [as a sign of dismay]. The hoopoe then descended, and she noticed that a letter was tied to its wing. She opened the letter and read it. The text was as follows:

> From me, Solomon the King, who sends greetings. Peace unto you and your nobles, Queen of Sheba! No doubt you are aware that the Lord of the Universe has made me king of the beasts of the field, the birds of the sky and the demons, spirits, and Liliths. All the kings of the East and West, and the North and South, come to me and pay homage. If you would come greet me [that is, pay homage], I will honor you more than any kingly guest of mine, but if you refuse and do not appear before me to pay homage, I shall send out against you [my] generals, contingents, and riders. You ask, "What generals, contingents, and riders has King Solomon?" Then know that the beasts of the field are my generals, the birds in the sky are my riders, and the demons, spirits, and Liliths are my contingents who will strangle you in your beds. The beasts will slay you in the fields, and the birds of the sky will consume your flesh.

When the Queen heard the words of the letter, she again tore her clothes. Then she sent for her elders and notables and said to them, "Do you know what King Solomon has sent me?" They answered, "We know not of King Solomon nor do we respect his rule." She, however, had no faith in them and so she did not listen to them. She summoned all the ships and loaded them with gifts—pearls and precious stones. The queen also sent him six thousand young boys and girls who were born in the same year and month and on the same day at the same hour. Moreover they were all of the same stature and build and were dressed alike in purple raiment. Then she wrote a letter for Solomon and sent it along with them. The text read as follows: From the city of Kitor to the Land of Israel is a journey of seven years. Because of my questions and requests, I shall come in three.

And so, after three years the Queen of Sheba came to King Solomon. When he heard of her arrival, he sent Benaiah son of Jehoiada to meet her. He was as handsome as the morning star shining brightly in the firmament and as elegant as the lily that graces the pond's edge. When she saw Benaiah son of Jehoiada, the queen dismounted, and so he asked, "Why do you dismount?" "Are you not King Solomon?" she asked. "I am not King Solomon," he replied, "only one of those who serve him." At once, she turned to her notables and offered the following based on a [well-known] proverb: "If you do not see the lion, you see his lair. So, if you do not see Solomon, then see the handsomeness of the man that stands before him." Benaiah son of Jehoiada then escorted her to the king.

When Solomon heard that she was coming to him, he went and sat in a court (*bayt*) of glass. When the Queen of Sheba saw that, she said to herself, "The king is sitting in water." So she raised her garment to wade across the water at which point she exposed her legs and the king noticed that they were hairy. As a result, he said to her, "You're a beautiful woman but hairiness is for men. You look absolutely disgraceful." Then the Queen of Sheba said to him, "My lord king! I shall present you with three riddles. Should you solve them I will know that you are a wise man. If not, then you are like all other men."

"What is it? A basin of wood and a pail of iron; it draws stones but pours out water." "A cosmetic box," he replied. She asked again, "What is it? It comes as dust from the earth and it feeds on dust. It is poured like water but lights the house." He answered, "Naptha." She asked once more, "It precedes all things; it wails and cries; it bends like a reed; it is the glory of the nobles and the disgrace of the poor; the glory of the dead and the disgrace of the quick; it is the delight of the birds but the distress of the fishes. What is it?" "Flax," he says. At that, she exclaimed: *I did not believe the reports until I came and saw with my own eyes that what had been told me was not even the half of it. Your wisdom and wealth surpass the reports which I have heard. How fortunate are your people and servants, those* [*who stand always before you and listen to your wisdom*].

Following that, Solomon brought her to an apartment of the royal abode. When she saw the greatness and wealth (of King Solomon), she praised God and said: *Blessed be the Lord your God* who delighted in you and set you on the ruling throne to rule with righteousness and administer justice. She then presented the king with gold and fine silver and he gave her all her desires.

E. *Pseudo Ben Sira on the Queen's Visit*

[Manuscript A]

Nebuchadnezzar asked Ben Sira how the rabbit's head was made smooth. He answered, "Miracle [*nes*] in lime." The king then asked what that was and Ben Sira answered, "A shaving cream that permits one to pluck out hair. It is made in the following fashion: One mixes a solution of lime with arsenic. That is 'miracle in lime.' But if you [really] want to know, ask your mother and she'll tell you how it's made." "My mother!" Nebuchadnezzar blurted out. Ben Sira explained:

"When your mother, the Queen of Sheba arrivied with tribute [*minhah*] to listen to Solomon's wisdom, he found her beautiful and wished to have intercourse with her. But he found her exceedingly hairy—that was a time when no Israelite woman had hair on those parts of her body ordinarily covered by garments. And so, Solomon declared to his servants, 'Bring me lime and arsenic.' They took the lime [solution] and sifted it in a sieve. Then they ground the arsenic and mixed the two together. They did this so that when Solomon then saw your mother, her skin was made pure and completely free of hair. Following that, he did with her as he wished.

"Immediately after that, she spoke up saying, "I did not believe the things [I had heard about you] until I came and saw with my own eyes that what I had been told was not even the half of it. Your wisdom and wealth surpass the reports which I have heard.' " At that, Nebuchadnezzar asked Ben Sira, "Who told you that?" "I came upon that by myself," he responded, "because I am a prophet and the son of a prophet."

[Manuscript B]

Nebuchadnezzar asked Ben Sira how the head of this rabbit was made smooth. He answered, "Miracle in lime." The king then asked how they make this "miracle in lime" of which you speak. Ben Sira responded, "It is made with arsenic. There you have it. But if you wish, ask your mother and she'll tell you how it's made." The king then asked, "How does she know that?" And so, Ben Sira related:

"Because [the following happened] when your mother, the Queen of Sheba, visited King Solomon in order to test [lit. see] his wisdom. When Solomon wanted to have intercourse with her, he found her excessively hairy. At that very time, no Israelite was fully covered with hair, as it is written: *I am a smooth man.* Solomon, given his wisdom, immediately instructed his servants to 'go and bring me lime and arsenic.' They brought it to him right away and he then sifted it in a sieve. The arsenic was ground on a tile. He mixed the two forming 'miracle in lime,' which he prepared for your mother, the Queen of Sheba. She took a beauty bath and all her [unwanted] hair was removed.

"Soon after that, she spoke up saying, 'I did not believe the things [I had heard about you] until I came and saw with my own eyes.' At that, Nebuchadnezzar asked Ben Sira, "Who told you that?" He answered, "[I came upon that] by myself because I am a prophet."

F. *The Yemenite Tale of Saadiah Ben Joseph*

(The Story of the Queen of Sheba: How She Acquired the Realm

The Queen of Sheba heard of Solomon's fame . . . and she came to test him with riddles. The learned scholars say that this Queen of Sheba's mother was descended from the jinn. She married the King of Sheba and when he died, the Arabs, having perceived her intelligence and understanding—there was at the time no one wiser than she—chose her to be their ruler.

Her father was in the service of the king. Now, the King of Sheba used to present riddles to all the notables. The riddles had to be solved within a prescribed period of time. Whoever failed to solve the riddle in time had to forfeit his wealth. And so, all the great men of the kingdom became impoverished.

After a while, the King of Sheba presented her father with a riddle. When he was unable to provide a solution in time, the king said, "I know that you are not in possession of great wealth, nor do I wish to kill you. So, you will do as I command you. You will go to such and such a province, which is three month's distance. But he who mounts one of the steeds bred of the royal mares can make that journey in thirty days. Should you complete that journey, your debt will be wiped clean." "I'll go!" he responded.

So, the king supplied him with a swift steed and set for him a time schedule: ten days going; ten staying; ten days returning—thirty days in all. That is what he did.

En route to his destination, the king's emissary saw two snakes fighting: one black, one white. The black snake, which sought to kill its adversary, was about to emerge victorious because the latter was exhausted from lack of drink. Whereupon, the white snake, parched with thirst, approached the man, and he gave it water until it became sated. Then, the snake went on its way.

Right off, the two snakes stood poised to do combat [once again]. [This time,] the white snake overcame the black and killed him. The king's agent then continued on his mission, arriving safely at his appointed destination. Having done that, he delivered the dispatches to the governor of that very province. The latter read them, took responsibility for the contents, and said, "All that which the king commands, I shall carry out."

Without delay, he answered all the emissary's questions, attended to all his requests and needs, and then sent him on his way filled with joy and contentment. At the very moment he was four days distant from that city, he was approached by a handsome man with an impressive bearing that reflected honor and majesty. The latter was flanked by servants.

The handsome man took hold of him and said, "You will not budge from this place until you visit me at my home so that I may honor you and reciprocate a previous act of loving kindness. For you have saved me from death." The emissary asked, "Who are you, sir, that you hold me in such esteem?" "I will not reveal [myself] at present nor will I tell my story until you desire to accompany me," was the response. And so, the [puzzled] traveler went off with the man and entered his abode.

All the people of the household, the great and the small, women and infants as well, came to greet the guest and kiss his hands and feet. The king's emissary was astounded at all the honor that was bestowed upon him.

He spent the night at the man's home. The following morning, he wished to depart. He explained to his host that the king had placed him on a [rigid] schedule and that he had only ten days left [in which to return. By remaining where he was,] he was being delayed while much pressed [for time].

"No need for you to show concern about that," was the reply. "Because, in an instant, I can lead you to the heart of city. That is, we are jinn; I was the white snake that you found locked in combat with the black. He was a slave of mine who sought to kill me and commit incest with [members of] my household. Because of that, I went out to do combat with him, but he fled and I only caught up with him at that place [where we met]. He was about to emerge victorious and would have killed me had you not appeared and given me a little water. And so, my strength and spirit were renewed and [it was] I

[who] killed him. All that good fortune is on your account. For had he killed me, he would have returned and laid this place waste. Our strength would not have been revived nor would we be alive but for you. Now, have no concern, because we know everything that the king is doing to all of you including the riddles that he poses and the confiscation of your wealth.

Therefore, I'll marry you to my sister, a young virgin whose beauty is unrivaled in all the world. Furthermore, as she is possessed of great wisdom, she can immediately enrich you with that wisdom and her advice. She will provide you with the solution to all the riddles that the king proposes. And so, she will save [his] subjects and all the inhabitants of your city from death and the confiscation of their wealth. Know this! The truth is: The wife you had that day when you departed has died [leaving you free to marry again]."

Upon hearing that, he married that very same maiden and remained with the jinn for seven happy days. After the seven days had passed, the jinn mounted the bride on the ringed snake and he took to his swift steed. Then they gave the couple heaps of clothing, great quantities of spices, and other gifts, and proceeded to escort him, whereupon he immediately reached his city.

They told him once again, "Don't let anything concern you; we won't be far away. That is, we'll all be making periodic visits to see our sister. We'll take care of anything that's too difficult for you to handle." The emissary then appeared before the king and, after prostrating himself, delivered the dispatches. The king read them, was happy with their contents, and gave orders for the man to return to his home in peace.

From time to time, the king would sit on his throne and present the usual riddles. The people would then come to that man, and he in turn would question his wife. She would then solve the riddles, for which he accepted a contribution from each of them depending on their rank and generosity. In such fashion, they were saved from the king's grasp. The king was astonished at the turn of events.

Now, that woman became pregnant and gave birth to a daughter, the likes of whom was not to be found in all the world. And when that daughter was then seen by the entire populace, they knew that the king's servant had taken a wife. It also became known that she was a jinni.

The daughter grew up and when she was twelve years old [that is the age of marriage], she gladdened the heart of the king as she was [even] more comely and wise than her mother. Her beauty was unmatched throughout the world and she was more able at solving riddles. And so, she would give the answers to those very people who came [to her mother] in search of a solution. [She would say:] "It appears to be such and such" or "Such is the answer." This went on until the king was amazed.

Finally, he asked her father for her hand in marriage and then married her. He made her royalty. Placing a crown of the realm on her head, the king made her queen for as long as he lived and put her in charge of all his possessions. [As regards her mother:] All her kin, her people [among the jinn] and her relatives, and all the officials that were governed by them would visit her. They would ask about her welfare, and attend to all her needs. Then when her mother died, the queen's entire family courted her [as they did her mother], and she too was regarded by them as royalty and a queen just as she was among the humans. And so, her fame and character became known in all the lands.

When her husband, the King of Sheba died, she sat on the throne and all the notables, their lieutenants and the provincial governors bowed down to her. With little fighting, she conquered large fortified cities to an extent that her husband never did. That was because the jinn aided her.

Moreover, among the various birds she ruled was the hoopoe.

(Solomon's War with One of the Island Kings)

When King Solomon wished to do combat with some distant king or governor, or one that was across the sea, he would immediately send word to the commander of the wind with express orders to have the wind come and transport him between Heaven and Earth. Furthermore, he ordered that the wind carry his troops while the wild animals take the land route beneath his camp and every species of bird flies above spreading their wings on those below. It were as though [those in the camp] were sitting in their abodes.

One time, King Solomon heard of a ruler situated in one of the islands of the sea. He had an extremely comely daughter whose beauty was unmatched in all the world. So he wrote the king:

> I am Solomon son of David King of Israel, he who God, the Lord of Israel, annointed to be ruler [*nagid*] of his people. God, the Lord of the Heavens, granted me all the kingdoms of the earth as He did the jinn who serve me. For He has empowered me over them and given me control of the animals and birds as well as the rulers of nations. So now, take heed and guard yourself diligently lest your pride deceive you or your brother the son of your mother entice you saying: "Who is this Solomon son of David?" Thus, I must take your daughter for my woman. She will become royalty. [As for you:] I need you to adopt our faith, to accept the unicity of God may His name be blessed and to worship Him as we do in order that we may become one people.

This aforementioned king had a certain idol in which there was a certain jinni. The king would bow down to that idol, light incense, and offer sacrifices before it. [Having received Solomon's missive,] a visibly agitated king set straight for the idol. "What's this panic in your face?" the jinni asked. He answered, "King Solomon has sent me word to give him my daughter in marriage so that she might serve him. That doesn't mean anything to me but there is one thing that does. He told me to smash the idol and embrace the Jewish faith."

When the jinni heard that, he immediately became enraged and said, "Pay no heed to his words, for he speaks falsely. He lacks what it takes to deal with me or [even] you. I shall gather all my jinn and order the wind to destroy the vessel by which he might come. I too have a mind as he does. Fear not! Do not be apprehensive! We shall indeed prevail for our people and the cities of our God." Upon hearing that, the island king became emboldened. And so, he raised his hand and swore by his God that he would wage extensive war with King Solomon.

The king sent Solomon a letter addressing the latter's dreams [of dominance] and answering his words. He wrote:

> Do not be swayed by your wisdom, your kingdom, your silver, or gold. Because I have that many times over. Cease opposing [the God] who is with me lest he destroy you. I will not bow down or bend before your God. Nor will I give my daughter to be your woman. Do as you will!

When Solomon heard that evil answer, he became enraged; his anger burned within him. And so, he lifted his hand and swore that he [Solomon] would not remain still and would not rest until he rendered massive judgment in the land of the island king. He would continue until he threw the king's carcass and those of his people to the birds of the sky and the wild beasts of the field. He would not rest until the king's idol was smashed. At that, he sent for the commanders of the wind and said unto them, "Let the four winds come and lift the camp and everything in it and all the wild animals and beasts of the field, and let them place the camp on such and such an island." Then he sent for all the wild animals and the birds of the sky who were to fly over the camp thus providing it with cover.

They came from all directions, from East and West and from the North and from the direction of the Sea [meaning the South] and the wind transported them between heaven and earth. Then it landed them on that island. [There they were] the king and all his camp, the wild animals, and the birds.

The island shook mightily at the sound of the steeds neighing and at the roar of the young lions and wild animals. A shaken and confused island king ran immediately to his idol and relayed what was happening, for the king still held fast to his wickedness. The jinni egged him on saying, "Assemble all your troops and take the field against him. Behold! I declare [myself] his adversary and go forth to gather my forces. I shall wage war against him." And so, that is what they did.

The [armies] gathered in the midst of that island from the north and from the Sea, whereupon Solomon immediately ordered the wild animals [to attack]. The animals penetrated the enemy camp, tearing it apart and leveling the tall cedars and cypress trees. The survivors fled to the hills. Solomon's forces captured the king [whom they brought back] alive and annihilated the entire populace. They brought the captive king to Solomon who rendered judgment upon him. The Israelite asked, "Who persuaded you to send word to me that 'I will not bend to your God. Nor will I give you my daughter [to be your woman]?'" He responded, "I have a certain idol. He persuaded me to do those things. For he said, 'Do not let David's son sway you with his machinations. He can do nothing for I have greater means at my disposal than they do.'"

At that, Solomon sent one of his jinn for the idol saying, "Who among you [jinn] influenced the king so that he presumed to defy the armies of the Living God, and in doing so, defied me as well and sought to do me harm? Who is it that said to me [upon receiving my missive] that he cannot abide by folly and madness? So now, wherever you might find him, seize him and bring him to me alive so that I might render judgment upon him. I shall know what to do with him."

When the [rebellious] jinni heard that, he fled in order to save himself from Solomon. But Solomon's jinn pursued him, seeking him here and there, as does a tracker in the wilderness. They found him and brought him to King Solomon who rendered judgment upon him. Then Solomon commanded his servants, the jinn, and the officers of his army to escort that jinni to the very spot where they had apprehended him. The Israelite king gave them an iron beam upon which was inscribed the ineffable name of God and said, "Hang him from it." That they did, and so he is suspended there until this very day.

Solomon then laid that island waste and made off with the young maiden after hanging her father.

(King Solomon and the Queen of Sheba)

When Solomon returned and took stock of what had happened, he noted that the hoopoe had not set off with him nor had it entered the fray [later]. So he sent for the officers and lords of the birds and said to them, "The hoopoe did not come to God's aid. Go now and bring me its lord and officers so that I might take revenge and punish the entire species."

The lords and officers of the birds then went off [to carry out the king's orders]. When the hoopoes appeared, they submitted themselves to Solomon saying, "O patron king and man of God! Do not think of us in that way. God forbid! We are not about to rebel against your rule or defy your wisdom. Nor are we about to deny those gifts that God has granted you; gifts with which he has granted you dominion over all his creatures great and small alike. It just so happens that we did not hear [of your proclamation to mobilize] nor has any [official] directive of yours reached us yet. There was this certain woman who is known as the Queen of Sheba—she has ruled over the Shebans since the death of her husband. Wise, charming, kind, knowledgeable, and beautiful [as well], she judges us with justice and fairness and has brought much goodness and righteousness to that land. Moreover, she has raised us from our youth until the present day. She has been a mother unto us, hence, we submit to her not [as subjects] in awe of [a] ruler, but as sons respecting her righteousness." When the king heard their sincere plea expressed so eloquently, he immediately bade them to go in peace.

The hoopoes then returned to the Queen of Sheba and informed her of Solomon's exploits. They spoke of his bravery and his campaigns and how he vanquished the island king and its God. They also told her that he had annihilated the island's populace and laid it bare, putting everything to the torch. As for the island jinni, the birds related that

Solomon had him hung at the very place where he had been found [fleeing the Israelite force] and that he remains alive and suspended there until this very day. Then they informed her of their good fortune, for Solomon had "taken compassion on us when we appeared before him brokenhearted. [For it is said:] 'Through forebearance a ruler can be won over; a gentle tongue can break bones.' " [Finally, they spoke of how] Solomon immediately "bade us to return home in peace."

When the Queen of Sheba [and her subjects] heard all that and all the stories of his power and bravery as well as the full account of Solomon's greatness, they were overcome with awe of him and their hearts were filled with utter dismay. It were as though those hearts melted and turned to water. And so, she said, "I shall go to him and hear directly his wisdom and see [firsthand] the wonderful and awesome things that he alone among humans can accomplish." For it is said: *He was wiser than all other men; wiser than Ethan the Ezrahite, and Heman, Chalkol, and Darda, the sons of Mahol,* (etc.) It is also said: "Solomon's wisdom surpassed that of all the wise men of the East."

She took with her one hundred twenty talents of pure gold, a very great quantity of spices, precious stones, and sandalwood and set out for the king in Jerusalem. Upon arriving, she tested him with riddles. And so she asked, "What are they? Seven depart and nine enter; two give succor but only one partakes?" He replied, "You come to test me with the [idle] prattle of women chatting in the moonlight? Nevertheless, I will respond lest you become haughty and say, 'I asked King Solomon and he didn't answer my question.' Did I not say in my own book: 'Answer a dullard in accord with his folly lest he consider himself wise.' "

[And so, he gave answer to her riddle:] "Seven depart refers to days of 'wearing of white' [when women examine themselves for lingering signs of menses and all means of contact with men is forbidden]. Nine enter refers to the nine months of pregnancy. After the woman gives birth, the two breasts succor the child."

Following that, she asked [the following] of him: "[What does this signify:] A child asked his mother, 'Who is my father?' She answered, 'Your father is my father and your grandfather is my husband. You are my son and I am your sister.' " Solomon responded: "No doubt the reference is to Ammon and Moab who were descended from Lot by way of his [incestuous] daughters."

After that answer, she took very young boys and girls and dressed and bejeweled them alike [so that one could not tell the difference between them]. Having done that, she asked Solomon, "Distinguish the males from the females." What did King Solomon do? He placed before them for their taking nuts and roasted grains. The boys grabbed them by the handful and ran off. The girls placed them in their laps and acted well behaved. And so, he said to her, "Those are boys and those girls."

She then asked him, "Tell me! What is it? A copper basin, an iron pitcher, it raises dust and sucks water." "A cosmetic box [*quvta d^ekohala*]," he answers. When she perceived his unlimited wisdom, knowledge, and understanding, she acknowledged his [status], as it is said: *Solomon had answers for all of her questions, there was nothing that he did not know nor anything to which he could not give an answer . . . She said to the king, "The report that I heard in my own land about you and your wisdom was true. But I did not believe the reports until I came and saw with my own eyes that what had been told me was not even the half of it.* You have surpassed your wisdom and reputation."

The king immediately perceived her to be exceedingly beautiful. As she was unmarried, he spoke of laying with her. But, when he heard that she was the daughter of a jinni and thus had hairy legs, he said, "What shall I do?" At once, he had a place made of inlaid marble two hundred cubits square. He placed a orchard on one side and splattered water over the marble thus giving the impression that the stone flooring was [a pond of] water. Then he ordered her to cross to the other side and enter the orchard. Convinced that [the surface] was all water, she lifted her garment and Solomon saw that her legs were indeed hairy. And so, he sent her cosmetics and a depilatory, which she used in making herself ready. She came to him and he lay with her. As a result, she gave birth to Nebuchadnezzar. Concerning that, it is said: *Those who ravage you and leave you waste shall* issue forth *from you.* Afterwards, he sent her away and she returned to her place. *King Solomon satisfied all of* her *desires in addition to what he gave her in his official capacity as king. Then she and her retainers left and returned to her own land.*

G. *Recent Jewish Folklore and Folkloric Texts*

(H. N. Bialik's Rendering of Solomon and the Hoopoe)

The Arabians tell the following story of Solomon: It came to pass that after the prophet of God, Solomon son of David, built the temple, he had the urge to wander about the earth. And so, he mounted the flying carpet. He took with him humans, jinn, and spirits, and all means of wild animals and birds, a great company that extended for a hundred parasangs. He then commanded the gentle wind which lifted them [skyward]. The birds flew along to service them.

Among the birds that set out [with Solomon] was the hoopoe, whose task was that of finding water for the camp in the wilderness. That is because the hoopoe had an eye that allowed it to see water in the belly of the earth as a human looks through glass.

Now, whenever the company would encamp at a given place, the company of winged creatures would also halt and hover above the heads of Solomon and his people thus shielding them with their wings from the blazing sun while the hoopoe would go off in search of water. When it found what it was looking for, it would go and tell Solomon. Throughout the journey, it would perform this task.

After journeying some days, the king arrived in the land of Yemen. There, he saw a bright and beautiful landscape, lush with all means of vegetation. The spot pleased him, and he and all his camp disembarked on the green grass at noontime.

But there was no water throughout that place. And so, the hoopoe said to itself, "I shall fly off, find water, and return before the king and his camp set up their tents."

At that, the bird spread its wings and took to the sky. It so happens, as it looked hither and yon, suddenly it gazed upon a green garden on the ground below. It made its way there, swooping towards the garden to land among the herbiage. It thus came upon another hoopoe, this one native to that land. For a moment, the two winged creatures remained silent and looked at one another in surprise.

Then the Yemenite hoopoe began to speak and asked the stranger, "What's your name, my friend? Where have you come from and where are you going?" Solomon's hoopoe replied, "My name is Ya'purah and I have come from the camp of Solomon son of David." The Yemenite asked, "Who is Solomon son of David?" "Really," replied Ya'purah, "That Solomon who rules over humans, jinn, and spirits, and over wild beasts and birds. It is he who rules on land and sea and over the four winds in the skies. And you, my sister, who are you and what is your name?" "My name is 'Afayrah and I am native to these parts," answered the Yemenite. Ya'purah continued, "Who is their king?" The answer, "A woman rules over them." At that, Ya'purah inquired, "What is her name?" The answer, "Her name is Balqīs. If the kingdom of your lord is vast and powerful, then know that hers is its equal. She has twelve thousand commanders and one hundred thousand fighting men for each of them. Will you journey with me to see her domain?" Ya'purah replied, "I fear that if I delay, the king will become short tempered with me because he will ask for water and it will not be found." "Do not fear," was the Yemenite's reply, "because your king will also be gladdened when you bring him tidings of this queen and her land."

When Solomon and his entourage had finished setting up their tents, it was time for afternoon prayer (*minhah*). At that, Solomon sought water in order to wash his hands but he did not find any. Moreover the people and cattle accompanying him were exceedingly thirsty. And so, there was a great outcry in the camp. He glanced towards the birds above his head. Behold, there was a gap that had developed there because the hoopoe was absent from its place. The king called out to the commander of the birds, that is, the eagle, and asked him about the hoopoe. He replied, "May God cause the king to be at ease! I know not where it went and where it is, nor have I sent it anywhere." The king became enraged and exclaimed, "As God lives, I will surely punish it or slaughter it if it cannot justify its behavior before me."

Solomon then called for the osprey and said to him, "Bring me the hoopoe immediately." The osprey took to the skies and canvassed the earth all around as a human sees a bowl [set] before him. While he was looking about, suddenly there was the hoopoe coming from the direction of the Yemen. The osprey swooped down intending to snatch it, but the hoopoe appealed for mercy saying, "I invoke God's protection from you whom He made strong and more powerful than I am, lest you assault me or do me harm." At that, the osprey let the hoopoe be and said, "Woe unto you! Your mother is about to become childless! The king is enraged at you and has sworn to punish or slaughter you."

The two flew on towards Solomon. When they reached the [other] birds, they were met by the eagle and all the other winged creatures. "Where have you been," they asked the hoopoe. Then they related to the hoopoe how Solomon in a fit of rage swore to inflict a cruel punishment upon it. A trembling hoopoe then inquired, "Is the prophet of God's decision to harm me final?" They answered, "Thus, spoke the prophet of God: If it cannot justify its behavior before me." "That being the case, I'm saved," remarked the hoopoe.

The two of them, the hoopoe and osprey, then went down to Solomon who was sitting on his throne. The osprey spoke, "Behold! O prophet of God! I have brought it." The hoopoe drew near trembling with fear, head bowed, tail lowered, and wings dragging along the ground. There it stood humbled and shamed. King Solomon then grabbed it by its crest and, drawing the hoopoe to him, said, "Where were you? Tell me lest I kill you this instant." The hoope responded, "O prophet of God! Remember that you stand before the Lord, the most mighty and high God." When Solomon heard those words, his anger abated and he said, "Tell me! Where were you and why were you late in coming?"

The hoopoe then related: "O prophet of God! I did indeed go out to seek water. It happened, that when I climbed on high, a new country was revealed to me, one of which you do not know. It is the Land of Sheba. Therefore, I said to myself, 'I'll go and wander about there investigating the place. Whatever is revealed to me about it, I'll pass along to my master.' This is what I found: The land is vast and blessed by God; it lacks for nothing. A woman rules over it; she has a great and most wonderful throne. But the queen and her subjects know not God. They worship the sun at its rising and setting. That is what I heard and saw. That is what I relate to my lord, the king."

"I shall see whether you have spoken the truth or have told me lies," said Solomon. At that he ordered a letter prepared for the Queen of Sheba. Meanwhile, the hoopoe moved about with Solomon's entourage in search of water, which it found beneath the ground of the valley. The jinn and spirits then dug in the valley exposing the water. Following that, humans and animals alike drank and sated their thirst.

The king's scribe finished composing the letter, which read as follows:

> From the servant of God, Solomon son of David to Balqīs, Queen of Sheba:
>
> In the name of God, the Merciful.
>
> Peace to them who walk in righteousness. I command in my own voice that you all present yourselves to me and thus give honor to God.

Solomon had the letter scented with musk and sealed it with his signet ring. He then instructed the hoopoe, "Fly with this letter to the Queen of Sheba. When you have delivered it into her hand, stand aside and listen to the discussion between her and her people. Then come back and tell me the precise nature of their reaction." The hoopoe said, "As commanded, I shall carry out the king's orders."

The hoopoe took the letter and after three days flight it reached Sheba in the morning. It then landed on the roof of the queen's palace. The palace was still tightly shut because the queen had not yet risen from her sleep. There was, however, an aperture built into the roof of the queen's bedroom. It faced her bed, so that when the sun rose, its light broke through the aperture and shone on the queen's face. She would then arise and bow down to the sun. Such was the queen's custom each and every morning.

Now, the hoopoe perched itself on the aperture and blocked it with its wings. Below lay the queen in an ivory bed with coverings of silk. Her eyelids were shut tight with morning slumber; her face was turned upward [towards the aperture]. The sun rose, but the queen was unaware that it had. The hoopoe dropped the letter from its beak, and it fell upon the queen's neck. A trembling Balqīs awoke and opened the letter. She smelled the sweet scent and when she read its contents and saw Solomon's seal, she shuddered and, lowering her head towards the ground, said, "The king who uses birds of the sky as his messengers is, indeed, a very great and powerful king. His kingdom is more powerful than mine." The hoopoe then stood aside to see what would happen.

The queen rose and went and sat on her throne. She hastily assembled the wisest of her commanders so that she might consult with them. It was her custom to speak to them while veiled, but when something caused her spirit to flag, she would reveal her face to them. And so it came to pass, that when the commanders arrived, she revealed her face and then revealed to them the entire contents of the letter.

She said, "O my commanders and chosen servants! Advise me now and instruct me as to what I should do. For I decide nothing until you take counsel with me." The commanders answered her, "We have the might and bravery to do battle but that is for you to decide. Command us and none will go against you." Balqīs responded, "This is my advise: I shall be sending Solomon tribute [*minhah*] with my messengers. If he is indeed a king, he will accept it and desist from bothering us. But, if he is a prophet, he will spurn our tribute and will not free himself from us until we come to him and pay obeisance to his God." As the queen's response seemed right to the commanders, they replied, "Do as you have spoken. May the queen live forever!"

Following that, Balqīs chose five hundred boys and girls. She dressed the girls in boy's clothing: tunics and girdles. The boys she dressed as girls. Morever, she placed bracelets of gold on their arms and gold chains about their necks. From their ears hung various types of earrings inset with precious stones. The boys were given horses to ride; the girls camels. There was a gold saddle for each horse and a [riding] cushion of gold for the camels. All the saddles and cushions were covered with embroidery and were encrusted with precious stones. She gave the boys and girls five hundred bricks of pure silver and an equal number of pure gold. In addition, there was a large gold crown, completely overlaid with pearls and opals, that was to be brought to Solomon. Moreover, there was musk and ambergris and aloes wood and ebony. All that was brought by them as tribute for Solomon. She then took a chest and put in it a perfect pearl without any perforation—it was very rare. She also placed in that chest a shell with a crooked perforation. Then the queen closed the receptacle and gave it and its contents to great and honorable officials, men of knowledge and wisdom, to bring to Solomon.

Her messengers also carried a letter from her saying:

> If you are a prophet of God, distinguish at once between the boys and girls; reveal the chest's contents before opening it; perforate the pearl evenly; and put a string through the crooked perforation of the shell. Do all this without assistance from either men or jinn.

Balqīs then instructed the boys and girls as follows: When you speak to King Solomon, alter your voices. The boys will speak softly and in a high pitched tones as do women; the girls in full-bodied and strong voice as do men. Then she commanded the leader of the boys, "When you come before Solomon, look at him. Should he gaze upon you in anger, fear not for he is only a king and I am mightier than he. But if the man be pleasant looking and goodhearted, then know that he is a prophet of God and show him proper respect." And so, the people took the tribute and precious things and went on their way. The hoopoe knew of everything that was happening and it returned and related all these things to Solomon.

(Israel Folklore Archives 1340)

[Informant: Avraham Benisti, Moroccan, Tangier:]

King Solomon invited the Queen of Sheba to his palace. The floor of the salon was built of mirrors, according to the king's instructions. Everything was decorated as befits a reception for the queen of a foreign country. And so, the Queen of Sheba arrived at King Solomon's palace.

After a reception party, the queen wanted to test Solomon's wisdom. She said, "Everywhere, you have a reputation as a wise man who knows everything. It's my wish for you to tell me what distinguishes my body." King Solomon smiled and replied, "You have very hairy legs." She said, "How do you know; you've never seen my legs?" Solomon answered her, "That's why I set the mirrors on the floor." The queen pondered how it would be possible [to carry out her plan] so that the king wouldn't guess the game (*ta'mulah*) that she's preparing for him.

The following morning, she assembled before him six of her people, all dressed alike and all the same height. Their faces were [also] hidden from view so that it was impossible to identify who was male and who was female. "Yes," said Solomon, "you have presented me with a difficult problem." He looked at them and they all appeared identical. The Queen of Sheba laughed and said to him, "This time, you will not guess who are the males and who are the females from among the six."

He ordered that a bag of nuts be brought to him. When he held it in his hand, he said, "Now, all of you stand in front of me." He called for the first of the six and said, "Take the nuts from my hand." That person offered Solomon two outstretched hands and he put the nuts in them. The king then said, "You will stand near the wall to the left." Solomon [then] called the second person in disguise and said, "Take the nuts from my hand." That person folded the edge of his dress and Solomon deposited the nuts there. Solomon said, "Stand near the wall to the right." Solomon demonstrated the same ploy to the Queen of Sheba until the last of them received nuts.

The Queen of Sheba said to him, "My king, you're trying, but this time you won't guess. This is all an act." Suddenly, her face betrayed amazement. Solomon said to her, "Those that I stood near the wall to the left are females; the three that I stood near the wall to the right are males." "That's right," said the queen. "Would you like to explain to me how you guessed that." "Very simple," Solomon responded. "When I told the first to take the nuts from my hand, she offered me her two hands so that I might place the nuts in them. I knew at once that this was a female. That is because she did not lift the hem of her dress. What female would do that? In contrast, the second lifted the hem of the dress immediately. I knew at once that this was a male for why shouldn't a male lift a part of the dress? Thus, I was able to guess who were the three males and three females."

(Israel Folklore Archives 8152)

[Informant: Alizah Anidjar, Moroccan, Tangier:]

At a certain time and in a certain city there lived the Queen of Sheba who worshiped the stars. One day, it just so happened, that Solomon heard about that. And so, he sent a certain bird with a letter for her. In the letter he wrote to her: "Do not worship the stars: [Worship] God alone, for there is a God in the heavens."

She got very angry and wrote to him in reply: "I am the Queen of Sheba! I do as I please! No one can tell me what to do! I like to worship the stars and will always worship them!" Then she sent the letter to him. King Solomon did not answer her. What did he do? He gathered all the birds from all over the world and said to them, "Go to the palace of the Queen of Sheba and blanket it so that she will see neither sun nor sky, only darkness."

Responding to Solomon's order, the birds flew off and blanketed the entire palace. When she wanted to worship the stars, she saw nothing except the darkened sky. She came to her wazīr and asked him, "What happened today that I cannot see the stars?" He answered, "My queen, don't you recognize King Solomon? That is King Solomon's trick [*kuntz*]!" "Ah!" she sighed.

Alright, what did she do? She wrote a letter to Solomon and said to him: "I would like to visit you." He answered, "Please do. I will be happy to greet you in my palace." What did she do? She took numerous precious stones—two boatloads of them. She also took along twenty children—ten boys and ten girls. All twenty were born on the same day and resembled one another as do two drops of water. She did that so he would not be able to distinguish the boys from the girls. She dressed them all as girls with skirts and white blouses. (The queen had hairy legs like those of a young man, but no one ever saw them.)

She came to Solomon, and a warm reception was arranged for her—music and so forth. With the king's troops forming an honor guard, she entered his palace. She had only to see King Solomon and she fell in love with him. She said to him, "I heard about you, but I wanted to see with my [own] eyes if that [which I heard] is correct." Solomon smiled at her and said, "Your every request will be made ready." "But," she said, "I want to make an agreement with you. I have two things that I want you to explain to me. If you know [the answers], I will marry you and my entire domain will be yours."

He said to her, "Everything you ask, I shall answer." She said to him, "First, what am I like?" He answered, "Those legs of yours are like a young man's but your face is that of a girl. Her jaw dropped as she expressed astonishment. She said to him, "You won as regards the first question. Now for the second: I want you to tell me. Of these twenty children, who are boys and who are girls." He took his servant aside and said to him, "I want you to bring me a bag of nuts and one of dates." They brought that to him. Then Solomon placed a pile of nuts and dates [before him] and called out to the first of the children, "Come here! Come, take!" offering him [the nuts and fruit].

The child put his hands to the hem of the skirt and stretched the garment and Solomon deposited the fruits in the skirt. He [then] called out to the second, "Take!" as he offered the child fruits. What did the second child do? The child took a kerchief and placed it between the forearms. The nuts were [then placed] inside the kerchief. [This was repeated until] all twenty came forward. Solomon [then] said, "You go here, and you there." To the right, he placed the ten who gathered [the fruits and nuts] in their kerchiefs; to the left, those who gathered them in their skirts. Thus, they stood, ten to a side.

Solomon said to the queen, "You see, I will immediately tell you who is a boy and who is a girl. Alright, these are girls and those are boys." How did he know? The boys didn't care about raising a skirt in order to take [fruits and nuts], but the girls, being modest, did not stretch the hems of their skirts.

And so, the Queen of Sheba married Solomon according to their agreement.

(Excerpts from Israel Folklore Archives 723)

[Informant: Simeon Gabbai, the Yemen:]

King Solomon was erudite in all matters pertaining to the world. Every day, he prayed for God to give him wisdom and understanding. Thus, God gave him wisdom and understanding and [in addition] bestowed upon him vast amounts of silver and gold. Kings of the West and those of the East came to him in order to hear his words of wisdom. They brought with them very valuable gifts for him. In such fashion, Solomon became rich, the richest of all the kings.

(Solomon would go to the mountains of darkness and not die. Solomon would fly in an aeroplane and not die.) The kings bowed before him and called out, "There is none as wise as you under the sun!" And so, Solomon became haughty. He opened the book of laws and read therein: *He shall not have many horses, nor shall he return the people to Egypt. He shall not have many wives, nor shall he have much silver and gold.*

One day, he made a great party for all his officials, and when he was good and drunk, he exclaimed, "It is written in the Torah: *He shall not have many horses, nor shall he return the people to Egypt. He shall not have many wives, nor shall he have much silver and gold.* [But] I have acquired many horses and women and similarly much silver and gold. You see me! I am right because my wisdom is the greatest in the world. Surely, this statute in the Torah is not for us to know."

After this declaration of the king, the room became silent and the words reached the heavens. God became angry and said, "Solomon and a thousand like him will perish for making light of the words of the Torah, but not a single dot of the Torah's statutes will perish." And so, God called for Ashmedai, King of the Jinn, and ordered him, "Go to Solomon the wastrel."

The King of the Jinn went to Solomon and asked, "Are you Solomon?" He answered promptly, "I am Solomon the King." Now Solomon knew the language of the birds and paid attention to them in his gardens. From those [winged] friends of his he learned that Ashmedai was on the earth. The king wanted to build a temple and sanhedrin but he did not know how to build it because iron [implements] were not allowed to touch the temple stones. But who would bring Ashmedai to Solomon?

Benaiah son of Jehoiada gathered his troops and reached the desert, but he did not see there the King of the Jinn. In the meantime, Ashmedai checked into a hotel and ate to his heart's content and drank until he was sated. Following that, he descended into the pit which was [then] blocked. With God's help, Benaiah son of Jehoiada found it [the pit], opened it, and fettered Ashmedai with chains of iron. "Who has fettered me?" cried Ashmedai, as he shook his body. But he lacked the strength to move [from that place]. And so, Benaiah son of Jehoiada removed him from the pit and took him to Jerusalem.

While going through its streets, Ashmedai touched its buildings and towers and collapsed everything with which he came into contact. When they reached the house of a certain widow, she went into the street and pleaded for mercy, "My lord! Please do not destroy my house! I am poor and feeble so that I have not the strength to build myself a new house." Ashmedai heard her voice and prostrated himself. One of his ribs was broken. This incident gave rise to the verse: *A gentle tongue can break bones.* Benaiah son of Jehoiada and Ashmedai then continued on their way until they appeared before King Solomon.

They [Solomon and Ashmedai] competed with each other as regards wisdom, and Solomon gained the upper hand. In the end, Ashmedai requested, "Please remove my chains. You're a wise man whose wisdom is greater than mine." Solomon removed Ashmedai's chains but in that he erred. It was his [Solomon's] custom to wear a ring on which was engraved the ineffable name of God. The very instant that he freed Ashmedai of his chains, the latter snatched the ring and tossed it into the sea. Solomon's power and wisdom disappeared. Ashmedai than removed him from the throne and sat in his place. The hawk [then] dove earthward, and after snatching Solomon in its sharp talons, brought him to the desert.

> *At this point the narrative turns to Solomon's wanderings. He protests that he is indeed Solomon but none pay him heed. He then becomes involved in a number of adventures, all typical of folkloric accounts of a person who has erred and thus lost his or her sense of identity. Finally, he becomes a rich king's personal waiter with responsibility for preparing food—this for five gold coins daily. It appears that, despite his exile, Solomon retained his culinary gifts.*

[While Solomon was thus employed by the king,] it happened, that one day the fishermen went without catching any fish. Now, Solomon sought, as was his custom, to cook a fish for the king's meal. After nary a fisherman came to the royal kitchen, Solomon sent a young lad to the market to fetch some fish. But the lad returned as he left, with empty hands. At that, Solomon himself made off for the fishermen's market. "Why didn't you bring fish today to the king's kitchen," he asked one of them. The man shrugged his shoulders and said, "There isn't a single fish. There are no fish for the royal kitchen. What can you do?" "Go out to the sea a second time. I'll go with you. We'll see what fish is available for us." The surprised fisherman answered, "You'll sail the sea with us? Have you the strength for this kind of work? You don't look to me as being the least bit suitable." "Nothing to worry about! Grab the nets and we'll shove off!"

These words were perceived as if they were a command, and the fisherman did not dare go against them. He called out to his colleagues and they [all] went to the shore. There, they embarked on the wide fishing boat and set sail. Not long after they sailed, Solomon commanded them to anchor and dropped their net. In a very short time, he commanded them to raise the net and, behold, it was heavy from the weight of the great catch. The catch was deposited in the boat's hold, and Solomon chose the largest of the fish when he said, "This fish! Give it to me! I'll take it with me to the palace kitchen." They gave him the fish.

When Solomon returned to his place of work, he [split] open the fish and, behold, in it was his ring that had been tossed into sea by Ashmedai. Solomon put on the valuable ring and continued to prepare the fish for the king's meal.

> *The story continues. The king's daughter is smitten with Solomon and wishes to marry him, but he is still considered a slave. Despite the girl's protestations and her mother's intervention, the king will not sanction the match. Moreover, there are rumors that the two have consummated their love. This leads to*

much melodrama. They are first banished from the palace and then from the kingdom. And so Solomon returns to Jerusalem with the girl. There Solomon received handouts from people who thought him down and out.

Ashmedai, who had taken on Solomon's shape and appearance, took for himself all the women of the harem. Every single one of Jerusalem's inhabitants was [therefore] certain that it was Solomon who sat on the throne of the kingdom. On that very day that Solomon had returned to Jerusalem, Ashmedai went to visit [Solomon's mother] Bathsheba. "Peace be upon you," he blessed her. When Solomon's mother gazed at him, she knew in her heart that, despite the great resemblance, it was not her son that had entered her chamber. She asked Ashmedai to sit down and she conversed with him, but after a short while she hinted that he should leave her be. After Ashmedai had departed from the room, Bathsheba hastened to the Sanhedrin. "I am mourning my son Solomon," she said, "The man who presently sits on the ruling throne is not my son!" [The judges asked,] "How can that be? How do you know that this is not your son?" "I don't know [for sure," she responded,] but I shall do everything that we may determine the truth."

And so, Solomon's mother left the Sanhedrin and took a bag of ashes, which she scattered along Ashmedai's usual route. After this act, she took to the side of the road and awaited Ashmedai's arrival. After a while, he came and passed over the ashes, leaving traces of a human foot and that of a donkey. Bathsheba then returned to the Sanhedrin and relayed to them what she had done and what she had seen with her own eyes. "You are right, my lady. The man that sits on the ruling throne is not your son, but Ashmedai himself." And so, they called to Benaiah son of Jehoiada, "Are you aware of King Solomon's whereabouts?" An astonished Benaiah son of Jehoiada answered, "The king has not summoned me to consult with him for some time. Perhaps the man who has been coming to the [city] gates for the last few days; perhaps he is Solomon."

Benaiah son of Jehoiada went to the market. There, he met Solomon and then brought him to the Sanhedrin. That very day, a new ring was fashioned and the ineffable name of God was inscribed upon it. The ring was given to Solomon, and thus, the kingdom was restored to him.

When Solomon returned to his palace, Ashmedai came to him. [Ashmedai said,] "What business have you here? Away with you!" He [Ashmedai] became infuriated and called everywhere for the hawk so that the bird might return Solomon to the desert. But the hawk lacked the power to harm him. Ashmedai cursed Solomon in the vilest terms, but the curses did him no harm. Solomon smiled sadly and said, "You are smart. Perhaps you will show me that you are indeed Ashmedai by transforming yourself into a grain of barley."

Ashmedai's honor was offended and so he made himself into a grain of barley in order to convince Solomon that he was indeed who he was. At that, Solomon took the grain and placed it into a box, which he closed and sealed with his ring. Then, he threw it into the sea.

> *The story concludes with Solomon hosting a large affair for his fellow sovereigns. It is at this party that he confronts the king who had banished him and his daughter. The king realizes the error of his ways and agrees to a marriage. And so, Solomon married the daughter of the King of Ammon who gave birth to Rehoboam.*

H. *Various Qur'ānic Texts*

(From "The Ant": Sūrah xxvii: 15–44

(15) We gave knowledge (*'ilm*) to David and Solomon and they said: Praise be to God who has favored us over many of his servants, the believers. (16) Solomon inherited from David and said: O people, we have been taught the speech of birds and something of everything has been bestowed upon us. This is indeed preference made clear. (17) Gathered unto Solomon were his hosts consisting of jinn, humans, and birds. They were arranged according to rank. (18) Until they came to the Valley of the Ants, when an ant said: O ants, enter your dwellings lest Solomon and his hosts crush you inadvertently. (19) And so, he smiled, laughing at its words and said: My Lord! Hold me in order that I might give thanks for the beneficience that You have bestowed upon me and my parents, and that I may act righteously in a manner that will please You. Admit me by your compassion to the company of your righteous servant. (20) He [Solomon] reviewed the birds and said: Why don't I see the hoopoe. Can it be that he is among the missing? (21) I shall surely punish him severely or slaughter him unless he brings me a clear excuse. (22) He [the hoopoe] lingered nearby and said: I have encompassed what you have previously not encompassed. And come to you from Sheba with tidings true. (23) I have found a woman ruling over them. She has had something of everything bestowed upon her and has a great throne. (24) I found her and her people bowing down before the sun rather than God. Satan has made their deeds seem pleasing to them and has kept them from the [true] path. Thus they are not rightly guided. (25) So they do not bow down to God who brings forth what is hidden in heaven and earth and knows what you conceal and reveal. (26) Allāh! There is no God but He, Lord of the mighty throne. (27) He said: We shall see if you have spoken the truth or are among the liars. (28) Go with this letter of mine and deliver it to them. Then turn away and see what they come back with. (29) She said: O ye leading men, a noble letter has been delivered to me. (30) It is from Solomon and reads: In the name of God the Merciful and Compassionate. (31) Do not be haughty! Come to me submitting as Muslims. (32) She said: O ye leading men, advise he in my affair. I only decide matters when you bear witness. (33) They said: We are possessed of power and fierce fighting spirit. But the matter is yours [to decide]. (34) She said: Indeed, when rulers conquer a city, they corrupt it, transforming the greatest of its people into the most debased. (35) Indeed, I shall be

sending them a gift and shall see what the envoys bring back. (36) When they came to Solomon, he said: You reach out to me with wealth? Has not God given me better than what he has given to you? And yet, it is you who rejoice with your gift. (37) Return to them, for we will most certainly come to them with contingents too powerful for them. We shall indeed expel them from it [the city] debased. (38) He said: O ye chiefs, which of you can bring me her throne before they come to me submitting as Muslims. (39) An 'ifrīt, one of the jinn, said: I will bring it to you before you arise from your place. For indeed I have the power to do it and am trustworthy. (40) One who had knowledge of the book then spoke: I will bring it to you in the twinkling of an eye. When he [Solomon] then saw it standing before him, he said: This is the grace of my Lord in order to test me. Shall I give thanks or be ungrateful? If one gives thanks, he does so for his own sake. If one is ungrateful, indeed my Lord is rich and generous. (41) He said; Disguise her throne for her. We shall see if she is truly guided or is one of those not truly guided. (42) When she arrived, [she] was asked: Is this the likes of your throne? She said: It is as if it were. Knowledge was brought to us prior to her. For we were Muslims. (43) Her worship of others than Allāh turned her away [from the true faith]. For she was from a people of unbelievers. (44) She was told: Enter the court (*ṣarḥ*)! When she saw it, she reckoned it to be a pool and she uncovered her ankles. He said: It is a court made smooth with slabs of glass. She said: My Lord! I have wronged myself. I submit through Solomon to Allāh, the Lord of the Universe.

(From *Ṣād* Sūrah xxxviii:30–36)

(30) We gave to David, Solomon, an excellent servant. Indeed, he was in the habit of turning [to Us]. (31) Behold there were brought before him at eventide swift horses that stand on three legs while brushing the ground with the fourth. (32) He said: Instead of mentioning My Lord, I have loved the love of good [things] until it [the sun] was concealed by the veil [of night]. (33) Bring them [the horses] back to me! Then he began to pass his [hand] over shanks and necks. (34) We tried Solomon and placed a body on his throne. Then he [Solomon] repented. (35) He said: O My Lord! Forgive me and bestow upon me rule [the likes of which] will be unsuitable to any [ruler] after me. Indeed, You are the Bestower.

(From *Sabā'* Sūrah xxxiv:12–14)

(12) To Solomon [we subjected] the wind [which carried him] a month's journey in the morning and a month's journey in the evening. We made a spring of [molten] brass for him and there were jinn who worked for him with his Lord's permission. Whichever of them turned aside from Our command, we made him taste the punishment of the Blazing Fire. (13) They made for him what he wished: prayer-niches, images, bowls [as large] as cisterns, and pots that stood firm. Work, family of David with thanks! But few of My servants are grateful. (14) And when We ordained that it was time for him [Solomon] to die, only the earthworm gnawing away at his staff revealed his death to them. When

he fell down, the jinn realized that if they had known the unseen, they would not have remained humiliated by their punishment.

(From *The Prophets* Sūrah xxi:79, 81–82)

(79) We gave Solomon understanding. To both of them [Solomon and David] We gave judgment and knowledge. We subjected the mountains and birds to sing Our praise as did David. And We were active. (81) To Solomon [We subjected] the strong wind so that it flowed [gently] at his command until reaching the land which We had blessed. We had Knowledge of everything. (82) Of the satans, some dived for him and did other work [as well]. We kept watch over them.

I. *Tha'labī's Version of Sulaymān and Bilqīs, the Queen*

God, may He be exalted, says (in the Qur'ān): *He* [*Solomon*] *reviewed the birds and said: Why don't I see the hoopoe. Can it be that he is among the missing?* (Qur'ān xxvii:20). Scholars versed in the history of the ancient peoples relate: When Solomon son of David—may peace be upon them both—finished building the temple, he decided to leave for the sacred precinct (*arḍ al-ḥaram*). Preparing for the journey, he gathered his retinue of humans, jinn, satans, birds, and wild animals, an army that extended one hundred parasangs (*farsakh*). He then commanded the gentle wind which carried them to their destination. Arriving at the sacred area, he remained as God wished, offering sacrifices and fulfilling the rites of pilgrimage. To his people, Solomon brought glad tidings of the coming of our Prophet, Muḥammad—may God pray for him and keep him! He informed them that Muḥammad is [to be] the Lord and Seal of the Prophets, and that that [truth] is fixed in their sacred scripture.

After that, Solomon decided on a journey to the land of Yemen. Leaving Mecca on the morn, he traveled to the Yemen, guiding himself by the star Canopus, and arrived at Ṣan'ā' [that day] when the sun was high. That was [for ordinary people] a month's journey. He saw a gleaming beautiful land lush with green foliage, whereupon he favored camping there in order to worship and partake of the midday meal. They sought water but didn't find it. The hoopoe was Solomon's guide. He could see water under the ground as one of you sees [it in] the cup in your hand. Scrutinizing the ground, he would disclose the place and depth of the water at which point the satans would strip the surface as one strips a hide and then draw the water from the ground.

Sa'īd b. Jubayr: When Ibn 'Abbās related this tradition, Nāfi' b. al-Azraq said to him, "How can he see water underground when he can't [even] see the trap laid for him under a few fingers of dirt." "Woe unto you!" Ibn 'Abbās responded, "When fate intervenes, sight turns to blindness."

Qatādah related on the authority of Anas b. Mālik: The Messenger of God said, "You are prohibited from killing the hoopoe because he was Solomon's guide to water."

So Solomon sought the hoopoe and, as he did not find the bird, he threatened him. When the hoopoe came, following that, he said [to his master]: *And* [*I*] *come to you from Sheba with tidings true. I have found a woman ruling over them* (Qur'ān xxvii:22–23). The reason for this comment was as follows: When Solomon camped, the hoopoe said to himself, "Solomon is surely busy setting up camp." With that, he lifted himself up to the sky and looked right and left over the length and breadth of the earth. When he saw the garden of Bilqīs [the Queen of Sheba] he made for the green and landed there. Suddenly, he came upon the hoopoe of the Yemen and touched down next to him. Solomon's hoopoe was named Ya'fūr, the hoopoe of the Yemen, 'Afīr. The latter questioned Ya'fūr, "Where have you come from and what do you want?" "I have come from Syria with my master Solomon son of David," he replied. The local hoopoe continued his questioning, "And who is Solomon son of David?" "The ruler of the jinn and of men and of satans and of wild animals and the winds," Ya'fūr replied. "And where are you from?" Solomon's hoopoe asked, Declared 'Afīr, "I am from this land." When Ya'fūr then asked, "Who rules it?" the hoopoe of the Yemen replied, "A woman." The [visiting] bird then probed further, "What's her name?" "She is called Bilqīs," was the answer. 'Afīr continued, "If your master possesses a mighty domain, Bilqīs has no less than he. For she is ruler of all the Yemen. Twelve thousand provincial rulers [*qayl*] serve at her behest and each is served by one hundred thousand fighting men—a *qayl* in the language of the Yemenites is the equivalent of a *qā'id* [among the Northern Arabs]. "Why not join me so you can have a look at her rule." The [visiting] hoopoe responded, "I fear Solomon will miss me at the time of worship when he has need of water." But, declared the Yemenite hoopoe, "He will surely be gladdened if you bring him news of this queen." So the hoopoe went off with 'Afīr until he came to Bilqīs and saw her domain. He did not return to Solomon until the time of the evening prayer.

Our source continued: When Solomon had camped, it was time for the evening worship and he sought the hoopoe. This was because he camped in a place without water. He asked the men about water and they answered, "We don't know if there is any here." Then he asked the jinn and satans and they [too] responded, "We don't know." At that point, Solomon put out a search for the hoopoe. When he did not find him, he threatened the bird.

Ibn 'Abbās related in a number of accounts attributed to him: One of the sun's rays fell upon Solomon's head, so he looked [up] and, behold, he saw that the place of the hoopoe was vacant. He summoned the bird who was the officer in charge of muster (*'arīf*), that is, the vulture, and asked him about the hoopoe. "May God set things right for the King!" replied the vulture, "I do not know where he is, nor have I sent him anywhere." Solomon grew angry at that and said: *I shall surely punish him severely or slaughter him* (Qur'ān xxvii:21).

Scholars disagree as to this severe punishment. According to most exegetes: He was going to have his feathers and tail plucked, and would then be laid bare on an anthill to be stung. But al-Ḍaḥḥāk said: [In effect Solomon threatened:] I will surely pluck him [clean], bind his feet, and expose him to the sun. Muqātil is of the opinion [that Solomon meant]: I will surely smear him with tar and expose him to the sun. The following interpretations [of what Solomon meant] are also offered: I will surely cage him; I will surely banish him from his species; and *I will surely prohibit him from serving me unless he brings me a sulṭān mubīn* (Qur'ān xxvii:21), that is, a clear excuse (*ḥujjah wāḍiḥah*). 'Ikrimah related on the authority of Ibn 'Abbās: Every time *sulṭān* is mentioned in the Qur'ān, it means excuse (*ḥujjah*).

Our source continued: Following that Solomon summoned the eagle, lord of the birds, and said, "Bring the hoopoe to me at once!" The eagle lifted himself beyond the sky until he clung to the outer reaches of space. Scanning right and left, he looked at the world as if it were a bowl placed before me or you. Suddenly, he came upon the hoopoe approaching from the direction of the Yemen. The eagle dove towards the hoopoe, seeking to [catch] him. When the hoopoe noticed that the eagle sought him with a mind to do him harm, he invoked God's protection saying, "By the law of Him who has empowered you and made you stronger than I am, would you not pity me and approach me without harmful intent." The eagle then turned aside and said, "Woe unto you! Your mother is about to become childless because the prophet of God, Solomon, has sworn that he will punish you or slaughter you." Then the two set off, flying towards Solomon.

Upon reaching the encampment, they were met by the vulture and all the other birds. They said to the hoopoe, "Where have you been today? Solomon, the prophet of God, has already threatened you." Then they informed the hoopoe of what Solomon had said, whereupon the hoopoe asked, "Didn't the prophet of God allow for an exception?" "Indeed," they replied, "He said: *unless he brings me a clear excuse*." The hoopoe and the eagle then flew on until they came to Solomon who was seated on his throne. The eagle spoke, "I have brought him to you O prophet of God." When the hoopoe then approached the prophet, he lifted his head and lowered his tail and wings, dragging them on the ground in humility before Solomon. Solomon stretched out his hand towards the hoopoe's head and pulled it forward. Then he said: "Where have you been? I will surely punish you severely!" The hoopoe replied, "O prophet of God! Remember, you are standing before Allāh." Solomon trembled on hearing that and forgave him.

I was thus informed by al-Ḥusayn b. Muḥammad al-Thaqafī through his chain of transmitters going back to 'Ikrimah: Solomon decided against slaughtering the hoopoe only out of mercy for the bird's parents.

When that [the prophet's anger] had passed, he asked the bird, "What kept you from me?" The hoopoe replied as God relates (in the Qur'ān): *I have encompassed what you have previously not encompassed*—that is, I have learned something that you do not know. *And come to you from Sheba with tidings true. I have found a woman ruling over them. She has had something of everything bestowed upon her* (Qur'ān xxvii:22–23).

Our source continued: Her name was Bilqīs, daughter of al-Bashrakh, he who was [nicknamed] al-Hadhhādh. It is also said: She is Bal'amah daughter of Sharāḥīl b. Dhī Jadan b. al-Bashrakh b. al-Ḥārith b. Qays b. Ṣan'ā' b. Sabā' b. Yushjib b. Ya'rib b. Qaḥṭān. Bilqīs's father, the one named al-Bashrakh and nicknamed al-Hadhhādh, was a king possessing great influence. Ruler of all the Yemen, he would proclaim to the provincial dynasts (*mulūk al-aṭrāf*), "There is not one among you who is my equal." As he refused to marry among their people, they paired him off to a woman of the jinn called Rayḥānah bt. al-Shukr—at that time men could see the jinn and have intercourse with them. She subsequently bore him Bal'amah, that is, Bilqīs. He had no other offspring. The proof of this [genealogy] is found in what Ibn Maymūnah related through his chain of transmitters going back to Abū Hurayrah and then the Prophet, who said, "One of Bilqīs's parents was a jinni."

The authorities related: When Bilqīs's father died, leaving no other offspring, she coveted rule and sought to have her people render the oath of allegiance to her. One group obeyed Bilqīs but others turned against her. They chose a man in preference to her and made him their ruler. And so, the people [of the Yemen] split into two factions, each holding dominion over part of the land. But the man they had chosen to rule them behaved abominably towards the people of his kingdom, having gone so far as to violate the womenfolk of his subjects. As a result, his followers wished to depose him, but they were powerless to do so.

When Bilqīs saw this, she was horrified and [concoting a ruse] she sent word to the king offering herself to him. The king responded favorably saying, "I would have initiated a proposal had I not despaired of your [likely] refusal." She answered, "I cannot turn away from you [now] for you are surely equal to me in nobility. So gather my notables and people and propose marriage through them." With that, he gathered them and, addressing them [directly], he proposed marriage to her. "We do not envision her doing this," was their response. "But," he countered, "it was she who first contacted me! I would indeed like to hear her [own] response. So bear witness [to these proceedings] and testify before her [as to my intentions]." When they came to her and mentioned that, she exclaimed, "I loved the boy. I did not respond to him previously because I preferred not to marry, but now I give my consent to him." And so, they married her off to him.

She left with a vast retinue of servants and attendants when she was brought to him as part of the bridal procession. So vast was her retinue that his residences and palaces were crammed with those serving her. When finally she came to him [in his private chamber], she offered him wine until he became drunk. Then she cut off his head and slipped away from his dwelling in the darkness of the night. Upon greeting the morning, the notables saw that the king was slain and that his head had been hung from the gate of the palace. Then they knew that these nupitials were a deception concocted by her. Gathering to her they said, "You are worthier than anyone of this kingship." She responded, "Were he not branded by his disgrace, I would not have killed him. But, when I saw that his corruption had become widespread, I was seized with rage and did with him as I did." They chose her to govern them and her rule became firmly established throughout the [entire] kingdom.

Ibn Maymūnah related through his chain of authorities going back to al-Ḥasan b. 'Alī and then Abū Bakr, who said, "I mentioned Bilqīs in the presence of God's Messenger and he remarked, 'No society (*qawm*) prospers that allows a woman to rule over them.' " The authorities related: When Bilqīs assumed rule, she built a palace and throne of her own.

(Description of the Palace that Bilqīs Built)

Al-Sha'bī: It has been reported that when Bilqīs assumed rule, she ordered the construction of a palace. Five hundred columns of marble were brought to her, each fifty cubits in length. At her command, they were erected at spaced intervals of ten cubits on a hillock near the city of Ṣan'ā'. She then covered the structure with a ceiling of marble slabs arranged in order and joined together with lead so that the entire ceiling looked as if it were a single slab. Above this she built a squire palace of burnt brick and gypsum. At each corner of the palace was a gold cupola that extended towards the sky. Among the structures framed by these domes were audience halls whose walls were made of gold and silver encrusted with varieties of square gems. She also provided the palace—that is, at the palace gate contiguous to the city—a tower of white, red, and green marble. Along the sides of the palace were rooms for her chamberlains, security patrols, guards, servants, and attendants, each arranged in order of their rank.

(Description of Her Throne)

The front of her throne [platform] was made of gold inset with rubies and emeralds; the rest was of silver encrusted with various kinds of gems. It had four supports: one consisting of rubies, one of green corundum, one of emeralds, and one black pearls. The seat was covered with sheets of gold. Leading to the platform were seventy chambers, each protected by a locked gate. The [entire] throne [structure] was eighty cubits in length as well as height. Regarding that, God Mighty and Powerful says (in the Qur'ān); *She had something of everything bestowed upon her*—that is the implements required for ruling—*and has a great throne*—that is, a beautiful and solid couch (Qur'ān xxvii:23).

I found her people bowing down before the sun rather than God (Qur'ān xxvii:24). That is to say, she had asked her wazīrs, "What did my ancestors worship?" "They worshiped the Lord of Heaven," was their reply. She then asked, "And where is he?" They responded, "He is in Heaven, but his sign is [here] on earth." She continued [to probe], "How shall I worship him when I cannot see him? I know of nothing more powerful than the light of the sun. We should give precedence to the sun as the object of our worship." So she worshiped the sun rather than Almighty God and obligated her people to do likewise. They would bow down to it when it rose and when it set.

Our source continued: When the hoopoe related that to Solomon, *He said: We shall see if you have spoken the truth or are among the liars* (Qur'ān xxvii:27). Afterwards, the hoopoe guided them to water, whereupon they dug out the *rakāyā*—these are natural cisterns (*ābār*) beneath every dried out river bed. The people and pack animals who had already grown thirsty were therefore able to quench their thirst. When that was done, Solomon wrote the following letter:

> From God's servant, Solomon son of David, to Bilqīs the Queen of Sheba: *In the name of God the Merciful and Compassionate* [Qur'ān xxvii:30]. Peace is for those who follow the rightly guided path. *Do not be haughty. Come to me submitting as Muslims* [Qur'ān xxvii:31].

Ibn Jurayj and others reported: The letter was as Almighty God relates it [in the Qur'ān]. Solomon added nothing. He was the most elegant of men when it came to [composing] his letters, but he was also the most concise when it came to dictating them. So it was with [all] the prophets. They would write in summary fashion rather than long, detailed accounts.

The authorities related: When Solomon had written his letter, he dabbed it with musk, and sealed it with the impression of his signet ring. Having done all that, he said to the hoopoe: *Go with this letter of mine and deliver it to them. Then turn away,* but stay close to them *and see what they come back with* (Qur'ān xxvii:28), that is, the answer that they give in response. The hoopoe took the letter and took it to Bilqīs who was at a place called Ma'rib some three days journey from Ṣan'ā'. He reached her at her palace where she had already locked the gates and gone to bed. When she went to sleep, she would lock the gates and, taking the keys, would place them under her head. The hoopoe came to her as she slept on her back and dropped the letter on her neck. That is the statement of Qatādah. But Muqātil reported: The hoopoe carried the letter in his bill and flew about until he was directly above the woman. Then he flapped his wings for a while, attracting the attention of the notables, until she lifted her head, at which point he dropped the letter on her bosom. Wahb b. Munabbih related: She had a window, that is an arched aperture facing the direction of the sun. At sunrise, light would strike the window [and enter the chamber]. Upon seeing the sun, she would bow down before it. The hoopoe came to the window and blocked it with his wings so that the sun rose and she did not know it. Sensing the delay in the sun's coming, she got up in order to look, at which point the hoopoe dropped the letter in her lap.

The authorities continued: Bilqīs took the letter—she was from the people of Ṭubba' b. Sharāḥīl al-Ḥimyarī and was literate in Arabic. When she saw the seal, she trembled and bowed down because Solomon's ruling power was in his signet ring and she thus knew that the sender of this letter was a greater sovereign than she. "Any ruler who uses birds as his emissaries is indeed a great ruler," she said. Then she read the letter as the hoopoe lingered not far away. Following that, she went and sat on her throne and gathered the leading men among her people. They were twelve thousand provincial rulers (*qayl*), each of whom was served by a hundred [thousand] fighting men. She would [ordinarily] speak to them veiled, but when some matter distressed her she'd strip the veil from her face.

When they came and took their places in the assembly, Bilqīs addressed them: [*O ye leading men*], *a noble letter has been delivered to me* (Qur'ān xxvii:29). That is, the letter was noble (*sharīf*) because of the nobility (*sharaf*) of the sender. Al-Ḍaḥḥāk said: She labeled it noble because it was sealed. This interpretation is indicated by an account related to me by Abū Ḥāmid al-Warrāq through his chain of authorities going back to Ibn 'Abbās and then the Prophet, who said, "The noble quality of a letter is in its seal." It is also said: She labeled it noble because the letter was introduced: "In the name of God the Merciful and Compassionate." Regarding that, God, may He be exalted, says (in the Qur'ān): *It is from Solomon and reads: In the name of God the Merciful and Compassionate. Do not be haughty. Come to me submitting as Muslims* (Qur'ān xxvii:31–32). Then *she said: O ye leading men, advise me in my affair* and offer me counsel concerning that which has been proposed to me. *I only decide matters when you bear witness* (Qur'ān xxvii:32), that is when you are present. *They said* in response to her: *We are possessed of power and fierce fighting spirit* when called to combat. *But the matter is yours* [to decide]. *Consider that which you will command* (Qur'ān xxvii:33). You will find us obeying your order. When they offered themselves for combat, Bilqīs declared: *Indeed, when rulers conquer a city, they corrupt it, transforming the greatest of its people into the most debased* (Qur'ān xxvii:34). That is, they humble its nobles and great men so that authority can be established on their [own] behalf. God has verified her statement, for he says: *That is what they do* (Qur'ān xxvii:34).

Capturing this sense [of the verse], Abū al-Qāsim al-Junayd recited [the following poem] to me on the authority of his father:

> Wheresoever kings come to settle they vanish
> There will be no shelter for you under their wings.
> What hopes do you entertain from a group enraged
> They oppress you, impatient, even if you satisfy them.
> Praise them, and they suppose you deceive them
> They find you burdensome as they do everything.
> Ask God that for your sake you do without their portals
> For he who stands at their door is surely debased.

In retelling her story, God, may he be exalted, says: *Indeed I* [*the Queen of Sheba*] *shall be sending them a gift* (Qur'ān xxvii:35). Bilqīs said that because she was a sensible and intelligent woman. She had already trained the leading men of her people to conform [to her wishes] and was experienced at command and manipulating authority. When she said: *Indeed I shall be sending them a gift,* that is, to Solomon and his people, she meant a gift with which I will dissuade him from seizing my authority and through which I will determine whether he is king or prophet. Should he be a king, he will take the gift and depart. But, if he is a prophet, he will not be satisfied until we follow his religion. Following that, she sent him a gift of slaves consisting of young lads and maidservants (*wuṣafā'* and *waṣā'if*).

Ibn 'Abbās related: She dressed them alike so he wouldn't be able to tell male from female. But Mujāhid said: She dressed the young lads (*ghilmān*) as maidservants (*jawārī*) and the maidservants as young lads. The authorities disagreed as to their number. Thus, al-Kalbī reported: ten maidservants and ten young lads, while Muqātil indicated: One hundred young lads and one hundred maidservants. Mujāhid contended: Two hundred of each, and Wahb, who said five hundred each, also indicated: She sent him as well five hundred sheets (*ṣafīḥah*) of gold. There was [additional] disagreement as to how much gold was sent and in what form.

As to God's statement: *Indeed I shall be sending them a gift,* I received a tradition by way of Ibn Maymūnah, who reports it through his chain of authorities going back to Thābit al-Bunānī. The latter said: She made him a gift of sheets of gold placed in brocade sacks. When word of that reached Solomon, he issued an order to the jinn and they fashioned for him bricks of gold (*ājurr*). Then, at his command, the bricks were strewn everywhere along the road so that they were seen by the emissaries as they approached [Solomon's camp]. They said, "We have come bearing something [precious] which we see strewn about indiscriminately." What they were bringing now seemed trivial to them—it is said that they brought four bricks (*labinah*) of gold.

Wahb b. Munabbih and others who read scripture related: Bilqīs called for five hundred maidservants and an equal number of young lads. She dressed the former as young lads in tunics and sashes. The latter she dressed as maidservants, placing bracelets and necklaces of gold around their forearms and necks. In their ears she inserted earrings for the upper and lower lobes, each inset with various kinds of gems. Then she placed the maidservants on five hundred steeds and the young lads on an equal number of nags. Each steed was covered with a gold saddle inset with gems and a brocade blanket of many colors. Bilqīs also sent Solomon five hundred bricks (*labinah*) of gold, the same of silver, and a crown ornamented with valuable pearls and rubies. In addition, they sent musk, ambergris, and various kinds of aloes wood. She also called for a box and placed in it a costly pearl (*durrah*) without perforation, as well as a shell (*kharazah*) that had been perforated, but whose perforation had been crooked. Bilqīs then summoned a man, one of the notables among her people. He was called al-Mundhir b. 'Amr. Picking from among the other notables, she attached to his service men of reason and intellect. Having done that, she wrote a letter containing an inventory of the presents and sent it along with them.

In the letter she stated, "If you are a prophet, distinguish between the maidservants and young lads, tell us what is in the box before opening it, perforate the pearl evenly, and string the crooked shell." Following that, Bilqīs ordered the young lads, "If Solomon addresses you, speak to him in an effeminate way, as if imitating the speech of women." [Similarly] she ordered the slavegirls to speak to him roughly in a tone that resembles the speech of men. Then she said to her emissary, "Look at the man when you enter into his presence. If he gives you an angry look, then know that he is a [mere] king and do not let his gaze frighten you, for I am greater than he. But, if you find him to be pleasant and kind, then know that he is a prophet that has been sent [by God]. So understand his words and return with his response." The emissaries then departed with the gifts.

When the hoopoe saw that, he hurried [back] to Solomon and told him the entire story. Solomon ordered the jinn to make him bricks (*labinah*) of gold and silver and they did. Then he ordered them to use such bricks in paving a single review ground that extended nine parasangs from the spot he occupied. Around the review ground, they were to place a prominent wall of gold and silver. This they [also] did. Then he asked them, "Which beasts of burden are the most beautiful that you have ever seen?" They responded, "O prophet of God! Indeed we have seen in such a sea multicolored animals possessing wings, combs, and forelocks." Solomon commanded, "Bring them to me immediately!" They brought the animals to him and he said, "Hitch them to the right and left of the review ground on the bricks of gold and silver and scatter fodder on it for them." Following that, he ordered the jinn, "Bring me your children!" A large throng gathered, and he positioned them to the right and left of the review ground. With that done, Solomon sat on his throne in his [place] of assembly and had four thousand chairs placed to his right and an equal number to the left. He ordered the satans to form rows several parasangs long, and ordered the same for the men, the wild animals, the beasts of prey, the reptiles, and the birds. All formed rows to the right and left of him. When the emissaries approached, drawing near to the review ground, that is, when they beheld Solomon's domain (*mulk*) and saw the pack animals, the likes of which they had never seen, defecating on the gold and silver bricks, they panicked and threw aside the gifts that they were carrying.

Some reports indicate that when Solomon ordered the review ground paved with bricks of gold and silver, he commanded the jinn to leave along the way [an empty] space equal to the number of bricks carried by Bilqīs's agents. When the emissaries then saw that the place for these bricks was empty while the rest of the ground was paved, they feared that they would be accused [of having taken them]. So they placed what bricks they were carrying in that [empty place].

Our source continued: When they came to the review ground and saw the satans, the queen's representatives were greeted by an awesome look that frightened them. They were told, however, "Enter without fear." Passing squadron after squadron of jinn and of men, of birds and of beasts of prey and wild animals, they finally stood before Solomon. Looking kindly upon them and with cheerful countenance, he spoke, "What is your purpose?" The leader of the delegation indicated to Solomon what they had brought and gave him the queen's letter. After looking at the letter and reading it aloud, Solomon asked them, "Where is the box?" When it was brought to him, he shook it, whereupon the [angel] Gabriel came and informed him of its contents. So Solomon said, "It contains a costly pearl without perforation and a shell that is perforated but whose perforation is crooked." "Correct," said the emissary. "Now perforate the shell and string the pearl."

Solomon called out, "Who can perforate this for me?" He asked the men but they lacked the knowledge to do it. Then he asked the jinn but they [too] lacked the knowledge thereof. After that, he sent for the satans who replied, "Send for the earthworm." And so he did. When the earthworm came, it seized a hair [and placing it] in its mouth, it passed through the pearl until exiting at the other side. Solomon said to the earthworm, "Ask! Whatever you need is yours." The earthworm responded, "That my daily sustenance (*rizq*) be provided by the brush [I inhabit]." "Done!" he said to the earthworm. Then he asked, "Who can thread this shell?" A white fruitworm spoke up, "I can do it O prophet of God." The worm then took the thread in its mouth and, after entering the perforation, exited at the other side. Solomon asked the fruitworm, "Ask! Whatever you need is yours." The fruitworm responded, "That my daily sustenance be provided by the fruits." "Done!" he said to the fruitworm.

That accomplished, Solomon distinguished the maidservants from the young lads by ordering them to wash their hands and faces. For, as a rule, a maidservant takes water from a vessel with one hand and, after transferring it to the other, splashes it on her face. Moreover, a maidservant pours [water] on the inside of her forearms while a young lad does it on top. Also, a maidservant [actually] pours water, whereas a young lad lets it run down his forearms. Thus, did Solomon distinguish among them.

Then Solomon returned all the gifts saying: *You reach out to me with wealth. Has not God given me better than what he has given you? And yet, it is you who rejoice with your gift* (Qur'ān xxvii:36) because you are a people given to boasting and the acquisition of material wealth. You know nothing else. The earthly world is not among my needs, for God, may His name be exalted, has already allowed me to possess that. He has bestowed upon me riches that he has given to no one else in the universe. Were that not enough, God, may He be praised and exalted, honored me with the gifts of prophecy and wisdom. After that, Solomon said to al-Mundhir b. ʿAmr, the leader of the delegation: *Return to them* [with the gifts], *for we will most certainly come to them with contingents too powerful for them. We shall indeed expel them from it* [*the city*] *debased. And they shall be humbled* (Qur'ān xxvii:37) if they do not come to me submitting as Muslims.

Our authority related: When Bilqīs's emissaries returned to her after having been with Solomon and informed her [of what had happened], she exclaimed, "By God! This is no king! We are powerless to deal with him." So she sent word to Solomon, "I am coming to you with the rulers of my people in order to consider your command and the calling of your religion." Bilqīs then ordered that her throne be placed in the most remote of her palaces in the last of seven chambers each enclosing one another. Following that, she locked the gates and appointed a security force to stand guard. Then she spoke to the deputy [that she had] left behind to look after her domain (*sulṭān*): "Guard what is before you and the seat of my rule. Let no one have access to it or [even] see it until I return to you." Bilqīs now ordered a herald to make announcements to the people of her kingdom apprising them of the journey. Having done all that, she set off for Solomon with twelve thousand provincial rulers from among the kings of the Yemen, each of whom was served by one hundred thousand fighting men.

Ibn ʻAbbās related: Solomon was a cautious man who never undertook anything until he himself inquired about it. One day, he sat on his throne and suddenly saw a cloud of dust approaching. "What's this?" he asked. They replied, "Bilqīs! O messenger of God." He then inquired, "Has she encamped at this place in order to meet with us?" "Yes," they said.

Ibn ʻAbbās pointed out: [Solomon was separated from Bilqīs by a line equal to] the distance between al-Ḥīrah and al-Kūfah [which] was one parasang. Solomon then went to his contingents and asked: *Which of you can bring me her throne before they come to me submitting as Muslims* (Qur'ān xxvii:38), that is obedient and subservient.

The authorities disagreed as to why Solomon ordered the throne brought [to him]. Most said: Because Solomon knew that when she submitted to Islam, her property would be forbidden to him. Therefore, he wished to seize her throne before her conversion. But Qatādah said: It was because he was amazed at the hoopoe's description of the throne and thus wished to see it before he saw her. It has also been said: [He did it] so that he could demonstrate to her, through the miraculous delivery of her throne, the power of God, may He be exalted, and the greatness of His dominion.

An ʻifrīt, one of the jinn, the most powerful of the spirits, spoke: *I will bring it to you before you arise from your place* (Qur'ān xxvii:39), that is, from the assembly at which you issue judgments. Ibn ʻAbbās said: Every morning Solomon held an assembly, issuing judgments until midday. The authorities also disagreed as to the ʻifrīt's name. Wahb said that it was Kūdā but Shuʻayb indicated Kūdhān.

[The ʻifrīt continued:] *For indeed I have the power to do it,* that is, the power to transport the throne *and am trustworthy* (Qur'ān xxvii:39)—trustworthy in addition to being capable because of the jewels that embellished the throne. Solomon said, "I want it faster than that." *One who had knowledge of the book then spoke* (Qur'ān xxvii:40). There is disagreement concerning the speaker. Some said: It was Gabriel; others: It was an unspecified angel that God had sent to assist his prophet; still others held: It was rather a human being. Those scholars who maintained that the speaker was human disagreed as to his identity. Most exegetes opined: It was Asaph son of Berechiah son of Shimea son of Malchijah. A truthful man, he knew the mightiest of God's names. When he summoned the Lord with that name, God answered. If asked anything when summoned by that name, God granted it.

I was informed by Ibn Maymūnah through his chain of authorities going back to Ibn ʻAbbās: When Asaph prayed and summoned God [invoking his mightiest name], he said to Solomon, "Look afar and make out what you can at a glance." Solomon then looked far to the right, and God sent the angels on their mission. They carried the throne, tunneling underground, until they burst from the earth, the throne appearing before Solomon.

The authorities disagreed also concerning Asaph son of Berechiah's invocation at the time the throne was brought. It has been related by way of 'Ā'ishah and her father that the mightiest name [of God] invoked by Asaph was Yā Ḥayy Yā Qayyūm. On the other hand, the following tradition was related on the authority of al-Zuhrī who said: The invocation of the *one who had knowledge of the book* was, "Our Lord and Lord of everything. The Lord is One. There is no Lord but You. Bring me her throne." Muhāhid said: [He summoned God by calling out] "O Possessor of greatness and generosity."

Ibn Maymūnah related the following through his chain of authorities going back to Zayd b. Aslam, the client of 'Umar b. al-Khaṭṭāb: The *one who had knowledge of the book* was a righteous man (*rajul ṣāliḥ*) from one of the sea islands. On that day, he went forth to observe the inhabitants of the earth to see how they did or did not worship God. As a result, he found Solomon and when he invoked one of God's names, there was the throne already transported. It had been brought to Solomon *in the twinkling of an eye* (Qur'ān xxvii:40).

Quoting from his chain of authorities going back to Mujāhid, Ibn Maymūnah said: I have been informed by Suhayl b. Ḥarb as follows: Ibn Abī Baradah maintained that the *one who had knowledge of the book* was Usṭūm. The author continues: Qatādah stated: His name was Malīḥā. But, according to Muḥammad b. al-Munkadir: It was rather Solomon [himself] to whom God had given knowledge (*'ilm*) and understanding (*fiqh*). Thus, one of the authorities among the Israelites told Solomon: *I shall bring it to you in the twinkling of an eye*. When Solomon responded, "Do so!" the Israelite then said, "You are a prophet and the son of a prophet. There is none more highly regarded by God than you. Were you to call God, you would have it." "You are right," said the prophet, whereupon he did just that and the throne was brought to him immediately.

When Solomon saw the throne standing before him—it had been brought in the twinkling of an eye, a slight period of time—he said: *This is the grace of my Lord in order to test me. Shall I give thanks or be ungrateful* (Qur'ān xxvii:40)? He who gives thanks does so on his own behalf. That is, by giving thanks he himself profits, as thanks are necessary for consummating and then continuing [the act of] beneficence (*ni'mah*). Thanks is the shackle of beneficence that exists and the object sought of a beneficence that is lacking. As to he who is ungrateful, *indeed my Lord is rich* without his thanks *and generous* in granting favor even to one who withholds thanks for His beneficence (Qur'ān xxvii:40).

Solomon then said: *Disguise her throne for her.* That is, add to it and take away from it by substituting the upper and lower parts for one another. *We shall see if she is truly guided* to her throne and recognizes it or is among the ignorant, [meaning] *those not truly guided* to it (Qur'ān xxvii:41). Solomon did this in order to test her intelligence.

According to Wahb b. Munabbih, Muḥammad b. Ka'b, and other authorities: Solomon was led to this [test of her intelligence] because the satans feared that he would marry her and make her desirous of having his offspring. She would then disclose to him the secrets of the jinn, and they would never rid themselves of their subservience to Solomon and his offspring to follow. Wishing to incite him against her, they distorted what was praiseworthy [about her], saying, "There is something [wrong] with her intelligence and her feet are like the hooves of a mule." Thus, Solomon wanted to test her intelligence by disguising her throne and wished to examine her feet by building the palace. When Bilqīs arrived, [*she*] *was asked: Is this the likes of your throne? She said: It is as if it were* (Qur'ān xxvii:42). Then she compared the [altered] throne to the one she had left behind in a chamber of seven locked gates—she retained the keys. She did not confess that [it was hers] nor did she deny it, whereupon Solomon knew the extent of her intelligence. Al-Ḥusayn b. al-Faḍl related: She was uncertain of them and they of her, so she retorted curtly to their questions. If they asked, "Is this your throne?" She would simply say, "Yes!"

Solomon spoke: *Knowledge was brought to us* of her obedient arrival *min qablihā,* that is, [knowledge was brought to us of her] *prior to her* coming. *For we were Muslims,* obedient and subservient to God, may He be exalted (Qur'ān xxvii:42). This is the interpretation of Mujāhid and others. Some maintain, however, that the statement is [not Solomon's but] Bilqīs's. Upon seeing her throne in Solomon's presence, she said, "I recognize this. *Knowledge was brought to us* verifying the prophethood of Solomon by wonders *prior to this* [min qablihā]," that is, *prior to this* wonder. *For we were Muslims,* that is, we had been guided to you in accordance with your command [even] before we came to you.

When she arrived in Solomon's presence, *she was told: Enter the court* (Qur'ān xxvii:44)! The reason for this was as follows: When Bilqīs drew near in search of him, Solomon ordered the satans to build him a court (*ṣarḥ*). That was a palace (*qaṣr*) of glass resembling white waters in which they placed [real] water stocked with fish beneath the [floor]. Following that, he had his throne placed along the central axis (*fī ṣadrihi*). Then he sat, the birds, jinn, and humans arrayed about him.

He ordered the construction of the court because the satans said to one another, "Whomsoever God has made subservient to Solomon, He has made subservient [according to His wish]. Bilqīs is the Queen of Sheba. If Solomon marries her, she will give him a son, and [our] servitude [to the prophet] will forever be unbreakable." Hence, they wished to incite him against her. And so they said, "Her feet are like the hooves of a mule and she has hairy ankles, all because her mother was a jinni." Solomon wished to learn the truth concerning that and to look at her feet and ankles. So he ordered the building of the court.

Wahb b. Munabbih related: Solomon built the court only to test her intelligence and understanding. Thus, he presented her with a puzzle just as she did him in sending the lads and maidservants in order that he might distinguish between the males and females. When Bilqīs arrived, she was told: *Enter the court! When she saw it, she reckoned it to be a pool* most of which was filled with water. *And* so, *she uncovered her ankles* (Qur'ān xxvii:44) to wade through the water on her way to Solomon. Solomon gazed at her. Behold! She had the most beautiful ankles and feet that any human could have, but her ankles were most certainly hairy. When Solomon saw that, he turned his eyes from Bilqīs and called out to her that *it is a court made smooth with slabs of glass* (Qur'ān xxvii:44) and there [actually] is no water [on the surface]. When she was seated, she said to him, "O Solomon, I wish to ask you something." "Ask," he responded. She continued, "I wish to ask you about [drinking] water which is neither in the ground nor in the skies." Now, when something came up that Solomon did not know, he asked the humans. If they had knowledge of that, good and well, if not, he would ask the jinn. If they knew, fine, and if not, he would ask the satans. So he asked the satans about her question and they said, "Simple! Order horses to race and then fill the vessels with their sweat." Solomon replied, "The sweat of horses." "Correct," she said. She continued [to probe], "Tell me about your Lord's [very] being." At that, Solomon leapt from his throne, prostrated himself, and lost consciousness. She stood aside as his contingents broke ranks [in panic], whereupon Gabriel came to him and said, "O Solomon, your Lord is speaking to you. Whatever you want is yours." The prophet answered, "O Gabriel, my Lord Knows better of what she said." The angel then proclaimed, "God orders you to return to your throne. Then you will send for her and those of your contingents and hers that were present [when she asked her question]. You will ask her and them as well what she asked of you."

Solomon returned to his throne and when they [that is, all who had been present] settled down about him, he inquired of Bilqīs, "What was it that you asked me about?" "About water that is neither in the earth nor in the sky," she responded. He continued, "What else did you ask?" "I asked nothing else," she said. Following that he asked [the same of] the contingents and they responded as she did, for God, may He be exalted, caused them to forget her query. Thus, God protected Solomon from having to answer.

Now, Solomon called upon her to become a Muslim. Having witnessed what had happened concerning the hoopoe, the gifts, the messengers, the throne, and the court [of glass], she responded affirmatively saying: *My Lord! I have wronged myself* through unbelief. *I submit through Solomon to Allāh, the Lord of the Universe* (Qur'ān xxvii:44).

The authorities disagree as to what happened to Bilqīs after her conversion to Islam. Most report: When Bilqīs became a Muslim, Solomon wished to marry her. But, when he mulled over the idea, he became disenchanted; that was because of her thick ankle hair. "How disgusting this is," he said. Then he asked the humans, "How is [ankle] hair removed?" "With a razor," they answered. The woman protested, "No blade has ever touched me." So Solomon was against [using] a razor. He said, "She'll cut her ankle." He turned to the jinn, but they responded, "We don't know [how to remove hair without a razor]." Finally, he asked the satans who feigned ignorance and said the same. When pressed by Solomon, however, they said, "We'll employ a technique for you that will make her ankles appear like highly polished silver." And so, they prepared her depilatory and bath.

Ibn 'Abbās related: That was the first time a depilatory was used. Solomon then married her. Ibn Maymūnah related [a tradition] based on his chain of authorities going back to Abū Mūsā and then the Prophet, who said, "The first to take [hot] baths was Solomon." When he was backed up against the [scalding] wall, he remarked, "Ow! That's a sign of God's chastisement."

The authorities [that is, those who believed that the prophet and queen had wed] reported: Solomon was very much in love with Bilqīs when he married her and established her [as ruler] over her dominion. At his command, the jinn build three fortresses in the land of Yemen, the likes of which were never seen as regards height and grandeur. They were: Salḥīn, Ghumdān and Baynūn. Following that, he would travel back and forth from Syria to the Yemen, visiting her once a month and remaining for three days—that was after he returned her to her domain.

Muḥammad b. Isḥāq reported the following on the authority of some scholars quoting Wahb b. Munabbih: Solomon said to Bilqīs when she submitted to Islam—his business done with her—"Choose a man from your own people so that I might marry you off to him." She answered, "O prophet of God, should the likes of me marry among [mere] men when I have already possessed such authority as I have in my domain and among my people." "Yes," he said, "submission to Islam requires that you not prohibit what God has declared as lawful." "If there is no other way," she replied, "marry me off to Tubba' the Elder, King of Hamdān." And so, he married them. He returned her to the Yemen and established Dhū Tubba' as ruler there. When he did that, he summoned Zawba'ah, the commander (*amīr*) of the Yemenite jinn and said, "Do whatever I require of you for Dhū Tubba' in the Yemen." The latter remained there, ruling with a free hand until Solomon died.

When the year had passed and word of Solomon's death reached the jinn, one of them came forward and crossed Tihāmah. Then, when he was in the inner reaches of the Yemen, he cried out at the top of his lungs, "O noble jinn, Solomon, the Prophet of God, has died, so raise up your hands." At that, the jinn made off for two massive rocks where they wrote the following inscription in the *musnad,* that is, the Ḥimyarite script:

> We built Salḥīn and Baynūn
> We built Sirwāḥ and Mirwāḥ and
> Fanqūn and Hindah, Hunaydah and Dalūm.
> These were fortresses in the Yemen built by
> The satans for Dhū Tubba'. Were it not for

Someone crying out in Tihāmah, they
Would not have raised their hands.

The jinn were thus set free and dispersed as the rule of Dhū Tubba‘ and Bilqīs came to an end with that of Solomon. [As to the truth of these divergent views] God knows best.

J. *Passages from al-Kisā'ī*

(Solomon's Birth)

Wahb b. Munabbih related: When David had been confirmed as king and prophet, he looked to the heavens and said, "O God! My Lord! You have given me of your kingdom and have blessed me with your grace. I now ask you to give me a righteous son so that he may inherit these and succeed me." At that, God revealed the following to David, "I have already responded to your prayer and have fulfilled your request." David received the glad tidings (*istabashara*) and rejoiced thereupon. At the time, David already had all his other children: Absalom, whose mother was Saul's daughter, Amnon, Ibhar, Adonijah, Shepatiah, Ithream, Elishua, Shobab, Nathan, and Daniel. David arose and bathed and following that entered into the presence of his wife Bathsheba daughter of Jeshua. He penetrated her, whereupon she became pregnant with Solomon.

A call went out, "O Iblīs! On this night, a man has been conceived. He will be responsible for your sorrow and your children shall be his servants [*khādim*]." Iblīs became filled with rage and gathered the ‘ifrīts and satans from the East and West and informed them of what he had heard. Then he said to them, "Sit tight here until I come to you with news." Following that, he went to David and behold, the standards of the angels had already been set up around David's Tower. An unseen herald proclaimed, "Bathsheba is pregnant with Solomon, who will rule the kings of mankind." And so, Iblīs asked the angels, "Who is this Solomon?" They answered, "David's son, at whose hands you and your seed shall perish." Iblīs then returned to his troops melting from grief as a lead is melted by fire.

When the pregnancy ran its course, Solomon's mother gave birth. She looked at him and behold she saw that he was exceedingly fair skinned, had a round face, delicate eyebrows, and the most mature eyes. Radiating from his visage was a dazzling light. The satans lost their senses completely and were as if dead for seventy days. As for Iblīs, he sank into the Great Sea, where he remained submerged for seventy days. Then he emerged and went ashore where he saw the world laughing and the wild animals bowing towards David. The latter hastened to his house and saw the angels arranged in order of rank, proclaiming, "O David! Since our Lord has created us, we have descended from the heavens and come to earth [as a group] only for the birth of Abraham and for this birth of your son Solomon." With that, David fell fully prostrate. He rendered effusive thanks to his Lord and offered a great sacrifice.

Ka‘b continued: The earth laughed on the day Adam first walked upon it and it continued to laugh until Cain killed his brother Abel. Then it did not cease crying until

Abraham was born. It laughed [again] until he was thrown into the fire and then it cried continuously until Solomon was born.

(Excerpts on the Prophet's Childhood)

When Solomon reached the age of three, David ordered food brought and summoned to his presence Israelites who were reciters of scripture. Whenever David recited something from the Psalms or Torah, Solomon commited it to memory instantly until he [that is, Solomon] absorbed the Torah in less than a year. By the time he was four years old, he performed one hundred *rak'ah*s a day while reciting a verse from the Psalms and the Torah. When he walked, he would hear all about him and from below, "Blessed are you O son of David! You have been granted a domain to minister [for God] the likes of which had not been granted your ancestor Adam." As a result, David sought Solomon's counsel in all matters and ruled in accord with his advice.

It is reported that one day, his mother saw an ant on his garment and said, "Kill it!" He picked it off his garment and replied, "Every creature will have its say on the Day of Resurrection. I would not wish this ant to say, 'Solomon, the son of David killed me.'"

Wahb related: One day, when Solomon was in the presence of his father, a dove appeared landed in front of him [that is, Solomon]. The dove spoke, "O son of David! I am one of the doves of this house but I have not been given any chicks to hatch." So Solomon passed his hand along her womb and said, "Go forth and may God bring forth seventy chicks from your womb. May your progeny increase until the Day of Resurrection." It was a turtledove and all the turtledoves that have been and will be born until the Day of Resurrection are descended from that one.

The Israelite chieftains saw [young] Solomon sitting in his father's presence and they became jealous. So God revealed to David that he should make Solomon a preacher in order that he might allow the chieftains to hear [for themselves] the wisdom that God had graciously bestowed upon Solomon and know thereby his superiority to them. As a result, David gathered the various holy men from the wilderness and clothed Solomon, who was then twelve years old, with the white woolen garb of a prophet. Then Solomon was given permission to ascend the pulpit of his father. Having done that, he praised God and mentioned His greatness and power. Following that, he spun a parable for each one of them, citing the life of Adam as well as the chronicles of Seth, Abraham, Enoch, and Moses. Then he offered commentary on the Torah and the Psalms so that the people were amazed at his eloquence, his knowledge, and his wisdom. At that point, Solomon bowed before God in gratitude saying, "Praise be to Him who bestows wisdom on whomever He wills."

The people then came to David and said, "Indeed, it is right for someone such as him to sit at your right side when you render judgment. And it is right for you to accept his advice for he speaks with wisdom as regards all matters." Thereafter, they looked upon Solomon with the utmost of respect.

(Solomon's Test)

When Solomon was seventeen years old, Gabriel came down to David with a gold scroll and said, "O David! God greets you and says unto you, 'Gather your children and read to them the riddles contained in this scroll. Whoever gives you the correct answers will be your successor.' David then informed his [older] sons of what Gabriel had said but none among them knew the answers. They confirmed in this way their failure [to achieve their father's rule]. And so, David turned to Solomon, "O my boy! I shall be asking you these riddles. Tell me what you think." "Ask, my father," said Solomon, "I hope to God that He will guide me rightly to the answers." (And so, David presented Solomon with all the riddles and when the latter answered) David confirmed that he had been correct as regards each and every riddle. When the matter of the riddles had ended, David said to the learned men, "Do you reject anything that my son Solomon has said?" They responded, "We reject nothing." At that, David proclaimed, "I am satisfied that Solomon will be my successor, to rule over you after I am gone. What do you say [to that]?" They answered, "Yes! We are satisfied with him."

(The Story of Solomon's Investiture)

When David died, [the angel] Gabriel came down to Solomon and said to him, "Verily God asks you, 'What is more precious to you—rule or knowledge?'" Solomon prostrated himself before the Lord and answered, "O Lord! Knowledge is more precious to me than rule." God then revealed to Solomon, "Indeed, I am giving you rule, knowledge, reason, and a perfect disposition."

Following that, the four winds came and stood before Solomon saying, "O Prophet of God! Allāh has indeed made us subservient to you. So, ride us to any place you desire." Then came the beasts of prey and birds saying, "God has already given us orders to be obedient to you. So, do with us as you please." With that done, Gabriel came forward with the seal of the Vice Regent which he had taken from Paradise. It shone as brightly as the Milky Way and had four points. On the first was written: "There is no God but Allāh." The second: "Everything perishes save his countenance." The third contained: "His is the Kingdom, the Power, and the Glory." And on the fourth was written: "Blessed be God, the Best Creator."

Each point signified [dominion over] a different order of creation. Thus, the first was for the rebellious jinn; the second was for the beasts of prey and the birds; the third for the monarchs of the earth; and the fourth for the inhabitants of the seas and mountains. Gabriel gave the ring to Solomon and said to him, "This is the gift of rule, the emblem of the prophets, [the symbol of] humankind's obedience as well as that of the jinn, the beasts of prey, and the rest of [God's] creations." That [investiture] took place on Friday, the third day before the end of the month Ramaḍān.

When the signet ring fell into Solomon's palm, he was unable to look at it because of the intense brilliance that it emitted—that is, until he recited, "There is no God but Allāh." Having said those words, he was able to look at it. God had given him the power to do so and [also] added light to his vision. The seal had been Adam's while he was in Paradise. But when he was expelled, the signet ring flew from his finger and returned to Paradise [where it remained] until Gabriel brought it down to Solomon.

Solomon then commanded the Israelites to take up arms and they all answered his call. He had with him twelve thousand breastplates made by his father David. Following that, Gabriel spread one of his wings to the east and the other to the west, whereupon the jinn and satans swarmed from everywhere. The angel moved them along as does a shepherd his flock until they appeared before Solomon. There were represented that day by four hundred and twenty sects, each with its own distinctive religious observance. The prophet looked at their diverse appearances; there were among them blonds, redheads, whitehaired, and black. Some of them took the forms of horses, mules, donkeys, and other pack animals; others were like wild animals. Among them were those resembling lions, hyenas, dogs, and [other] beasts. There were those with trunks, tails, long ears, and hooves. There were bodiless heads and headless bodies.

Solomon began asking them about their tribes and names and of their kin and dwelling places. Then he said, "I see that you have different forms and yet your father is al-Jann." "O prophet of God," they replied, "That is because of our sins and because Iblīs has comingled with us. And so, our religious observances have become diverse. There are those among us who worship fire, others who worship trees or the sun or the moon." Each one of us says that he is right." At that, Solomon put his stamp upon their necks and sent them off respectively to their dwelling places.

None disobeyed him except Ṣakhr the Rebellious. He had hidden himself on an island in the sea. As for Iblīs, he remained without assistants and on the run until Solomon found him and said, "What makes you think you can escape me?" Iblīs replied, "I did not humble myself to your progenitor Adam so why should I humble myself to his progeny? Indeed, I have been made immortal until the first blast of the [heavenly] trumpet and have been given mastery over the sons of Adam and daughters of Eve, save those whom God protects from me."

Solomon dispersed the rebellious jinn, assigning to them various tasks of working with iron, copper, wood, and stone. They were given the job of building villages, cities, and fortresses. He ordered their women to spin silk, cotton, linen, and wool, and to weave carpets. He also had the women of the jinn make clay bowls and pots—a thousand men could eat from each of those bowls. He put a contingent to work diving for coral and pearls in the sea. Some of the jinn were ordered to dig wells and extract treasures from the depths of the earth. Following that, Solomon created [distinctive] emblems, each reflecting one of four orders of jinn. The warrior jinn wore green turbans and red belts; the servants in the ranks wore immaculate multicolored garments. There were also the servants of the Israelites and those assigned to other tasks. [They too were distinguished by their raiment.]

(Solomon's Temple)

God commanded Solomon to build the temple at the Ascension Rock [where Muḥammad later made his night journey to heaven]. And so, he gathered the rebellious satans and the demons (*'ifrīt*) among the jinn as well as the wise men. He singled out the satans for cutting the stones, laying marble, and similar tasks. The prophet then ordered that the foundations be dug until they reached water. At that, he gave the command to build the temple [itself], but the water forced the foundations to give way. As a result, the jinn made spheres of copper and lead upon which they wrote, "There is no God but Allāh." As a result, the foundations became firm, and the structure was raised.

The people complained of the din created by the cutting of the rock. So Solomon asked, "O ye rebellious [jinn]! Do you know how to cut rock without making noise?" "We don't," they replied, "but Ṣakhr the Rebellious has the expertise for that." And so, Solomon said to the satans, "Bring him to me!" They answered, "We have no means of forcing him but we can trick him. That is, he comes at the beginning of each month to drink from a [certain] spring. The idea is to fill the spring with wine so that he'll become intoxicated, at which point, we'll seize him and bring him to you." Solomon then gave them permission to carry out that scheme.

They filled the spring with wine. When Ṣakhr became thirsty, he came to the spring and, finding it filled with wine, he shouted, "O good wine! You dull the senses and make the wise ignorant. By God! I will not partake of you." And so, he left the wine untouched and went on his way. But his thirst fatigued him, so he came back a second day only to find the spring as it had been [the day before]. He called out, "Of what use is precaution against fate?" Then he looked at the spring ravaged by thirst and drank all its contents. At that, the satans came forward, fettered him in irons, and transported him to Solomon.

Tongues of flame leapt from his nostrils, but when he saw Solomon's ring, he prostrated himself and said, "O prophet of God! As great as your dominion is, it will pass from you." "You speak the truth," said Solomon. "Now tell me what is the most wondrous thing about humankind that you have witnessed." Ṣakhr replied, "One day I passed by a man who had bound a pack animal with a threadbare rope nearly eaten through by locusts. I realized that he lacked sense. Then I passed by another man espousing the occult. As God knows best of hidden things, I was amazed as well by his lack of sense. Solomon laughed and reminded him how the people complained about the noise made by the jinn when they cut stones. "O prophet of God! I know how to handle that," said Ṣakhr. He went on, "Bring me an eagle's nest and eggs." And so, these were brought to him. Ṣakhr now called for a glass dome, which he placed over the eagle's nest. When the eagle came, it could not reach its nest, and so it flew east and west. Then it returned the following day with a piece of a diamond (*sāmūr*), which it dropped on the glass thus splitting the dome. Following that, the eagle made off with its nest leaving the stone behind, whereupon Ṣakhr brought the diamond to Solomon. The latter asked, "Where did you get this stone." "O prophet of God!" answered the jinni, "It is from a lofty mountain situated at the most western reaches [of the earth]—an inaccessible mountain called Jabal Sāmūr." Solomon then dispatched the satans to that place and they gathered all the stones that they needed. And so, they [were able to] cut stones without [anyone] hearing noise.

Solomon then took to building the temple and he made it a tall structure which he covered with onyx and a variety of precious stones. In it he placed a thousand marble columns each of which featured a lamp of reddish gold. He finished building it in forty days because every day he employed a thousand demons, and an equal number of satans and humans. Following that, he hung in it a thousand lamps of reddish gold with lustrous silver chains. Then he offered a magnificent sacrifice, saying, "My Lord and Master! You have indeed clad me in the garments of prophethood and have granted me a great domain. I would ask You to grant me in building Your holy house that which You granted Your friend Abraham in building the Ka'bah." The angels then requested permission of their Lord to visit the temple and God agreed. It is said that they visit there every year, every month, and every Friday and that it will be a place of blessings until the Day of Resurrection. Solomon then selected servants for the temple from among the Israelites. Later, rulers from the most distant regions heard of the temple and came to visit and were amazed at its beauty and [the quality of] worksmanship.

Following that, Solomon had twelve thousand chairs built of ivory and aloes wood. Each scholar had his own chair, and none of these seats was higher than any other. For Solomon, Ṣakhr made a throne of magnificent ivory with legs of gold. On it he placed representations of wild beasts, lions, and birds. It was encrusted with pearls each of which was the size of an ostrich egg. On the first step was a gold grapevine with emerald leaves and clusters of precious stones made to look like grapes. To the right and left of the throne, he fastened palm trees of gold upon which were peacocks, birds [of various sorts], and vultures. They were hollow and encrusted with precious stones, and when the wind blew through their hollow cavities, they whistled, giving off bird songs the likes of which no one had ever heard. On the second step, he fastened [representations of] two mighty lions and on the third birds, peacocks, and eagles. When Solomon would mount the first step, the vultures and birds would flap their wings and spray musk over him. Then when he ascended the second step, the wild beasts and lions would roar and a voice behind him could be heard saying, "O son of David! Thank God for this mighty domain that He has granted you." When he climbed the fifth step, he heard the voice of a herald proclaim: *Indeed God sees what you do* (Qur'ān ii: 110). When he reached the seventh step, the throne seat itself rotated about the attached elements, and when it stopped rotating, Solomon sat upon it as the birds sprayed musk and ambergris on him.

Whenever litigants came to the prophet seeking judgment, the lions would gaze at them as if they were speaking [about them], the birds would flap [their wings], and the jinn would cause them to be apprehensive. The litigants were then so awestruck that they were powerless to do anything but tell the truth.

(The Origins of Bilqīs)

Following Ibrāhīm al-Rākis there ruled Sharākh b. Sharāḥīl the Ḥimyarite who decreed that his subjects provide him each week with a maiden from among their daughters. He would ravage the girl and then return her to them in exchange for another. The king had a wazīr called Dhū Sharkh b. Hudād, a strikingly handsome man who was an avid hunter. One day, the wazīr happened upon a heavily wooded place where he heard voices reciting poetry. He knew therefore that this was Valley of the Jinn. And so, he called out in his strongest voice, "O assemblies of the jinn! I would spend the night with you. Do let me hear your poems." And so, they recited a verse of their poetry, whereupon 'Umārah, daughter of the king of the jinn, appeared before him. The wazīr was smitten at first sight, but she disappeared from his view. Nevertheless, she had captured his heart. "Who is this maiden?" he inquired of them. "She is the daughter of our king," they said. He then remarked, "I would like you to take me to the king so that I may see him."

The jinn escorted him to their ruler. The wazīr spoke, "Long life and honor to you O generous ruler!" The king replied, "We say the same to you. Now, who are you?" "I am the wazīr of the master of the city of Sheba," he answered. [The wazīr continued,] "Would you marry me to your daughter?" The king approved of him because he was strikingly handsome, and so he gave her to him in marriage. The wazīr had intercourse with her and she became pregnant with Bilqīs.

Wahb b. Munabbih relates: When her pregnancy ran its course, she gave birth to a girl as radiant as the brightest sun. The girl was named Bilqīs. Later, when her mother died, the child was raised by the daughters of the jinn and grew up to be so beautiful that she was called "Venus of the Yemen." When she reached maturity, she said to her father, "O father of mine! I have grown to despise living among the jinn. Would you not take me away to the land of the humans?" "O daughter!" he said tenderly, "The humans have a tyrannical ruler who angrily ravages the virgins of their land. I fear for you because of him." She then said, "O father of mine! Build me a palace outside his city and install me there. You shall then see what happens between me and the king." And so, her father built her a palace, provided her with an ivory throne, and moved her into that place where she remained for a long time.

Afterward, news of her reached the king and he rode off and approached the palace. He had his stewardess enter and after seeing how strikingly beautiful was Bilqīs, she hurried back to the king and informed him of that. As a result, the king summoned his wazīr and declared, "You built this palace and did not inform me of that." "O king!" he responded, "I built this palace a short while ago when the daughter of the king of the jinn was blessed with this child—the mother has since died. She despised living among the jinn so I moved her into this palace." The king then said, "I want you to marry her to me." "Gladly!" replied the wazīr, "But I must first ask her for consent." And so, the wazīr returned to his daughter saying, "O daughter! What I feared for you has befallen me. The king has asked me for your hand in marriage." At that, she declared, "O father of mine! Marry me to him! I'll kill him before he lays a hand on me!" The wazīr then returned to the king and informed him of her consent.

The king was gladdened by what he heard and wrote her a letter in which he said, "As a result of your reputation [for great beauty], I fell madly in love with you [even] before setting eyes on you. When you have read my letter, hasten to me." Bilqīs replied, "I do indeed long to [come and] see your face, but this palace of mine is constructed by the jinn and I have already installed in it for you a number of conveniences [*marātib*] suitable for the likes of yourself. [So why not first come to me?]" When her letter arrived, he sprang into action and put on his finest garments, which he had laid out. Then he rode off accompanied by his nobles. When he approached the palace, Bilqīs told her father to go out to the king and inform him to enter the palace alone. And so, her father went out and informed the king of that, whereupon he dismissed his troops and made for the palace by himself.

The palace had seven gates, each attended by a daughter of the jinn as radiant as the rising sun. They held trays of gold containing silver and gold coins. Bilqīs instructed them to shower the king with them when they caught sight of him. Thus, when the king entered, he was showered by coins, causing him to say to each one of them, "Are you my beloved?" At that point, they answered, "No! I am [only] her servant. You have yet to see her." This went on until he finally reached the last of the gates.

When Bilqīs emerged and he saw her striking beauty, he just about lost his senses. She set for him a gold table filled with all varieties of food. "I have no need of these," he said. So she had drinks brought and poured them for him; he partook of them and began to moan. Then she offered him wine and he fell into a drunken stupor, laying absolutely motionless on the ground. At that, Bilqīs arose and cut off his head. She then turned to her servant girls and ordered them, "Take this ungrateful cur and hide his body in the sea. Tie him to a rock lest he surface above the water." The servants carried out her commands.

Following that, she sent word to the king's treasury with instructions to transfer all the wealth and money contained therein. When the letter reached the treasury, the officials gathered all the wealth that they had and sent it along to Bilqīs's palace. With that done, she summoned the wazīrs. Bilqīs offered them drinks, which they imbibed, and then she declared, "The king says that you should send him your women and daughters." They became furious and retorted, "All [the women] that he's had up till now aren't enough for him?" When she realized that their anger had taken control of them, she said, "I shall return [to him] and apprise him of your anger." Then she absented herself for a while. When she returned, she told them, "I informed him of what you had said and he replied, "I'll have it no other way.'" They became [even] more furious, whereupon she said, "Do you wish for me to kill him, ridding you all thereby of his evil, in which case I would rule over you?" They agreed to her proposal and swore allegiance to her. Then she took leave of them [once again] and when she returned after a while, she had the king's head. They were overcome with joy and appointed her their ruler. And so, she ruled for seventeen years.

(Solomon and the Hoopoe)

Wahb b. Munabbih related: One day, Solomon was journeying on his [flying] carpet. The hoopoe, who was his guide to water, said to himself, "It's time for Solomon to land and ask me to find water." So he took to the high reaches of the sky to locate a place with water, when suddenly he came upon the hoopoe of the Yemen. And so, he asked the latter, "From where have you come?" He answered, "I am from the region of the Yemen," whereupon Solomon's hoopoe declared, "I come from Syria, from the army of Solomon, ruler of humans and jinn." "As for me," said the Yemenite hoopoe, "in my country there is a mighty queen who commands ten thousand princes [*qā'id*], each of whom commands a like number of fighting men. Were you to journey with me to the Yemen, you would see how she rules." At that, Solomon's hoopoe said, "Yes!" and went off with his compatriot to the Yemen. Finally, Solomon's hoopoe landed at the palace of Bilqīs where he observed her manner of rule.

Solomon had already discovered that the hoopoe was missing and could not find him. So he sent the vulture to bring the hoopoe to him. The vulture flew east and west and [finally] found him in hurried flight. Then he brought the hoopoe to Solomon. The latter was concerned that his feathers would be plucked and so he said, "O prophet of God! Remember that tomorrow you will be standing [and awaiting judgment] between Paradise and Hellfire." At that, Solomon let him go.

The hoopoe [then explained his absence, saying]: I come to you from Sheba with tidings true. *I have found a woman ruling over them. She has had something of everything bestowed upon her. I found her and her people bowing down before the sun rather than God* [etc.] (Qur'ān xxvii:22–24). *He* [Solomon] *said: We shall see if you have spoken the truth or are among the liars* (Qur'ān xxvii:27). Following that Solomon asked the hoopoe about water, and he replied, "O prophet of God! There is water beneath one of the legs of your throne." Solomon gave orders for the throne to be moved and the hoopoe then pecked away at the ground with his beak, whereupon water came gushing out. And so, Solomon and his cohort were able to perform the ritual ablutions and pray. When he was finished with prayer the prophet instructed the hoopoe: *Go with this letter of mine and deliver it to them. Then turn away* [but stay close to them] *and see what they come back with* (Qur'ān xxvii:28).

The prophet then called for gold quire and instructed Asaph b. Berechiah, "Write that *it is from Solomon and is: In the name of God the Merciful and Compassionate* [etc.] (Qur'ān xxvii:29). *Do not be haughty. Come to me submitting as Muslims*" Qur'ān xxvii:31). Following that, he sealed the letter with musk and gave it to the hoopoe who flew until he reached to Bilqīs's palace. He found her sleeping on her throne couch and dropped the letter on her chest. Then he flew to the aperture where he remained perched. It is also said that she awakened from her slumber and saw the hoopoe with the letter in his beak. And so, he tossed it to her.

She summoned her people and read them the letter. Then she said, "O my people! What do you think? We have been ordered to submit." *They said* [in response]: *We are possessed of fierce power and fighting spirit. But the matter is yours to decide* [etc.] (Qur'ān xxvii: 33). *She said: Indeed, when rulers conquer a city, they corrupt it, transforming the greatest of its people into the most debased* [etc.] (Qur'ān xxvii:34). She continued: *Indeed, I shall be sending them a gift and will see what the envoys bring back* (Qur'ān xvii:35). "If he is one of those insincere prophets who seeks material gain, we shall satisfy him with wealth and good riddance to him. But, if he is a true prophet, only our obedience will satisfy him." She then ordered that the gifts be made ready while the hoopoe observed all that she did.

The bird returned to Solomon and explained everything that had transpired. The prophet then summoned the jinn and instructed them saying, "This queen wishes to send me a gift of gold and silver. I want you to pave the review ground with alternating bricks of silver and gold." Bilqīs had already prepared for him one hundred gold bricks and an equal number of silver; one hundred young pages dressed in the attire of maidservants and one hundred servant girls dressed as slave boys. She also made ready a hundred horses with [saddle blankets of] magnificent brocade and silk patchwork. In a gold box, she placed a perfectly smooth pearl along with a unique piece of onyx that was unevenly perforated. The queen sent the gifts with one of her wazīrs with orders to watch his tongue in Solomon's presence.

In a letter to Solomon, she wrote: "I have sent you servant girls and slave boys to [see if you can] distinguish male from female without uncovering their private parts. I have sent as well a perfectly smooth pearl. I would like you to string it without using any implement. There is also a perforated piece of onyx through which I want you to run a thread. Finally, there is a jar. Fill it with water that has neither fallen from the sky nor sprung from the ground!"

When the wazīr came to Solomon and saw his review ground and the treasure with which it had been paved along with the horses tied round about, his heart sank. Then he entered into Solomon's presence and handed over the letter, but the prophet informed him of its contents before even bothering to read it. Then he called for a gold vessel filled with water and ordered the slave boys and servant girls to wash their hands. Slave boys trickle water on the backs of their hands and then let it run off the side; servant girls pour water on the inside of their forearms. Hence, Solomon was able to tell the difference between them. Following that, he called for the silkworm, who pierced the pearl and threaded the onyx. Finally, he called for horses and ran them until they sweat, whereupon their sweat was collected as water in a receptacle.

Solomon then turned to the wazīr saying, "Return to your mistress with your gifts and tell her: *You reach out to me with wealth. Has not God given me better than he has given to you?*" [etc.] (Qur'ān xxvii:36). And so, the wazīr returned with the gift(s) to Bilqīs and informed her of what he had seen as regards Solomon. She said to her people, "You now know that my idea was better than yours. By God! He *is* a prophet. We have no means of resisting him." At that, she gathered her clients and treasures and carried them with her, save her throne, which she locked behind seven gates. Thus, she proceeded to Solomon in order to pay obeisance to him.

The news reached Solomon and he asked his companions: *Which of you can bring me her throne before they come to me submitting as Muslims? An 'ifrīt said: I will bring it to you before you arise from your place* (Qur'ān xxvii:38–39). "I want it faster than that," Solomon replied. *The one who had knowledge of the book*—that is, Asaph son of Berechiah—*then spoke: I shall bring it to you in the twinkling of an eye* (Qur'ān xxvii:40). When the prophet saw the throne standing before him, he exclaimed: *This is the grace of my Lord* (Qur'ān xxvii:40). Then he said: *Disguise her throne for her. We shall see if she is truly guided* [etc.] (Qur'ān xxvii:41).

An 'ifrīt called out, "O prophet of God! I shall make for you a court of glass. Whoever sees it will think that it contains water stocked with fish." Solomon gave permission to have the court built. It had been mentioned to him that Bilqīs had hairy ankles [and he wanted to see if that was true]. When the 'ifrīt had finished, Bilqīs arrived and drew near the court. She saw her throne and was bewildered. [*She*] *was asked: Is this the likes of your throne? She said: It is as if it were* [etc.] (Qur'ān xxvii:42). Following that, she ascertained that it was indeed her throne.

When she drew near the court, *she reckoned it to be a pool* [of water]. *And* so, *she uncovered her ankles* (Qur'ān xxvii:44). Solomon then informed her that *it is a court made smooth (with slabs of glass). She said: My Lord, I have wronged myself* [*with unbelief*]. *I submit through Solomon to Allāh, the Lord of the Universe* (Qur'ān xxvii:44). After that, Solomon married her and she bore him a son whose name was Rehoboam. The latter's arms reached his knees, which is a sign of leadership.

Wahb continued: Bilqīs remained with Solomon for seven years and seven months. Then she died and Solomon buried her beneath the walls of Palmyra, which is in the Land of Syria.

(The Daughter of the Defeated Island King)

News reached Solomon that a king from one of the islands of the sea—he was called Nūriyah—had attached to his service a contingent of jinn and satans. The prophet found that unbearable, and so he and his military forces took to his [flying] carpet until they looked down at King Nūriyah's island. Then he killed Nūriyah and, seizing the king's daughter, Shajūbah, he returned to Syria. Shajūbah was unbelievably beautiful. When Solomon proposed that she accept Islam, Shajūbah complied, whereupon the prophet married her and set aside a separate palace, which he designated her domicile.

She asked Solomon to order the satans to make her an image of her father and mother so she might take comfort [in their absence] and overcome her loneliness. And so, Solomon commanded Ṣakhr the Rebellious and he made images of the two in her palace. She began to bow down to them and Asaph son of Berechiah learned of this, whereupon he asked Solomon for permission to preach among the Israelites. And so, Asaph mounted the pulpit (*minbar*). He gave thanks to God and praised Him, and prayed for each of the prophets who preceded Solomon and lauded their virtues. But when it came time to mention Solomon, he immediately became silent and did not praise him. Then he climbed down from the pulpit. Solomon scolded him for that and Asaph retorted, "How can I praise you when you have married a woman who worships idols in your [own] house?" As a result, Solomon became enraged; he divorced Shajūbah and destroyed the two idols.

Ṣakhr the Rebellious built Solomon a palace along the coast and lived there with him. The jinni already knew that the secret of Solomon's dominion was in the prophet's signet ring, so he harbored secret intentions of obtaining it. Solomon had a maidservant called al-Amīnah, "the faithful one," who never left him. When he desired privacy with his women, he would hand over his ring to her for safekeeping. [One day,] when Solomon entered the women's quarters and handed over his ring to the maidservant as was his custom, Ṣakhr appeared to her, having taken on Solomon's form. He approached her for the ring and she turned it over to him thinking that he was Solomon. And so, Ṣakhr went and sat on Solomon's throne.

The prophet emerged, but God had already changed his form so that he now resembled Ṣakhr. When he approached the girl for the ring, she exclaimed, "God protect me against you O Ṣakhr! Solomon has already taken his ring so be off!" Thus, Solomon knew that he had given in to temptation and had been tried [for that], so he fled the palace.

Ibn 'Abbās related: Ṣakhr could handle neither Solomon's women nor his treasury. As a result the birds and wild beasts broke ranks with him, and the people began to hear stories of his behavior the likes of which were never linked to Solomon.

[Returning to the account of] Wahb b. Munabbih: Solomon grew hungry and entered a village where he said, "O people! I am Solomon! My dominion has been taken from me because of a sin [that I committed]. I'm hungry. Would you give me something to eat? God will surely return my dominion to me and I'll [then] reward anyone who gives me some food." Then Solomon called out, "O my Lord! You have afflicted the prophets [in the past] but never have you taken away their sustenance. O my Lord! Would you not have mercy on me for I shall return penitent to you."

Still, Solomon remained without tasting food for forty days. Then he found a piece of dry bread and went to the sea in order to moisten it. But a wave snatched it from his hand and it was gone. Following that, he found some fishermen and asked them for a piece of fish, but they drove him off saying, "We've never seen anyone more repulsive than you." "O people," he cried, "I am Solomon." At that, one of them came over to him and struck him on the head with a staff saying, "You tell lies about Solomon!" When that happened, the angels wept out of compassion for him and God told them to quiet down because this was an affliction of mercy and not one of torment.

Following that, God cast his compassion into the hearts of the fishermen and they gave him a fish. When Solomon split open this fish's belly, he found in it his signet ring. He then washed it and placed it upon his finger. As a result, his handsome features were immediately restored, and he went off seeking his palace. Everything that Solomon passed bowed down before him, including Ṣakhr the Rebellious, who then fled. Solomon sat on his throne, and the jinn and humans and the birds and the wild beasts all gathered about him as before. He had Ṣakhr fettered in irons and covered him with two boulders, which he sealed with his ring. With that done, the prophet ordered that he be thrown into a lake. It is said that he shall remain there until the end of time.

(Concerning the Death of Solomon and His Legacy)

Ibn 'Abbās relates: When Ṣakhr the Rebellious sat on Solomon's throne, he realized that the situation was temporary, and so he wrote a magic formula and placed it under the throne. Thus, when Solomon died, the satans said that Solomon was a sorcerer and that [the key to] his magic was under his throne. But the learned men told them, "This [document] is not the work of Solomon." [Later,] when God sent our Prophet Muḥammad, He revealed to him the truth about Solomon. The Jews of Medina had said, "Are you not startled by Muḥammad? How does he claim that Solomon was a prophet when he was but a sorcerer?" Hence, God revealed to Muḥammad: [*And when a messenger came to you from Allāh confirming what you already know* (that is, what is written in your own scripture), *a group of those who were given the Book, the book of God, cast it aside as if they did not know. And you follow what the satans were told concerning Solomon's rule*]. *Solomon was not an unbeliever* [etc.] (Qur'ān ii: 102).

It is said that Solomon lived for sixty years and that after him, the Israelites split into three groups: a group of apostates that embraced witchcraft; a group that remained [politically] neutral saying, "We'll follow no one after him"; and a group that followed Rehoboam, who was a king but no prophet. When the latter died, he was succeeded by his son Abijam, who was an obdurate tyrant. To him, God sent a prophet named Daniel—this, however, is not Daniel the Wise; he lived in the time of Nebuchadnezzar. Abijam, who called upon his people to worship idols, had a son called Asa. The latter was a believer who hid his faith out of fear for his father. When Daniel heard that, he dressed himself in a woolen cloak and went to the palace of Abijam the king only to discover that the king had died during the night. The prophet exclaimed, "Praise to Him that keeps him [Abijam] far from His mercy!" Then he said to Asa, the king's son, "Cling to the faith of your ancestors!" As the latter responded, "Yes," Daniel was gladdened. And so, Asa commanded his people to do what is right and eschew what is wrong, but they neither listened nor obeyed right up to his death.

Abbreviations

AIED	*Annales de l'Institut des Études Orientales*
AJSL	*American Journal of Semitic Languages*
AJSR	*Association for Jewish Studies Review*
AO	*Acta Orientalia*
AOS	American Oriental Series
ARNA	*Avot d^eRabbi Natan A*
ArO	*Archiv Orientalni*
BA	*Biblical Archeologist*
BAR	*Biblical Archeology Review*
BGA	Bibliotheca Geographorum Arabicorum
BJS	Brown Judaica Series
BI	Bibliotheca Islamica
BM	*Bet Ha-Midrash*
BR	*B^ereshit Rabbah*
BSOAS	*Bulletin of the School of Oriental and African Studies*
BT	*Babylonian Talmud*
BWANT	Beiträge zur Wissenschaft vom Alten und Neuen Testament
CAD	*Chicago Assyrian Dictionary*
CBQ	*Catholic Biblical Quarterly*
EI	*Encyclopedia of Islam*
EI²	*Encyclopedia of Islam*, New Edition
EJ	*Encyclopedia Judaica*
EM	*Encyclopedia Miqra'it*
ER	*Seder Eliahu Rabbah*
ET	*Encyclopedia Talmudit*
FHA	*Fragmenta Historicorum Arabicorum*
GAL	C. Brockelmann, *Geschichte der arabischen Litteratur*
GAS	F. Sezgin, *Geschichte des arabischen Schrifttums*
GO	*Graecolatina et Orientalia*
HSS	Harvard Semitic Studies
HTR	*Harvard Theological Review*
HUCA	*Hebrew Union College Annual*
IC	*Islamic Culture*
IEJ	*Israel Exploration Journal*
IFA	Israel Folklore Archives
IJH	*Israelite and Judaean History*, ed. J. Hayes and J. Miller
IJMES	*International Journal of Middle East Studies*
IOS	*Israel Oriental Studies*

IS	*Islamic Studies*
JA	*Journal Asiatique*
JAAR	*Journal of the American Academy of Religion*
JAOS	*Journal of the American Oriental Society*
JBL	*Journal of Biblical Literature*
JCS	*Journal of Cuneiform Studies*
JESAI	*Jerusalem Studies in Arabic and Islam*
JJS	*Journal of Jewish Studies*
JNES	*Journal of Near Eastern Studies*
JQR	*Jewish Quarterly Review*
JRAS	*Journal of the Royal Asiatic Society*
JSOT	*Journal for the Study of the Old Testament*
JSOTS	*Journal for the Study of the Old Testament,* Supplement Series
JSS	*Journal of Semitic Studies*
LOS	London Oriental Studies
MG	*Miqra'ot G*^{e}*dolot*
MGWJ	*Monatsschrift für Geschichte und Wissenschaft des Judenthums*
MR	*Midrash Rabbah*
MW	*Muslim World*
OC	*Oriens Christianus*
OIP	Oriental Institute Publications
PAAJR	*Proceedings of the American Academy of Jewish Research*
PAPS	*Proceedings of the American Philosophical Society*
PIFAO	Publications de l'Institut Française d'Archélogie Orientale du Caire
REI	*Revue des Études Islamique*
REJ	*Revue des Études Juives*
RMM	*Revue du Monde Musulman*
SI	*Studia Islamica*
SPDS	*Studies in the Period of David and Solomon,* ed. T. Ishida
TS	*Targum Sheni*
TTHS	Trierer Theologische Studien
VT	*Vetus Testamentum*
VTS	Supplements to *Vetus Testamentum*
WHJP	*World History of the Jewish People,* ed. E. A. Speiser et al.
WZKM	*Wiener Zeitschrift für die Kunde des Morgenlandes*
YJS	Yale Judaica Series
ZA	*Zeitschrift für Assyriologie*
ZAW	*Zeitschrift für die Alttestamentliche Wissenschaft*
ZDA	*Zeitschrift für Deutsches Altertum*
ZDMG	*Zeitschrift der Deutschen Morgenländischen Gesellschaft*

Notes

For complete bibliographic data, see Bibliography.

Chapter One

1. The most detailed accounts of the legendary King Solomon, those of M. Grünbaum and G. Salzberger, were produced around the turn of the century. A new and extensive literary treatment of the midrashic texts in relation to Muslim accounts is certainly in order. See M. Grünbaum, *Neue Beiträge zur semitischen Sagenkunde;* G. Salzberger, *Die Salomo-Sage in der semitischen Literatur.* On Solomon's wisdom and knowledge as described in the Hebrew Bible, see M. Noth, "Die Bewährung von Salomos 'Göttlicher Weisheit' "; R. B. Y. Scott, "Solomon and the Beginning of Wisdom."

2. I Kings 5:9–15.

3. I Kings 10:1. The word translated as "riddles" is Heb. *hidot,* which has that meaning in Judges 14:12–18 describing the riddles of Samson. See H. P. Müller, "Der Begriff 'Rätsel' im Alten Testament"; also the more broadly based but antiquated W. Hertz, "Die Rätsel der Königin von Saba"; A. Wünsche, *Die Rätselweisheit bei den Hebräern.*

4. I Kings 10:8.

5. This passage, which gave rise to sexual nuances (see chap. 1, sec. E), is probably based on the language of a business transaction. See M. Elat, "Trade and Commerce."

6. For a general review of the times, see B. Mazar, "The Era of David and Solomon"; and in the same volume D. N. Freedman, "The Age of David and Solomon." See also the studies of A. Malamat, "The Kingdom of David and Solomon and Its Contact with Egypt and Aram Naharaim"; "A Political Look at the Kingdom of David and Solomon and Its Relations with Egypt"; "Aspects of the Foreign Policy of David and Solomon." Also J. A. Soggin, "The Davidic-Solomonic Kingdom"; H. Donner, "The Interdependency of Internal Affairs and Foreign Policy during the Davidic-Solomonic Period"; E. W. Heaton, *Solomon's New Men: The Emergence of Ancient Israel as a Nation State.*

7. See I Kings 3:1, 11:1–3.

8. I Kings 11:3.

9. For a very concise description of the legendary Solomon, see L. Ginzberg, *Legends* 4:125–172.

10. The account of the queen's visit is found on pp. 40–41 of the Wilna edition edited by S. Buber and pp. 3–7 of the more recent and complete edition of Visotzky. See also chap. 6, sec. C.

11. Job 28:12.

12. *M. Mishle* (Buber), 40; (Visotzky), 4–5.

13. For the story of Lot's daughters, see Gen. 19:31–35.

14. *M. Mishle* (Buber), 41; (Visotzky), 5–6.
15. *M. Mishle* (Buber), 41; (Visotzky), 6–7.
16. The reference is to Num. 24:15–16 where Balaam exlaims: "The word of Balaam son of Beor . . . who sees the vision of the Almighty, prostrate but with opened eyes."
17. Job 12:3.
18. Edited with translation and brief annotation by S. Schechter in "The Riddles of Solomon in Rabbinic Literature." See also chap. 6, sec. C.
19. Gen. 38:6–30. For an extensive discussion of this tale, see M. A. Friedman, "Tamar, a Symbol of Life: The 'Killer Wife' Superstition in the Bible and Jewish Tradition."
20. I Kings 5:13. Note the specific reference to the famous cedars of Lebanon: "He [Solomon] spoke of trees from the cedar of Lebanon to the hyssop that grows out of the wall and he spoke of beasts, birds, things that crawl, and fishes."
21. Schechter, "Riddles," 349. For the sources of the midrash, see chap. 6, sec. C. Riddles 14, 15, and 17 reflect an Aramaic tradition. See trans. in Appendix C.
22. The *Targum Sheni* has been edited several times, but the editions have all been based on a limited number of manuscripts. These include the following texts, which I have been able to examine: L. Munk (Berlin, 1876), M. David (Cracow, 1898), and the text which is found in the Supplement to the volume on the Five Scrolls in *Miqra'ot Gᵉdolot,* the compendium of medieval Jewish exegetical traditions dealing with the text of the Hebrew Bible. The edition of *MG* is cited here as it is the most easily accessible to readers. A new edition based on far more variants than hitherto used is being prepared by B. Grossfeld, who provides a translation and commentary in his *The Two Targums of Esther.* P. Cassel has also translated the targum into English as Appendix 1 to his commentary on Esther; a more accurate translation into German accompanied by useful annotation is that of A. Sulzbach, *Targum Sheni zum Buche Esther.*
23. *Targum Sheni* in *MG* 6:2a–b. The interpolation of the Solomonic story into the tale of Ahasueras and Esther is suggested by Solomon's famous throne. It was upon this throne that Ahasueras sat during the celebrated feast.
24. Esther 1 esp. 7–10.
25. *MG* 6:2a. The symmetry between the absence of the bird and that of Queen Vashti in the biblical tale could not have been lost on readers of the text.
26. In contrast to the fabulous wealth of Solomon described in I Kings 11:14–24. Note verse 21: ". . . silver counted for nothing in Solomon's days."
27. *MG* 6:2b.
28. Note I Kings 11:24: "All the world came to pay homage to Solomon . . ."
29. See esp. chap. 3, sec. E.
30. That is Benaiah son of Jehoiada, the king's political ally and right hand.
31. Ginzberg understands the hair to signify that the queen was a jinni. See *Legends* 4:289 n.41.
32. *MG* 6:2b.
33. Ginzberg understands the references to bending and wailing as the sound of sails (made of flax) beaten by the wind. See *Legends* 6, 290–91 n.47.
34. I have relied on the recent edition of E. Yassif (Jerusalem, 1984). For other editions see *EJ* 4:548–50. The Yassif text, the most complete of the editions, is entitled *Sippure Ben Sira* and is henceforth referred to as Ps. Ben Sira, as distinct from the Ben Sira of antiquity. See also chap. 6, sec. C. The text of the Queen of Sheba's visit is found on pp. 217–18.
35. Ps. Ben Sira, 212–13.

36. Ibid., 214.

37. The reference is to II Kings 6:8–23 where the King of Aram besieges the Israelites and gives orders to have Elisha taken and brought to him. When the enemy horsemen and chariots ring the town, the prophet calls upon his Lord who blinds the Arameans. They were later led to the King of Israel who returned them to their master, "and the Aramean bands stopped invading the Land of Israel." Note also 7:1–7 where calamity befalls the horsemen of Ben Haddad.

38. Jer. 27:6.

39. Ps. Ben Sira, 214–15.

40. See Num. 22:15 in reference to Balak who sent "other dignitaries more numerous and distinguished than the first."

41. Ps. Ben Sira, 215–16.

42. I Kings 1:4–11.

43. Amos 7:14.

44. The Islamic prophetic tradition includes a number of biblical figures that are not considered as prophets among the Jews, David and Solomon among them.

45. *nes b^esid.* The meaning of this expression is problematic, but the author leaves no doubt that he speaks of a depilatory.

46. Ps. Ben Sira, 217–18.

47. Ibid., 217, invoking Gen. 27:11: ". . . my brother Esau is a hairy man but I am smooth skinned."

48. *BT Sanhedrin* 21a relates that David's son Amnon became entangled in the pubic hair of Tamar and became mutilated. As distinct from the daughters of Israel who had no pubic hair, Tamar, who was the daughter of a concubine (*y^efat to'ar*), was hairy. It is instructive of changing attitudes towards women in postbiblical times that Tamar is found blameworthy in this respect by the rabbis. The biblical account (II Samuel 13) clearly indicates that Amnon was infatuated with his half sister, the virgin Tamar, and following a ruse to get her to his bedside, he raped her. Her brother Absalom then concocted his own ruse and exacted revenge, taking Amnon's life. The linking of women's pubic hair to mutilation of men's genitalia is a powerful image reflecting the worst nightmares of castration and blaming women for that fear. Note also that, having raped Tamar, Amnon comes to loathe her. The attempt of F. van Dijk-Hemes to link this Tamar and her story to that of Tamar and Judah in Genesis 38 (the Genesis story is regarded by her as a "midrash" on II Samuel 13) strikes me as straining the clearest meaning of both texts. See her "Tamar and the Limits of Patriarchy," 153–55. On Tamar and Judah, see n. 19 above.

49. Ps. Ben Sira, 218.

50. Ibid.

51. Ibid., 231–32, 289–90; also Yassif's comments, 10, 13, 27, 25, 29, 58, 63ff., 126, 128, 143, 179–80. See also G. Scholem, "P^erakim hadashim me-inyane Ashm^eday v^e-Lilit"; *EJ* s.v.; and Ginzberg, *Legends* 6:289. A. Rösch's attempt to link etymologically Lilith with Bilqīs, the Arab Queen of Sheba in Islamic sources, cannot be accepted. See *Königin von Saba,* 28ff. See also chap. 1, sec. F for ancient parallels. For an example of a Jewish amulet from the Islamic period, see P. Schäfer, "Jewish Magic Literature in Late Antiquity and the Middle Ages," 84ff.

52. Gen. 1:28. For ancient and medieval interpretations of this text see the learned study of J. Cohen, *Be Fertile and Increase, Fill the Earth and Master It.*

53. Gen. 9:1–17. In articulating a monotheist vision of the world and how it came to be, the chosen people marked their universe as being different from that of the

"other," their pagan neighbors. Thus, thematically similar accounts that share details also reflect an intended dissonance. Note the ancient Mesopotamian flood story of Atrahasis with its cranky and capricious Gods, anxious lest they be well fed, sated, and rested; its demons that kill infants before they have a chance to grow into adulthood; and, more generally, its pronounced emphasis on population control rather than procreation. See W. G. Lambert and A. R. Millard, eds., *Atra-Hasis: The Babylonian Story of the Flood;* also E. Lichty, "Demons and Population Control." In contrast, the world, reflecting God's schema, is seen by the ancient Israelites as an orderly place imbued with an overarching moral vision that permeates covenantal arrangements between them and their Lord.

54. Gen. 17:1–2, 6–8.

55. Gen. 17:19–21, 28:3–4, 35:11–12, 47:27, 48:3–4; also Lev. 26:9; Jer. 3:16, 23:3, Ezek. 36:9–11. For a discussion of these passages, see Cohen, "*Be Fertile and Increase,*" 25–35. Of particular interest is Ezekiel's description of a restored Israelite state: ". . . the cities will be resettled and places laid waste shall be rebuilt [10]. I shall multiply men and animals and they shall increase and be fruitful. I will restore you to your previous state and shall make you more prosperous than before. I am the Lord [11]." The prophet's words suggest that the well-being of the Israelite polity depends on guarding more than religious or ideological boundaries. The anxiety about foreign ideas and practices (see n. 53 above) is matched by that of defending real frontiers against incursions by foreign armies. God's blessing is thus linked to the need of human resources. See C. Meyers, *Discovering Eve.* She contends that the hill country of premonarchic Israel was underpopulated and gave rise to a complex interweaving of societal resources and needs that encouraged large families. For Meyers, the end result was the value system embodied in the Genesis narratives, which valorize procreation. See also n. 56 for the need of human resources in the postbiblical period.

56. Cohen, *Be Fertile and Increase,* 124–165. The need to preserve a critical mass was pressing for Jewish communities in the postbiblical period, particularly after the complete dissolution of the Jewish polity. Thus the concern with the integrity of the family.

57. *BT Yebamot* 64a.

58. *MG* I Kings, 6:29; see also E. Ullendorff, *The Bawdy Bible,* 428. Note also *BT Sanhedrin* 21b, reflecting on the disaster occasioned by Solomon's marriage to the daughter of the Pharoah of Egypt (I Kings 3:1). At the moment of the union, the angel Gabriel descended and placed a reed in the sea. The reed then gathered a sand bank around it, upon which was built the great city of Rome. That is, the marriage to the foreign queen, the descendant of the former enemy of Solomon's ancestors, gave rise to the future enemies of Israel, the polity that would destroy the second temple and Jewish sovereignty. The long-range implications of involvement with foreign women are deemed deadly.

59. See chap. 6, sec. H and Appendix G.

60. IFA, 7248.

61. Prov. 12:4, 31:10; also Ruth 3:11. The number of scholarly and popular works dealing with women in the Hebrew Bible has grown enormously. A useful survey is that of P. Bird, "Images of Women in the Old Testament."

62. See Meyers, *Discovering Eve,* on the social transformations of Israelite women, particularly those under a monarchy that occasioned increased urbanization and a complex bureaucracy. Her observation that "urban women became the chief referents for

many of the negative images in the Bible, especially in Proverbs" strikes me as convincing (p. 191). See also Postscript.

63. Judg. 4:17–22, 5:24–27.

64. Judg. 5:30.

65. Jael's actions and the larger tale of the Israelite rebellion told in Judges 4–5, which has been cobbled together from two traditions, has been subjected to commentary by literary critics as well as philogists. See C. Rabin, "Judges V,2 and the 'Ideology' of Deborah's War"; M. Coogan, "A Structural Analysis of the Song of Deborah"; Y. Zakovitch, "Sisseras Tod"; B. Halpern, *The First Historians: The Hebrew Bible and History,* 76–103; M. Bal, *Murder and Difference: Gender, Genre, and Scholarship on Sisera's Death;* also her *Death and Dissymmetry,* 144–48, 197–231 esp. 206–17; M. Steinberg, *The Poetics of Biblical Narrative,* 270–83; also B. Margulies, "An Exegesis of Judges V 8a." The authors address the salient, indeed surprising feature of the biblical narrative, namely, the active role of the two women, Deborah and Jael, in bringing about Sisera's demise. See S. Niditch, "Eroticism and Death in the Tale of Jael"; R. Alter, *The Art of Biblical Poetry,* 43–39; Bal, *Murder and Difference* and *Death and Dissymmetry;* also J. Bruns, "Judith or Jael." Niditch (pp. 45, 52) describes Jael as "warrior and seducer, alluring and dangerous . . . and bloodthirsty" and states that "Jael is a symbolization of self-assertion, a force of change, one who breaks through from oppressive and suppressive forces." All that may be true for a current feminist reader, but it strikes me as teasing far more meaning out of this fragile text than it can comfortably yield. In this connection, see also G. Taylor, "The Song of Deborah and Two Canaanite Goddesses." Bal's reading of Judges 5, the Song of Deborah, as a female composition seems to me plausible but not nearly as significant to the larger understanding of the text as maintained by feminist scholars. Note the studies of R. Rasmussen; S. Hanselman; and J. Shaw in Chapter 2 of *Anti-Covenant,* 79–132. Rasmussen, "Deborah and the Woman Warrior," 85–93, argues that the female personae of the (original) tale have been made to share power in the current version by patriarchal writers. They certainly do share power in Judges 4,5. That there was an earlier tale with women linked to goddesses is a conjecture that requires much more support than Rasmussen can muster. As it were, the rabbis thought that Deborah had too much power (see n. 70 below). S. Hanselman, "Narrative Theory, Ideology and Transformation in Judges 4," 96–112, invokes recent literary theory to link Jael and Anath, the goddess warrior of Ugaritic mythology (see also Niditch, Taylor, and n. 97 below). The point, as in other feminist studies cited, is to find echoes of an ancient (proto-Israelite) religion which places emphasis on women as full "actants." The desire to establish activist credentials for women and, more generally, to give credence to an Israelite culture featuring goddesses who privileged the position of Israelite women is a function of a modern ideology that has been projected back into ancient times. The evidence in support of that culture is, at best, highly problematic. J. Shaw's "Constructions of Women in Readings of the Story of Deborah," 113–32, discusses the recasting of the story as a modern tale by feminist ideologues. I am left with the general impression that the literary critics, nonfeminists and feminists, underestimate how this text, cobbled together from two disparate traditions, resists the interpretation of modern readers and would have occasioned problems of interpretation for ancient readers as well.

66. Summarized in Ginzberg, *Legends* 4:35–39.

67. Judg. 4:9.

68. Judg. 5:7.
69. Judg. 5:28–31.
70. Ginzberg, *Legends* 6:196 n. 74 quoting *Zohar* 3:19b. As to whether women are eligible to be judges, see Tosafot *Niddah* 50a, and more generally Maimonides view on women ruling in his MT Hilkhot M^elakhim. Note also the disparaging remarks about women prophets in *BT Megillah* 14a.
71. *BT Megillah* 14a; *ER,* 48; also Ps. Jerome on Judg. 5:1 cited by Ginzberg, *Legends* 6:196 n. 73.
72. *BT Megillah* 14a; *ER,* 48.
73. *BT Megillah* 14b; *Pesahim* 66b; also *BR* 40.4, and *Zohar* 3:21b–22a cited in Ginzberg, *Legends* 6:196 n. 77.
74. For the story of Samson (Judg. 13–16), see J. Blenkinsopp, "Structure and Style in Judges 13–16"; J. Crenshaw, "The Samson Saga: Filial Devotion or Erotic Attachment?"; Bal, *Lethal Love,* 33–67, and her *Death and Dissymmetry,* 135ff., 200–206. See also B. Meredith, "Desire and Danger," 63–78, linking the stories of Samson and Delilah and Judith and Holefernes; J. C. Exum, "The Theological Dimension of the Samson Saga," and her "Aspects of Symmetry and Balance in the Samson Saga"; Margolith, "Samson's Riddles and Samson's Magic," and "More Samson Legends."
75. Judg. 15:15.
76. Judg. 16:21.
77. Judg. 16:5.
78. For Ahab and Jezebel, see I Kings 16:29–22:52, II Kings 9:19–37; also F. Anderson, "The Socio-Juridical Background of the Naboth Incident"; R. Bohlen, *Der Fall Nabot. Formen, Hintergrund und Werdegang einer alttestamentlichen Erzählung (I Kg. 21).* I have not seen H. Kraus, "Ahabs Gewalttat an Naboth (I Kon. 21): Das Eigentum als Problem evangelischer Sozialethik." For references to the rabbis' views of Jezebel, see Ginzberg, *Legends* 7:258.
79. According to the rabbis, Ahab and his family are to have no portion in the world to come. See for example *ER,* 49, where his fate is linked to the corrupt Jezebel. Note that in certain respects the rabbis make Ahab an analogue to Solomon, although I know of no explicit statement linking the two. Like Solomon, Ahab was considered a world conqueror and a king of extraordinary wealth. See *BT Megillah* 11a; *ER,* 9 (world conqueror) and *BT Berakhot* 61b; *ER,* 9 (wealth).
80. II Kings 10:30.
81. II Kings 10:22.
82. II Kings 10:32–37. The text indicates that Jehu originally intended to give her a burial as befits a queen, but only her skull, feet, and hands remained. At that, he recalled Elijah's prophecy: "The dogs shall devour the flesh of Jezebel in the fields of Jezreel; and the carcass of Jezebel shall be like dung on the ground in the field of Jezreel so that none will be able to say, 'This was Jezebel.'" The story may suggest that Jehu's comments to Joram about the queen's witchcraft and whoring (see n. 81 above) had a real sense of immediacy. I am informed by T. Abusch that, in his opinion, witches were not buried in ancient Mesopotamia for fear that they could rise from the dead. Rather, their bodies were mutilated and thrown to the dogs. On incantations and ceremonies against witches in the ancient Near East, see his *Reallexikon des Assyriologie,* s.v. Maqlu; T. Abusch, "The Demonic Image of the Witch in Standard Babylonian Literature"; also his "Mesopotamian Anti-Witchcraft Literature"; and his reworked studies with new material in *Babylonian Witchcraft Literature: Case Studies.*
83. Noting that she was the daughter of a king (I Kings 16:31), the rabbis considered

her a reigning queen along with Semiramis, Vashti, and her own daughter (or sister-in-law) Athaliah. That is to say, she was the king's consort. See *ER,* 51. The *Midrash Shᵉmuel,* 24, states that Jezebel was the daughter of priests (*komᵉrim*).

84. The biblical tradition alternately maintains that Athaliah was the daughter of Omri and of Ahab, Omri's son. II Kings 8:18 (daughter of Ahab), 26 (daughter of Omri), 11:1–20 (Omri's daughter); Chron. 21:6 (sister of Ahab). See J. Begrich, "Atalja, die Tochter Omris"; H. J. Katzenstein, "Who Were the Parents of Athaliah?"; J. Miller, "The Fall of the House of Ahab"; M. Noth's suggestion that the name Athaliah is derived from Akkad. *etelu* "to be manly" is an interesting gloss on her behavior given the scope of our inquiry on the Queen of Sheba. Whether Noth's suggestion is probable, I leave for others to decide. See his *Die israelitischen Personennamen im Rahmen der gemeinsemitischen Namengebung,* 191.

85. II Kings 11:1–20. In postbiblical times there is Salome Alexandra, who ruled as sole monarch following the death of her husband, Alexander Yannai. Accusations are recorded that she plotted the death of her first husband Aristobulus's brother but the veracity of the claim is considered doubtful. In any case she enjoyed the support of the populace, having been identified with the general prosperity of the times. See *EJ* s.v.; also S. Zeitlin, "Queen Salome and King Jannaeus Alexander."

86. See n. 79 above.

87. As regards the ancient Arab world, see N. Abbot, "Pre-Islamic Arab Queens." See also I. Eph'al, *The Ancient Arabs,* index, 249 s.v. Arab(s) with reference to queens. As regards the Queen of Sheba (pp. 63–64), he notes, "most scholars, assuming that this account has a kernel of authenticity, locate the homeland of Solomon's royal visitor in northern Arabia [as opposed to the Yemen] and connect her with the Sabaeans" known from Assyrian inscriptions and Job 1:15 (citing J. A. Montgomery, *Arabia and the Bible,* 180–81). Eph'al nevertheless believes that the queen was based in the south of Arabia and came to Solomon with regard to the lucrative spice trade mentioned in the biblical account. He does not seem to be convinced of his own argument which is based entirely on archeological evidence that has uncovered sedentary populations organized as kingdoms in southern Arabia at the beginning of the first millennium B.C.E. In any case, the Muslims certainly associated the land of Sheba and its queen with the Yemen. For the Jewish Salome Alexandra, see n. 85 above. Jews and Muslims were aware of women rulers from surrounding lands. It is not clear, however, what larger impressions may have been formed about female rulers as a result of that. For Muḥammad's derogatory comment about female rulers, see Tha'labī, *'Arā'is,* 313, among others. For postbiblical Jewish attitudes, see n. 70 above.

88. Lev. 19:31, 20:6, 20:27; Deut. 18:10–12; (prohibiting necromancers and wizards); I Sam. 28:3–24; I Chron. 10:13 (Saul consults the witch of En-dor, an act which earns the author's disapproval); II Kings 21:6 (Manasseh's practice of soothsaying and divination); Is. 8:19, 19:3, 29:4 (Israelite practices); II Kings 23:24 (Josiah against witchcraft). The practice of witchcraft was punishable by death according to both biblical and rabbinic legislation. See *BT Sanhedrin,* 53a.

89. The alleged uniqueness of biblical historiography and the ideology that informs it is a point much discussed. For a detailed summary of the issues, see J. van Seters, *In Search of History.* See also C. Conroy, "Hebrew Epic: Historical Notes and Critical Reflections"; F. M. Cross, *Canaanite Myth and Hebrew Epic;* the essays in R. Dentan, ed., *The Idea of History in the Ancient Near East;* J. J. Finkelstein, "Mesopotamian Historiography"; A. K. Grayson, "Histories and Historians of the Ancient Near East: Assyria and Babylonia"; and in the same volume, H. A. Hoffner, Jr., on the Hittites;

J. J. Roberts, "Myth versus History: Relaying the Comparative Foundations"; E. A. Speiser, "The Biblical Idea of History in Its Common Near Eastern Setting."

90. I Kings 11:1–14; also Deut. 7:3–4, 23:4 and Exod. 34:15–16. Intermarriage was forbidden to the Israelites after entering Canaan. See Josh. 23:12. The admonition of Solomon in Kings reflects the language of the Deutronimist reformist historians). The need for reforms would seem to indicate that intermarriage and the practice of foreign ways had spread deeply at least in certain circles.

91. II Kings 11:12–13.

92. For a survey of current views, see R. Oden, *The Bible Without Theology;* M. Smith, *The Early History of God.*

93. II Kings 21:6. In addition he "rebuilt the shrines that his father Hezekiah had destroyed; he erected altars for Baal and made a sacred post, as King Ahab of Israel had done. He bowed before all the host of heaven and worshiped them, and he built altars for them in the two courts of the House of the Lord" (3–5).

94. See n. 83 above.

95. Prov. 2:16–19; also 5:3–15, 7:5, and note also 9:18.

96. For Anath, see U. Cassuto, *The Goddess Anath;* W. F. Albright, *Yahwe and the Gods of Canaan;* A. S. Kapelrud, *The Violent Goddess.* On parallels to Proverbs, see R. Clifford, "Proverbs IX: A Suggested Ugaritic Parallel"; and more expansively B. Lang, *Wisdom and the Book of Proverbs: A Hebrew Goddess Redefined;* C. Camp, *Wisdom and the Feminine in the Book of Proverbs.*

97. Concerning various demonic creatures and a possible linkage to Lilith, see T. Abusch, *Reallexikon der Assyriologie,* s.v. Lamaštu esp. 4 and 5 and Lilu esp. 2; also *CAD,* s.v. for references to texts and additional bibliography. There seems to be little question that Lilith is an analogue of the more ancient demons and may indeed be related etymologically to Lilu (Lilitu). The fear of female demons who tamper with the biological imperatives of women and endanger men and humankind runs deep and has a long and widespread history.

98. See, however, P. Hayman, "Monotheism—A Misused Word in Jewish Studies." He argues that true monotheism was only achieved in the Middle Ages. The rabbis in his view were still battling the cumulative effects of paganism.

99. Pertaining to this view, see I. Jacobs, "Elements of Near Eastern Mythology in Rabbinic Aggadah." The residual effects of ancient Near Eastern cultures on rabbinic Judaism is a compelling subject worthy of serious study by scholars skilled in both disciplines.

100. For a concise summary of the story of Solomon and the Queen of Sheba in the Ethiopic and Western Christian traditions, see J. B. Pritchard, ed., *Solomon and Sheba.* Note that the story plays a central role in the Ethiopian national epic.

Chapter Two

1. As in Tha'labī, *'Arā'is,* 311ff.

2. For the importance of the juxtaposition of the queen's throne (*arsh 'aẓīm*) and the throne of God (*al-'arsh al-'aẓīm*), see chap. 5, sec. E.

3. See chap. 5, sec. A.

4. Most translations, following the Arabic lexicographers and exegetes, render Arb. *ṣarḥ* as "palace." Some indicate it to be "tower" or "glass tiles." In these instances it is the Qur'ānic text which gives meaning to *ṣarḥ*. T. Nöldeke opts for a derivation from an Ethiopic word meaning "room" and sometimes "palace" or "temple." See his *Neue Beiträge zur semitischen Sprachwissenschaft,* 51. This suggestion is endorsed by

A. Jeffery, *The Foreign Vocabulary of the Qur'ān,* 196–97, arguing against a proposed Arm. etymology of S. Fraenkel, *Aramäischen Fremdwörter,* 237. Jeffery also rejects a linkage to the Targum to Judg. 9:49 which gives Arm. *ẓariaḥ* as "citadel" or "fortified place." Jeffery points out that *ẓariaḥ* is the equivalent of Arb. *ḍarīḥ* meaning a deep cavity in a rock, that is a place easily defended. The story as told by the Muslim exegetes follows the lines of the *Targum Sheni* and clearly indicates some sort of courtyard disguised as a pond of water.

5. Chap. 1, sec. D.
6. *MG Targum Sheni* 6:2a.
7. Qur'ān 27:15.
8. Qur'ān 27:37.
9. Qur'ān 27:24.
10. Qur'ān 27:32.
11. Qur'ān 27:44.
12. I Kings 11:4.
13. I Kings 11:10–12. Note that the Muslim tradition also admonishes Solomon for his indiscretions about idolatry and also indicates that, as a result, his kingdom would be split following his death. See Ya'qūbī, *Historiae* 1:64, which follows the biblical text. The author's history of Solomon (pp. 20–24) paraphrases the Hebrew account and even translates from it. See Chap. 5, sec. B. Other Muslim accounts (via Jewish midrashic texts) report Solomon's rather lax attitude towards idolatry, here as well brought about by association with foreign women, see Ṭabarī, *Annales* 1/2, 588–91; Tha'labī, *'Arā'is,* 322–23; Kisā'ī, *Qiṣaṣ,* 290–93; Balkhī, *Bad'* 2:107; Bal'amī, *Ta'rīkh* (Zotenberg) 4:24–26; also M. Grünbaum, *Sagenkunde,* 222, and chap. 6, sec. F.
14. Sūrahs 2:96, 4:161, 6:84, 21:78–81, 34:12–14, 38:30–36.
15. Qur'ān 27:41.
16. Qur'ān 27:42.
17. Ibid.
18. See D. H. Müller, *Propheten* 1:20–60, 211ff.
19. See Sūrahs 16:103 and 26:195. The process of collating and editing the various versions of the Qur'ān was first treated in great detail by T. Nöldeke et al., *Geschichte des Qorans,* esp. vol. 2, revised by F. Schwally, *Die Sammlung des Qorans,* and vol. 3 revised by G. Bergsträsser and O. Pretzl, *Die Geschichte des Qorantexts.* See also the studies of E. Beck, "Der 'Utmānische Kodex in der Koranlesung des zweiten Jahrhunderts"; "Studien zur Geschichte der kufischen Koranlesung in den beiden ersten Jahrhunderten"; "Die Zuverlässigkeit der Überlieferung zum 'Utmanischen Varianten bei al-Farrā' "; "Die Mas'ūdvarianten bei al-Farrā' "; J. Burton, *The Collection of the Qur'ān;* A. Jeffery, *Materials for the History of the Text of the Qur'ān* and the *Index* to that work published later.
20. The traditional views: a) The loss of so many Qur'ān reciters (*qurrā'*) in battle led to the fear that the text would be lost to the faithful. As a result, the first Caliph, Abū Bakr commissioned Zayd b. Thābit to collect various written materials and oral testimony to establish an authorized version. This version was then given for safekeeping to the Prophet's widow Ḥafsah. The story is contradicted by other Arabic sources that indicate very few *qurrā'* were lost and that the process of establishing a canonical version was completed by Abū Bakr's successor, 'Umar b. al-Khaṭṭāb or begun by 'Umar and finished by his successor, 'Uthmān b. 'Affān (summed up in T. Nöldeke (rev. by F. Schwally), *Geschichte* 2:11–27, and analyzed by Burton, *The Collection of the Qur'ān,* 117–37). b) Various regional centers of the Islamic state used different

versions, causing discontent. The caliph set about establishing an authoritative version that was to supersede the texts floating about. The recension in Ḥafṣah's possession served as the basis for establishing the canonical version. It was left to Zayd and a commission of editors to establish a text in keeping with the dialect of Quraysh, the Prophet's tribe. This story is also problematic (summed up by T. Nöldeke (rev. by F. Schwally); *Geschichte* 2:47–119, and criticized esp. by Burton, 138–60 who maintains that text was known in the Prophet's time and that the traditions of the canonical editing were in fact later inventions to serve a variety of hermeneutical needs). In any case, most western scholars hold that the text, as we currently have it, was more or less available by the time of 'Uthmān. For a fuller bibliography, see n. 19 above.

21. See J. Wansbrough's *Quranic Studies.* He maintains that the authoritative text was not fixed until the ninth century. The traditions of the editing process were therefore later inventions designed to establish the legitimacy of the ninth-century version. Similarly, the various noncanonical codices attributed to contemporaries of the Prophet must be seen as inventions of a later time. Just what purpose would have been served by the later collection of the noncanonical material is not clear to me. For the codices, see T. Nöldeke (rev. by F. Schwally), *Geschichte* 2:27–47; A. Jeffery, *Materials;* and the studies of Beck in n. 19. In any case, Wansbrough (p. 49) is prepared to say that "it is neither possible nor necessary to admit that the material of the canon did not, in some form, exist prior to that period of intensive literary activity [ninth century], but establishment of a standard text such as is implied by the 'Uthmānic recension traditions can hardly have been earlier." Note, however, M. Cook and P. Crone, *Hagarism,* where the model of back projection used by Wansbrough serves to completely alter our understanding of early Islamic history and civilization, the text of the Qur'ān included. For those who hold to the thrust of this last view, the current versions of Muslim scripture are highly fragmented texts that have been cobbled together and are bound to obscure meaning and cause problems of interpretation.

22. Oral communication of M. Sharon of the Hebrew University, Jerusalem.

23. This would certainly be true of the use of short, didactic statements. Marked by rhythmic assonanced prose, they are often interpolated into the narrative and give it pungency. The power of the language was in this case perhaps as important if not more important than a message clearly stated.

24. See n. 18 above.

25. One may wish to speculate how reader response would have varied if the language of the Qur'ān a) were originally colloquial and only later rendered into the classical language (following K. Vollers, *Volkssprache und Schriftsprache im alten Arabien;* and P. Kahle, "Arabic Readers of the Qur'ān"); b) reflects the language of poetic *koine* (Nöldeke, *Neue Beiträge,* 2–4); or c) reflects poetic *koine* of classical Arabic poetry with some allowance for the Meccan dialect (C. Rabin, *Ancient West Arabian,* esp. 1–4; "The Beginnings of Classical Arabic"; M. Zwettler, *The Oral Tradition of Classical Arabic Poetry,* 112–72). Note, however, J. Wansbrough (*Quranic Studies,* 85–118) who maintains that there is no solid point of entry to discuss the language of the Qur'ān.

26. Qur'ān 16:103, 26:195.

27. Muslim authors saw Sulaymān as a genuine Arabic name and understood it to be the diminutive of Salmān from the root *s-l-m.* Salmān, along with Salamān, does appear in pre-Islamic times. See Ibn Manẓūr, *Lisān* s.v. *s-l-m.* Some western scholars agree with this view (P. de Lagarde, *Übersicht über die Bildung der Nomina,* 86; M. Lidzbarski, *Das Johannesbuch der Mandäer,* 1:74 n.1). Jawālīqī, *Mu'arrab,* 85, sees it as a

borrowing from Hebrew. Most western scholars maintain that the name Sulaymān is derived from Syriac Shelomon and is thus of Christian origin (summed up in A. Jeffery, *Foreign Vocabulary of the Qur'ān,* 178). J. Horowitz indicates that Sulaymān as a personal name existed in pre-Islamic times only among the Jews of Medina. See his *Koranische Untersuchungen,* 118, and his "Jewish Proper Names and Their Derivatives in the Qur'ān," 167–69 (pp. 23–25 in the Hildesheim reprint as a separate monograph). This indicates for him that Arabian Jews also made use of the Arabicized form by way of Syriac. One should not draw too many conclusions on the basis of only two Jewish names that he cites. In any case, whatever language the name Sulaymān may be derived from, the stories of the Qur'ān and its exegesis reflect Jewish sources, whenever identifiable.

Chapter Three

1. See chap. 6, sec. C.

2. For a summary of views on the dating of the *Targum Sheni,* see *EJ* s.v. and chap. 6, sec. C. Suffice it to say, the language of the various manuscripts offers no conclusive proof for preferring one date to another. Neither is context all that useful because we are dealing with texts that are likely repositories for elements of older traditions, some of which are no longer extant. B. Grossfeld of the University of Wisconsin-Milwaukee, who is preparing the most complete edition to date of the targum, informs me that versions of *TS* can be traced back to the Byzantine milieu of the sixth century C.E. If he is correct in his dating, one can easily imagine how the legendary Jewish material of the queen's visit could have made its way to Arabia, which was, at that time, sensitive to cultural stimuli from the North.

3. Ibn 'Asākir's history (*Ta'rīkh Dimashq*), as yet unpublished, similarly contains numerous legends and chains of authority, many of which are also found in Ibn Kathīr's *Qiṣaṣ*.

4. One parasang (*farsakh*) equals three Arabic miles (*mīl*) or 2 km. See W. Hinz, *Islamische Masse und Gewichte* s.v. Nasafī, *Tafsīr* 4:157 adds that it was also one hundred *farsakh* wide and that the force was divided equally among humans, jinn, birds, and animals. See also Ṭabarī, *Annales* 1/2, 575, and his *Jāmi* 19:141; Ṭabarsī, *Majma'* 19:206; Zamakhsharī, *Kashshāf,* 1020.

5. In Muslim sources Solomon's control of the winds and various jinn is first indicated in Qur'ān, 24:12–14, 21:81–82 and 38:36–37. For more details of Solomon's flying carpet, his bizarre army, and his mastery over the jinn, see chap. 4, sec. B.

6. Qur'ān 3:75(81) indicates that all the prophets preceding Muḥammad took an oath to God, the so-called "Covenant of the Prophets [*mīthāq al-nabīyīn*]." They did that to foretell his future coming, thus assisting Muḥammad [in his eventual mission]. The significance of this verse and its extended commentary for Muslim-Jewish polemics is referred to in chap. 5, sec. I. For a full discussion, see J. Lassner, "The Covenant of the Prophets: Muslim Texts, Jewish Subtext."

7. See Yāqūt, *Mu'jam* s.v.

8. The geographical formation of Arabia is that of a tilted shelf of mountains and watersheds. The rains in the northern regions where Mecca is situated are irregular. That area is thus characterized by oases and various forms of desert. On the other hand, the high mountains of the Yemen force monsoon rain clouds to water the area below. As a result, the Yemen has been a region of rich cultivation, as is reflected in our text.

9. Some Muslim scholars were skeptical about the hoopoe's ability to determine the site and depth of the water. When Ibn 'Abbās related this tradition, Nāfi' b. al-Azraq

reportedly said, "How can it see water under the ground when it cannot see a trap laid under a few inches of dirt?" See Tha'labī, *'Arā'is,* 311 (> Sa'īd b. Jubayr); Ṭabarī, *Jāmi'* 19:144; Ṭabarsī, *Majma'* 19:213 (> al-'Ayyashī indicating that the question was rendered to Abū Ḥanīfah by Abū 'Abdallāh).

10. *'Arā'is,* 311.

11. She is also referred to in spoken Arabic as Balqīs. Note that the name of the queen is not indicated in the Qur'ān nor in the accounts of the Hebrew Bible and midrashim. The etymology is uncertain. Suggestions of Heb. *pilegesh* "concubine" or Naukalis, the Greek name used by Josephus are not convincing. See *EI²* s.v. Bilqīs. Tha'labī reports that she was known also as *Bal'amah,* that is the female Balaam. See *'Arā'is,* 312; Ṭabarī, *Annales* 1/2, 576 (*ylmqh;* C *blmqh* BM *?l'mh*); Ibn al-Athīr, *Kāmil* 1:121 (*blqmh*); Ibn Kathīr, *Bidāyah* 2:22 (*tlqmh*) and his *Qiṣaṣ* (Q), 498. It cannot be said that there is an intended linkage between Bilqīs and the biblical Balaam who journeyed to the tents of Israel and was overwhelmed by them and their God (Num. 22–24; also Deut. 23:5–6; Josh. 24:9–10). Note also that the example of Balaam is cited by Solomon in the *Midrash Mishle* (chap. 1, sec. B) to put the queen in her place.

12. The bird's comment is, to say the least, puzzling as Solomon was the most learned of men. Nasafī, *Tafsīr* 4:158–59, sees it as a sort of test for Solomon, and Bayḍāwī, *Anwār,* 66, indicates that God wished for Solomon to understand that there were limits to his knowledge. See also Diyārbakrī, *Khamīs* 1:276. Similarly, in the account of the *Targum Sheni,* the hoopoe brings Solomon information that is new to the great and all-wise monarch, namely, the existence of a polity not yet ruled by him. See chap. 1, sec. D. Solomon's need to conquer all the regions inhabited by humankind is echoed in Ṭabarī, *Annales* 1/2, 574 and his *Jāmi'* 19:159.

13. *'Arā'is,* 312–13.

14. The full pedigree is given in the translation. See Appendix I. A Rösch's attempts to link Bilqīs's ancestors to persons and deities known from other regions and ages in the Near East reflects an approach characteristic of nineteenth-century scholarship, but largely abandoned today. See his *Königin von Saba,* 18ff.

15. Dīnawarī, *Akhbār,* 22, indicates that the mother of Bilqīs was herself the daughter of a king, that is the King of the Jinn. One might thus be led to believe that a marriage to a regional prince would have compromised her genealogy on both maternal and paternal sides. He also indicates that she was thirty years old at the time of her father's death, that is to say, she was well beyond the ordinary age for an arranged marriage. Lest we believe that Bilqīs's ascension to rule could be considered ordinary, Dīnawarī and other authorities remind us that she was nominated by her father to succeed to the throne only because his nephew Yāsir Yun'im had not yet reached his majority. Her rule was to end when he came of age. See also Ya'qūbī, *Historiae* 1:222; Ṭabarī, *Annales* 1/2, 684 (Yāsir b. 'Amr, called Yāsir An'am); Mas'ūdī, *Murūj* 3:173 (Yāsir b. Yun'im b. 'Amr); Ibn al-Athīr, *Kāmil* 1:233 (has him killed by two relatives of hers); Ibn Kathīr, *Bidāyah* 2:21; Nasafī, *Tafsīr* 4:158 (father has no other offspring); Diyārbakrī, *Khamīs* 1:276. According to Dīnawarī, 25, Yāsir Yun'im did in fact succeed her [upon coming of age] and then launched expeditions, reaching territory where no ruler had been before. Note, however, the tradition that she eventually married Dhū Tubba', King of Hamdān, who then became the ruler of the Yemen. See sec. G of this chapter; also n. 16.

16. The reference to "the boy" suggests that the Yāsir Yun'im of other sources (see n. 15 above) contested Bilqīs's authority and, according to Tha'labī, was killed by her (*'Arā'is,* 313). Note, however, Mas'ūdī, *Murūj* 2:152, who cites unnamed historians

claiming that Bilqīs killed her father's successor, Tubba' I, presumably Dhū Tubba', King of Hamdān, whom she married, according to Tha'labī after her encounter with Solomon. According to Mas'ūdī, *Murūj* 3:173, she ruled for seven years, was succeeded by Solomon who ruled for twenty-three; he in turn was succeeded by his son Rehoboam and the latter was replaced by Yāsir b. Yun'im. Diyārbakrī, *Khamīs* 1:282, preserves a tradition that she lived seven years after her conversion. Kisā'ī, *Qiṣaṣ,* 287, indicates that the husband was Sharakh b. Sharāḥīl al-Himyarī and that she was the daughter of a wazīr. See also Ibn al-Athīr, *Kāmil,* 1:233. There is, needless to say, confusion about these "historical" events and the identity of Bilqīs's first husband. See also chap. 4, sec. C.

17. *'Arā'is,* 313; Ibn Kathīr, *Bidāyah* 2:22, and his *Qiṣaṣ* (H), 499; see also Ṭabarī, *Jāmi'* 19:152 (one parent was a jinni but no reference to Prophet). The most detailed account of Bilqīs's mother is that of Diyārbakrī, *Khamīs* 1:276–77. It is said that the Prophet was referring at the time to the Sasanian Empire, as he had heard that a daughter of one of the emperors had been made ruler. Ibn Kathīr had doubts about the tradition because one of the links in the chain of authorities (*isnād*) was considered weak (*ḍa'īf*), but he verified it by way of other authorities (Bukhārī, Tirmidhī, Nasā'ī) who produce *isnād*s that are sound in all respects. The same view of the tradition is found in Ibn Kathīr.

18. *'Arā'is,* 313–14.

19. Ibid., 305–306.

20. As distinct from the legitimate right to rule which Solomon possessed. This distinction is discussed in chap. 4, sec. C.

21. *'Arā'is,* 315.

22. See Yāqūt, *Mu'jam* s.v.

23. The ring of Solomon is the subject of considerable attention in Jewish and Muslim lore. See chap. 4, sec. B.

24. See *EI*[2] s.v. al-Djunayd.

25. *'Arā'is,* 316 (> Wahb b. Munabbih and others from the *ahl al-kutub*). The *isnād* would seem to indicate that, in this case, the "people of the books" were readers of texts in the original.

26. The number of girls and boys is the subject of considerable discussion among the Muslim authorities as Tha'labī, *'Arā'is,* 316, indicates: Ten of each (> al-Kalbī); one hundred (> Muqātil); two hundred (> Mujāhid); five hundred (> Wahb). See also Muqātil, *Tafsīr* 3:304 (100); Kisā'ī, *Qiṣaṣ,* 291 (100); Ṭabarī, *Jāmi'* 19:155 (200 > Mujāhid); Ṭabarsī, *Majma'* 19:221 (500 of each); Jazā'irī, *Qiṣaṣ,* 426 (100 > Ibn 'Asākir); Zamakhsharī, *Kashshāf,* 1026 (500); Nasafī, *Tafsīr* 4:161 (500); Bal'amī, *Ta'rīkh* (Zotenberg) 4:16 (100); Diyārbakrī, *Khamīs* 1:278–79 (500 > Tha'labī).

27. According to Tha'labī, *'Arā'is,* 316, this too was a matter of dispute. The tradition cited here follows Wahb b. Munabbih. The reported cross-dressing is also attested in a tradition attributed by Tha'labī to Mujāhid. Note, however, a third tradition going back to Ibn 'Abbās in which the girls and boys were dressed identically. Ṭabarī, *Jāmi'* 19:155, preserves both traditions: cross-dressing (> Mujāhid, Ibn Zayd, and Ibn Jurayj) and that all were dressed alike (> Ibn 'Abbās and al-Ḍaḥḥāk); Muqātil, *Tafsīr* 3:304 (identically dressed but with different hairstyles); Ṭabarsī, *Majma'* 19:220–21 (identically dressed > Ibn 'Abbās; cross-dressing > Mujāhid); Kisā'ī, *Qiṣaṣ,* 291, and Nasafī, *Tafsīr* 4:161, indicate cross-dressing. Diyārbakrī, *Khamīs* 1:278–79 (cross-dressing > Tha'labī). Note parallels in the Jewish sources that have the children all dressed alike. See the *Midrash Mishle,* the *Midrash ha-Hefez,* and the *Targum Sheni* to the Book of

Esther in chap. 1 (*TS* puts the number at 6,000 children and adds that they were all born in the same year and at the same hour and moment and were of the same stature [to ensure that they would look alike in disguise]). Later Jewish folklore follows the midrashim in reporting that the boys and girls were born at the same time, were of equal stature, and were dressed alike. See IFA 1340, 8152.

28. Tha'labī gives the inventory of the gifts (*'Arā'is,* 316) which included, in addition to the gifts already mentioned, various quantities of gold (see n. 30); bars of silver; a crown ornamented with precious gems; musk; ambergris; and various types of aloes wood. Ṭabarsī, *Majma'* 19:221, indicates that the crown was encrusted with emeralds; Ṭabarī, *Jāmi'* 19:157, adds to the list full-blooded Arabian horses. This is presumably suggested by Solomon's legendary affection for horses, stated initially in the Hebrew Bible (I Kings 4:26: "Solomon had 4,000 stalls for chariots and 12,000 horses.") and later in the Qur'ān 38:30–36. A more interesting gift in light of possible Jewish parallels is reported in Jazā'irī, *Qiṣaṣ,* 427. His report, based on an anonymous authority (*qīla*), indicates that the queen sent him a staff that the Kings of Ḥimyar [her ancestors] inherited from one another. Solomon was then asked to identify the top from the bottom. There is the obvious presumption that the ability to distinguish between the two gives him the right that had previously accrued to the rulers of the Yemen and that she currently holds. Solomon hurls it to the sky and determines that the bottom is the end that touched the ground. The scientific principle underlying this decision is not clear but it is clearly the correct answer. Note the similarity of this tale with the riddle posed to Solomon in the *Midrash ha-Hefez* (see chap. 1, sec. C). In the Hebrew text, a sawn log is tossed into the water and the end that sank was determined to be the bottom. There is certainly the possibility that the Jewish and Muslim sources are somehow linked. Ṭabarsī, *Majma'* 19:222, also relates the story of the staff and indicates that the riddle of the horses and drinking water was asked at this time (see n. 54 below).

29. *'Arā'is,* 316, continuing the account of Wahb.

30. *'Arā'is,* 316–17. In response to the queen's gift. *Ājurr* indicates "baked bricks,' which were of sounder construction than the *labinah* "mud bricks." Tha'labī, *'Arā'is,* 316, indicates disagreement among the authorities as regards the number and shape of the gold objects sent to Solomon. Hence: sheets of gold in coverlets of brocade without reference to number (> Thābit al-Bunānī; five hundred *labinah* "bricks," that is, bars of gold (> Wahb b. Munabbih). Ṭabarsī, *Majma'* 19:220–21 (sheets of gold in coverlets and citing a second tradition: 500 bars of gold and an equal number of silver); see also Kisā'ī, *Qiṣaṣ,* 291 (100 bars of gold and equal number of silver); Ṭabarī, *Jāmi'* 19:156 (bricks of gold > Abū Ṣāliḥ); Jazā'irī, *Qiṣaṣ,* 426 (sheets of gold in coverlets of brocade > Mujāhid); Nasafī, *Tafsīr* 4:161 (one thousand bars of gold and silver).

31. Nasafī, *Tafsīr* 4:162, reports the review ground to have been seven parasangs in length. Ṭabarsī indicates several parasangs and that the *maydān* and enclosure wall were made of bricks of gold *and* silver.

32. The story of the wondrous animals is told as well by Nasafī, *Tafsīr* 4:162. For the significance of the animals and of Solomon's preparations for the queen's emissaries, see chap. 4, sec. D.

33. *'Arā'is,* 317. Note the similarity to the story of Joseph and Benjamin as told in both the Hebrew Bible and the Qur'ān. Joseph gains the edge on the visiting delegation of his brothers by deftly placing a precious object in the bag of a sibling, Benjamin, which was used to accuse them of theft. See Gen. 44; Qur'ān 12:70.

34. Gabriel is generally assigned to assisting God's prophets in their moment of need. He appears on two, and according to some authorities three, occasions to allow Solomon

victory over his antagonist: The episode of the box; the more critical moment when Solomon is about to lose the game of wits as he cannot describe the essence of God (*'Arā'is*, 320–21); and, according to some authorities, the angel was responsible for transporting the Queen's throne to Solomon "in the twinkling of an eye," thus allowing him the opportunity to turn the tables and question her (pp. 318–19). This Gabriel did by invoking God's "mightiest name." For a detailed discussion of this last episode, see chap. 5, secs. E and F.

35. See also Jazā'irī, *Qiṣaṣ*, 427. On the larger significance of this test, see chap. 4, sec. D.

36. The exegesis to this critical verse is dealt with in detail in the preliminary remarks of Chapter 5.

37. *'Arā'is*, 318–321.

38. *'Arā'is*, 318, indicates 12,000 *qayl* from among the rulers (*mulūk*). Previously (p. 311) he explained that *qayl* in the language of the Yemenites is the equivalent of *qā'id*, that is "military commander" [in Classical Arabic]. Ṭabarī, *Jāmi'* 19:154, indicates that *qayl* in the language of the Yemen means ruler (*malik*). In mentioning *qayl*, the tradition is apparently calling attention to the provincial rulers or petty dynasts (*mulūk al-aṭrāf*) that are mentioned by the chroniclers. See for example the indices to Ṭabarī, *Annales*. Note that Bilqīs's father refused to marry any daughter from among these provincial rulers, and Bilqīs in turn refused marriage to any of them, as they were clearly subordinate to the ruler of all the Yemen. In the *Jāmi'*, 154, Ṭabarī (> Mujāhid) confirms the numbers of dynasts and fighting men given in the *'Arā'is*. But he also mentions a second tradition that puts the figures at 100,000 each (> Mujāhid > Ibn 'Abbās); Nasafī, *Tafsīr* 4:160 (12,000 commanding many thousands); Kisā'ī, *Qiṣaṣ* 290 (10,000 commanders and an equal number of troops). Rāzī, *Mafātīḥ* 5:84 (12,000 *malik* and 100,000. Note the figures of Ṭabarsī, *Majma'* 19:214, 217. He speaks of 313 *qayl* each commanding 1,000 men; Muqātil, *Tafsīr* 3:306 (313 *qā'id* and 100,000 men) also Diyārbakrī, *Khamīs* 1:275 (12,000 *qā'id* and 100,000 men), 278 (12,000 and 100,000 > Muqātil; 100,000 each > Ibn 'Abbās; also 313 (and 10,000), 280 (many thousands). The most complicated set of figures is that of Ibn al-Athīr, *Kāmil* 1:233–34 (400 rulers [*malik*] of regions [*kūrah*] each with four thousand fighting men [*muqātil*]. She also had 12,000 commanders [*qā'id*] each commanding 12,000 men. He then cites other accounts: 12,000 commanders [*qayl*] and 100,000 men [*muqātil*], each fighting man commanded 7,000 units [*jaysh*], and in each unit there were 70,000 champions for individual combat [*mubāriz*]. The author regards these reports as fantasies). The numbers in all instances are intended to give emphasis to the strength commanded by Bilqīs and her influence over powerful men.

39. *'Arā'is*, 318. See also chap. 5, secs. A and B.

40. Ibid. (> Qatādah). One could read Tha'labī's comment as indicating nothing more than the curiosity of one great ruler towards another's property. Note, however, Ṭabarī, *Jāmi'* 19:160, who links two seemingly conflicting views. He indicates that Solomon's interest in the throne was aroused by the hoopoe's description and as a result he wanted the throne before her conversion to Islam.

41. See also Ṭabarī, *Jāmi'* 19:161. He also reports that Solomon wanted her throne to test her intelligence (see n. 49 below). Note the tests presented to Bilqīs in the form of her altered throne. See *'Arā'is*, 319, and chap. 5, sec. A.

42. *'Arā'is*, 318, identifies the 'ifrīt as either Kūdā (> Wahb) or Kūdhān (> Shu'ayb). See also Bayḍāwī, *Anwār*, 68: Dhakwān or Ṣakhr—the latter being the familiar spirit who is the analogue to the Jewish Ashmedei and who appears in other

Solomonic accounts (see chap. 4, sec. A); Ṭabarī, *Jāmiʿ* 19:161–62 gives Kūzān (> Shuʿayb and Ibn Isḥāq > various [unnamed] authorities); Zamakhsharī, *Kashshāf,* 1028, has Kūdhān; Nasafī, *Tafsīr* 4:162, Kūwān; Diyārbakrī, *Khamīs* 1:280 names Kūdhā (> Wahb), Dhakwān, (> *qīla*), and Ṣakhr the jinni; Muqātil, *Tafsīr* 3:307 names the ʿifrīt "al-Ḥaqīq" (Ms. A: *al-ḥqbq,* Z: *ḥnqwq*); Ibn Kathīr (H), *Qiṣaṣ* 439, and *Bidāyah* 2:23 state that he was a believer among the jinn.

43. A full discussion of this verse is found in chap. 5, secs. E and F. A slightly different treatment of the issues appears in J. Lassner, "The 'One Who Had Knowledge of the Book' and the 'Mightiest Name' of God. Qur'ānic Exegesis and Jewish Cultural Artifacts."

44. *'Arā'is,* 318–19. See also chap. 5, secs. E and F.

45. Ṭabarī, *Jāmiʿ* 19:163, reads Balīkhā (> Qatādah); Bayḍāwī, *Anwār,* 69, adds al-Khiḍr to the list of humans who assisted Solomon; Ṭabarsī, *Majmaʿ* 19:226 reads Balīkhā (> Mujāhid); Usṭūm (> Qatādah); al-Khiḍr (> Abū Lahīʿah); Gabriel, whom God sent to bring the throne; and Solomon himself to demonstrate to the ʿifrīt the beneficence of God. This last tradition concerning the ʿifrīt is treated skeptically by the exegete. See also Diyārbakrī, *Khamīs* 1:280 (an angel, Gabriel; al-Khiḍr; Solomon himself; Asaph; and an unnamed Israelite who spoke to Solomon > Ibn al-Munkadir). For the linking of the legendary al-Khiḍr (or al-Khaḍir) and the mysterious visitor from the island and the identity of Usṭūm (or Asṭūm?) see chap. 5, sec. E.

46. See also Ibn Kathīr, *Qiṣaṣ* (Q), 502, and *Bidāyah* 2:23; Ṭabarī, *Jāmiʿ* 19:163, who believes that Qaṭādah, in mentioning the one with knowledge of the book, indicated that he was an Israelite; Zamakhsharī, *Kashshāf,* 1028, explicitly mentioning Solomon himself as having the special knowledge to summon God. Ṭabarsī, *Majmaʿ* 19:230, indicates that Solomon did indeed have the requisite knowledge but that he allowed Asaph to play the role of interlocutor so as to groom him for leadership.

47. *'Arā'is,* 319 ("Yā Ḥayy . . ." > 'Ā'ishah and her father, i.e., Abū Bakr), ("Our Lord . . ." > Zhurī), ("O Possessor . . ." > Mujāhid). See also Muqātil, *Tafsīr* 3:307 ("O Possessor . . ."); Ṭabarī, *Jāmiʿ* 19:163 ("Our Lord . . ." > Zuhrī) and ("O Possessor . . ." > Mujāhid); Zamakhsharī, *Kashshāf,* 1028, and Diyārbakrī, *Khamīs* 1:280–81, list all three formulae. Nasafī, *Tafsīr* 4:162, seemingly combines "Yā Ḥayy! Yā Qayyūm!" and "O Possessor of Greatness and Generosity" as one formula. Ṭabarsī, *Majmaʿ* 19:226 (A formula invoking Allāh and al-Raḥmān "The Merciful"), ("O Possessor . . ." > Mujāhid), ("O Lord . . ." > Zuhrī), and "Yā Ḥayy! Yā Qayyūm!" linked to Hebrew formula transliterated into Arabic characters. For this formula and "Yā Ḥayy! Yā Qayyūm!" see chap. 5, secs. E and F.

48. For the meaning of this verse in relation to the larger story dealing with issues of gender, see chap. 4, sec. D.

49. *'Arā'is,* 319–20. See also Ṭabarī, *Jāmiʿ* 19:166; Ṭabarsī, *Majmaʿ* 19:225; Bayḍāwī, *Anwār,* 69; Ibn Kathīr, *Qiṣaṣ* (Q), 503; Rāzī, *Mafātīḥ* 5:87.

50. *'Arā'is,* 320 (> Wahb and Muḥammad b. Kaʿb among others). Similarly in the Jewish *Targum Sheni* (see chap. 1, sec. D). Note that the jinn were said to be hybrid creatures who took on various characteristics of animals. See Kisā'ī, *Qiṣaṣ,* 279 (some jinn are like donkeys; some have hooves. They are hybrids as a result of the jinn fornicating with Iblīs, the Devil). In Jewish sources, the jinn were said to possess the feet of chickens. See Ginzberg, *Legends* 6:301 n. 32; and *BT Berakhot* 6a; *Zohar,* 3:309a.

51. *'Arā'is,* 320.

52. Ibid.

53. Kisā'ī, *Qiṣaṣ,* 292, indicates that an ʿifrīt volunteered to construct it. On the

meaning of *ṣarḥ,* see chap. 2, n. 4. See also Ṭabarī, *Jāmi'* 19:168; Bayḍāwī, *Anwār,* 70; Nasafī, *Tafsīr* 4:163–64; Ibn Kathīr, *Qiṣaṣ* (Q), 503; Bal'amī, *Ta'rīkh* (Zotenberg) 4:18; Diyārbakrī, *Khamīs* 1:281, indicates that the *ṣarḥ* was constructed to verify Solomon's prophethood. He is also most explicit in identifying the *ṣarḥ* as a court (*ṣaḥn*) rather than an enclosed structure. See also Rāzī, *Mafātīḥ* 5:89, indicating that *ṣarḥ* is the court of a chamber (*ṣaḥn al-dār*) for some authorities. In a Jewish Yemenite tale of the eighteenth century (Appendix F), Solomon put down a marble floor and splashed water over it.

54. *'Arā'is,* 320–21. Muqātil, *Tafsīr* 3:305; Ṭabarsī, *Majma'* 19:222; and Bal'amī, *Ta'rīkh* (Zotenberg) 4:16–17, indicate that this riddle was presented by the queen's envoys during their initial meeting with Solomon. According to Bal'amī, only the sweat of horses was correct because only their sweat is not salty.

55. *'Arā'is,* 320–21; Ṭabarī, *Jāmi'* 19:168. See chap. 4, sec. D for the significance of this last event.

56. *'Arā'is,* 321–22.

57. See also Ṭabarī, *Jāmi'* 19:69–70 (> 'Ikrimah and Abū Ṣāliḥ); Ṭabarsī, *Majma'* 19:229 (composition of paste and innovative use); Balkhī, *Bad'* 3:106 (innovative use of depilatory), 108 (composition of paste); Ibn Kathīr, *Qiṣaṣ* (Q), 503, and *Bidāyah* 2:23; Diyārbakrī, *Khamīs* 1:281 (> Tha'labī); Suyūṭī, *Awā'il,* 285. Note also the use of a depilatory in the Jewish account of Pseudo Ben Sira (see chap. 1, sec. E). For legal issues regarding the Muslim use of depilatories, see Suyūṭī, *Ḥāwī* 1:339ff. esp. p. 343. I am indebted for this last reference to J. Sadan of Tel Aviv University.

58. *'Arā'is,* 321 (> Ibn 'Abbās); Kisā'ī, *Qiṣaṣ,* 292–93 (indicates that he married her and she bore him Rehoboam); Muqātil, *Tafsīr* 3:309 (she bore him a child called David); Diyārbakrī, *Khamīs* 1:281 (indicates that David perished before Solomon died—the implication being that the otherwise unaccounted for David could not have been a factor in the succession; also that Solomon forced her to marry and so she reluctantly chose Dhū Tabba' > Wahb); Nasafī, *Tafsīr* 4:164; Bayḍāwī, *Anwār,* 70 (indicates that there was a dispute among scholars as to whether Solomon married her or whether she married Dhū Tubba', King of Hamdān); Ibn Qutaybah, *Ma'ārif,* 268–69 (both versions); Ibn Kathīr, *Qiṣaṣ* (H), 440 and *Bidāyah* 2:24 (both versions); Balkhī, *Bad'* 3:108 (both versions); Ṭabarsī, *Majma'* 19:229 (both versions); Rāzī, *Mafātīḥ* 5:89 (both versions). He adds that there is some dispute as to whether Solomon married her before or after she uncovered her ankles. I find no trace of this dispute, which would be inconsistent with the general thrust of the story.

59. Yāqūt, *Mu'jam* 1:801–802 (Baynūn); 3:115 (Salḥīn), and 811–12 (Ghumdān). Ibn Kathīr, *Qiṣaṣ* (H), 440 (Sāliḥīn and Baytūn); Ṭabarsī, *Majma'* 19:229 (no names). See also Diyārbakrī, *Khamīs* 1:281. The geographical dictionary of Yāqūt reports that Baynūn was a large fortress near Ṣan'ā' that had been built by Solomon along with Salḥīn. He, nevertheless, prefers a second explanation, namely that it had been built by one of the Tubba's, the local rulers. He indicates that this second tradition is found in the chronicles of Ḥimyar and among the poets. According to him, it was destroyed during the Abyssinian conquest of the Yemen (in the sixth century C.E.). The place is not to be confused with Baynūnah, which is between Oman and Bahrein. Similarly, scholars conjecture (*za'amū*) that Salḥīn was built for Dhū Tubba', the King of Hamdān when Solomon arranged for his marriage to Bilqīs. Here, too, Yāqūt prefers an explanation unencumbered by the supernatural. He holds that, as with Baynūn, Salḥīn was built by the Tubba's. The same was true for Ghumdān, although Yāqūt, faithful to the Solomonic tradition, briefly mentions the account that the great Israelite had built it.

Yāqūt describes the enclosure wall of Ghumdān as having a different color for each side. Inside was a palace built on multiple platforms, each separated by forty cubits (approx. sixty feet). It was of such great height that it cast a shadow for many miles. On the upper section he built an audience hall of grained marble. Each of the pillars featured a fierce lion. The wind passed through the lions [simulating the lions' roar]. It was also fitted with lamps that lit up the night as does lightning. It was allegedly destroyed in the time of the Caliph 'Uthmān (d. 656 C.E.). When 'Uthmān learned that the soothsayers of the Yemen predicted the death of whomsoever destroys it, he attempted to build anew, but the project proved too expensive and was abandoned. 'Uthmān was later assassinated, fulfilling that prophecy.

60. *'Arā'is,* 321–22 (> Wahb). See also n. 58 above.

61. See n. 9 above.

Chapter Four

1. Lassner, *Islamic Revolution,* 1–33 esp. 19–29 dealing with the highly tendentious early historical traditions.

2. For an overview of the Babylonian Akitu Festival, see S. A. Pallis, *The Babylonian Akitu Festival;* T. Jacobsen, "Religious Drama in Ancient Mesopotamia"; and the article by H. Tadmor in *EM* s.v. Rosh ha-shanah (b^{e}Mesopotamiah).

3. Unlike the Jews who intercalate a month every fourth year into their lunar calendar, Muslims allow the months to rotate through the seasons. Thus, there is no convenient way for Muslims to link agricultural concerns with specific calendrical dates. Still, Muslims were obviously aware of the links between seasonal change and agriculture. Note, for example, the various celebrations that revolve around the river Nile described in chap. 4 of the forthcoming study of Fatimid ceremonial by P. Sanders, *Ritual, Politics, and the City in Fatimid Cairo.*

4. *'Arā'is,* 313.

5. Ibid., 294ff.; Kisā'ī, *Qiṣaṣ,* 273.

6. Kisā'ī, *Qiṣaṣ,* 267–68 (> Wahb).

7. Ibid., 269, 272.

8. For example, Kisā'ī, *Qiṣaṣ,* 271–72, describes a dispute concerning a parcel of land on which was found money that neither the former owner nor the man to whom he had recently sold the parcel wanted to claim. Solomon resolves the dispute for his father by arranging a marriage between the two families and dividing the find. For Jewish parallels, see Salzberger, *Salomo-Sage,* 48ff. Similarly, Kisā'ī relates a story (> Wahb) about the sheep of a tribe that had eaten the harvest on land not belonging to the tribe. Solomon proposes a more equitable solution than that of his father. The account is based on Qur'ān 21:78. See the various commentaries on that verse and Ṭabarī, *Annales* 1/2, 573 (> Ibn Mas'ūd); Ibn Kathīr, *Bidāyah* 2:26–27; also Salzberger, 44–38. For other examples of Solomon's early displays of wisdom, see Salzberger, 43–63. For a brief survey of Solomon's wisdom in rabbinic sources, see Ginzberg, *Legends* 4:130–142.

9. Kisā'ī, *Qiṣaṣ,* 272.

10. Jazā'irī, *Qiṣaṣ,* 405.

11. Solomon's youth at the time of his succession is suggested by I Kings 3:7, which describes his dream at Gibeon. Offered kingship by God, Solomon replies: "I am but child." This passage of the Hebrew Bible was rendered into Arabic by Ya'qūbī, *Historiae* 1:61. See also Tha'labī, *'Arā'is,* 292 (thirteen years old > Muqātil); Kisā'ī, *Qiṣaṣ,* 272 (twelve); Balkhī, *Bad'* 3:103ff. (twelve). For non-Islamic traditions of Solomon's youth when assuming rule, see Salzberger, *Salomo-Sage,* 70ff.

12. Kisā'ī, *Qiṣaṣ,* 272–73.
13. Ibid., 278–79.
14. The Jewish tradition is based on Solomon's dream at Gibeon. See I Kings 3:5–14 esp. 11–13: "And God said to him [Solomon], 'Because you have asked for this [wisdom to rule] and not for long life or wealth or for the lives of your enemies; because you have asked for wisdom to discern judgments, [11] behold I will have done according to your word. Behold, I have given you a wise and understanding heart, so that there were none like you before you and there shall be none like you hereafter. [12] I have also given you what you have not asked: both wealth and honor so that there will be no king like you all your days' " [13]. Note that this text of the Hebrew Bible was known to Muslims. It is partially translated or, to be more precise, is rendered into a faithful paraphrase by Ya'qūbī, *Historiae* 1:61. See n. 11. On the biblical dream see, G. von Rad, *Wisdom in Israel,* 296–97. I have not been able to obtain the study of P. Reymond, "Le rêve du Salomon (I Rois 3, 4–15)," *Hommage à Wilhelm Wischer,* Montpellier, 1960: 210–215.
15. Kisā'ī, *Qiṣaṣ,* 278–79. See also n. 21 on Solomon's command of the winds.
16. This tradition seems to mirror *M. Genesis Rabbah,* 34.12, which indicates that the power lost by Adam over the animal world after his failing (see Genesis 1:28 giving Adam dominion over the Earth) was given later to Solomon. Note, however, that Solomon also lost this dominion as a result of his failings. Previous to that, he was the lord of all celestial and terrestrial beings. See *BT Sanhedrin* 20b. See also Salzberger, *Salomo-Sage,* 115ff.
17. The Jewish ring was five-sided and had the tetragrammaton, God's ineffable name engraved on it (for the tetragrammaton, see Chap. 5, n. 113). According to Jewish mystical sources, possession of the ring enabled Solomon to learn the heavenly mysteries. See *Zohar* 3:233a–b. The ring was given to Solomon by the archangel, and he used it to subdue the demons and compel them to build the temple in Jerusalem. See Ginzberg, *Legends* 4:150ff. For Solomon's dominion over all of creation, see *M. Exodus Rabbah,* 15.6, 30.16; *M. Numbers Rabbah,* 11.3 and n. 16 above.
18. Kisā'ī, *Qiṣaṣ,* 279.
19. Ibid., 279. Solomon's use of spirits for practical concerns is indicated in the Qur'ān 21:82, 34:12–13. See various commentaries. Kisā'ī, *Qiṣaṣ,* 282, indicates how Ṣakhr was captured and forced to assist Solomon in the construction of the temple in Jerusalem. This account of Ṣakhr's captivity is linked to the Jewish legends of Ashmedai. See Ginzberg, *Legends* 4:166–67; *JE* s.v. Asmodeus.
20. Kisā'ī, *Qiṣaṣ,* 279.
21. Ibid., 279–80.
22. Solomon's mastery of the winds is derived from Qur'ān 34:12 and 38:36. See the various commentaries to those passages. Constructed by the jinn, the flying carpet or platform was an elaborate structure that contained space and supplies, not only for all of Solomon's terrestrial army, but also for his wives and concubines. His throne also was transported when the prophet traveled. For the flying carpet or platform, see Kisā'ī, *Qiṣaṣ,* 285; Tha'labī, *'Arā'is,* 293ff.; Jazā'irī, *Qiṣaṣ,* 407, 412, 421; Balkhī, *Bad'* 3:109; Ibn Kathīr, *Qiṣaṣ* (H), 443–45 and *Bidāyah* 2:27; Ṭabarī, *Annales* 1/2, 574ff. and *Jāmi'* 19:141; Ṭabarsī, *Majma'* 19:206–207; Nasafī, *Tafsīr* 4:157; Zamakhsharī, *Kashshāf,* 1020; Diyārbakrī, *Khamīs* 1:272; Bal'amī, *Ta'rīkh* (Zotenberg) 4:13.
23. Tha'labī, *'Arā'is,* 312 (> Ibn 'Abbās).
24. For example, Tha'labī, *'Arā'is,* 312—it is said (*qīla*) that the hoopoe will be separated from his species. The discussion of the bird's punishment serves as a com-

mentary to Qur'ān 27:21: "I will surely punish him severely or slaughter him." For a full discussion of this verse and its exegesis, see chap. 5, sec. C.

25. Qur'ān 27:17: "Gathered unto Solomon were his hosts . . . They were arranged according to rank (*yuza'ūna*). The exegetes understood this to mean that they were arranged to prevent the lead troops from pulling away and stragglers from being left behind. See for example Ṭabarsī, *Majma'* 19:206; Zamakhsharī, *Kashshāf,* 1020; Ibn Kathīr, *Bidāyah* 2:19 (each of the troops knew their place) and *Qiṣaṣ* (H), 434. For references to the arrangement of Solomon's army while traveling, see n. 22 on the flying carpet. Note also Tha'labī, *'Arā'is,* 317; Ṭabarī, *Annales* 1/2, 577; Jazā'irī, *Qiṣaṣ,* 413, describing the arrangement of Solomon's host at his court while awaiting the Queen of Sheba.

26. Regarding the *Amṣār* of Iraq, see J. Wellhausen, *Arabische Reich;* S. A. al-'Alī, "Minṭaqat al-Ḥīrah"; and his *Tanẓīmāt,* which deals with Baṣrah in the first Islamic century; M. Hinds, "Kufan Political Alignments and Their Backgrounds in the mid-7th Century A.D."; Lassner, *Abbasid Rule,* 143–51. On the military reforms of the Abbasids, see D. Ayalon, *Military Reforms;* and Lassner, *Abbasid Rule,* 102–136, 208–223 (composition of the armies and patterns of urban settlement at Baghdad). See also M. Sharon, *Black Banners.*

27. For the hoopoe as Solomon's guide to water, see chap. 5, sec. C. More generally, see the commentary to Qur'ān 27:20, for example, Tha'labī, *'Arā'is,* 311; Ṭabarī, *Jāmi'* 19:144; Ṭabarsī, *Majma'* 19:213.

28. Tha'labī, *'Arā'is,* 312–13 (construction of bricks and fashioning of review ground), 322 (palaces in the Yemen). See chap. 3, secs. E and G. There are numerous references to Solomon utilizing the jinn in construction. Note Kisā'ī, *Qiṣaṣ,* 279–80 and n. 19. On the division of labor and places of settlement for the jinn, see Jazā'irī, *Qiṣaṣ,* 409ff. (in building Jerusalem). The disposition of the jinn in the urban setting described by Jazā'irī recalls the arrangement of the military cantonments at Baghdad and Sāmarrā where the Abbasid caliphs sought to control their armies by assigning them discrete locations. See J. Lassner, *Topography,* 138–54, and his "The Caliph's Personal Domain: The City Plan of Baghdad Reexamined," 103–118, and expanded in his *Abbasid Rule,* 208–223. For Sāmarrā, see Ya'qūbī, *Buldān,* 255ff.; also Ayalon, *Military Reforms.*

29. Qur'ān 27:39 and its various commentaries. Note the exegetical comment of Tha'labī, *'Arā'is,* 318. Note that Kisā'ī, *Qiṣaṣ,* 292, also mentions that an 'ifrīt was used in constructing Solomon's court of glass.

30. Tha'labī, *'Arā'īs,* 317; Ṭabarsī, *Majma'* 19:221; Nasafī, *Tafsīr* 4:162; Ṭabarī, *Annales* 1/2, 579 (one insect pierces a smooth gem); Jazā'irī, *Qiṣaṣ,* 423 (a gem to be pierced without fire or iron).

31. Kisā'ī, *Qiṣaṣ,* 268–69 (> Ka'b). See also n. 16 above for Jewish parallels.

32. Kisā'ī, *Qiṣaṣ,* 269–70.

33. Ibid., 270; Diyārbakrī, *Khamīs* 1:273. For Ka'b al-Aḥbār, see *EI*² s.v.

34. Tha'labī, *'Arā'is,* 295.

35. Jazā'irī, *Qiṣaṣ,* 411; see also the variant in 418.

36. Tha'labī, *'Arā'is,* 312–13. Detailed and conflicting accounts of her relationship to the jinn are found in Kisā'ī, *Qiṣaṣ,* 287ff., and Diyārbakrī, *Khamīs* 1:276ff. The latter's account can be traced back to Ibn al-Athīr, *Kāmil* 1:231–32, and a shorter version of Mas'ūdī, *Murūj* 3:152. The Mas'ūdī-Diyārbakrī version is also echoed in an eighteenth-century Jewish folkloric account from the Yemen. See chap. 6, sec. E.

37. As regards the queen's name, see chap. 3, n. 11. Her genealogy, as described in the sources is contradictory and the readings of various names is conjectural.
38. Tha'labī, *'Arā'is,* 313.
39. Ibid.
40. Ibid.
41. Ibid.
42. Ibid.
43. Ibid.
44. Ibid.
45. Ibid., 313–14.
46. Khaṭīb, *Ta'rīkh Baghdad* 1:74ff. On brick technology, see R. J. Forbes, *Ancient Technology* 1:72–74.
47. For the architectural features of the palace of the Round City at Baghdad, see E. Herzfeld and F. Sarre, *Archäologische Reise* 2:103ff.; K. A. C. Creswell, *Early Muslim Architecture* 2:4ff.; note the corrections to their reconstructions suggested in J. Lassner, *Topography,* 141–49 and in his "The Caliph's Personal Domain," 103–18.
48. That is to say, the functional arrangements would have been the same in both the Abbasid palace and that of Bilqīs. The point of the arrangement was to demonstrate the legitimacy and authority of the inhabitant. For Baghdad, see J. Lassner, *Topography,* 128–37 and his "Some Speculative Thoughts on the Search for an 'Abbāsid Capital," *MW* 55 (1965): 135–41, 203–310, and his revised views in *Abbasid Rule,* 161–83.
49. Tha'labī, *'Arā'is,* 305–306; Bal'amī, *Ta'rīkh* (Zotenberg) 4:23.
50. Ibid., 314–15.
51. A detailed description of Solomon's throne (see n. 49 above) indicates a linkage between Muslim and Jewish sources. For a summary of the Jewish legends of Solomon's throne, see Ginzberg, *Legends* 4:157–160; for the sources 6:296–98. Note esp. the account of the *Targum Sheni* in *MG* 6:1b, and the descriptions of the midrashim collected by A. Jellinek, *BM* 2:83–85, 5:34–37. The throne of Solomon also excited the interest of Christians. The Byzantine emperor Theophilus (tenth century) sat on "The Throne of Solomon." Like the Muslim and Jewish descriptions of the throne, Theophilus's structure featured mechanical devices. See G. Brett, "The Automata in the Byzantine Throne of Solomon." Theophilus was likely to have been directly influenced by contacts with the Islamic world. See A. Grabar, "Le success des arts orientaux a la cour byzantine sous les Macedoniens."
52. Tha'labī, *'Arā'is,* 314 (soundness of construction); According to Ṭabarsī, *Majma'* 19:211, the structure was 30 × 30 × 30 cubits (> Ibn 'Abbās). The length of the Islamic cubit varied but was approximately 1.5 feet. See W. Hinz, *Islamische Masse und Gewichte,* 54ff.; also *EI*² s.v. dhirā'. Bayḍāwī, *Anwār,* 65 (30 × 30 × 80 cubits. The height equals that of the reconstructed throne rooms in the walls of the Round City at Baghdad. See Herzfeld, *Archäologische Reise* 2:125; K. A. C. Creswell, *Early Muslim Architecture* 2:12; note, however, J. Lassner, *Topography,* 242 n. 31, calling for a height of fifty cubits, as in the Khaṭīb, *Ta'rīkh Baghdād* 1:74); Diyārbakrī, *Khamīs* 1:278 (solid construction and 30 × 30 × 30 cubits > Ibn 'Abbās, 80 × 80 × 80 > Muqātil, > 40 × 40 × 30 > anonymous); Nasafī, *Tafsīr* 4:161 (eighty cubits in height); Zamakhsharī, *Kashshāf,* 1023 (some say eighty in height, some thirty); *Jāmi'* 19:148.
53. Tha'labī, *'Arā'is,* 311.
54. See Chap. 1, sec. D.

55. Brevity was considered the style of prophetic discourse. See Tha'labī, *'Arā'is,* 314; Rāzī, *Mafāṭīh* 5:86; Zamakhsharī, *Kashshāf,* 1025.

56. Ibid., 314–15; Ṭabarī, *Annales* 1/2, 578–79, and *Jāmi'* 19:153; Ṭabarsī, *Majma'* 19:217; Rāzī, *Mafātīḥ* 5:85; Zamakhsharī, *Kashshāf,* 1025; Diyārbakrī, *Khamīs* 1:278.

57. Tha'labī, *'Arā'is,* 314–15; Ṭabarī, *Annales* 1/2, 578–79. See also n. 65 and chap. 5, sec. B.

58. See chap. 1, sec. D.

59. Tha'labī, *'Arā'is,* 315–16.

60. Tha'labī, *'Arā'is,* 315.

61. Ibid. 316: *Wahb b. Munabbih wa-ghayruhu min ahl al-kutub.* For Wahb, see the study of R. G. Khoury, *Wahb b. Munabbih.*

62. Tha'labī, *'Arā'is,* 316; Muqātil, *Tafsīr* 3:304; Kisā'ī, *Qiṣaṣ,* 291; Ṭabarī, *Jāmi'* 19:155; Ṭabarsī, *Majma'* 19:221; Jazā'rī, *Qiṣaṣ,* 426; Zamakhsharī, *Kashshāf,* 1026; Nasafī, *Tafsīr* 4:161; Bal'amī, *Ta'rīkh* (Zotenberg) 4:16; Diyārbakrī, *Khamīs* 1:278–79. See also chap. 3 n. 27 for Jewish parallels.

63. See n. 30 above; also chap. 3, sec. E.

64. Tha'labī, *'Arā'is,* 317. One Arabic *mīl* equals 2,000 meters making it somewhat longer than an English mile. See Hinz, *Islamische Masse und Gewichte* s.v. mīl.

65. Tha'labī, *'Arā'is,* 318ff.; Ṭabarī, *Annales* 1/2, 580ff. and *Jāmi'* 19:159–60 (explicit instructions to guard the throne against the worshipers of Allāh); Zamakhsharī, *Kashshāf,* 1028; Bal'amī, *Ta'rīkh* (Zotenberg) 4:17; Diyārbakrī, *Khamīs* 1:278.

66. The manner in which the queen's throne was disguised calls to mind the destruction of the royal Sasanian palace, the great Īwān Kisrā, at al-Madā'in and the redeployment of its architectural members in the construction of the caliphal palace, the Tāj (tenth century), at Baghdad. According to Yāqūt, the incident created quite a stir. What had originally been the battlements of the Sasanian structure became the base of the new retaining wall of the Muslim structure; the base of the old palace in turn became the upper register of the Tāj walls. The symbolic meaning of this reverse use of architectural material was apparently clear and is reflected in several verses attributed to the poet al-Buḥturī that are judiciously placed by Yāqūt in his account. The poet reflects on the frailty of earthly power in a world turned upside down. See Yāqūt, *Mu'jam* 1:109, 808–809; Ibn al-Jawzī, *Muntaẓam* 5/2, 144; also Lassner, *Abbasid Rule,* 177–78; also C. Wendell, "Baghdad: *Imago Mundi* and Other Foundation Lore," 127; G. Makdisi, "The Topography of Eleventh-Century Baghdad: Materials and Notes," 134 n. 2; G. Le Strange, *Baghdad During the Abbasid Caliphate,* index, 368, map 8, ref. no. 2.

67. See chap. 3, sec. F and chap. 5, sec. B.

68. Note Ibn Kathīr, *Bidāyah* 2:23 identifies her throne explicitly as the symbol of her rule.

69. Tha'labī, *'Arā'is,* 320–21; Ṭabarī, *Annales* 1/2, 582ff. and *Jāmi'* 19:168; Ibn Kathīr, *Qiṣaṣ* (Q), 503, and his *Bidāyah* 2:24; Diyārbakrī, *Khamīs* 1:281; Rāzī, *Mafātīḥ* 5:89; Nasafī, *Tafsīr* 4:164; Bal'amī, *Ta'rīkh* (Zotenberg) 4:18.

70. Tha'labī, *'Arā'is,* 320; Kisā'ī, *Qiṣaṣ,* 292 ('ifrīt offers to build court of glass); Ṭabarī, *Annales* 1/2, 583 (floor of green glass), and *Jāmi'* 19:168 (indicates *ṣarḥ* was the form of a *saṭḥ,* that is a flat area; for the meaning of *ṣarḥ,* see chap. 2 n. 4); Ibn Kathīr, *Qiṣaṣ* (Q), 503 (fish and other creatures), and *Bidāyah,* 2:24; Ṭabarsī, *Majma'* 19:220, 228 (*ṣarḥ* = structures of glass or smooth stone; described here as an open area with no ceiling, that is, a court); Bayḍāwī, *Anwār,* 70 (*ṣarḥ* = court); Nasafī, *Tafsīr* 4:164; Diyārbakrī, *Khamīs* 1:281 (*ṣarḥ* = *saḥn,* that is, court); Rāzī, *Mafātīḥ*

5:89 (*ṣarḥ* = *saḥn*); Bal'amī, *Ta'rīkh (Zotenberg) 4:18 (court of crystal 100 × 100 cubits).*

71. See chap. 2, sec. D.

72. See chap. 3 n. 54.

73. Tha'labī, *'Arā'is,* 321; also chap. 3 n. 57 for further references, particularly to the use of depilatories. Note Bal'amī, *Ta'rīkh* (Zotenberg) 4:18, who indicates that "Even today it is the custom that when a man wishes to take a woman, he has her expose her ankles."

74. It may also signify, albeit in symbolic fashion, pollution. Note the Jewish accounts of Solomon's recklessness in bedding foreign women while they were menstruating or still observing themselves for residual traces of blood. See chap. 6, sec. G.

75. Note also the Jewish account of Pseudo Ben Sira, which calls for the use of a depilatory made of lime laced with arsenic (chap. 1, sec. E). Note that the same composition for the depilatory paste is given in Muslim sources. See Ṭabarsī, *Majma'* 19:229; Balkhī, *Bad'* 3:108.

76. Tha'labī, *'Arā'is,* 321 (> Ibn Isḥāq > various scholars > Wahb). See also chap. 2 n. 58 for other references to the queen's marriage.

77. Tha'labī, *'Arā'is,* 321.

78. Ibid.

79. I Kings 11:3. The biblical numbers are found in the Islamic sources although the relationship of wives to concubines is sometimes reversed. Note, however, Ibn Kathīr, *Bidāyah* 2:29–30, also indicates 600 wives and 400 concubines > Isḥāq b. Bishr > Abū Hurayrah; his *Qiṣaṣ* (Q), 511–12 reverses the figures to 400 wives and 600 concubines.

80. For the story of Solomon's potency, see Ibn Kathīr, *Qiṣaṣ* (H), 446 (70 women > al-Bukhārī, 90 > Shu'ayb, 100 > Abu Ya'lā and Aḥmad b. Ḥanbal); similarly his *Bidāyah* 2:29 (invoking the same authorities and tracing various accounts back to Abū Hurayrah); Zamakhsharī, *Kashshāf,* 1036 (70 women).

81. Kisā'ī, *Qiṣaṣ,* 287–89.

Chapter Five

1. *'Arā'is,* 314.

2. See for example Kisā'ī, *Qiṣaṣ,* 14. For a summary of the Jinn, see *EI*^{2} s.v. Djinn.

3. Tha'labī, *'Arā'is,* 314.

4. Ṭabarī, *Jāmi'* 19:167; Ibn Kathīr, *Bidāyah* 2:24, and *Qiṣaṣ* (Q), 503; Zamakhsharī, *Kashshāf,* 1023 (a Magian); Diyārbakrī, *Khamīs* 1:278 (her people were Magians).

5. Put most explicitly by Tha'labī, *'Arā'is,* 321 (she submits recognizing her idolatry); Ṭabarī, *Jāmi'* 19:170 (recognizing the unicity of God).

6. See chap. 3, sec. D.

7. *EI*^{2} s.v. Basmalah.

8. See chap. 1, sec. D.

9. Tha'labī, *'Arā'is,* 315; Ṭabarī, *Jāmi'* 19:152; Ṭabarsī, *Majma'* 19:217; Nasafī, *Tafsīr* 4:160; Ibn Kathīr, Qiṣaṣ (H), 437–38; Diyārbakrī, *Khamīs* 1:278 (> Qatādah); Rāzī, *Mafātīḥ* 5:86; see also Zamakhsharī, *Kashshāf,* 1025, and Kisā'ī, *Qiṣaṣ,* 290 (she sees the bird at the aperture and he drops the letter on her neck).

10. In the *Targum Sheni* the birds, sent as an army, blacken the sky. See chap. 1, sec. D.

11. Ṭabarī, *Annales* 1/2, 574, and his *Jāmi'* 19:159 (Solomon can tolerate no independent rulers); Jazā'irī, *Qiṣaṣ,* 407. Note that Solomon was considered one of four

conquerors of the world. He and Alexander the Great were the conquerors who were believers; Nimrod and Nebuchadnezzar were the unbelievers. See, for example, Tha'labī, *'Arā'is,* 292; Ibn Qutaybah, *Ma'ārif,* 32 (> Wahb); Dīnawarī, *Akhbār,* 24 (kingdoms that he conquered); Balkhī, *Bad'* 3:45–46; Ṭabarsī, *Majma'* 19:206 (rules the entire world).

12. Tha'labī, *'Arā'is,* 318.

13. See chap. 3, sec. F.

14. Tha'labī, *'Arā'is,* 318; Ṭabarī, *Jāmi'* 19:161 (also Solomon's prophethood); Ṭabarsī, *Majma'* 19:225 (to demonstrate Solomon's prophethood > Wahb); Nasafī, *Tafsīr* 4:162; Jazā'irī, *Qiṣaṣ* 428; and Zamakhsharī, *Kashshāf,* 1028 (also Prophethood); Diyārbakrī, *Khamīs* 1:280; Rāzī, *Mafātīḥ* 5:87.

15. See chap. 5, sec. E.

16. Tha'labī, *'Arā'is,* 320; Ṭabarī, *Jāmi'* 19:167 (> Mujāhid); Ṭabarsī, *Majma'* 19:228 (> Mujāhid); Nasafi, *Tafsīr* 4:163; Bayḍāwī, *Anwār,* 69; Ibn Kathīr, *Qiṣaṣ* (H), 440. Note also the puzzling tradition in Ṭabarī, 158, which claims that Solomon sent for the queen's throne after receiving news of her from the hoopoe, that is, even before he had sent her his missive calling on her to submit to him and to Allāh. The arrival of the throne was to be "proof" that the bird had indeed spoken the truth. This view fits neatly into that episode of the story, but it makes all that follows illogical.

17. Tha'labī, *'Arā'is,* 320; Ṭabarsī, *Majma'* 19:228; Nasafī, *Tafsīr* 4:163; Zamakhsharī, *Kashshāf,* 1029.

18. So stated in Ṭabarsī, *Majmā'* 19:228.

19. Most explicitly in Nasafī, *Tafsīr* 4:163.

20. Note Ṭabarī, *Jāmi'* 19:159–60, who states that her people were still polytheists at the time of her arrival at Solomon's court.

21. See chap. 3, sec. F and chap. 4, sec. D. One hardly had to state that Bilqīs's throne was indeed the quintessential symbol of her rule as well as her rebellion against the authority of men and God, but some Muslim exegetes are explicit in this judgment. Note Ibn Kathīr, *Bidāyah* 2:24; Ṭabarsī, *Majma'* 19:217 (> Abū Muslim); and Rāzī, *Mafātīḥ* 5:87, indicating that the throne is symbol of her rule; see also Zamakhsharī, *Kashshāf,* 1023.

22. See chap. 2, sec. C.

23. Tha'labī, *'Arā'is,* 318 (> most authorities); Ṭabarī, *Jāmi'* 19:161 (> Ibn Jurayj); Nasafī, *Tafsīr* 4:162; Jazā'irī, *Qiṣaṣ,* 428; Zamakhsharī, *Kashshāf,* 1028; Ṭabarsī, *Majma'* 19:225 (also because he was amazed at the hoopoe's description of the throne > Qatādah); Bayḍāwī, *Anwār,* 68; Rāzī, *Mafātīḥ* 5:87 (> Qatādah).

24. Ṭabarī, *Jāmi'* 19:154; Nasafī, *Tafsīr* 4:162; Bayḍāwī, *Anwār,* 67–68; Ibn Kathīr, *Qiṣaṣ* (H), 438.

25. Ibn Kathīr, *Qiṣaṣ* (H), 438. Note, however, the account of Bal'amī, *Ta'rīkh* (Zotenberg) 4:16, where the queen asks her advisors about Solomon. They respond that he is a great ruler in the Land of Syria (al-Shām) who practices the faith of the Israelites. They add that he is a prophet of God who rules over satans, jinn, birds, and wild animals. Bilqīs then recites the verse of conquerors entering a city and decides to try diplomacy instead of war. Bal'amī would seem to be indicating that she was swayed in her decision by their objective assessment of the situation.

26. See chap. 3, sec. E.

27. Tha'labī, *'Arā'is,* 318; Ṭabarī, *Jāmi'* 19:160; Ṭabarsī, *Majma'* 19:225. This tradition is only understandable in light of Ṭabarī's earlier statement that Solomon

had the queen's throne brought before sending her his ultimatum. He did that in order to verify the hoopoe's report. See n. 16 above.

28. See chap. 4, sec. E.

29. Ibid.

30. *'Arā'is,* 321. See also *EI* s.v. al-Shām and *EI²* s.v. Filasṭīn.

31. Tha'labī, *'Arā'is,* 321.

32. Jazā'irī, *Qiṣaṣ,* 408; also Ṭabarsī, *Majma'* 19:205; Zamakhsharī, *Kashshāf,* 1020; Diyārbakrī, *Khamīs* 1:272. For Solomon's legendary potency see chap. 3 n. 80, which discusses the tradition that he set out to impregnate all his wives in a single evening and succeeded in having intercourse with anywhere from forty to all one thousand of them.

33. Kisā'ī, *Qiṣaṣ,* 292–93.

34. *'Arā'is, 292; also Bayḍāwī, Anwār,* 65; Nasafī, *Tafsīr* 4:156; Diyārbakrī, *Khamīs* 1:272; Zamakhsharī, *Kashshāf,* 1019.

35. *Qiṣaṣ* (H), 433, also his *Bidāyah* 2:18.

36. Qur'ān 27:16.

37. Ibn Kathīr, *Bidāyah* 2:18, and his *Qiṣaṣ* (Q), 494; also Tha'labī, 'Arā'is, 292; Ṭabarī, *Jāmi'* 19:141; Ṭabarsī, *Majma'* 19:205; and Rāzī, *Mafātīh* 5:81–82 (indicates that the matter of Solomon's inheriting wealth was disputed among scholars); Nasafī, *Tafsīr* 4:156; Diyārbakrī, *Khamīs* 1:272; Bayḍāwī, *Anwār,* 65; and numerous others commenting on Qur'ān 27:16.

38. Explicitly stated in Ibn Kathīr, *Bidāyah* 2:21 and *Qiṣaṣ* (Q), 495–96 (> Ibn 'Abbās), but also apparent from all the other references to Solomon's air corps.

39. See chap. 2, sec. B.

40. See chap. 3, n. 9.

41. As regards the prohibition of killing the hoopoe, see for example Tha'labī, *'Arā'is,* 311 and 297 (lists other species whose lives are protected by Muḥammad's dictum).

42. See chap. 1, sec. D and chap. 3, sec. B.

43. Ṭabarsī, *Majma'* 19:213, indicates that the bird's absence without good reason would have been considered "rebellion' (*'iṣyān*), a serious offense. There is, however, nothing in the story to justify this view.

44. That is, other than Tha'labī. See *Kashshāf,* 1022. Ṭabarī, *Jāmi'* 19:146, notes that slaughtering the bird actually meant an intention to kill (execute?) the hoopoe (*qtl*) but offers no further comment.

45. For example Tha'labī, *'Arā'is,* 312 (in addition to plucking out feathers and placing him in anthill, hanging him exposed to the sun with wings plucked [> al-Daḥḥāk], tarred and hung in the sun [> Muqātil], imprisoned, exiled from his species, and banished from Solomon's service). These punishments are also discussed in sum or in part by other authorities. Note Kisā'ī, *Qiṣaṣ,* 290; Tabari, *Jāmi'* 19:145–46; Ṭabarsī, *Majma'* 19:213 (same as Tha'labī [> Ibn 'Abbās, Qatādah, and Mujāhid]); Nafasī, *Tafsīr* 4:158; Ibn Kathīr, *Bidāyah* 2:21; Bayḍāwī, *Anwār,* 66; Rāzī, *Mafātīḥ* 5:83; Bal'amī, *Ta'rīkh* (Zotenberg) 4:15.

46. *'Arā'is,* 312.

47. Tha'labī, *'Arā'is,* 311 (both versions); Kisā'ī, *Qiṣaṣ,* 289; Ṭabarsī, *Majma'* 19:213 (> Ibn 'Abbās; also version of missing place in patrol > Wahb); Nasafī, *Tafsīr* 4:157 (both versions); Ibn Kathīr, *Qiṣaṣ* (H), 436 and by *Bidāyah* 2:21; Zamakhsharī, *Kashshāf,* 1021–22 (both versions). For the hoopoe missing in the patrol without citing

need for water at time of prayer, see Jazā'rī, *Qiṣaṣ,* 423. Note also Ṭabarī, *Jāmi'* 19:143–44, which also indicates that Solomon was initially unaware of the hoopoe's talent for finding water and was apprised of that only after lengthy consultations with various elements of his entourage.

48. Tha'labī, *'Arā'is,* 312; Diyārbakrī, *Khamīs* 1:276; Kisā'ī, *Qiṣaṣ,* 290: "standing between Paradise and the Hellfire."

49. *'Arā'is,* 302; Jazā'irī, *Qiṣaṣ,* 421–22; Ibn Kathīr, *Qiṣaṣ* (H), 441–42 and his *Bidāyah* 2:25–26; Bal'amī, *Ta'rīkh* (Zotenberg) 4:32–33. See also the more formal exegesis to the Qur'ānic verses in question.

50. Tha'labī, *'Arā'is,* 302 (Naṣībīn > al-Kalbī; inherited from David > Muqātil; winged creatures from the sea > al-Ḥasan).

51. Note, however, Jazā'irī, *Qiṣaṣ,* 421, who indicates that God kept the sun from setting so that the prophet could still say his prayers. Ibn Kathīr, *Qiṣaṣ* (H), 441 adds that Muḥammad also missed saying the 'aṣr prayer during the Battle of the Trench. See also his *Bidāyah* 2:25–26. Note Bal'amī, *Ta'rīkh* (Zotenberg) 4:32, who states that according to the Torah and the ancient prophets, the afternoon prayer was not a religious obligation. It was Solomon who prescribed it for his people. It thus became the middle prayer, i.e., between the morning-noon and evening-night prayers. Hence, Qur'ān 2:238: "Guard strictly your prayers, especially the middle prayer, and stand before Allāh devout."

52. Tha'labī, *'Arā'is,* 302, explicitly mentions sacrifice; Ibn Kathīr and Jazā'irī mention the killing of the horses. To compensate Solomon for the sacrifice of the horses, God gave the prophet dominion over something swifter, namely the winds. See for example, Tha'labī, 304.

53. Ibid.

54. See also Jazā'irī, *Qiṣaṣ,* 421–22, who is more explicit as regards the linkage. He relates that in order to do penance Solomon went off by himself and gave his famous signet ring to one of his servants, who was then duped into giving it up by one of the satans. The satan, impersonating Solomon, then took over rule, and the Israelite was forced to experience a humiliating exile for forty days until he was fortuitously restored to his throne. Most authorities place this story of Solomon's exile in a different setting. See nn. 57 and 58.

55. Tha'labī, *'Arā'is,* 304 (> al-Zuhrī), and Ibn Kathīr, *Qiṣaṣ* (H), 441, also cite a minority opinion that the "passing of hands" refers to Solomon lovingly wiping the sweat from the swift horses that had paraded before him. There is also disagreement as to the number of horses. For example, Tha'labī, 302, gives the figure at one thousand, nine hundred of which were paraded before Solomon before he realized his error. Those were sacrificed; the remaining hundred were spared. He also cites the account of Ka'b indicating the number at only fourteen, all of which were killed. Ibn Kathīr, 441, puts the number of horses at ten thousand or twenty thousand, of which twenty had wings. In addition, he cites a tradition concerning Muḥammad who had come upon his child bride, 'Ā'ishah, playing with a "toy" winged horse. When asked about it, she quoted the appropriate verse from the Qur'ān, and the Prophet split his sides laughing. Bal'amī, *Ta'rīkh* 4:32, indicates one thousand horses. Tha'labī, *'Arā'is,* 304 (> Ibn 'Abbās), and Bal'amī, 33, cite a tradition attributed to 'Alī b. Abī Ṭālib commenting on the Qur'ānic verse. 'Alī contended that Solomon sacrificed a number of the horses; the others he spared to ensure the continuity of the species. Needless to say this view is consistent with Solomon's reputation as the quintessential ecologist (see chap. 4, sec. A).

56. For example, Tha'labī, *'Arā'is,* 302 (> al-Ḥasan); Ibn Kathīr, *Qiṣaṣ* (H), 442 and his *Bidāyah* 2:25.

57. Tha'labī, *'Arā'is,* 322–25; Ṭabarī, *Annales* 1/2, 586ff.; Diyārbakrī, *Khamīs* 1:283–84 (> Wahb), 285 (> al-Suddī); Kisā'ī, *Qiṣaṣ,* 293–95. See also formal commentary on Qur'ān 33:34–35. The relationship of this tradition to a Jewish Yemenite tale is explored in chap. 6, sec. F. The loss of Solomon's ring and throne is an ancient Jewish motif. For a comparative view, see Salzberger, *Salomo-Sage,* 94ff. The temporary removal of a legitimate king and his replacement with a figure of dubious character is a convention with deep roots in the world view and political ritual of the Near East.

58. Ibn Kathīr, *Qiṣaṣ* (H), 442.

59. That is certainly the conclusion to be drawn from Jazā'irī, *Qiṣaṣ,* 421–22.

60. *Jāmi'* 19:144.

61. See chap. 4, sec. B.

62. I Kings 3:5–14. The critical passage (3:7) is loosely translated or, if you prefer, faithfully paraphrased in Ya'qūbī, *Historiae* 1:61. There is no question that in this instance we are dealing with direct borrowing from the Hebrew text. See chap. 4, n. 14.

63. I Kings 3:7.

64. I Kings 3:9.

65. Kisā'ī, *Qiṣaṣ,* 278.

66. See chap. 4, sec. B esp. nn. 17, 19.

67. Tha'labī, *'Arā'is,* 318–19; Ṭabarī, *Jāmi'* 19:162–64; Ṭabarsī, *Majma'* 19:226; Nafasī, *Tafsīr* 4:162; Ibn Kathīr, *Qiṣaṣ* (Q), 502, and his *Bidāyah* 2:23–24; Jazā'irī, *Qiṣaṣ,* 427; Diyārbakrī, *Khamīs* 1:280–81; Bayḍāwī, *Anwār,* 68–69; Zamakhsharī, *Kashshāf,* 1028; Bal'amī, *Ta'rīkh* (Zotenberg) 4:218. Note also Ṭabarī, *Annales* 1/2, 508, in reference to Balaam.

68. Tha'labī, *'Arā'is,* 319; Diyārbakrī, *Khamīs* 1:280.

69. Tha'labī, *'Arā'is,* 319; Ṭabarsī, *Majma'* 19:226 (Gabriel was appointed by God to serve Solomon in bringing God's throne); Nasafī, *Tafsīr* 4:162; Ibn Kathīr, *Qiṣaṣ* (Q), 502, and his *Bidāyah* 2:23; Bayḍāwī, *Anwār,* 69.

70. Tha'labī, *'Arā'is,* 319; Diyārbakrī, *Khamīs* 1:280 (unspecified angel); Bayḍāwī, *Anwār,* 69; Zamakhsharī, *Kashshāf,* 1028.

71. See *EI*[2] s.v. Djibrā'īl.

72. Tha'labī, *'Arā'is,* 317, 320–21; Ṭabarī, *Annales* 1/2, 581–82.

73. Tha'labī, *'Arā'is,* 319; Ṭabarsī, *Majma'* 19:226; Zamakhsharī, *Kashshāf,* 1028. Read perhaps "Aṣṭūm" or "Iṣṭūm."

74. Tha'labī, *'Arā'is,* 319 (Malīḥā); Ṭabarī, *Jāmi'* 19:163 (Balīkhā); Ṭabarsī, *Majma'* 19:226 (Balīkhā).

75. Bayḍāwī, *Anwār,* 69; Ṭabarsī, *Majma'* 19:226; Diyārbakrī, *Khamīs* 2:280. See Qur'ān 27:59–81 and relevant commentary for al-Khiḍr or al-Khāḍir as Moses's companion. Briefly put, Moses seeks a servant of God to teach him. He is instructed to obey his mentor regardless of what happens. This is of course a well-known theme in the didactic literature of the Near East and beyond. See *EI*[2] s.v. al-Khaḍir for extensive bibliography of the primary and secondary sources. For Khiḍr being wiser than Moses, see Ṭabarī, *Annales* 1/2, 417, and his *Jāmi'* 15:164; Diyārbakrī, *Khamīs* 1:121. For Khiḍr living on an island, see Ṭabarī, *Annales* 1/2, 422, and Diyārbakrī, 1:121, who portrays him as the guardian of seafarers. There is considerable controversy among the Muslims as to his origins, his lifespan, and his activities. There are reports of his being a human, a prophet, and a celestial being. For a summary of these views, see Diyārbakrī, 121–22.

76. Tha'labī, *'Arā'is,* 319; Kisā'ī, *Qiṣaṣ,* 292; Muqātil, *Tafsīr* 3:307; Ṭabarī, *Jāmi'* 19:163; Ṭabarsī, *Majma'* 19:226, 230 (Solomon also knew God's mightiest name but allowed Asaph to carry on as he was being groomed to replace the prophet); Nasafī, *Tafsīr* 4:162; Zamakhsharī, *Kashshāf,* 1028 (Asaph is Solomon's scribe); Ibn Kathīr, *Bidāyah* 2:23 (son of maternal aunt), and his *Qiṣaṣ* (Q), 502; Jazā'irī, *Qiṣaṣ,* 422 (son of maternal aunt); Diyārbakrī, *Khamīs* 1:280 (wazīr and scribe); Bayḍāwī, *Anwār,* 69 (wazīr); Bal'amī, *Ta'rīkh* (Zotenberg) 4:26.

77. See n. 76 above.

78. Ibid.

79. Kisā'ī, *Qiṣaṣ,* 290.

80. Jazā'irī, *Qiṣaṣ,* 428, 434–35; Ṭabarsī, *Majma'* 19:230.

81. Tha'labī, *'Arā'is,* 322–24; Jazā'irī, *Qiṣaṣ,* 429; Diyārbakrī, *Khamīs* 1:284–85; Ya'qūbī, *Historiae* 1:63–64; Ṭabarī, *Annales* 1/2, 588; Jazā'irī, *Qiṣaṣ,* 422; Bal'amī, *Ta'rīkh* (Zotenberg) 4:25.

82. Jazā'irī, *Qiṣaṣ,* 425; Zamakhsharī, *Kashshāf,* 1028.

83. See n. 82 above.

84. Tha'labī, *'Arā'is,* 319.

85. See *EJ* s.v.

86. II Kings 18:37; Isaiah, 36:3, 22.

87. II Sam. 8:18, 23:20–23 = I Chron. 18:17, 11:22–25 (warrior for David); I Kings 1:8–44, 2:25, 29–34, 46 (supports Solomon's cause); I Kings 2:35, 4:4; I Chron. 27:5–6 (commander of Solomon's army).

88. See *MG* 6:2b.

89. I Chron. 15:17, 19. Note that Ezra 2:4 and Neh. 7:44 classify the descendants of Asaph separately from the Levites, but Ezra 3:10 seems to suggest that the singers were a subcategory of the Levites.

90. I Chr. 16:4–5, 7, 37; II Chr. 5:12, 35:15.

91. Ezra 3:10; II Chr. 35:15.

92. See *EJ* s.v. Asaph; *EI*² s.v. Āṣaf.

93. See *EI* s.v. Zabūr.

94. Note Tha'labī, *'Arā'is,* 311; and, more generally, concerning the importance of the Zabūr for Muslims, Kister, "Ḥaddithū," 230ff.

95. I Chron. 25:1–2; II Chron. 29:30.

96. Bal'amī, *Ta'rīkh* (Zotenberg) 4:18, correctly identifies Asaph as one of the great Israelites and a descendant of Levi, but he offers no further comment about his temple activities.

97. *Qiṣaṣ,* 425. Note that Muslim mystics invoked the *ism al-a'ẓam* when in need of divine intervention, no doubt a measure of their higher spirituality.

98. *BT Kiddushin* 71a. See also A. Marmorstein, *The Old Rabbinic Doctrine of God* 1:28. Numerical combinations of God's name were also used on amulets and had magical properties. For pre-exilic amulets containing the divine name, see A. Yardeni, "Remarks on the Priestly Blessing on Two Ancient Amulets from Jerusalem"; also G. Barkay, "The Divine Name Found in Jerusalem." For later numerical combinations, see the Geniza text in J. Naveh and S. Shaked, *Amulets and Magic Bowls,* 238. See also J. Trachtenberg, *Jewish Superstition and Magic,* 92–94.

99. Tha'labī, *'Arā'is,* 319; Ṭabarī, *Jāmi'* 19:163; Ṭabarsī, *Majma'* 19:226; Nasafī, *Tafsīr* 4:162; Zamakhsharī, *Kashshāf,* 1028; Diyārbakrī, *Khamīs* 2:280–81.

100. See n. 99. Note Nasafī combines this formula with *Yā Ḥayy! Yā Qayyūm!*

101. Tha'labī, *'Arā'is,* 319; Ṭabarsī, *Majma'* 19:226 (also additional formula invok-

ing Allāh and al-Raḥmn̄ "The Merciful"); Nafasi, *Tafsīr* 4:162 (combines with "O Possessor . . ."); Zamakhsharī, *Kashshāf,* 1028; Diyārbakrī, *Khamīs* 1:280–81.

102. Qur'ān 27:23, 26. See also Ibn Kathīr, *Bidāyah* 2:22.

103. Rāzī, *Mafātīḥ* (Beirut) 4:2ff.

104. Note esp. Kisā'ī, *Qiṣaṣ,* 287ff., and Diyārbakrī, *Khamīs* 1:276, 277ff. The latter account is clearly linked to an eighteenth-century C.E. Jewish folkloric tale from the Yemen. See chap. 6, sec. E.

105. See M. Ayoub, *The Qur'ān and Its Interpreters* 1:246–56.

106. Ṭabarsī, *Majma'* 19:226; Diyārbakrī, *Khamīs* 1:280; and Zamakhsharī, *Kashshāf,* 1028, identify the book with either the *Lawḥ maḥfūẓ* or *K. al-maqādir.*

107. See Ṭabarī, *Jāmi'* on Qur'ān 2:255.

108. *Mafātīḥ* (Beirut) 4:8.

109. Dan. 6:26.

110. S. Lieberman, *Greek in Jewish Palestine,* 65.

111. M. A. Friedman, *Jewish Marriage in Palestine* 2:429.

112. See A. Murtonen, *Philological and Literary Treatise of Old Testament Divine Names.* See also D. N. Freedman, "The Name of the God Moses," commenting inter alia on W. F. Albright, 54 (1935): 173–93, and 67 (1948): 377–81; R. Abba, "The Divine Name Yahwe," esp. 324.

113. Marmorstein, *Rabbinic Doctrine* 1:17–40; J. Lauterbach, "Substitutes for the Tetragrammaton." See also *EJ* s.v. God "names of."

114. Exod. 20:7 = Deut. 5:11.

115. See Marmorstein, *Rabbinic Doctrine* 1:20–32. He believes that the prohibition against pronouncing "The Name" altogether was observed but that certain compromises were effected in Hellenistic times. As a result, the tetragrammaton was pronounced by the priests. The practice of pronouncing it was limited, however, to the temple precinct. Elsewhere, a substitute (*kinui*) was employed. Even when allowed, caution was advised. Note the observation of Rabbi Tarfon in *BT Kiddushin* 71a that when he and his uncle approached the priests he heard the High Priest literally "swallow" God's ineffable name, that is, it was pronounced but not distinctly. See also n. 98 above.

116. *BT Sotah* 37b–38a; *BT Yoma* 66a–b. Reference to these events and the texts describing them is found in the Musaf or additional service for Yom Kippur, the Day of Atonement. A full text is preserved in all the traditional High Holiday prayer books. The priestly blessing is based on Num. 6:24–26: "May *YHWH* bless you and keep you. May *YHWH* make His countenance shine upon you and be gracious to you. May *YHWH* turn towards you and give you peace." A later and more expanded version is found in the Dead Sea Scrolls (IQ Serekh I,2). Note also that the priestly blessing is found on ancient amulets dated before the destruction of the temple (586 C.E.), and the pronunciation of the tetragrammaton is called for in ancient incantations in order to secure blessings and ward off evil. See Yardeni, "Remarks," 184 and n. 98 above.

117. Apparently in a muted and somewhat garbled manner. See n. 115 above.

118. *Majma'* 19:226.

119. Hebrew *'ehye asher 'ehye.*

120. The meaning of these passages has given rise to considerable commentary. Some scholars prefer to read *a-h-y-h* as a causative even though the hiph'il form does not exist for *h-y-h.* Most intriguing is Abba's contention that the vocalized *'ehye* is the imperfect and signifies the continuing, indeed eternal presence of Israel's God in the affairs of the people. Thus it should be understood as "I Shall Be what I Shall Be." See n. 112 above.

121. The only text that I know of linking Asaph to the temple is Bal'amī's brief reference to the Israelite as a descendant of Levi. See *Ta'rīkh* (Zotenberg) 4:18. According to Num. 6:23, only the Aaronid priests offered the priestly blessing in which God's name was pronounced. On the other hand, Deut. 10:8 and 21:5 indicate that all the Levites blessed the people. One can hardly believe that this division of opinion in the Hebrew Bible is the source for Muslim's elevating Asaph as intercessor on Solomon's behalf before God.

122. See M. J. Kister, "Ḥaddithū," and the additional notes to the reprint in his *Studies in Jāhilliya and Early Islam.*

123. The complexities of this polemic are illustrated in J. Lassner, "The Covenant of the Prophets: Muslim Texts, Jewish Subtexts." See also his "The Origins of Muslim Attitudes Towards Jews and Judaism." The point of departure for all studies of Muslim-Jewish polemics remains M. Steinschneider, *Polemische und apologetische Literatur in arabischer Sprache.* More recently, there have been the studies of M. Perlmann, whose researches are summarized in his "The Medieval Polemics between Islam and Judaism."

124. For the development and meaning of the term "Islam," see EI^2 s.v.; also D. H. Baneth, "What Did Muḥammad Mean When He Called His Religion Islām? The Original Meaning of Aslama and Its Derivatives"; H. Ringgren, *Islam Aslama and Muslim* (reviewing the previous literature); M. Bravmann, *The Spiritual Background of Early Islam,* 7–26.

125. See n. 122.

126. *EI^2* s.v. Khaybar.

127. *'Arā'is,* 311.

128. Chap. 3, sec. A.

129. *EI^2* s.v. al-Ḥaramayn.

130. *EI^2* s.v. Ka'ba.

131. *EI^2* s.v. Ibrāhīm and Ḥanīf.

132. Ibn Kathīr, *Qiṣaṣ* (Q), 506–507, and his *Bidāyah* 2:26; Kisā'ī, *Qiṣaṣ,* 285 (Mecca preferred to all other settlements); and relevant commentary to Qur'ān 38:25. A detailed study of the sanctity of Mecca in relation to other holy settlements can be found in M. J. Kister, "'You Shall Only Set Our For Three Mosques'—A Study of an Early Tradition" (additional notes in the reprint of his studies titled *Studies in Jāhilliya and Early Islam*). One could argue that this tradition is not directed specifically towards the Jews but towards the Umayyad caliph, 'Abd al-Malik, who, during the revolt of the Zubayrids in the Ḥijāz, sought to promote Jerusalem as a holy settlement. According to this view, he erected the Dome of the Rock in Jerusalem and made the city an alternative center for the pilgrimage to counter his rival, 'Abdallāh b. al-Zubayr, who exploited the sanctity of Mecca (see I. Goldziher, *Muslim Studies* 2:32–35). The argument for 'Abd al-Malik's policy, which rests largely on a single source (Ya'qūbī, *Historiae* 2:311), is denied by S. D. Goitein in his "Sanctity of Jerusalem and Palestine," 135–148. The inscriptions from the Dome of the Rock would seem to indicate that the building was erected to counter the sacred claims of the Byzantines. See O. Grabar, "The Umayyad Dome of the Rock in Jerusalem." There is, nevertheless, a plethora of old traditions that show concern over the general tendency of Muslims to make additional pilgrimages to sites other than the Ḥaramayn. Over the course of time, these traditions, for and against additional pilgrimages, could easily have served various functions, including an anti-Jewish polemic.

133. Ibn Kathīr, *Qiṣaṣ* (Q), 506–507, and his *Bidāyah* 2:26; also Diyārbakrī, *Khamīs* 1:274, and relevant commentary to Qur'ān 38:25. For a tradition linking the sanctity of Mecca and the Prophet's authority as the seal of the prophets, see Kister, "Three Mosques," 178. Quoting various authorities: "I am the Seal of the Prophets and my mosque is the seal of the mosques of the prophets . . ."

134. *'Arā'is,* 311.

135. *Kashshāf,* 1021; for the sacrifices, see also Diyārbakrī, *Khamīs* 1:274. See also Jazā'irī, *Qiṣaṣ,* 409 (Solomon covers the sanctuary).

136. *'Arā'is,* 311; also Diyārbakrī's more extensive comment (*Khamīs* 1:274), which has Solomon offering a description of Muḥammad, the future prophet who will appear a thousand years hence, and predicts as well that Muḥammad will be victorious against all who resist him. He also notes, as does Tha'labī, that Muḥammad will be the "Lord and Seal of the Prophets."

137. Jazā'irī, *Qiṣaṣ,* 412.

138. See Lassner, "Covenant of the Prophets," 209–220.

Chapter Six

1. A. Geiger, *Was hat Mohammed aus den Judenthume aufgenommen?*

2. See for example, M. Grünbaum, *Neue Beiträge zur semitischen Sagenkunde;* H. Hirschfeld, *Jüdische Elemente im Koran;* M. Maas, *Bibel und Koran;* I. Schapiro, *Die haggadischen Elemente im erzählenden Teil des Korans;* D. Sidersky, *Les origines des légendes musulmanes;* H. Speyer, *Die biblischen Erzählungen im Qoran;* G. Weil, *Biblische Legenden der Muselmänner* and the English version, *The Bible, the Koran and the Talmud;* The most recent work that attaches importance to vague similarities in Jewish and Muslim traditions is that of A. Katsh, *Judaism in Islam.* The study of Jewish influence in Islam has again become a subject of interest. There is every reason to expect that contemporary scholars will have a more complex view of cultural transactions.

3. Much has been said recently of orientalists and of "orientalism." See the influential work of E. Said, *Orientalism.* Said's work, which has stirred much controversy, is seriously flawed by not considering the German contributions to Islamic studies and, related to that, by its failure to draw necessary distinctions between early and mid-nineteenth-century scholarship and the work of scholars following T. Nöldeke and I. Goldziher, the founders of the modern discipline. Said also draws no significant distinction between the "orientalist" discourse of political functionaries and traveling romantics and the scholarship of academicians from the universities of Europe. A full history of nineteenth-century scholarship on Islam remains a desideratum. As regards Jewish scholars of Islam, see the essay of B. Lewis, "The Pro-Islamic Jews." See also L. Conrad, "The Dervish's Disciple: On the Personality and Intellectual Milieu of the Young Ignaz Goldziher" (using Goldziher's published diaries, various rare publications, and R. Simon's biography: *Ignac Goldziher: His Life and Scholarship as Reflected in his Works and Correspondence*). Note also Conrad's "The Near East Study Tour Diary of Ignaz Goldziher." The latter article serves to correct the faulty annotation of R. Patai, the editor of Goldziher's *Oriental Diary,* which supplements Goldziher's more detailed *Tagebuch.*

4. Kister, "Ḥaddithū."

5. In addition to Kister, note 4 above, see Goldziher, *Muslim Studies* 2:131 n. 3; G. Vajda, "Juifs et Musulmans selon le ḥadīt," 115–20; also *EI*[2] s.v. Isrā'īliyyāt.

6. A study of the Muslim understanding of the Hebrew Bible by H. Lazarus-Yaffe is

currently in press. See F. Rosenthal, "The Influence of the Biblical Tradition on Muslim Historiography," esp. 40ff.; W. M. Watt, "The Early Development of the Muslim Attitude to the Bible."

7. For a general overview of the problem and various viewpoints, see C. C. Torrey, *The Jewish Foundation of Islam;* H. Z. Hirschberg, *Yisrael ba-'Arav;* and most recently G. Newby, *A History of the Jews of Arabia.*

8. The argument for Christian influence on the development of early Islam is forcefully argued by R. Bell, *The Origin of Islam in its Christian Environment.*

9. Oral communication of I. Shahid of Georgetown University.

10. See the detailed study of S. D. Goitein, "Mi Hayuu Rabbotav ha-Muvhaqim shel Muhammad," on the extent of Muhammad's learning of Judaica and the means by which he was likely to have acquired that education. These views are summed up in his *Ha-Islam shel Muhammad,* a course reader circulated for students of the Hebrew University.

11. Concerning the possible influence of early Jewish converts on the Islamic tradition and the social dynamics of conversion and its influence on the transmission of cultural artifacts, see Lassner, "Covenant of the Prophets," 234ff. esp. 234–35.

12. For a general overview of Jewish-Muslim and Jewish-Christian disputes, see S. W. Baron, *History* 5:86–137. Among the Jewish converts to Islam who engaged in polemics against their former coreligionists were Samau'al al-Maghribī (fl. 12th century) and 'Abd al-Ḥaqq al-Islāmī (fl. ca. 14th century). See the excellent summary in M. Perlmann, "The Medieval Polemics between Islam and Judaism"; and his "'Abd al-Ḥaḳḳ al-Islāmī: A Jewish Convert."

13. For Ka'b, see *EI*[2] s.v. The bibliography should be augmented by I. Wolfensohn, *Ka'b al-Aḥbār und seine Stellung in Hadīt und der islamischin Legendenliteratur.* For 'Abdallāh b. Salām, see *EI* s.v. 'Abd Allah b. Salām.

14. This subject is taken up by H. Lazarus-Yafeh in her soon to appear work on Muslims and the Hebrew Bible.

15. The reference is to H. Ben-Shammai, "Observations on the Beginnings on Judaeo-Arabic Civilization," which was presented at The Jews of Medieval Islam: Community, Society, Identity, an international conference held in London in June 1992. I am currently unaware of any plans to publish this stimulating paper.

16. An exception is 'Alī b. Rabban al-Ṭabarī (fl. 9th century). See D. S. Margoliouth, "On 'The Book of Religion and Empire' by 'Alī b. Rabban al-Ṭabarī"; F. Taeschner, "Die alttestamentlichen Bibelzitate vor allem aus dem Pentateuch in Aṭ-Ṭabarīs Kitāb ad-dīn wad-daula und ihre Bedeutung für die Frage nach der Echtheit dieser Schrift."

17. Ya'qūbī, *Historiae* 1:61.

18. This view is adopted with interesting results by R. Firestone in his recent study of the evolution of the Abraham-Ishmael legends in Islamic exegesis. See his *Journeys in Holy Lands,* 6–21 esp. 15–18.

19. See chap. 1, secs. B through E.

20. *M. Proverbs,* 2–12 esp. 8–12. These comments are found in the terse introduction to Visotzky's translation for the Yale Judaica Series. A far more extensive analysis is found in the introduction to volume 1 of his doctoral dissertation which is, as the title indicates, "A Critical Edition Based on Manuscripts and Early Editions with an Annotated English Translation of Chapters One through Ten." The date and place of origin is discussed (pp. 5–55—sums up in great detail all the previous scholarship); as is style

(pp. 56–77); and the text and manuscript traditions (78–112). Volume two, the critical edition appeared as a separate publication, which continues the text through chapter 31.

21. Visotzky, "Critical Edition," 139–49.

22. The reference is to the first riddle concerning birth and nurture. See *Ekha Rabbah,* 1.11.

23. Chap. 1, sec. D.

24. The analysis of the Solomonic material is discussed in chap. 1, sec. E. The most recent treatment of the manuscript traditions is discussed in the introduction to E. Yassif's edition. See Ps. Ben Sira, 7–19. Yassif's edition is not a composite text but one that preserves two distinct but related versions. The divergence in detail between the different sources would seem to indicate a much earlier common source. A systematic breakdown of all the sources utilized by the redactors of the Ben Sira tradition would be extremely useful. It is, nevertheless, clear from Yassif's footnotes that the current text is a repository of older rabbinic material.

25. Ibid., 19–29.

26. See his "Das Herz auf dem Lande."

27. The name Baghdad actually predates the Islamic city. The Arabic lexicographers have many fanciful explanations for it. It is, however, safe to say that the place called Baghdad that was chosen by al-Manṣūr to be his imperial capital was not previously the site of an important city. For the name Baghdad, see *EI*[2] s.v.; for the city of al-Manṣūr, see Lassner, *Topography,* 138–54, and his *'Abbāsid Rule,* 184–203.

28. Ps. Ben Sira, 217–18; for detail see chap. 1, sec. E. The Muslim version is discussed in chap. 3, sec. G, and chap. 4, sec. E.

29. Ṭabarsī, *Majma'* 19:229; Balkhī, *Bad'* 3:108.

30. *BT Hullin* 88b.

31. Chap. 1, sec. D.

32. B. Grossfeld, *The Two Targums to Esther.* The annotated translation of the second targum using MS *Sassoon* 282 as the skeletal text is found on pp. 96–195; the segment on Solomon on 103–117. Note that this translation is apparently based on a somewhat different text than that which is printed in the editions of *MG,* the compendium of bible commentaries read by learned Jews. The latter serves as the basis for my translation in the appendix.

33. Ibid., 3–7.

34. Ibid., 7–12, 199–201.

35. Summed up by Grossfeld, 199–201.

36. Ibid., 14–16. Note esp. the views of S. Gelbhaus, *Das Targum Scheni zum Buche Esther,* 24ff.

37. *MG* 6:5a–b.

38. For a summary of Byzantine rule in Palestine at the time and its effects on the Jews, see M. Gil, *Erez* 1:4ff.

39. Ibid., 5–6, citing the account of the monk Antiochus Eustratios, known by his shortened name Strategios. The monk's anti-Jewish account of their collaboration with the Persians was repeated in later sources. Note, however, Gil's reservations as to the veracity of Strategios's report.

40. Note Qur'ān 30:2–3 in the Sūrah called "al-Rūm." The verses reflect upon the Byzantine defeats at the hands of the Sasanians and predict that the former will rebound, a seeming reference to the reconquest of Jerusalem under Heraclius.

41. See chap. 5, sec. I.

42. See chap. 5, sec. C. For other instances of Islamization see chap. 5, secs. D–I.
43. See chap. 1, sec. B.
44. See chap. 1, sec. A.
45. IFA, 724.
46. Y. Avida, "Ma'aseh Malkat Sheva," 1–17.
47. JTS Enelow, 874.
48. Avida, "Ma'aseh," 1. Avida's contention that the author was not very literate nor a great grammarian does not do justice to the exquisite manner in which he occasionally uses scriptural allusions to reinforce his point. Saadiah, if nothing else, was a skilled storyteller, as Avida is forced to acknowledge.
49. Ibid. Avida's despair at recovering the Muslim substratum is not entirely warranted. See chap. 6, secs. E and F.
50. Avida, "Ma'aseh," 1.
51. Ibid., 5–7, 11–15.
52. I Kings 1:10.
53. Avida, "Ma'aseh," 5.
54. The play is on I Kings 10:13 where Solomon satisfies all the queen's desires.
55. See chap. 2, sec. C.
56. Avida, "Ma'aseh," 7.
57. Diyārbakrī, *Khamīs* 1:276–77. See also Ibn al-Athīr, *Kāmil* 1:231.
58. Mas'ūdī, *Murūj* 3:152.
59. Avida, "Ma'aseh," 7–9, 15–17.
60. For Muslim parallels, see chap. 3 n. 22.
61. Avida, "Ma'aseh," 8.
62. The seeming allusion is to I Sam. 10:1: "Then Samuel took the vial of oil and poured it upon his head and kissed him saying, 'Is it not that the Lord has anointed you as prince [*nagid*] over His land [*nahalah*]?'" The reference in Samuel is to the anointing of Saul.
63. Based on Ezra 1:2: "Thus said Cyrus King of Persia, 'All the kingdoms of the earth *YHWH,* the Lord of the Heavens, gave me; and he charged me with building a house for him in Jerusalem, which is in Judah.'"
64. Avida, "Ma'aseh," 8, based on II Sam. 10:12: "We shall indeed prevail for our people and the cities of our God; *YHWH* will do as He sees fit to do." The reference here is to Joab's campaign against the enemies of the Israelites. By omitting the reference to the God of the Israelites, Saadiah can utilize the passage to suit his own purposes.
65. Avida, "Ma'aseh," 8. The reference to "bowing" may be a humorous play on Dan. 3:17–18: "[17] If our God whom we serve is able to deliver us, He will deliver us from the fiery furnace and out of your grasp O King. [18] If not, let it be known to you, O King, that we will not serve your gods or bow down to the golden image which you have erected." If there is a linkage between the biblical text and Saadiah's rendering of the island king's response, then the author has stood the meaning of Dan. 3:18 on its head. That is, it is the idol-worshiping king that invokes his god's protection against the King of the Israelites and his God.
66. The reference is to Esther 1:12: "But Vashti, the Queen, refused to comply with the king's command delivered by the chamberlains; whereupon the king was livid and burned with anger." The use of the passage from Esther foretells the demise of the recalcitrant king. It also links Saadiah's account with that of the *Targum Sheni,* which he later cites in connection with the Queen of Sheba's visit to Solomon's court.

67. Based on Jer. 19:7: "And I will void the counsel of Judah and Jerusalem in this place; and will cause them to fall by the sword before their enemies and by the hand of those who seek their lives; and I shall give their carcasses as food to the birds of the sky and the beasts of the earth." See also the imagery of Solomon's letter of demands to the Queen of Sheba in the *Targum Sheni* (see chap. 1, sec. D).

68. Avida, "Ma'aseh," 9, based on Jer. 8:17 speaking of the Lord's vengeance: "From Dan is heard the snorting of his horses; the whole land shook at the sound of his neighing steeds; they came and devoured the land and all in it, the city and its inhabitants."

69. See Num. 22:32.

70. Avida, "Ma'aseh," 9, based on Jer. 37:24 in response to the boasts of Sennacherib, the Assyrian King: "You have taunted the Lord through your servants, saying, 'With the multitude of my chariots, I climbed to the mountain tops; I reached the innermost parts of the Lebanon and have leveled its tall cedars and choice cypress trees; I have reached its greatest height, the forest of its fruited field.'" Here again the author reverses the meaning of the text. It is not an enemy of the Israelites such as Sennacherib that utters these words but Solomon who, acting as God's servant, will defeat and utterly annihilate the boastful island king.

71. Gen. 14:10 in reference to the flight of the kings of Sodom and Gomorrah.

72. Based on I Sam. 15:8: "And he took Agag, the king of the Amalekites alive and annihilated all the people by the sword." The author thus calls attention to Saul, who, contrary to God's command, spared the Amalekite while killing all of his people. Solomon will not make this mistake.

73. Seemingly based on Jer. 39:5–9, where Nebuchadnezzar rendered judgment against the captured Zedekiah, killing his sons, putting out his eyes, and destroying the Israelite polity.

74. Avida, "Ma'aseh," 9.

75. See chap. 5, sec. F.

76. Tha'labī, *'Arā'is,* 322ff.; Kisā'ī, *Qiṣaṣ,* 293–95; Ṭabarī, *Annales* 1/2, 586–94; Ya'qūbī, *Historiae* 1:63–64; Ibn al-Athīr, *Kāmil* 1:238ff.; Diyārbakrī, *Khamīs* 1:283–84; Zamakhsharī, *Kashshāf,* 1236; Bal'amī, *Ta'rīkh* (Zotenberg) 4:24–26. For Jewish parallels, see Salzberger, *Salomo-Sage,* 94ff.

77. *Qiṣaṣ,* 293.

78. Tha'labī, *'Arā'is,* 322 (followed by all other authorities naming the king). Note also Diyārbakrī, *Khamīs* 1:283, who gives Ṣaydūn as the name of the island (reference linked somehow to Sidon?).

79. For example Tha'labī, *'Arā'is,* 322; see also n. 43 above.

80. Ibid.

81. *Qiṣaṣ,* 293.

82. See chap. 5, sec. F.

83. Avida, "Ma'aseh," 9–11, 17.

84. Ibid., 10.

85. Prov. 25:15. That is to say, they quoted Solomon's own book in his presence.

86. Based on Esther 10:2: "And all the acts [*ma'aseh*] of his power and bravery as well as the full account of Mordecai's greatness, for the king made him great, are they not inscribed in the chronicles of the kings of Media and Persia?"

87. Referring to Josh. 7:5: "And they smote among them, the men of Ai, some thirty-six men; and they chased them before the gate even until Shebarim; and they smote them at the descent; and the hearts of the people melted and turned to water."

There is an apparent play on words here. The reference to the people of Ai can be understood as a reference to the pursuit and extermination of the island people mentioned above. Note "island" in Hebrew is *'i,* which orthographically is the same as *'Ai.* That is, Solomon's victory over the island king caused the dismay of the Shebans.

88. I Kings 10:9.

89. See chap. 1, sec. B.

90. I Kings 5:10–15.

91. Avida suggests a connection to *BT Berakhot* 3a. Note also the expression *moz^erot bi-lvanah.*

92. Based on Lev. 15:19–33, 18:19; Ezek. 18:6, 22:10. See *EJ* s.v. Niddah for a summary of these complex issues; also H. Eilberg-Schwartz, *The Savage in Judaism,* esp. 177–95, combining the insights of anthropology with a reading of the traditional Jewish sources on ritual pollution; and the anthropologist M. Douglas, *Purity and Danger,* linking broadly laws of purity to the condition of the body politic. Despite the informing discussion of anthropologists, the laws of ritual purity remain problematic to scholars.

93. Lev. 18:19.

94. *ARNA,* 8ff., which also notes that it is not even possible for an unclean woman to sleep on a couch next to her husband fully clothed or to dress or apply makeup in a way that will make her alluring to men.

95. Prov. 26:5.

96. See chap. 1, sec. B.

97. Ibid., and chap. 1, sec. C.

98. Ibid. For the Islamic accounts see chap. 3, sec. E and chap. 4, sec. D. Note also the Jewish folklore below (chap. 6, sec. H).

99. See chap. 1, sec. B.

100. See chap. 2, sec. C.

101. There may be an echo here of the affair between Solomon's parents: David and Bathsheba. It will be recalled that the latter was still married to Urriah the Hittite when an infatuated David impregnated her. That required the death of Urriah, so as to allow the king license to marry the woman he loved. The entire episode was condemned by Nathan the Prophet in his famous parable and resulted in God taking retribution on all of Israel and on the ruling family. See II Sam. 11–12.

102. That is, the *Targum Sheni;* Ps. Ben Sira; and the various Muslim sources esp. Tha'labī. See chap. 1, secs. D and E, chap. 3, sec. G, chap. 4, sec. D.

103. See n. 102 above.

104. Other accounts speak of a court of glass.

105. See chap. 1, sec. E.

106. Neh. 13:26. Referring to the previous verse: ". . . You shall not give your daughters unto their sons, nor shall you take their daughters for your sons or for yourselves." And continuing (26): "Did not Solomon sin as regards that . . ."

107. *MR Song of Songs,* 9. In the larger discussion of Solomon's behavior there is the suggestion that in his activities with women he was not sensitive to Jewish practice. Note the commentary on I Kings 11:1–2: "King Solomon loved many foreign women . . . of the nations concerning which the Lord said, 'You shall not mingle with them nor shall they mingle with you; for surely they will turn away your heart after their gods'; Solomon cleaved to them [the women] out of love." Rabbi Joshua Ben Levi understood this to mean that Solomon took up with these foreign women against Deut. 7:3: "You shall not marry among them nor give your daughter to their son or take for your son

their daughter. [(4) For they will turn your son from me and he shall worship foreign gods; wherupon the wrath of God will be upon you and He will quickly destroy you.]" Rabbi Simeon Ben Jochai understood love to mean fornication, that is Solomon was driven by unbridled passion. A different view is that of Rabbi Jose Ben Halafta who suggests that Solomon loved them in order to "draw them close, convert them and bring them under the wings of the Divine Presence."

108. Anecdotal evidence suggests that the Yemenites are particularly stringent as regards the laws of ritual purity.

109. IFA, 8152.

110. IFA, 1340.

111. Bialik, *Vayᵉhi ha-Yom,* 111–23 (trans. of Tha'labī), 107–110 (adapted from Jewish sources); *Sefer ha-Aggadah,* 95–98. E. Spicehandler informs me that among Bialik's juvenalia is a poem about the Queen of Sheba and that the story also made its way into the Yiddish folklore of *Zena u-Re'na,* a work read by women.

Postscript

1. *Discovering Eve.*
2. Ibid., 122–88.
3. Ibid., 189–96.
4. Ibid., 190.
5. Ibid., 191.
6. An example of this kind of scholarship is J. Wegner, "The Image and Status of Women in Classical and Rabbinic Judaism," 68–93.
7. See Frymer-Kensky, *Goddesses,* 203–20.
8. Meyers, *Discovering Eve,* 196.
9. I Kings 21:1–29.
10. See R. Kraemer, "Jewish Women in the Diaspora World of Late Antiquity," 43–67.
11. For a highly schematic survey of Jewish women in the Middle Ages, see J. Baskin, "Jewish Women in the Middle Ages," 94–114. For the Geniza materials, see S. D. Goitein's magisterial five-volume study, *A Mediterranean Society.*
12. Note the recent studies of D. Spellberg, "Political Action and Public Example: 'A'isha and the Battle of the Camel," 45–57; and L. Ahmad, "Early Islam and the Position of Women: The Problem of Interpretation," 58–73. More appropriate to an understanding of what can be gleaned from literary sources is F. Rosenthal's pathbreaking, "Sources for the Role of Sex in Medieval Muslim Society," 3–22.

Bibliography

The bibliography is alphabetically ordered with no consideration given to the Arabic definite article (*al-*), which is often prefixed to a given name. Thus the exegete al-Ṭabarī appears as though his name were written Ṭabarī. The same principle applies to the Hebrew definite article (*ha-*). Works are listed under the name of the author, with the exception of compilations and editions of anonymous works, which are listed by title. Where more than one edition of a work was used, both are noted. The bibliography is essentially limited to works cited in the text and is therefore not to be considered inclusive. It is divided into primary and secondary sources; translations of original texts that are copiously annotated are listed among the primary sources.

Primary Sources

Abot dᵉRabbi Nathan [A and B]. Edited by S. Schechter. Vienna, 1887; [A] translated by J. Golden as *The Fathers According to Rabbi Nathan*. YJS 10. New Haven, 1955. [B] translated by A. Saldarini. Leiden, 1975.

Aggadat Bᵉreshit. Edited by S. Buber. Cracow, 1902.

Aggadat Shir ha-Shirim (*Song of Songs*). Edited by S. Schechter. Cambridge, 1896.

Aggudat Aggadot. Edited by H. Horowitz. Frankfurt a.M., 1881.

Alphabetum Siriacidis; see Pseudo Ben Sira.

al-Baghdādī, ʿAbd al-Qāhir b. Ṭāhir. *Al-Farq bayn al-firaq*. Edited by M. Badr. Cairo, 1910; translated and annotated as *Moslem Schisms and Sects*. 2 vols. K. Seelye, trans., vol. 1. New York, 1920. A. Halkin, trans., vol. 2. Tel Aviv, 1935.

Balʿamī. See Zotenberg, H.

al-Balkhī, Aḥmad b. Sahl. *K. al-badʾ wa al-taʾrīkh*. Edited by C. Huart. 6 vols. Paris, 1899.

Batte Midrashot. Edited by A. Wertheimer. 4 vols. Jerusalem, 1893–97. 2d ed. by S. Wertheimer. 2 vols. Jerusalem, 1967.

al-Bayḍāwī, ʿAbdallāh b. ʿUmar. *Anwār al-tanzīl wa-asrār al-taʾwīl*. Edited by H. O. Fleischer. 2 vols. in 1. Leipzig, 1846–48.

al-Bayhāqī, Ibrāhīm b. Muḥammad. *K. al-maḥāsin wa al-masāwī*. Edited by F. Schwally. Giessen, 1902.

Bet ha-Midrash. Edited by A. Jellinek. 6 vols. Leipzig, 1853–77.

al-Dhahabī, Muḥammad b. Aḥmad. *K. tadhkirat al-ḥuffāẓ*. 5 vols. Hyderabad, 1915–16.

al-Dīnawarī, Muḥammad b. Aḥmad. *K. al-akhbār al-ṭiwāl*. Edited by V. Guirgass. Leiden, 1888; indexes by I. Kratchkovsky, 1912.

al-Diyārbakrī, Ḥusayn b. Muḥammad. *K. al-Khamīs*. 2 vols. Cairo, 1302/1884.

Estori Parhi. *Kaftor va-Ferah*. Edited by A. Luncz. Jerusalem, 1897–98.

Ibn ʿAbbās, ʿAbdallāh. *Tanwīr al-miqbās min tafsīr Ibn ʿAbbās*. Beirut, n.d.

Ibn ʿAbd Rabbihī, Aḥmad b. Muḥammad. *Al-ʿIqd al-farīd*. 6 vols. Cairo, 1965.

Ibn al-Anbarī. *Al-Bayān fi gharīb al-Qur'ān*. Cairo, 1390/1970.
Ibn al-Athīr, 'Alī b. Muḥammad. *Al-Kāmil fi al-ta'rīkh*. 13 vols. Beirut, 1385–87/1965–67.
———. *Al-Lubāb fī tahdhīb al-ansāb*. 3 vols. Cairo, 1357/1938.
Ibn Ḥazm, 'Alī b. Muḥammad. *K. al-faṣl fī al-milal*. Cairo, 1317/1903; translated and annotated by I. Friedlander. "The Heterodoxies of the Shiites." *JAOS* 28 (1907): 1–80; 29 (1908): 1–83.
Ibn Hishām. *K. sīrat Rasūl Allāh*. Edited by T. 'Abd al-Ra'ūf. 4 vols. Beirut, n.d.; translated by A. Guillaume. *The Life of Muḥammad*. London, 1955.
Ibn Isḥāq; see Ibn Hishām.
Ibn al-Jawzī, 'Abd al Raḥmān b. 'Alī. *Al-Muntaẓam fi ta'rīkh al-mulūk wa al-umam*. Vols. 5^2–10. Hyderbad, 1938–39.
Ibn Kathīr, Ismā'īl b. 'Umar. *Al-Bidāyah wa al-nihāyah*. 14 vols. Cairo, 1351–1359/1932–1940.
———. *Qiṣaṣ al-anbiyā'*. Beirut (Dār al-Qalam), 1405/1985; Beirut (Dar wa Maktabat al-Hilāl), 1405/1985.
———. *Tafsīr al-Qur'ān al-'aẓīm*. 4 vols. Beirut, 1405/1984.
Ibn Khayyāt, Khalīfah al-'Uṣfurī. *Ta'rīkh*. 2 vols. Najaf, 1967.
Ibn Manẓūr, Muḥammad b. Mukarran. *Lisān al-'Arab*. 3 vols. Beirut, n.d.
Ibn Qutaybah, 'Abdallāh b. Muslim. *K. al-ma'ārif*. Edited by F. Wüstenfeld. Gottingen, 1850.
———. *Tafsīr gharā'ib al-Qur'ān*. Cairo, 1378/1958.
———. *Ta'wīl mushkil al-Qur'ān*. Cairo, 1393/1973.
———. *'Uyūn al-akhbār*. 4 vols. Cairo, 1373/1953.
Ibn Sulaymān, Muqātil. *Tafsīr*. 5 vols. Cairo, 1988.
Ibn Ṭabāṭabā, Muḥammad b. 'Alī. *Al-Kitāb al-fakhrī fi al-ādāb al-sulṭānīyah wa al-duwal al-islāmīyah*. Edited by H. Derenbourg. Paris, 1895; translated and annotated by E. Amar. *Histoire des dynasties musulmanes depuis la mort de Mahomet jusqu'à la chute du Khalifat 'Abbāside de Baghdadz*. Paris, 1910.
Ibn Taymīyah, Taqī al-Dīn. *Al-Tafsīr al-kubrā*. 7 vols. Beirut, 1401/1981.
al-Iṣfahānī, 'Alī b. Ḥusayn. *K. al-aghānī*. 20 vols. Beirut, 1390/1970. Vol. 21 edited by R. Brünnow. Leipzig, 1888.
al-Iṣfahānī, Ḥamzah b. al-Ḥasan. *Tawārīkh sinī mulūk al-arḍ wa al-anbiyā'*. Edited by J. M. E. Gottwald. 2 vols. Leipzig, 1844, 1848.
al-Jahshiyārī, Muḥammad b. 'Abdūs. *K. al-wuzarā'*. Cairo, 1357/1938.
Jawālīqī, Mawhūb b. Aḥmad. *Mu'arrab min al-kalām*. Leipzig, 1867.
al-Jazā'irī, Ni'mat Allāh. *Qiṣaṣ al-anbiyā'*. Beirut, 1398/1978.
al-Khaṭīb al-Baghdādī, Aḥmad b. 'Alī. *Ta'rīkh Baghdād*. 14 vols. Cairo, 1931; topographical introduction edited, translated, and annotated by G. Salmon as *L'Introduction topographique à l'histoire de Baghdadh*. Paris, 1904; translated and annotated by J. Lassner as *The Topography of Baghdad in the Early Middle Ages: Text and Studies*. Detroit, 1970.
al-Khū'ī, Abū al-Qāsim al-Mūsāwī. *Al-Bayān fi tafsīr al-Qur'ān*. Beirut, 1395/1975.
al-Kisā'ī, Muḥammad b. 'Abdallāh. *Qiṣaṣ al-anbiyā'*. Edited by I. Eisenberg. Leiden, 1922–23.
Ma'aseh ha-Nemalah. Edited by A. Jellinek in *BM* 5:22–26.
al-Mas'ūdī, 'Alī b. al-Ḥusayn. *K. al-tanbīh wa al-ishrāf*. Edited by M. J. De Goeje. BGA 8. Leiden, 1894.

———. *Murūj al-dhahab wa ma'ādin al-jawāhir.* Edited and translated by C. Barbier de Meynard and P. Courteille as *Les praires d'ôr.* 9 vols. Paris, 1861–77.

Midrash Abba Gorion. Edited by S. Buber in *Sefer d^eAggad^eta.* Wilna, 1886: 1–42.

Midrash Aggadah. Edited S. Buber. Vienna, 1894.

Midrash 'Aseret ha-Dibrot. Edited by A. Jellinek in *BM* 1:62–90.

Midrash B^ereshit Rabbati. Edited by H. Albeck. Jerusalem, 1945.

Midrash Ekha Rabbah. Edited S. Buber. Wilna, 1887.

Midrash Esther. Edited by H. Horowitz in *Aggudot Aggadot,* 56–75.

Midrash Exodus Rabbah, Midrash Numbers Rabbah. Wilno, 1887.

Midrash Lekah Tov. Edited by S. Buber in *Sifre d^eAggad^eta,* 85–112.

Midrash Mishle (Proverbs). Edited by S. Buber. Wilna, 1893; also edited by B. Visotzky. New York, 1990; translated by Visotzky with light annotation as *The Midrash on Proverbs.* YJS 27. New York, 1992; lengthy introduction and full annotation of the first ten of thirty-one chapters in his "Midrash Mishle: A Critical Edition Based on Manuscripts and Early Editions with an Introduction and Annotated English Translation of Chapters One through Ten." Vol. 1. Ph.D. diss., The Jewish Theological Seminary of New York, 1970.

Midrash Panim Aherim. Edited by S. Buber in *Sifre d^eAggad^eta,* 45–82.

Midrash Rabbah (Genesis-Deuteronomy). 11 vols. Edited by M. Mirkin. Tel Aviv, 1986.

Midrash Rabbah Shir ha-Shirim (Song of Songs). Edited by S. Dunsky. Jerusalem and Tel Aviv, 1980.

Midrash Sh^emuel (Samuel). Edited by S. Buber. Wilna, 1893.

Midrash Shir ha-Shirim (Song of Songs). Edited by S. Buber. Wilna, 1887.

Midrash Tanhuma. Edited by S. Buber. 2 vols. Wilna, 1885; enlarged edition published by N. Gaon. 2 vols. Jerusalem, 1948.

Midrash T^ehilim (Psalms). Edited by S. Buber. Wilna, 1891; translated by W. Braude. YJS 13. New Haven, 1959.

Midr^eshe G^eulah. Edited by Y. Even-Sh^emuel. Jerusalem and Tel Aviv, 1954.

Miqra'ot G^edolot. 10 vols. New York, 1951.

al-Muqaddasī, Muḥammad b. Aḥmad. *K. aḥsan al-taqāsīm fī ma'rifat al-aqālīm.* Edited by M. J. De Goeje. BGA 3. Leiden, 1877.

al-Nasafī, 'Abdallāh b. Aḥmad. *Tafsīr al-Qur'ān al-jalīl.* 4 vols. Cairo, 1343/1925.

al-Nasā'ī, Aḥmad b. Shu'ayb. *Tafsīr.* 2 vols. Cairo, 1410/1990.

Ozar ha-Aggadah. Edited by M. Gross. Jerusalem, 1954.

P^esikta d^eRav Kahana. Edited by B. Mandelbaum. 2 vols. New York, 1962; translated by W. Braude and I. Kapstein. Philadelphia, 1975.

P^esikta Rabbati. Edited M. Friedmann. Vienna, 1880; translated by W. Braude. YJS 18. New Haven, 1968.

Pirke d^eRabbi Eliezer. Edited Warsaw, 1852; translated by G. Friedländer. London, 1916.

Pseudo Ben Sira. *Sippure Ben Sira.* Edited by Eli Yassif. Jerusalem, 1984. Various traditions published by M. Steinschneider as *Alphabetum Siriacidis.* Berlin, 1858.

Pseudo Ibn Qutaybah. *Al-Imāmah wa al-siyāsah.* 2 vols. Cairo (?), n.d.

al-Rāzī, Muḥammad b. 'Umar Fakhr al-Dīn. *Al-Tafsīr al-kabīr (Mafātīḥ al-ghayb).* 6 vols. Bulāq, 1287/1870–71; 16 vols. Beirut, 1485/1985.

al-Ṣabī', Hilāl b. al-Muḥassin. *K. al-wuzarā'.* Beirut, 1378/1958.

———. *Rusūm dār al-khilāfah.* Cairo, 1383/1963.

al-Sakhāwī, Muḥammad b. Aḥmad. *Al-I'lān bi-l-tawbīkh liman dhamma ahl al-tawārīkh.* Translated by F. Rosenthal in *A History of Muslim Historiography.* 2d ed. Leiden, 1968.
Seder Eliahu Rabbah v^e^-Seder Eliahu Zuta. Edited by M. Friedmann. Vienna, 1904; translated by W. Braude and I. Kapstein as *Tanna Debe Eliyahu.* Philadelphia, 1981.
Sefer ha-Aggadah. Edited by H. N. Bialik and Y. Ravnitzky (Rawnizki). 6 parts in 1. Tel Aviv, 1987.
Sefer Zohar Hadash. Leghorn, 1866; translated by M. Simon and H. Sperling as *The Zohar.* 3 vols. London, 1931–34.
al-Shahrastānī, Muḥammad b. 'Abd al-Karīm. *K. al-milal wa al-nihal.* Cairo, 1321/1903.
Sifre d^e^Aggad^e^ta. Edited by S. Buber. Vienna, 1886.
Sifre d^e^darim (Deuteronomy). Edited by L. Finkelstein. New York, 1969; translated by R. Hammer. YJS 24. New Haven, 1984.
Sippure Ben Sira; see Pseudo Ben Sira.
Soher Tov; see *Midrash T^e^hilim.*
al-Suyūtī, Jalāl al-Dīn. *Al-Hāwī li-l-fatāwā.* Vol. 1, Cairo, 1402/1982.
———. *Tafsīr al-Jalalayn.* Damascus, 1385/1965.
———. *Al-Wasā'il ilā ma'rifat al-awā'il.* Cairo, 1980.
al-Ṭabarī, Muḥammad b. Jarīr. *Jāmi' al-Bayān 'an ta'wīl āy al-Qur'ān.* 30 vols. Cairo, 1954–65.
———. *K. akhbār al-rusul wa al-mulūk (Annales).* 13 vols. Edited by M. J. De Goeje et al. Leiden, 1879–1901.
al-Ṭabarsī, al-Faḍl b. al-Ḥasan. *Majma' al-bayān fī 'ulūm al-Qur'ān.* 30 vols. Beirut, 1954–57.
Tanne d^e^be Eliahu; see *Seder Eliahu Rabbah v^e^-Seder Eliahu Zuta.*
Targum Sheni (to Esther). Text in *MG* 6 (edition cited); D. Moritz. *Das Targum Sheni zum Buche Esther: Nach Handschriften herausgegeben.* Krakow, 1898; L. Munk. *Targum Scheni zum Buche Esther nebst Variae Lectiones nach handschriftlichen Quellen.* Berlin, 1876; A. Sulzbach. *Targum Sheni zum Buche Esther. Übersetzt und mit Anmerkungen versehen.* Frankfurt a.M., 1920; most recently translated and annotated by B. Grossfeld in *The Two Targums of Esther.* Collegeville, 1991: 95–195.
al-Tha'labī, Aḥmad b. Muḥammad. *'Arā'is al-majālis.* Beirut, n.d.
Yalkut Shimoni. Edited D. Hayman and Y. Shiloni. 8 vols to date. Jerusalem, 1984–.
al-Ya'qūbī, Aḥmad b. Abī Ya'qūb. *K. al-buldān.* Edited M. J. Goeje. BGA 7. Leiden, 1892; translated by G. Wiet. *Les Pays.* PIFAO 1. Cairo, 1937.
———. *Ta'rīkh (Historiae).* Edited by M. Houtsma. 2 vols. Leiden, 1883.
Yāqūt, Ya'qūb b. 'Abdallāh. *Mu'jam al-buldān.* Edited by F. Wüstenfeld. 6 vols. Leipzig, 1866–73.
al-Zamakhsharī, Maḥmud b. 'Umar. *Al-Kashshāf fi ḥaqā'iq al-tanzīl wa 'uyūn al-aqāwīl fī wujūh al-ta'wīl.* Edited by W. N. Lees et al. Calcutta, 1856.
Zohar; see *Sefer Zohar Hadash.*

Secondary Sources

Abba, R. "The Divine Name Yahwe." *JBL* 80 (1960): 320–28.
Abbot, N. "Pre-Islamic Arab Queens." *AJSL* 58 (1941): 1–22.
———. *Studies in Arabic Literary Papyri,* Vol. 2. *Qur'ānic Commentary and Tradition.* OIP 76. Chicago, 1967.

———. *Two Queens of Baghdad*. Chicago, 1946.
———. "Women and the State in Early Islam." *JNES* 1 (1942): 106–26, 341–68.
'Abd al-Raziq, A. *La femme au temps des Mamlouks en Egypte*. Paris, 1974.
Abusch, T. *Babylonian Witchcraft Literature: Case Studies*. BJS 132. Atlanta, 1987.
———. "The Demonic Image of the Witch in Babylonian Literature." In *Religion Science and Magic,* edited by J. Neusner et al., 27–58. New York and Oxford, 1989.
———. "An Early Form of the Witchcraft Ritual Maqlu and the Origin of a Babylonian Magical Ceremony." In *Studies in Ancient Near Eastern Literature in Honor of William M. Moran,* 1–57. HSS 32. Atlanta, 1990.
———. "Maqlu." In *Reallexikon der Assyriologie,* 346–51. Vol. 7.
———. "Mesopotamian Anti-Witchcraft Literature." *JNES* 33 (1974): 251–62.
Ahmad, L. "Early Islam and the Position of Women: The Problem of Interpretation." In *Women in Middle Eastern History,* edited by N. Keddie and B. Baron, 58–73. New Haven, 1991.
Albright, W. F. *Yahwe and the Gods of Canaan*. New York, 1968.
al-'Alī, S. A. "The Foundation of Baghdad." In *The Islamic City,* edited by A. H. Hourani and S. M. Stern, 87–101. Oxford, 1970.
———. "Minṭaqat al-Ḥīrah." *Majallat kullīyat al-ādāb*. Baghdad University 5 (1962): 17–44.
———. *al-Tanzīmāt al-ijtimā'īyah wa al-iqtiṣādīyah fī al-Baṣrah fī qarn al-awwal al-hijrī*. Baghdad, 1953.
Alter, R. *The Art of Biblical Narrative*. New York, 1981.
———. *The Art of Biblical Poetry*. New York, 1985.
Anderson, F. "The Socio-Juridical Background of the Naboth Incident." *JBL* 85 (1966): 46–57.
Arnaldez, R. "Controverse d'Ibn Hazm contre Ibn Nagrila le Juif." *RMM* 13/14 (1973): 41–48.
Ashtor, E. *The Jews of Moslem Spain*. 3 vols. Philadelphia, 1979.
Avida, Y. "Ma'aseh Malkat Shᵉva." In *Sefer Assaf,* edited by M. D. Cassuto et al. Jerusalem, 1953.
Ayalon, D. *The Military Reforms of al-Mu'taṣim: Their Background and Consequences*. Private circulation. Jerusalem, 1964.
Ayoub, M. *The Qur'ān and Its Interpreters*. Vol. 1. Albany, 1984.
Bal, M. *Death and Dissymmetry*. Chicago, 1988.
———. *Lethal Love*. Bloomington, 1987.
———. *Murder and Difference: Gender, Genre, and Scholarship on Sisera's Death*. Bloomington, 1988.
Baneth, D. H. "What Did Muḥammad Mean When He Called His Religion Islām? The Original Meaning of Aslama and Its Derivatives." *IOS* 1 (1971): 183–90.
Barkay, G. "The Divine Name Found in Jerusalem." *BAR* 9 (1983): 14–19.
Baron, S. W. *A Social and Religious History of the Jews*. Vol. 5. New York, 1957.
Baskin, J., ed. *Jewish Women in Historical Perspective*. Detroit, 1990.
Baskin, J. "Jewish Women in the Middle Ages." In *Jewish Women in Historical Perspective,* edited by J. Baskin, 94–114. Detroit, 1990.
Beck, E. "Die Mas'ūdvarianten bei al-Farrā." *Orientalia* n.s., 25 (1956): 353–83; 28 (1959): 186–205, 230–56.
———. "Studien zur Geschichte der kufischen Koranlesung in den beiden ersten Jahr-

hunderten." *Orientalia* n.s., 17 (1948): 326–55; 19 (1950): 328–50; 20 (1951): 316–28; 22 (1953): 59–78.
———. "Der 'Utmānische Kodex in der Koranlesung des zweiten Jahrhunderts." *Orientalia* n.s., 14 (1945): 335–73.
———. "Die Zuverlässigkeit der Überlieferung zur 'Utmānischen Varianten bei al-Farrā'." *Orientalia* n.s., 23 (1954): 412–35.
Beck, L. and N. Keddie, eds. *Women in the Muslim World.* Cambridge, Mass., and London, 1991.
Begrich, J. "Atalja, die Tochter Omris." *ZAW* 53 (1935): 78–79.
Bell, R. *The Origin of Islam in Its Christian Environment.* London, 1926.
Bellamy, J. "Sex and Society in Islamic Popular Literature." In *Society and the Sexes in Medieval Islam,* edited by A. L. El-Sayyid Marsot, 21–42. Malibu, 1979.
Beltz, W. "Über den Ur-Qur'ān." *Zeitschrift für Religions- und Geistgeschichte* 27 (1975): 169–71.
Bialik, H. N. *Vay^ehi ha-Yom.* Tel Aviv, 1964.
Bialik, H. N. and Y. Ravnitzky, eds. *Sefer ha-Aggadah.* Tel Aviv, 1987.
Bijlefeld, W. "A Prophet More Than a Prophet? Some Observations on the Qur'anic Use of the Terms 'Prophet' and 'Apostle.'" *MW* 59 (1969): 1–28.
Bird, P. "Images of Women in the Old Testament." In *Religion and Sexism: Images of Women in the Jewish and Christian Traditions,* edited by R. Ruether. New York, 1974.
———. "'Male and Female He Created Them': Gen. 1:27b in the Context of the Priestly Account of Creation." *HTR* 74 (1981): 129–60.
Blachere, R. *Introduction au Coran.* Paris, 1947.
———. "Les Principaux thèmes de la poésie érotique au siècle des Umayyades de Damas." *AIEO* 5 (1939–41): 82–128.
Blau, J. *The Emergence and Linguistic Background of Judeo-Arabic.* Oxford, 1965.
Blenkinsopp, J. "Structure and Style in Judges 13–16." *JBL* 82 (1963): 65–76.
Bohlen, R. *Der Fall Nabot: Formen, Hintergrund und Werdegang einer alttestamentlichen Erzählung (I Kg. 21).* TTHS 35. Trier, 1978.
Bowker, J. "Intercession in the Qur'ān and the Jewish Tradition." *JSS* 4 (1968): 183–202.
Bowman, J. "Banū Isrā'īl in the Qur'ān." *IS* 2 (1963): 447–55.
Boyce, A. "Moslem Women in the Capital of Persia." *MW* 20 (1930): 265–69.
Bravmann, M. *The Spiritual Background of Early Islam.* Leiden, 1972.
Brett, G. "The Automata in the Byzantine Throne of Solomon." *Speculum* 29 (1954): 477–87.
Brown, P. *The Body and Society.* New York, 1988.
Bruns, J. "Judith or Jael." *CBQ* 16 (1954): 12–16.
Bulliet, R. *Conversion to Islam in the Medieval Period.* Cambridge, Mass., 1979.
Burton, J. *The Collection of the Qur'ān.* Cambridge, 1977.
Cahen, C. "Coran IX-29: ḥattā yu'ṭū l-jizyata 'an yadin wa-hum sāghirūna." *Arabica* 9 (1962): 76–79.
Camp, C. *Wisdom and the Feminine in the Book of Proverbs.* Decatur, 1985.
Cassel, P. *An Explanatory Commentary on Esther.* Edinburgh, 1888.
———. *Zweites Targum zum Buche Esther.* Leipzig, 1885.
Cassuto, U. [M. D.]. *The Goddess Anath.* Jerusalem, 1971.
Chastel, P. "La legende de la reine de Saba'." *Revue de l'histoire des religions.* 119:204–225; 120:27–44, 160–74.
Clifford, R. "Proverbs IX: A Suggested Ugaritic Parallel." *VT* 25 (1975): 298–306.

Cohen, J. *"Be Fertile and Increase, Fill the Earth and Master It": The Ancient and Medieval Career of a Biblical Text.* Ithaca, 1989.

Cohen, M. "Islam and the Jews: Myth, Counter-Myth, History." *Jerusalem Quarterly* 38 (1986): 125–37.

Conrad, L. "The Dervish's Disciple: On the Personality and Intellectual Milieu of the Young Ignaz Goldziher." *JRAS* (1990): 225–66.

———."The Near East Study Tour Diary of Ignaz Goldziher." *JRAS* (1990): 105–26.

Conroy, C. "Hebrew Epic: Historical Notes and Critical Reflections." *Biblia* 61 (1980): 1–30.

Coogan, M. "A Structural Analysis of the Song of Deborah." *CBQ* 40 (1978): 132–66.

Cook, M., and P. Crone. *Hagarism, the Making of the Islamic World.* Cambridge, 1977.

Crenshaw, J. "The Samson Saga: Filial Devotion or Erotic Attachment?" *ZAW* 86 (1974): 470–504.

Creswell, K. A. C. *Early Muslim Architecture.* 2 vols. Oxford, 1940.

Crone, P. *Slaves on Horses.* Cambridge, 1980.

Cross, F. M. *Canaanite Myth and Hebrew Ethic: Essays in the History of the Religion of Israel.* Cambridge, Mass., 1973.

Cucchiari, S. "The Gender Revolution and the Transition from Bisexual Horde to Patrilocal Band: The Origins of Gender Hierarchy." In *Sexual Meanings,* edited by S. Ortner and H. Whitehead, 31–80. Cambridge, 1981.

Daum, W., ed. *Die Königin von Saba.* Stuttgart, 1988.

de Lagarde, P. *Übersicht über die im aramäischen, arabischen, und hebräischen übliche Bildung der Nomina.* Gottingen, 1889, 1891.

Dentan, R., ed. *The Idea of History in the Ancient Near East.* New Haven and London, 1955.

Donner, F. *The Early Islamic Conquests.* Princeton, 1981.

Donner, H. "The Interdependency of Internal Affairs and Foreign Policy During the Davidic-Solomonic Period." SPDS, 205–14.

Douglas, M. *Purity and Danger.* London, 1966.

Eilberg-Schwartz, H. *The Savage in Judaism.* Bloomington, 1990.

Elat, M. "Trade and Commerce." *WHJP* 4.2: 179ff.

Eph'al, I. *The Ancient Arabs.* Jerusalem and Leiden, 1982.

Exum, J. C. "Aspects of Symmetry and Balance in the Samson Saga." *JSOT* 19 (1981): 3–9.

———. "The Theological Dimension of the Samson Saga." *VT* 33 (1983): 30–45.

Fahmy, M. *La condition de la femme dans la tradition et l'évolution de l'Islamisme.* Paris, 1913.

Farnham, C. *The Impact of Feminist Research in the Academy.* Bloomington, 1987.

Fattal, A. *Le Statut légal des non-musulmans en pays d'Islam.* Beirut, 1958.

Finkelstein, J. J. "Mesopotamian Historiography." *PAPS* 107 (1963): 461–72.

Firestone, R. *Journeys in Holy Lands.* Albany, 1990.

Forbes, R. J. *Ancient Technology.* Leiden, 1955.

Fraenkel, S. *Die aramäischen Fremdwörter im Arabischen.* Leiden, 1886.

Freedman, D. N. "The Age of David and Solomon." *WHJP* 4.1: 101–25. Jerusalem, Ramat Gan, London, 1961–.

———. "The Names of the God Moses." *JBL* 79 (1960): 151–56.

Friedlander, I. "Jewish Arabic Studies." *JQR* n.s., 1 (1910–11): 183–215; 2 (1911–12): 481–516; 3 (1912–13): 235–300.

Friedman, M. A. *Jewish Marriage in Palestine.* 2 vols. New York and Tel Aviv, 1980.
———. "Tamar, a Symbol of Life: The 'Killer Wife' Superstition in the Bible and Jewish Tradition." *AJSR* 15 (1990): 23–62.
Fritsch, E. *Islam und Christentum im Mittelalter.* Breslau, 1930.
Frymer-Kensky, F. *In the Wake of the Goddesses.* New York, 1992.
Gaster, M. "Das Herz auf dem Lande." *MGWJ* 29 (1880): 475–80.
Geiger, A. *Was hat Mohammed aus dem Judenthume aufgenommen?* Bonn, 1833; translated by F. M. Young as *Judaism in Islam.* Madras, 1898.
Gelbhaus, S. *Das Targum Scheni zum Buche Esther.* Frankfurt a.M., 1893.
Gil, M. *Erez Yisrael ba-Tᵉkufah ha-Muslimit ha-Rishonah.* 3 vols. Jerusalem, 1983.
Ginzberg, L. *The Legends of the Jews.* 7 vols. New York, 1928.
Goedicke, H. and J. J. Roberts, eds. *Unity and Diversity: Essays in the History, Literature and Religion of the Ancient Near East.* Baltimore, 1975.
Goitein, S. D. "Bᵉne Yisrael u-Mahloktam." *Tarbiz* 3 (1932): 410–422.
———. "The Historical Background of the Erection of the Dome of the Rock." *JAOS* 70 (1950): 104–108. Expanded in his *Studies* as "The Sanctity of Jerusalem and Palestine," 135–48.
———. *Ha-Islam shel Muhammad.* Jerusalem, n.d.
———. "Isra'iliyat." *Tarbiz* 6 (1936): 89–101.
———. *A Mediterranean Society.* 6 vols. Berkeley, 1967–.
———. "Mi Hayyu Rabbotav ha-Muvhaqim shel Muhammad." *Tarbiz* 23 (1953): 146–59.
———. "'Olamah ha-Ruhani shel Yahadut ha-Mizrah bᵉTᵉkufat Prihatah." *Yᵉdion Yad Ben Zvi.* 2 (1973): 13–20.
———. "The Origin and Nature of the Muslim Friday Worship." *MW* 50 (1960): 23–29; reprinted in his *Studies,* 126–34.
———, ed. *Religion in a Religious Age.* Cambridge, Mass., 1974.
———. "Sanctity of Jerusalem and Palestine." In his *Studies in Islamic History and Institutions,* 135–148. Leiden, 1966.
———. *Studies in Islamic History and Institutions.* Leiden, 1966.
Golb, N. "The Topography of the Jews of Medieval Egypt: Inductive Studies Based Primarily on Documents from the Cairo Geniza." *JNES* 24 (1965): 251–70; 33 (1974): 116–49.
Goldziher, I. *Muhammedanische Studien.* 2 vols. Halle, 1895–90; translated and annotated by S. M. Stern as *Muslim Studies.* 2 vols. Chicago, 1966. London, 1971.
———. *Oriental Diary.* Edited and translated by R. Patai in *Ignaz Goldziher and His Oriental Diary.* Detroit, 1987.
———. *Tagebuch.* Edited by S. Scheiber. Leiden, 1978.
———. "Über Muḥammedanische Polemik gegen Ahl al-Kitāb." *ZDMG* 32 (1878): 341–87.
Grabar, A. "Le Success des arts orientaux a la cour byzantine sous les Macedoniens." *Münchner Jahrbuch der bildenen Kunst.* Ser. 3 (1951): 56.
Grabar, O. "The Umayyad Dome of the Rock in Jerusalem." *Ars Orientalis* 3 (1959): 33–62.
Grayson, A. K. "History and Historians of the Ancient Near East: Assyria and Babylonia." *Orientalia* 49 (1980): 140–94.
Grossfeld, B. *The Two Targums to Esther.* Collegeville, 1991.
Grünbaum, M. *Neue Beiträge zur semitischen Sagenkunde.* Leiden, 1983.
Halpern, B. *The First Historians: The Hebrew Bible and History.* New York, 1988.

Hanselman, S. "Narrative Theory, Ideology, and Transformation in Judges 4." In *Anti-Covenant,* edited by M. Bal. *JSOTS* 81 (1989): 95–112.
Hayman, P. "Monotheism—A Misused Word in Jewish Studies." *JJS* 42 (1990): 1–16.
Heaton, E. W. *Solomon's New Men: The Emergence of Ancient Israel as a Nation State.* London, 1974.
Heller, B. "Récits et personnages bibliques dans la légende mahometane." *REJ* 85 (1928): 113–36.
Hertz, W. "Die Rätsel der Königin von Saba." *ZDA* 27 (1883): 1–33.
Herzfeld, E., and F. Sarre. *Archäologische Reise im euphrat und Tigris Gebiet.* Vol. 2. Berlin, 1921.
Hinds, M. "Kufan Political Alignments and Their Backgrounds in the mid-7th Century A.D." *IJMES* 2 (1971): 346–67.
Hinz, W. *Islamische Masse und Gewichte.* Leiden, 1955.
Hirschberg, H. Z. *Jüdische und christliche Lehren im vor- und frühislamischen Arabien.* Cracow, 1939.
———. *Yisrael ba-'Arav.* Tel Aviv, 1946.
Hirschfeld, H. *Beiträge zur Erklärung des Ḳorān.* Leipzig, 1886.
———. "Historical and Legendary Controversies between Muḥammad and the Rabbis." *JQR* 10 (1897–98): 100–16.
Hoffner, H. A., Jr. "History and Historians of the Ancient Near East: The Hittites." *Orientalia* 49 (1980): 238–332.
Horovitz, J. "The Earliest Biographies of the Prophet and Their Authors." *IC* 2 (1928): 22–50, 164–82, 492–526.
———. "Jewish Proper Names and Their Derivatives in the Koran." *HUCA* 2 (1925): 145–227; reprinted as a separate monograph with cross-pagination. Hildesheim, 1964.
———. *Koranische Untersuchungen.* Berlin, 1926.
Jacobs, I. "Elements of Near Eastern Mythology in Rabbinic Aggadah." *JJS* 28 (1977): 1–11.
Jacobsen, T. "Religious Drama in Ancient Mesopotamia." In *Unity and Diversity: Essays in the History, Literature and Religion of the Ancient Near East,* edited by H. Goedicke and J. J. Roberts, 65–97. Baltimore, 1975.
Jeffery, A. *The Foreign Vocabulary of the Qur'ān.* Baroda, 1938.
———. *Materials for the History of the Text of the Qur'ān.* Leiden, 1937. *Index.* Leiden, 1951.
Johns, A. H. "Solomon and the Queen of Sheba: Fakhr al-Dīn al-Rāzī's Treatment of the Qur'ānic Telling of the Story." *Abr-Naharain* 24 (1986): 58–82.
Kahle, P. "Arabic Readers of the Qur'ān." *JNES* 8 (1949): 65–71.
Kapelrud, A. S. *The Violent Goddess.* Oslo, 1969.
Katsh, A. *Judaism in Islam.* New York, 1980.
Katzenstein, H. J. "Who Were the Parents of Athaliah?" *IEJ* 5 (1955): 194–97.
Khoury, R. G. *Wahb b. Munabbih.* 2 pts. Wiesbaden, 1972.
Kister, M. J. "'An yadin (Qur'an IX/29): An Attempt at an Interpretation." *Arabica* 2 (1964): 272–78.
———. "Ḥaddithū 'an banī Isrā'īla wa-la-ḥaraja." *IOS* 2 (1972): 215–39.
———. *Society and Religion From Jāhiliyya to Islam.* London, 1990.
———. *Studies in Jāhiliyya and Early Islam.* London, 1980.
———. "'You Shall Set Out Only for Three Mosques'—A Study of an Early Tradition." *Le Muséon* 82 (1969): 173–96.

Klausner, J. "Sh^e^lomo ha-Melekh u-Malkat Sh^e^va." *Ha-Shiloah* 13 (1904): 414–55.
Kraemer, R. "Jewish Women in the Diaspora World of Late Antiquity." In *Jewish Women in Historical Perspective,* edited by J. Baskin, 43–67. Detroit, 1990.
Kraus, H. "Ahabs Gewalttat an Naboth (I Kon. 21): Das Eigentum als Problem evangelischer Sozialethik." In *Kirche im Volk* 2:655–60. Essen, 1949.
Krauss, S. "Die Namen der Königin von Saba'" In *Festschrift* [Jakob] *Freimann,* 119–24. Berlin, 1937.
Lagarde, P.; see de Lagarde, P.
Lambert, W. G., and A. R. Millard, eds. *Atra-Hasis: The Babylonian Story of the Flood.* Oxford, 1969.
Lang, B. *Wisdom and the Book of Proverbs: A Hebrew Goddess Redefined.* New York, 1985.
Lassner, J. "The Caliph's Personal Domain: The City Plan of Baghdad Reexamined." In *The Islamic City,* edited by A. Hourani and S. M. Stern, 103–18. Oxford, 1970.
———. "The Covenant of the Prophets: Muslim Texts, Jewish Subtext." *AJSR* 15 (1990): 207–38.
———. *Islamic Revolution and Historical Memory.* AOS 66. New Haven, 1986.
———. "The 'One Who Had Knowledge of the Book' and the 'Mightiest Name' of God. Qur'ānic Exegesis and Jewish Cultural Artifacts." *Studies in Muslim Jewish Relations* 1 (1991).
———. "The Origins of Muslim Attitudes Towards Jews and Judaism." *Judaism* 39 (1990): 498–507.
———. *The Shaping of 'Abbāsid Rule.* Princeton, 1980.
———. "Some Speculative Thoughts on the Search for an 'Abbāsid Capital." *MW* 55 (1965): 135–41, 203–310.
———. *The Topography of Baghdad in the Early Middle Ages: Text and Studies.* Detroit, 1970.
Lauterbach, J. "Substitutes for the Tetragrammaton." *PAAJR* (1930): 39–67.
Lazarus-Yafeh, H. *Intertwined Worlds. Medieval Islam and Biblical Criticism.* Princeton, 1992.
———. *Some Religious Aspects of Islam.* Leiden, 1981.
Le Strange, G. *Baghdad During the Abbasid Caliphate.* London, 1900.
———. *Palestine Under the Moslems.* London, 1890.
Lewis, B. "An Anti-Jewish Ode: the Qasīda of Abū Isḥāq against Joseph Ibn Nagrella." In *Salo Wittmayer Baron Jubilee Volume,* edited by S. Lieberman. Jerusalem, 1975.
———. "An Apocalyptic Vision of Islamic History." *BSOAS* 13 (1949–51): 308–38.
———. *History—Remembered, Recovered, Invented.* Princeton, 1975.
———. *Islam and History.* London, 1973.
———. *The Jews of Islam.* Princeton, 1984.
———. "The Pro-Islamic Jews." In *Islam in History,* 123–37, 315–17.
Lewis, B., and P. Holt, eds. *Historians of the Middle East.* London, 1962.
Lichtenstader, I. *Women in the Aiyam al-'Arab.* London, 1935.
Lichty, E. "Demons and Population Control." *Expedition* 13 (1971): 22–26.
Lidzbarski, M. *Das Johannesbuch der Mandäer.* Vol. 1. Berlin, 1915.
Lieberman, S. *Greek in Jewish Palestine.* New York, 1942.
Lokkegard, F. *Islamic Taxation in the Classic Period with Special References to Circumstances in Iraq.* Copenhagen, 1950.
Maas, M. *Bibel und Koran.* Leipzig, 1893.

Makdisi, G. "The Eleventh Century Baghdad: Materials and Notes." *Arabica* 6 (1959): 178–197, 281–309.
Malamat, A. "Aspects of the Foreign Policy of David and Solomon." *JNES* 22 (1963): 1–17.
———. "The Kingdom of David and Solomon and Its Contact with Egypt and Aram Naharaim." *BA* 21 (1958): 96–102.
———. "A Political Look at the Kingdom of David and Solomon and Its Relations with Egypt." In *SPDS,* 189–204. Tokyo, 1982.
Malti-Douglas, F. *Woman's Body, Woman's Word.* Princeton, 1992.
Mann, J. *The Responsa of the Babylonian Geonim as a Source of Jewish History.* New York, 1973.
———. *Text and Studies in Jewish History and Literature.* 2 vols. New York, 1972.
Margoliouth, D. S. "On 'The Book of Religion and Empire' by 'Alī b. Rabban al-Ṭabarī." *Proceedings of the British Academy.* 16 (1930): 165–82.
Margolith, O. "More Samson Legends." *VT* 36 (1986): 397–405.
———. "Samson's Riddles and Samson's Magic." *VT* 36 (1986): 225–234.
Margulies, B. "An Exegesis of Judges V 8a" *VT* 15 (1965): 66–69.
Marmorstein, A. *The Old Rabbinic Doctrine of God.* 2 vols. London, 1927, 1937.
Masson, D. *Monothéisme coranique et monothéisme biblique.* Paris, 1976.
Mazar, B. "The Era of David and Solomon." *WHJP* 4.1: 76–99.
McAuliffe, J. *Qur'ānic Christians.* Cambridge, 1991.
Meredith, B. "Desire and Danger." In *Anti-Covenant,* Edited by M. Bal, 63–78. Sheffield, 1989.
Meyers, C. *Discovering Eve.* Oxford, 1988.
Miller, J. "The Fall of the House of Ahab." *VT* 17 (1967): 307–24.
Montgomery, J. A. *Arabia and the Bible.* New York, 1969.
Moore, H. L. *Feminism and Anthropology.* Minneapolis, 1988.
Morabia, A. "Ibn Taimiya, les juifs et la tora." *SI* 49 (1978): 91–122; 50 (1979): 77–107.
Moubarac, Y. *Abraham dans le Coran.* Paris, 1958.
———. "Les noms titres et attributs de dieu dans le Coran et les correspondents en épigraphie sud-sémitique." *La Muséon* 68 (1955): 93–135, 325–68.
Müller, D. H. *Die Propheten in ihrer ursprünglichen Form.* Vol. 1. Vienna, 1896.
Müller, H. P. "Der Begriff 'Rätsel' im Alten Testament." *VT* 20 (1970): 465–89.
Munajjid, S. *Al-Ḥayāt al-jinsīyah 'ind al-'arab.* Beirut, 1958.
Murtonen, A. *Philological and Literary Treatise of Old Testament Divine Names.* Helsinki, 1952.
Nagel, T. *Die Qiṣaṣ al-anbiyā'.* Bonn, 1967.
Naveh, J., and S. Shaked. *Amulets and Magic Bowls.* Jerusalem, 1985.
Neuwirth, A. *Studien zur Komposition der mekkanischen Suren.* Berlin, 1981.
Newby, G. "Abraha and Sennacherib: A Talmudic Parallel to the *Tafsīr* on *Sūrat al-Fīl. JAOS* 94 (1974): 431–37.
———. *A History of the Jews of Arabia.* Columbia, S.C. 1988.
———. *The Making of the Last Prophet.* Columbia, S.C., 1989.
———. "Tafsīr Isrā'īlīyāt." *Studies in Qur'ān and Tafsīr. JAAR,* Thematic Issue 47 (1979): 685–97.
Niditch, S. "Eroticism and Death in the Tale of Jael." In *Gender and Difference in Ancient Israel,* Edited by P. L. Day, 43–57. Minneapolis, 1989.

Nöldeke, T. *Neue Beiträge zur semitischen Sprachwissenschaft.* Strasbourg, 1910.

Nöldeke, T., et al. *Geschichte des Qorans.* 2nd. rev. ed. 3 vols. Vols. 1 and 2 revised by F. Schwally; vol. 3 revised by G. Bergsträsser and O. Pretzl. Leipzig, 1909–26.

Noth, A. *Quellenkritische Studien zur Themen, Formen und Tendenzen frühislamischer Geschichtsüberlieferung.* Bonn, 1973.

Noth, M. "Die Bewährung von Salomos 'Göttlicher Weisheit'." *VTS* 3 (1955): 225–37.

———. *Die israelitischen Personennamen im Rahmen der gemeinsemitischen Namengebung.* BWANT 3.10 (1928).

Obermann, J. "Islamic Origins: A Study in the Background and Foundation." In *The Arab Heritage,* edited by N. A. Faris, 58–120. Princeton, 1944.

Oden, R. *The Bible Without Theology.* Cambridge, Mass., 1987.

Ortner, S. "Is Female to Male as Nature is to Culture?" In *Women Culture and Society,* Edited by M. Rosaldo and L. Lamphere, 67–87. Stanford, 1974.

Ortner, S., and H. Whitehead, eds. *Sexual Meanings.* Cambridge, 1981.

O'Shaughnessy, T. "God's Throne and the Biblical Symbolism of the Qur'an." *Numen* 20 (1973): 20–21.

Pallis, S. A. *The Babylonian Akitu Festival.* Lund, 1928.

Paret, R. *Grenzen der Koranforschung.* Stuttgart, 1950.

———. "Der Koran als Geschichtsquelle." *Islamica* 27 (1961): 26–42.

———. *Der Koran: Kommentar und Konkordanz.* Stuttgart, 1971, 1977.

———. "Toleranz und Intoleranz im Islam." *Saeculum* 21 (1970): 344–65.

Patai, R. *Ignaz Goldziher and His Oriental Diary.* Detroit, 1987.

———. *Sex and Family in the Bible and the Middle East.* New York, 1959.

Pauliny, J. "Islamische Legende über Bukht-Nassar (Nebukadnezar)." *GO* 4 (1972): 161–83.

———. "Zur Rolle der Qussas bei der Entstehung und Überlieferung der populären Prophetenlegenden." *Asian and African Studies* (Bratislava) 10 (1974): 125–41.

Perlmann, M. "'Abd al-Ḥakk al-Islāmī: A Jewish Convert." *JQR* 31 (1940): 171–91.

———. "Another Ka'b al-Aḥbār Story." *JQR* 45 (1954): 48–51.

———. "Eleventh Century Andalusian Authors on the Jews of Granada." *PAAJR* 18 (1948–49): 269–90.

———. "A Legendary Story of Ka'b al-Aḥbār's Conversion to Islam." In *The Joshua Starr Memorial Volume,* 85–99. New York, 1953.

———. "The Medieval Polemics between Islam and Judaism." In *Religion in a Religious Age,* edited by S. D. Goitein, 103–129. Cambridge, Mass., 1974.

Pipes, D. *Slave Soldiers and Islam.* New Haven, 1981.

Pritchard, J. B., ed. *Solomon and Sheba.* London, 1974.

Rabin, C. *Ancient West Arabian.* London, 1951.

———. "The Beginnings of Classical Arabic." *SI* 4 (1955): 19–37.

———. "Judges V,2 and the 'Ideology' of Deborah's War." *JSS* 8 (1955): 125–34.

Rahman, F. *Major Themes in the Qur'ān.* Minneapolis and Chicago, 1980.

———. "Pre-Foundations of the Muslim Community in Mecca." *SI* 43 (1974): 44–66.

———. "The Religious Situation of Mecca from the Eve of Islam up to the Hijra." *IS* 16 (1977): 289–301.

Rasmussen, R. "Deborah the Woman Warrior." In *Anti-Covenant,* edited by M. Bal. *JSOTS* 81 (1989): 79–93.

Richter, G. *Das Geschichtsbild der arabischen Historiker des Mittelalters.* Tubingen, 1933.

Ringgren, H. *Islam Aslama and Muslim*. Lund, 1949.
Roberts, J. J. "Myth versus History: Relaying the Comparative Foundations." *CBQ* 38 (1976): 1–13.
Rosaldo, M., and L. Lamphere, eds. *Women, Culture and Society*. Stanford, 1984.
Rösch, A. *Die Königin von Saba als Königin Bilqīs*. Leipzig, 1880.
Rosenthal, F. *A History of Muslim Historiography*. 2d. ed. Leiden, 1968.
———. "The Influence of the Biblical Tradition on Muslim Historiography." In *Historians of the Middle East,* edited by B. Lewis and P. Holt, 35–45. London, 1962.
———. "Sources for the Role of Sex in Medieval Muslim Society." In *Society and the Sexes in Medieval Islam,* edited by A. L. al-Sayyid Marsot, 3–22. Malibu, 1979.
Rudolph, W. *Die Abhängigkeit des Korans von Judentum und Christentum*. Stuttgart, 1922.
Said, E. *Orientalism*. New York, 1978.
Salmon, G. *L'Introduction topographique à l'histoire de Baghdadh*. Paris, 1904.
Salzberger, G. *Die Salomo-Sage in der semitischen Literatur*. Berlin and Heidelberg, 1907.
Schäfer, P. "Jewish Magic in Late Antiquity and the Middle Ages." *JSS* 41 (1990): 75–91.
Schapiro, I. *Die haggadischen Elemente im erzählenden Teil des Korans*. Berlin, 1907.
Schechter, S. "The Riddles of Solomon in Rabbinic Literature." *Folklore* 1 (1890): 349–58.
Scholem, G. "P^e^rakim Hadashim me-inyane Ashm^e^day v^e^-Lilit." *Tarbiz* 19 (1948): 165–75.
Schreiner, M. "Die apologetische Schrift des Solomon b. Adret gegen einen Muhammedaner." *ZDMG* 48 (1894): 39–42.
———. "Sama'ual b. Jahya al-Magribi und Seine Schrift *Ifham al-Jahud*." *MGWJ* 42 (1898): 123–38, 170–80, 214–23, 253–61, 407–18, 457–65; 43 (1899): 521–27.
———. "Zur Geschichte der Polemik zwischen Juden und Muhammedanern." *ZDMG* (1888): 591–675.
Scott, R. B. Y. "Solomon and the Beginning of Wisdom." *VTS* 3 (1955): 262–79.
Sezgin, F. *Geschichte des arabischen Schrifttums*. Vol. 1. Leiden, 1967.
Shaked, S. *A Tentative Bibliography of Geniza Documents*. Paris, 1964.
Shamir, Y. "Allusions to Muḥammad in Maimonides' Theory of Prophecy in his *Guide of the Perplexed*." *JQR* 64 (1973–74): 212–24.
Sharon, M. *Black Banners from the East*. Jerusalem, 1983.
Shaw, J. "Constructions of Women in Readings of the Story of Deborah." In *Anti-Covenant,* edited by M. Bal. *JSOTS* 81 (1989): 113–32.
Sidersky, D. *Les origines des légendes musulmanes dans le Coran*. Paris, 1933.
Silberman, L. "The Queen of Sheba in Judaic Tradition." In *Solomon and Sheba,* edited by J. Pritchard, 65–84. London, 1974.
Simon, R. *Ignác Goldziher*. Leiden, 1986.
Smith, J. *An Historical and Semantic Study of the Term "islām" as Seen in a Sequence of Qur'ān Commentaries*. Missoula, 1975.
———. "The Meaning of Islam in Ḥadīth Literature." *IC* 48 (1974): 139–48.
Smith, M. *The Early History of God*. New York, 1990.
Soggin, J. A. "The Davidic-Solomonic Kingdom." *IJH*, 332–80. London, 1977.
Speiser, E. A. "The Biblical Idea of History in Its Common Near Eastern Setting." *IEJ* 7 (1957): 201–16.
Spellberg, D. "Political Action and Public Example: 'A'isha and the Battle of the

Camel." In *Women in Middle Eastern History,* edited by N. Keddie and B. Baron, 45–57. New Haven, 1991.

Spender, R. F. "The Arabian Matriarchate: An Old Controversy." *Southwestern Journal of Anthropology* 8 (1952): 478–502.

Speyer, H. *Die biblischen Erzählungen in Qoran.* Hildesheim, 1961.

Steinberg, M. *The Poetics of Biblical Narrative.* Bloomington, 1987.

Steinschneider, M. *Polemische und apologetische Literatur in arabischer Sprache.* Hildesheim, 1966.

Stern, G. *Marriage in Early Islam.* London, 1939.

Stillman, N. A. "The Story of Cain and Abel in the Qur'ān and Muslim Commentaries." *JSS* 19 (1974): 231–39.

Stowasser, B. "The Status of Women in Early Islam." In *Muslim Women,* edited by F. Hussain, 11–43. New York, 1984.

Streck, M. *Die alte Landschaft Babylonien.* Leiden, 1900.

Sulzbach, A. *Targum Scheni zum Buche Esther.* Frankfurt a.M., 1920.

Taeschner, F. "Die alttestamentlichen Bibelzitate vor allem aus dem Pentateuch in Aṭ-Ṭabarīs Kitāb ad-dīn wad-daula und ihre Bedeutung für die Frage nach der Echtheit dieser Schrift." *OC,* 3d. ser., 9 (1934): 23–39.

Taylor, G. "The Song of Deborah and Two Canaanite Goddesses." *JSOT* 23 (1982): 99–108.

Torrey, C. C. *The Jewish Foundations of Islam.* New York, 1967.

Trachtenberg, J. *Jewish Superstition and Magic.* New York, 1939.

Trible, P. *Texts of Terror: Literary-Feminist Readings of Biblical Narratives.* Philadelphia, 1984.

Tritton, A. S. *The Caliphs and Their Non-Muslim Subjects.* London, 1970.

———. "Islam and the Protected Religions." *JRAS* (1931): 311–38.

Ullendorff, E. *The Bawdy Bible.* Oxford, 1979.

Vajda, G. "Juifs et Musulmans selon le ḥadīṯ." *JA* 229 (1939): 57–127.

van Dijk-Hemes, F. "Tamar and the Limits of Patriarchy: Between Rape and Seduction." In *Anti-Covenant,* edited by M. Bal. *JSOTS* 81 (1989): 135–56.

Van Seters, J. *In Search of History.* Yale, 1983.

Vollers, K. *Volkssprache und Schriftsprache im alten Arabien.* Strasbourg, 1906.

Von Rad, G. *Wisdom in Israel.* London, 1971.

Wansbrough, J. *Quranic Studies.* LOS 31. Oxford, 1977.

———. *The Sectarian Milieu.* LOS 34. Oxford, 1978.

Watt, W. M. *Bell's Introduction to the Qur'an: Completely Revised and Enlarged.* Edinburgh, 1970.

———. "The Dating of the Qur'ān: A Review of Richard Bell's Theories." *JRAS* (1957): 46–56.

———. "The Early Development of Muslim Attitudes towards the Bible." In his *Early Islam.* 77–85, 195–97.

———. "Early Discussions About the Qur'ān." *MW* 40 (1950): 27–40.

———. *Early Islam.* Edinburgh, 1990.

———. *Muhammad at Mecca.* Oxford, 1953.

———. *Muhammad at Medina.* Oxford, 1956.

———. "The Queen of Sheba in Islamic Tradition." In *Solomon and Sheba,* edited by J. Pritchard, 85–103. London, 1974.

Wegner, J. "The Image and Status of Women in Classical and Rabbinic Judaism." In *Jewish Women in Historical Perspective,* edited by J. Baskin, 68–93. Detroit, 1990.

Weil, G. *Biblische Legenden der Muselmänner.* Leipzig, 1886; and *The Bible, the Koran and the Talmud.* New York, 1846.

Wellhausen, J. *Das Arabische Reich und sein Sturz;* translated by M. G. Weir as *The Arab Kingdom and Its Fall.* Calcutta, 1927.

Wendell, C. "Baghdad: *Imago Mundi* and Other Foundation Lore." *IJMES* 2 (1971): 99–128.

Wensinck, A. J. *Muhammad and the Jews of Medina.* Translated and edited by W. Benn. Freiburg, 1975.

Winkler, H. A. *Siegel und Charaktere in der muhammedanischen Zauberei.* Berlin and Leipzig, 1930.

Wolfensohn, I. *Ka'b al-Aḥbār und seine Stellung in Ḥadīt und der islamischen Legendenliteratur.* Frankfurt a.M., 1933.

Wunsch, A. *Die Rätselweisheit bei den Hebräern.* Leipzig, 1883.

Yardeni, A. "Remarks on the Priestly Blessing on Two Ancient Amulets from Jerusalem." *VT* 41 (1991): 176–85.

Zakovitch, Y. "Sisseras Tod." *ZAW* 88 (1976): 191–205.

Zeitlin, S. "Queen Salome and King Jannaeus Alexander." *JQR* 51 (1960): 1–33.

Zotenberg, H., trans. *Chronique de Abou Djafer Mo'hammad ben Djarir ben Yazid Tabari.* 4 vols. Nogent-le-Rotrou, 1867–74.

Zwettler, M. *The Oral Tradition of Classical Arabic Poetry.* Columbus, 1978.

Index of Scriptural Verses

Qur'ān

General Index

Abbasid Caliphate, 76–77, 130, 236n.28, 237n.48
'Abd al-Ḥaqq al-Islāmī, 248n.12
'Abd al-Malik, 43–44, 246n.132
'Abdallāh b. 'Abbās, 62–63, 187, 188, 189, 193, 194, 196, 201, 213, 214
'Abdallāh b. Salām, 125
Abihu, 164
Abijam, 214
Abraham, 22, 117, 164, 203, 207, 248n.18
Absalom, 202, 219n.48
Abū Bakr (first Caliph), 191, 225n.20
Abū Ḥāmid al-Warrāq, 193
Abū al-Ḥasan 'Alī b. al-Ḥusayn al-Mas'ūdī, 141
Abū Hurayrah, 190
Abū Ja'far 'Abdallāh b. Muḥammad al-Manṣūr, 130, 249n.27
Abū Mūsā, 201
Abū al-Qāsim al-Junayd, 193
Abyssinia, 123, 233–34n.59
Adam, 68, 70, 71, 111, 202; and Eve, 21, 22, 88, 158, 203, 235n.16
Adonijah, 103
'Afīr, 49, 78, 188. *See also* hoopoe: and Queen
Africa, North, 135
Agag, King, 251n.72
Ahab, 32, 222n.79, 224n.93; and Jezebel, 28
Ahasueras. *See* Esther: and Ahasueras
Ahaziah, King, 29
Ai, 251–52n.87
'Ā'ishah, 198, 242n.55
alcohol, Muslim prohibition against, 40, 134
Alexander the Great, 239–40n.11
Amalekites, 100, 251n.72
Amnon, 202, 219n.48
Amos, 6, 19
'Amr b. Mundhir, 55, 57, 194, 196
Anas b. Mālik, 187
Anath, 32, 33, 221n.65, 224n.96
Anidjar, Alizah, 153, 154, 180
"Ant" Sūrah, 36, 88, 185–86
Antiochus Eustratios, 249n.39
Aqhat, tale of, 24
Arabia, 40, 122, 133, 134, 223n.87, 227n.8
Arabic language, xii, 64, 124, 126, 127, 129, 131, 133, 135, 136, 145, 146
'Arā'is al-majālis, 47, 48
Aram, King of, 18, 219n.37
Aramaic language, xii, 14, 126–29, 131
Ark of the Covenant, 108, 114, 115; opening of, 12, 162, 163
Asa, 214
'aṣabīyah, 70–71
Asaph b. Berechiah, 58–59, 106–9, 144, 197, 198, 232n.46, 244n.96; and Solomon, 110, 210, 212, 213, 242n.50, 244n.99; and the Temple, 115, 244n.89, 246n.121
Ascension Rock, 206
Ashmedai, 69, 103, 182–84, 231–32n.42
Athaliah, 28–30, 32, 223n.84
Atrahasis, flood story of, 219–20n.53
Avida, Y., 135, 136, 147, 250n.48
Azariah, 164

Baal, 224n.93
Babylon, 130
Babylonia, 65, 122, 129, 151. *See also* Mesopotamia
Baghdad, city of, 76–77, 130, 236n.28, 237n.47, 238n.48, 238n.66, 249n.27
Balaam (pagan prophet), 12, 135, 162, 218n.16, 228n.11

Morocco, 153
Moroccan folktales, 154
Moses, 22, 31, 34, 106, 125, 203, 243n.75
Mot, 32
Muḥammad, the Prophet, 116–17, 125, 135, 187, 227n.6, 248n.10; and the Queen, 52; and Solomon, 48, 94, 118, 119, 187; traditions ascribed to, 42–45, 52, 96, 97, 121
Muḥammad b. Isḥāq, 201
Muḥammad b. Ka'b, 199, 202
Muḥammad b. al-Munkadir, 59, 104, 105, 198
Mujāhid, 194, 198, 199
Munk, S., 131
Muqātil b. Sulaymān, 188–89, 192, 194
mythology: ancient Near Eastern, 25, 32, 33, 221n.65; goddesses in, 24, 25, 32, 221n.65; and monotheism, 30–31

Nadab, 164
Nāfi' b. al-Azraq, 63, 187
Naṣībīn, 100
Nathan, 202, 252n.101
nature, Solomon's relationship with, 9, 14–16, 36, 39, 48, 56, 66, 69, 70–72, 102, 152, 175, 176, 178, 182, 187; *See also* hoopoe
Nebuchadnezzar, 18–20, 22–23, 26, 130, 239–40n.11, 251n.73; and the Queen, 151, 167–68, 175
Nimrod, 239–40n.11
Nineveh. *See* Jonah
Noah, 22, 125
numerology, use of, 244n.98
Nūriyah, King, 144, 212

Omri, line of, 28, 29, 223n.84
Onan, 165
Orientalism, 120–21, 247n.3
osprey, 176, 177

paganism, influences of, 31, 33
Palestine, 95, 117, 122, 129, 132, 157, 246n.132, 249n.38
Palmyra, 212
Perez, 164, 165
Persia, 132, 153
Philistines, 28
pietism: in Judaism and Islam, 6–7
polytheism, 30, 31, 41, 87, 88
Posner, S., 131
prayer: as religious obligation, 242n.51
priests, Israelite, 114, 115, 163, 246n.121. *See also* Levites
procreation, 162, 163, 164, 174
prophets: in Israel, 18
Proverbs, Book of, 24, 32. See also *Midrash Mishle*
Psalms, Book of, 108. *See also* Zabūr
Pseudepigrapha, 34
Pseudo Ben Sira, 11, 20, 22–23, 130, 167–68, 239n.75, 249n.24. See also *Stories of Ben Sira*
purity, ritual, 13, 6–7, 252n.92, 252n.94; and menstruation, 11, 148–49, 151–52, 239n.74. *See also* hair, body

Qatādah, 78, 187, 192, 198, 232n.46
Qumran, 34
Qur'ān, xii, 41–46, 225–26n.20, 226n.21, 226n.25
Quraysh tribe (Prophet's), 226n.20

rabbinic tradition, 25–27, 30, 32, 33–34, 122, 123, 130
rak'ahs, 67
Ramaḍān, 71
Rashi, comments of, 23
Ravnitzky, Y., 154
Rayḥānah bt. al-Shukr, 73, 190
al-Razī. *See* Fakhr al-Dīn Muḥammad b. 'Umar
Rehoboam, 96, 185, 212, 214, 228–29n.16, 233n.58
riddles, use of, 14, 17, 40, 129, 168–69, 217n.3; by the Queen, 9, 10–13, 17, 39, 40, 135, 137, 147–50; by Solomon, 40, 137, 139
ring, Solomon's, 10–11, 52–53, 66, 68, 71, 78, 103, 145, 184, 204, 206, 235n.17
Rome, city of, 220n.58
Rosenthal, F., xi
"al-Rūm" Sūrah, 249n.40

Saadiah b. Joseph, 136, 139–42, 144, 146–53, 168–75, 250n.48, 250n.64, 250n.65
"Ṣād" Sūrah, 99–102, 118